ABOUT CLSA BOOKS

CLSA Books is a new series of financial publications written by independent experts commissioned by CLSA Asia-Pacific Markets. As one of Asia's most independent brokers, CLSA recognises the value of going straight to the source. Being able to tap into unfiltered primary research is essential to making better-informed investment decisions.

CLSA's first effort to bridge the information gap resulted in CLSA U's executive education courses for institutional investors, led by independent experts. CLSA Books takes investment research even further, with even greater depth and breadth available to a wider audience. With independent research and an emphasis on outside sources, CLSA helps institutional investors draw their own conclusions.

A Financial Series by CLSA Asia-Pacific Markets

www.clsa.com

Tomorrow's Gold

Asia's age of discovery

by

Dr Marc Faber

Hong Kong Singapore New York London

Reprinted October 2003
Reprinted March 2003
Published in December 2002 by
CLSA BOOKS
CLSA Asia-Pacific Markets
18/F, One Pacific Place
88 Queensway, Hong Kong

The text of this book is set in Goudy, with the display set in Optima.

Printed in Hong Kong
ISBN: 962-86067-2-7

Our age cannot be completely understood if all the others are not understood. The song of history can only be sung as a whole.

JOSE ORTEGA Y GASSET

Those who don't study the past will repeat its error; those who do study it will find other ways to err.

CHARLES WOLF JR

Plus ça change, plus c'est la même chose.

ALPHONSE KARR

Contents

Acknowledgments

As a student in economics at the University of Zurich I spent more time on the slopes as a member of the Swiss University Ski Team than attending lectures. But, once in business, I began to study more profoundly the great economists - Adam Smith, David Ricardo, John Stuart Mill, Clément Juglar, Arthur Pigou, Joseph Schumpeter, Nikolai Kondratieff, Friedrich Hayek, Gottfried Haberler, Irving Fisher, Alfred Marshall, John Maynard Keynes, Ludwig von Mises - and economic and financial historians such as Fernand Braudel, Will Durant, Robert Sobel and William McNeill, to name just a few.

All my knowledge is entirely due to these luminaries' thorough research. Personally, I know only very little, but in my professional life I have been extremely privileged to meet some outstanding contemporary economists, strategists and historians - such as the late Sidney Homer, Henry Kaufman, Charles Kindleberger, Kurt Richebächer, Chuck Clough, Douglas Noland, the late Stan Salvigsen, Stephen Roach, Barton Biggs, Byron Wien, Ed Yardeni, Gary Shilling, Fred Sheehan, Ray Dalio of Bridgewater Associates, Tony Boekh, Warren Smith, Martin Barnes, Francis Scotland and Chen Zhao of the Bank Credit Analyst, Paul Schulte, Jim Walker, Christopher Wood, Peter Bernstein, David Shairp, David Scott, Charles Allmon, James Grant, Frank Shostak, Andrew Smithers and Charles and Louis Gave - from all of whose research, expertise and knowledge I have not only greatly benefited but also "profiteered".

In terms of financial markets I have learned a great deal from personal contact with market technicians such as Robert Prechter, Ralph Acampora, Robert Farrell, Richard Russell, Vince Boening and Michael Belkin; and in terms of security analysis from Jim Chanos, David Tice and Fred Hickey. Naturally, I have also gained much experience over the years from my clients - most of whom are very successful businessmen, value investors and hedge fund managers.

Lastly, I am very grateful to Gary Coull of CLSA for giving me the opportunity to write this volume; and Angelique Marcil for administering the entire project. I would like to thank Simon Harris, Aligo Mok and their production team for translating my draft into a readable text and creating an attractive book; as well as Jeffrey Marcil for his indexing skills. I am also grateful to my daughter Nantamada for lightening up the prose with some colourful illustrations.

Marc Faber
November 2002

Foreword

In the late 1990s, journalists, politicians and even some imprudent central bankers began to claim (again) that the US business cycle was dead. The rationale behind the claim was that the microprocessor revolution had transformed the economy into a smooth running, real-time information machine. Cycles were a remnant of the old economy - where information flows were slow and imperfect.

Well, they know better now. The current malaise in the global financial system is the direct result of the euphoria that accompanies the end of a business cycle. Too much credit fuelling too much speculation is the principal characteristic of the end of the boom. This is true always and everywhere. History is littered with burst bubbles.

Marc Faber gives example after example to this effect. But while this book is essentially about cycles - in business, in credit, in investment and in psychology - it is also about larger trends. That is the nature of the world economy, short cycles take place against the backdrop of long waves. These can be shifts caused by industrial revolution, political upheaval, or simply a change in conventional wisdom. Sometimes the cycle and the wave coincide and reinforce each other, sometimes they are moving in opposite directions and send mixed signals to investors and economic actors.

Japan is a perfect case in point. Although the last twelve years are widely seen as a period of constant decline, there have been two cyclical upturns in 1995-96 and 1999-2000. Growth petered out quickly when the banking system failed to support the upturn, but on both occasions the stock market rose by 30-40%. Investors failed to see that the secular trend had not changed course and concentrated instead on the short cycle. Some smart traders undoubtedly made money, but most investors lost as they mistook the cyclical upturn for a change in trend. This is an object lesson for us all; the trend is ultimately more powerful than the cycle but the latter tends to throw up more moneymaking opportunities. Unfortunately, despite many examples of investment fads, fashions and manias over the years, investors rarely learn from history and tend to make the same mistakes time and again.

This book will, we hope, help readers identify the telltale signs of investment bubbles, as well as pinpointing neglected assets that are about to run. It is about identifying trends and cycles. The author sees two asset classes, Asia (particularly China) and commodities, as particularly attractive at present. We, at CLSA, could not agree more.

Yet Dr Faber arrives at his conclusions independently of both Chris Wood, our global strategist, and myself. The common denominator among the three of us is that, to a large extent, we adopt the Austrian economic framework to formulate our views. This framework eschews formalised mathematical models and relies instead on deductive logic and an understanding of human nature. It is necessarily subjective, but that - whether the quasi-scientists in the economic mainstream like it or not - is reality. Ultimately, greed and fear are at the heart of most, if not all, investment decisions.

In our work over the last year, the CLSA economics and strategy teams have come to the conclusion that Asia is on the cusp of a strong cyclical upswing, driven by improving domestic-demand conditions. That, in itself, is reason to be positive on Asian stock markets. But Asia's cyclical positives are reinforced at this time by strong secular trends as well. The dragon of China has been unleashed. Growth in that country is taking off on the back of an invigorated private sector. As Marc Faber argues, before long, China will be the prime consumer of natural resources, the number one supplier of tourists, and dominate in joint ventures and takeovers. The rest of Asia will ride the back of this dragon, to its great benefit.

We have termed this secular trend "Asia's billion boomers". While much of the argument rests on Asia's favourable demographics, it is not entirely a 'baby boom' phenomenon. It is also about recovery from financial crisis and a realisation that tomorrow looks better than today. Confidence in Asia is rising again. Spending and investment will soon follow.

This book adds a new dimension to the story. It puts Asia, and emerging markets generally, in a historical context. It shows that they are overlooked assets at a point in time when there are no major investment themes in people's minds. As Marc Faber argues, "that is when they are most appealing". And as the Asian region begins to grow more strongly again, it will pull commodities out of their long decline as well. Asians, by and large, are still 'goods-poor'. With each incremental increase in income, Asians tend to buy goods rather than services - and goods are commodity-intensive. The coming Asian upturn, and it will be a long one, will be good news for commodity prices and commodity producers.

Faber's conclusions on Asia are welcome, but coincidental. This book is about investing and how to do it better. After all, tomorrow's gold, if history holds true, is likely to be a surprise to most of us. *Tomorrow's Gold* will help us all in identifying what that surprise might be.

Dr Jim Walker
CLSA Chief Economist
Hong Kong, November 2002

CHAPTER ONE

A world of change

The golden rule is that there are no golden rules.

GEORGE BERNARD SHAW (1856-1950)

Young people often visit my Hong Kong office. Frequently fresh to Asia, they like to tell me how fortunate I was to make the move here way back in 1973. Opportunities to make money, they say, were far better back then. It is true that, in the 70s and early 80s, Asia was right at the beginning of a major boom that lasted through to the financial crisis of 1997. But I totally disagree with holding any one age to be richer in opportunity than another. Openings always exist somewhere in the world and in some sectors of the economy.

When I moved to Asia, the communist countries were still closed but opportunities to participate in rapid expansion could be found in countries like Japan, Hong Kong, Taiwan, South Korea and Singapore. Today, China and Vietnam are liberalising their economies and Cambodia, Myanmar, North Korea and Laos will undoubtedly follow. India has abandoned its isolationism and self-reliance ethos to become far more market-oriented than it was in the 1970s.

Business and investment opportunities are now, in my opinion, even better than they were when I moved east. This is especially so since the 1997 crisis, as stock and real asset valuations are back to very low levels compared to similar assets in the West. But - and this is important - the opportunities today are vastly different to 30 years ago. There is a new Asia to discover. If I were twenty-six again, I would more likely move to Shanghai, Ho Chi Minh, Yangon or Ulan Bator. I would learn the local language to perfection, live with seven concubines and start a business.

* * *

This book is not about predicting economic disasters or colossal booms, but about highlighting opportunities in a world where economic, political and social conditions are continuously changing and accelerating with faster transportation, rapid communications and easier access to information.

With the breakdown of communism and socialism, and the end of self-reliance and isolationism, we are witnessing the most dramatic changes in the global economy since the discovery voyages at the end of the 15th Century and the Industrial Revolution of the 19th Century. Radical change in the markets of China and India have enlarged the world's economic sphere as much as did the discovery of the Americas, punctuating the Cold War economic equilibrium and throwing up marvellous opportunities for smart investors.

Finding the Americas and the trade route around the Cape of Good Hope altered the global established order radically and permanently. The economic centre of the world, until then concentrated around the Mediterranean, moved to Europe's Atlantic coast to capitalise on the rising movement of goods and people to the Americas and the Far East. Similarly, the rise of China, India and the rest of Asia with its three billion people must have a profound effect on the world's economic, social and geopolitical balance. The same will be true of the rise of Russia and the former states of the Soviet Union.

The richest cities and clusters of wealth of the present day are most unlikely to remain so in the future - and investors should not underestimate the rapidity of changes taking place right now!

The Industrial Revolution was also an agricultural transformation, as better productivity in the production of food allowed the global population to explode. Combined with the railroad, it led to urbanisation in the Western industrial countries and brought vast change in the economic environment of the 19th Century world. Thanks to our age of instant and almost free communication, the countries now joining the global economy, such as India and China, can capitalise on the technological achievements and knowledge of Western society at a much faster pace than ever. Therefore, the world will become a far more competitive place, in which new winners will emerge and quickly displace established regions of prosperity and corporate entities who fail to adapt to the new conditions.

A man who fell asleep and woke up 30 years later, in 2002, would hardly recognise cities like Hong Kong, Singapore, Taipei and Seoul. He would not be able to operate fax machines, cellular phones, PCs, printers, digital cameras and Bloomberg machines. He would be amazed at the explosion in world trade brought about by shipping containers, Boeing 747 freighters and the removal of foreign exchange controls. And if you took him to Shanghai or Moscow, he would think he was dreaming, as he could never have imagined communism coming to such an abrupt end and leading to a volcanic eruption in the economy of these cities.

We should be prepared for even more mind-boggling changes in the next 30 years, as the world becomes even more interconnected. The movement of people, goods and information is growing exponentially. This will have huge implications on investment returns. A very large number of companies will fail, while others, most probably not even existing today, will thrive. In fact, the only constant I expect for the future is continuous and rapid change in the world's political, economic and social conditions.

What is unlikely to change, however, is human nature. The historian Will Durant concluded that:

> . . . known history shows little alteration in the conduct of mankind. The Greeks of Plato's time behaved very much like the French of modern centuries; and the Romans behaved like the English. Means and instrumentalities change; motives and ends remain the same: to act or rest, to acquire or give, to fight or retreat, to seek association or privacy, to mate or reject, to offer or resent parental care. Nor does human nature alter as between classes: by and large the poor have the same impulses as the rich, with only less opportunity or skill to implement them. Nothing is clearer in history than the adoption by

> successful rebels of the methods they were accustomed to condemn in the forces they deposed
>
> *Will and Ariel Durant,* The Lessons of History*, New York, 1968, page 34*

* * *

In the following chapters, my modest attempt to highlight some of the changes that might occur is based partly on historical precedent and partly on current economic trends that I regard as almost irreversible. But I also emphasise that mankind will again and again fall prey to the same temptations and emotion. We are all still largely driven by basic instincts. At times, people will succumb to greed, credulity, unbound optimism, contagion, imitation and delusions of grandeur; at others they will be driven by fear, apprehension, desperation and pessimism. Thus, history will remain, as Voltaire remarked, "a collection of the crimes, follies and misfortunes of mankind".

In terms of methodology, I have combined observations about the present global environment with personal investment experience and economic history and theory. Inevitably, such an analysis cannot fulfil every reader's expectations as it remains incomplete and in many instances superficial. Since the global economy is the sum of every single economic decision made by every man, woman and child around the world, economics remains an enormously complex and "dismal" science, leaving much room for interpretation.

In Chapter 2, I analyse some long-term investment themes with a view to making some very tentative forecasts about likely economic and financial trends. In Chapters 3 and 4, I attempt to lower expectations by showing how investors have repeatedly incurred colossal losses - leaving the wealth pyramid fairly constant with many poor at the bottom and just a few rich at the top. The aim is to show that if people truly want to climb to the peak of the pyramid, they have to do something unusual and not conform to the majority. As JJ Rousseau remarked, "follow the course opposite to custom and you will almost always do well".

Chapters 5 to 8 deal largely with cycles in business, prices and stock markets. My aim is to show that economic activity and prices always fluctuate above and below an illusionary *equilibrium*. At times the economy will move into an "excursion of prosperity" and boom conditions while prices overshoot to the stratosphere. On other occasions, an "excursion of gloom" will bring sub-par growth, recession or even depression, while prices collapse to levels unimaginable during the boom. Similarly, high inflation or even hyperinflation will alternate with low inflation or deflation. And while I have offered explanations on the causes of such fluctuations, a precise answer remains elusive. Still, I find it indispensable for an investor to at least be aware of these cycles and the psychology of business people and investors at major economic inflection points.

In Chapter 9, I focus on Asia and its changes of the past 30 years. Chapter 10 discusses a special case in the investment universe - the opportunity high inflation and highly distressed economies can offer to thoughtful and rational investors. I have purposely devoted a full chapter to this complex issue because today's world has - in contrast to the early 1980s - become extremely complacent about inflation. However, after a 20-year-plus bear market in commodities, a pickup in the rate of price increases is - at least in some sectors of the economy - quite likely in future.

In Chapter 11, my aim is to analyse the enormous change the world has experienced since early times and show that further unimaginable shifts in economic geography are likely to occur in the period directly ahead. Chapter 12 takes a critical look at the US economy, the monetary system and current economic policies. The Austrian economist Friedrich Hayek remarked that, "the more the state 'plans' the more difficult planning becomes for the individual". As a like-minded free-market proponent, I take a very critical view of current Federal Reserve Board policies and other forms of government intervention. In light of the 11 September terrorist attacks and the response to them by the US, I am also analysing in Chapter 12, under the heading "The Curse of Empires", how in the past, empires have faced enormous and costly challenges in controlling their borders and territories, and how countries' imperial ambitions led to rising inflation rates and weaker currencies.

Chapter 13 and the Epilogue deal with some of the developments I envision for Asia and the world in the next few years. I am not a great believer in futurology and, to be frank, have very little knowledge about the past and the present - even less about the future. But that should not discourage us from meditating on the *issues* and preparing for the *types* of change that might characterise the road ahead - a road that might be rocky, but one that will always offer great excitement for those with an eye for opportunity.

The increased division of labour - brought about by the modern economy, where hundreds of industrial and service sectors, as well as countries and regions with a wide range of economic, social and political systems continuously interact with each other - makes any analysis of economic and financial trends incomplete and superficial. For this I apologise to the reader, but hope that some of the text in the following chapters will serve as a catalyst for more profound studies into the complexities of today's economic process.

CHAPTER TWO

Major future investment themes

> This currency, as we manage it, is a wonderful machine. It performs its office when we issue it: it pays and clothes troops and provides victuals and ammunition, and when we are obliged to issue a quantity excessive, it pays itself off by depreciation.
>
> *BENJAMIN FRANKLIN (1706-90)*
> In a letter to Samuel Cooper, 22 April 1779

Early in 2002, almost two years after the US bear market started, a well-known investment strategist wrote that, "the most frustrating aspect of being a portfolio manager these days is the lack of long-term themes". Investors want to identify an important fundamental industrial change, make a substantial commitment to a group of stocks benefiting from it, and lean back to watch it develop. But nothing like that seemed to be happening. In my opinion, however, it ought to be clear to all all investors that there is a huge pool of money sloshing around the world. In recent years, this pool has rapidly grown in volume as a result of credit expansion and an increase in the money supply - for which the central banks around the world, under the guidance of Alan Greenspan, the US Treasury and the International Monetary Fund (IMF), are responsible. And, whether or not this artificial stimulus from monetary authorities is healthy or will lead to further unimaginable problems, the fact remains that

- in a free market economy and in absence of foreign exchange controls - the pool of money will flow somewhere and boost some economic activity, and lead to inflation or a bull market in some asset class, somewhere in the world.

The problem with major investment themes

To understand this process better, visualise a gigantic flat bowl, perched on a very large bamboo tower on top of the earth. At its base, the tower is surrounded by investors (see inside front cover). A continuous supply of fresh water (money) flows into the bowl from a huge tap controlled by the world's central bankers. In what economists might call a state of "equilibrium" (which does not exist in the real world), the cash would overflow the bowl evenly unto the earth - economies around the world would expand and all asset classes would appreciate at about the same rate. However the bowl - being so large and perched on such a flexible tower - is unstable and will lean according pressure exerted on the tower by the investors below. If investors are collectively bullish on America, they will lean in such a way as to make the money overflow into the American continent. If they are optimistic about the Nasdaq, the bowl will be tilted to flow into the hi-tech, telecoms, media and biotech sectors, and so on. In short, the direction of the overflow will depend on the bias of investors, which in turn can be manipulated by opinion leaders, the media, analysts, strategists, politicians and economists.

Or think of the investment community as being very powerful due to its total size - similar to a herd of elephants, not very sophisticated when it comes to financial matters. The elephants, being rather docile, will listen to commands from their mahouts (keepers). With their strength and weight, they can bend the bamboo for quite some time in one direction or another. The mahouts aren't particularly sophisticated either - a group consisting of fund managers, stock brokers, economists, strategists and so on - but they have a keen interest to boost the productivity of their elephants and make as much money out of them as possible. Therefore, from time to time, they will give new instructions as to which side of the tower the elephants should lean. This is only natural, because mahouts' salaries depend on elephants' performance and on the volume of business they do. Each time the elephants receive new instructions, the water bowl overflows into a different region, industrial sector - or another asset class altogether.

The point is simply this: As long as the bowl is supplied from the central bankers' tap, and as long as the tower is buffeted by the mahouts and their elephants, there will always be assets that appreciate while others lose momentum. Under the present monetary system, which keeps the money flowing, there will always be major investment themes. So, what really frustrates investors is not a lack of themes, but their own inability to anticipate them.

The problem with major investment themes is that investors have as little imagination as our elephants and are conditioned to listen only to the instructions they receive from the likes of CNBC, Wall Street and government propaganda machines. As a result, investment themes only become obvious to most investors long after they have emerged - only once the bowl has been leaning and overflowing to one side for quite some time and created a bull market in a particular sector. Not surprisingly, we find that the largest flow of money into an asset class such as stocks, bonds, real estate or commodities will occur when just about everybody has fully understood the new theme - which will inevitably coincide with that sector's peak in popularity and prices. This has to be so, because once all the money has poured from the oversized bowl into one sector of the economy, that sector becomes grossly overpriced relative to sectors that haven't benefited from the torrential flows.

There then follows a further complication in the equation of money flowing from the bowl into a particular sector of the economy. In a market economy, the central bankers control the money tap. The mahouts, to a large extent, control the elephants. But none can control what the money will do once it hits earth. Sure, as the bowl leans to one side, the money pouring onto one sector will badly inflate it for a while. But then some smart people - some honest, some less so (I am thinking here of those analysts and corporate executives who, while continuing to paint a glowing picture about their companies, sell out of their own positions) - will notice the huge valuation differences between the inflated and relatively depressed sectors. They will begin to sell the former and move their money across. Thus, while the money continues to pour into the now-recognised major investment theme (recently "the new economy") the flow no longer boosts prices there, but instead leaks into other sectors of the investment universe.

This process will initially go unnoticed by most of the mahouts and their slow-moving elephants. Eventually, however, the public realises that the cheerleaders of the major investment theme have misled them. No matter how heavily they lean against the tower, or how much money pours onto their favourite sector, the leakage will suck up the money. This depresses the favourite investment theme while boosting the depressed sectors. The leak becomes a flood.

When the mahouts and their elephants finally recognise that no matter how much money they pour into one sector, it will no longer rise but, instead, will fall, a major shift takes place. The mahouts force their elephants to take a new position around the tower to shift the downpour into the newly appreciating asset class - but by that time they have already missed the first, most spectacular, gains in the new investment theme.

I regard the money leakage problem as the crux of the problem central banks face when they try to support a market or influence economic activity with monetary measures. Central bankers can regulate the quantity of money pouring into the bowl, but - fortunately for all of us, given their intellect and adherence to economic sophism - the market mechanism will itself control its ultimate direction.

The point to understand is that major investment themes are not obvious when they are their most attractive and promise the highest returns with the lowest risk - that is, at their nascence. When they become obvious to everyone, they are usually already in the final stage of euphoria, which inevitably ends the way we experienced with the hi-tech sector over the last two years. Figure 1 shows the net cashflows into technology funds between 1997 and 2002 to illustrate this observation. Investors only really started to pile into the tech funds at the end of 1999, when the Nasdaq was already above 3,000, and continued their buying binge in the first half of 2000. This was when the long-term theme of investing in "the new economy" was crystal clear to investors around the world (quite the opposite from today, when strategists claim a lack of clear long-term investment trends). But it was also one of the worst times to invest in the then seemingly "obvious" long-term tech, media and telecoms (TMT) story.

Figure 1

'NEW ECONOMY' EUPHORIA

Technology sector funds - Net cashflows (17-week average)

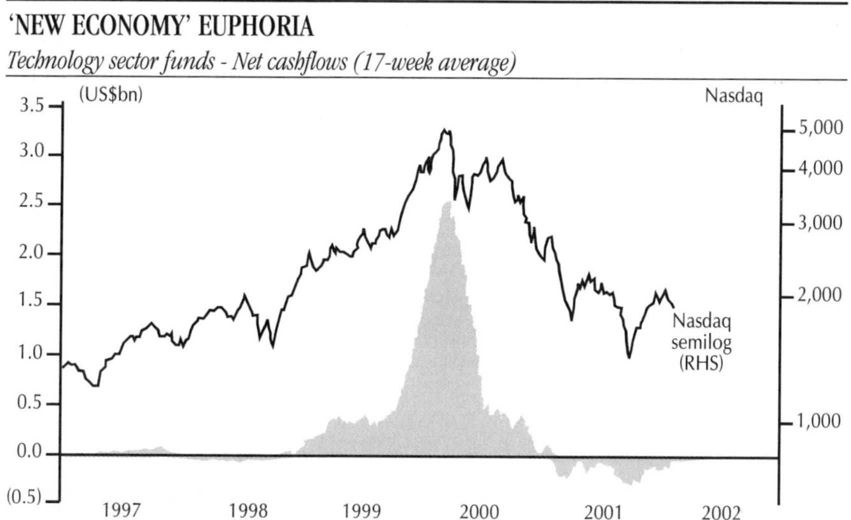

Source: The Leuthold Group - February 02.

I have studied all the major investment themes of the last 30 years - including gold, oil and gas and foreign currencies in the 1970s, Japanese stocks in the 1980s, emerging markets between 1985 and 1997, and US equities in the 1990s. In each case, investors were extremely slow to recognise the new major theme. They were too slow - to their detriment - to understand that the investment game is ever changing, requiring them to abandon the obvious and move to a totally new sector. A good example lies in the price movements of the emerging Asian markets between 1985 and 1997. The big move occurred between 1985 and 1990 (see Figures 2 and 3). By 1990 the party in Asia was almost over, and from 1994 the losses started to pile up, as by then all Asian markets bar Hong Kong had topped out. In US Dollar terms, South Korea, Taiwan, Indonesia and India all peaked between 1989 and 1991, while Malaysia, Thailand and the Philippines made their tops in 1994.

If you look at the money flows into Asia (see Figure 4), it is evident that foreign investors were largely absent during 1985-90 when Asian markets enjoyed their best performance and grew ten to twenty-fold. However, after their stellar performance, and on the back of the strong performance of the Japanese market in the 1980s, investors became enamoured with the region and enthusiastically endorsed the latest major investment theme: being overweight in Asia. I recall that in the early 1990s, and right up to the Asian Crisis in 1997, many financial institutions had more money invested in Asia than the United States.

Figure 2

TAIWAN'S TOP

Taiwan Weighted Index

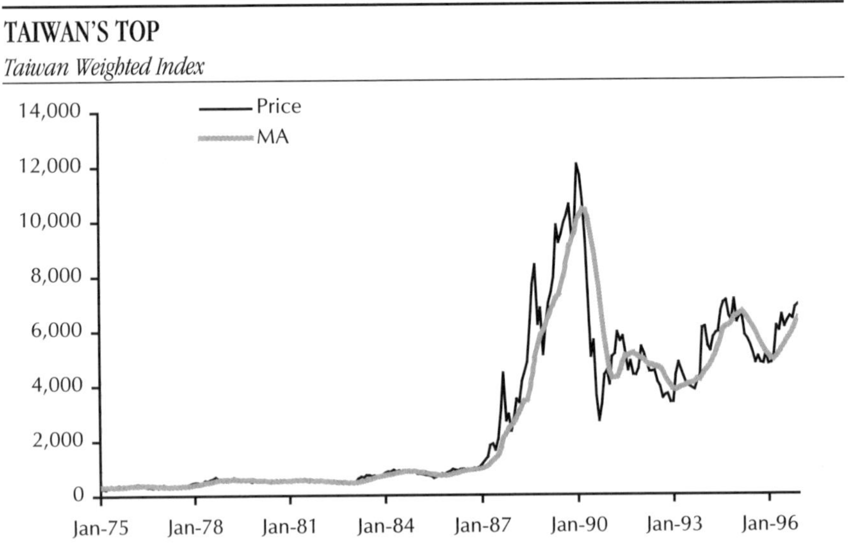

Source: Baring Securities.

Figure 3

INDONESIA'S INCLINE

Indonesia Jakarta Composite Index

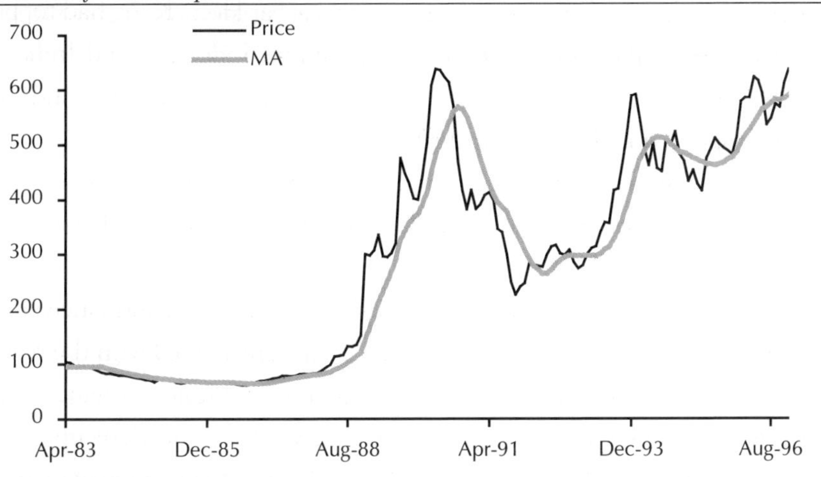

Source: Baring Securities.

Figure 4

ASIA'S BELATED LOVE AFFAIR

Emerging Asia: Net capital flows, 1980-2001

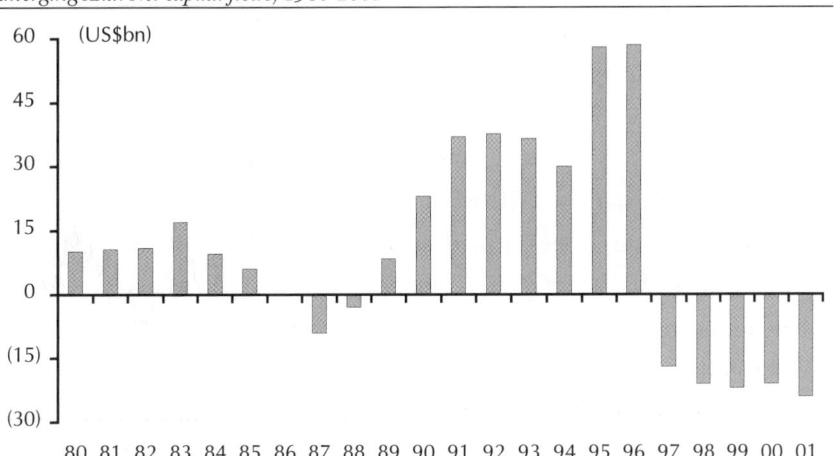

Source: Kim Eng Securities.

In fact, going back to Figure 4, it is remarkable that they not only increased their purchases of Asian securities after the great bull markets of 1985-90 had come to an end, *but foreign investors even stepped up their purchases right before the Asian Crisis of 1997.* I would therefore warn readers to be extremely cautious when investing in a widely accepted and highly popular major investment theme, because, once it is known to just about every investor around the world, the market is likely to enter its most speculative - and final - phase (see also Chapter 7). Admittedly, prices can rise almost vertically during this phase, as we saw the case of the Nasdaq. But this phase is also fraught with high risk and always ends in tears once the bubble bursts. In fact, I would make two additional observations regarding major investment themes.

When the investment community is fascinated by a major investment theme, outstanding opportunities arise elsewhere. Undervaluation must take place in sectors to which nobody is paying attention. In fact, the greater the mania in one sector of a market or in one stock market, the more likely that neglected asset classes elsewhere offer huge appreciation potential. This is one of the cardinal rules of investing, and will always work for the patient long-term investor.

In the 1970s, investors around the world focused increasingly on oil- and energy-related shares, as well as mining companies. They became such a major investment theme that, at their peak in 1980, energy stocks made up 28% of the S&P 500. At that time, a friend of mine worked in the corporate finance department of White Weld & Co. He would tell me about growing up in Sam Walton's neighbourhood, and how great a company Wal-Mart was. (It went public in 1970 with just 24 stores and US$46 million in sales). I paid little attention to my friend (who then owned 4,000 Wal-Mart shares - I hope he kept them), because at the time, few stocks outside energy and mining were performing well. In fact, because my friend was such a nice person I was rather sceptical of his investment acumen and (to my later embarrassment) never bought the stock. In any event, we all miss some great opportunities in life and now I also listen to the advice of some nice people. We all know how well Wal-Mart has done over the last 30 years (see Figure 5), having become the world's largest company in terms of sales (US$200 billion p.a.) and the dominant investment theme within the retailing universe. (Of course, having gained this status, it is now far less attractive from an investment point of view.)

Figure 5

MISSED OPPORTUNITIES

Wal-Mart Stores stock-price performance 1984-2002

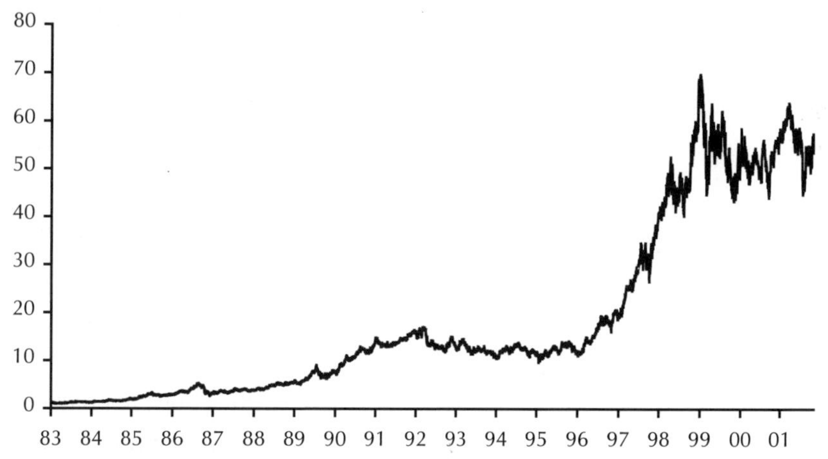

Source: The stock picture.

Another example of a major investment theme that created an outstanding opportunity right next to it was the Japanese market bubble of the late 1980s. At the time, investors were so focused on Japanese equities that they entirely missed the greatest bond market rally in financial history, during which yields on Japanese long-dated government bonds fell from over 6% in the early 1990s to a tad above 1% in 2002. I could go on and list countless other examples of a major investment theme creating tremendous opportunities in other sectors of the markets - including the recent Nasdaq bubble, which led to strong moves in "old economy" stocks and in the mid- and small-cap stock universe, which even produced a new high in the Value Line index in the spring of 2002. However, it is sufficient if we never forget that liquidity pouring from the large bowl into one sector of the economy will eventually - with as much certainty as night follows day - leak into other sectors and lead to sharp bull markets in those sectors.

My second observation with respect to major investment themes is that *the timing of the leakage from the popular and expensive sector into the neglected sector of the investment universe is difficult, if not impossible, to predict.* A popular sector, such as Japan in the late 1980s or the US market in the late 1990s, can captivate the imagination of the investment community for far longer than one might think, even after prices may have peaked. The timing problem is less pronounced when a major theme has just gone out of fashion and there is no obvious replacement in the minds of the investing community - as is the case in 2002, according to some strategists.

It is in this state of confusion that a new investment theme is most likely to emerge without too much delay. Thus, I would argue that from a timing point of view, it is precisely when there are no obvious major investment themes in the minds of investors that the opportunities for them are the most appealing, because in such an environment of general uncertainty the next major investment themes are born. I would therefore like to emphasise that, in both timing and magnitude of the forthcoming move, the opportunity is greatest for capital gains when there is an absence of major themes in the minds of investors.

I have stressed "in the minds of investors" because, in the real world, there is never a lack of major themes. It is just that the investment community does not perceive what is already in the process of fermenting and shaping up. The year 1982 is a case in point. The precious metals and energy boom of the 1970s had come to an end in 1980, and by 1982 investors were at a loss as to what to do with their money, as they all feared another wave of accelerating inflation. Investors had lost on just about everything, since US stocks were then no higher than they had been in 1964 (in inflation-adjusted terms they were down 70% from their mid-60s highs), bonds had tumbled, and since 1980 holders of energy and resource stocks had lost a ton of money. But it was in that environment of uncertainty and anxiety that the greatest bull market in stocks and bonds got under way, which lifted the S&P 500 from 102 to 170 (up 66%) within less than a year and Treasury bond futures from 56 in late 1981 to 83 in 1983! (By 1986 T-bond futures had almost doubled in price, and by 1987 the S&P 500 had risen by more than three times.)

In fact, one peculiarity of the 1982-83 bull market was that it was so sharp and brief that investors, waiting for a correction before piling in, missed most of the action. So, my point is that the longer a trend has been in place, the more time will be required after the turning point before the changes are perceived, even if the new investment themes immediately enjoy a very powerful bull market. The same happened after 1989 in Japan, when the stock market fell and investors continued to focus on stocks while they should have shifted their attention to the bond market.

Even since March 2000 and right up to the present, there have been some major investment themes. The most important was to stay out of, or short, the Nasdaq. Another was to avoid the S&P 500, which was weighted by large stocks and benefited until March 2000 from the process of indexation. On the long side, a major theme was to own small- and mid-cap stocks, which have strongly outperformed large stocks over the last two years. Another was to own the Asian emerging markets and Russia, which performed far better than the S&P 500 (see Figure 6). US and UK residential real estate was yet another major theme, since it has continued to appreciate - at least so far.

Figure 6

OUTPERFORMING THE S&P 500

Emerging markets versus global equities, 2000-2002

Source: BCA Research 2002.

Finally, the ownership of gold mining companies and of physical gold is a major theme - by mid 2002, mining companies had more than doubled over the previous 12 months and gold became the world's strongest major currency, rising from US$255/oz in August 1999 to over US$320 by the summer of 2002. So, there is never a lack of opportunities - particularly when the central banks are flooding the system with liquidity, which inevitably will lift the prices of at least one or several asset classes. What is lacking, however, when major secular trends change or when a major bull market reverses gear - a phase usually characterised by a number of strongly contradictory trends that obscure the event - is the comprehension by the investment community that the cards of the investment game have been reshuffled and a new game with new rules has begun.

Future major investment themes

What is important to understand is that once a major investment theme goes ballistic (gold in the late 1970s, Japan's stock market in the late 1980s and the Nasdaq until March 2000) and then ends with a severe bust, *the leadership always changes*, as investors finally shift into a new sector. In fact, I would argue that the greater the mania in one stock, or entire market (be it precious metals, agricultural commodities or real assets such as property, art and collectibles), the more likely it is that a burst bubble creates a permanent shift into another asset class. Therefore, I am inclined to rule out the Nasdaq and the S&P 500 as an asset class that will provide the future leadership. I shall explain in more detail in Chapter 12 why I doubt that US financial markets can provide the kind of leadership we are now trying to identify. Similarly, Western European stock markets, which are closely correlated to the S&P 500.

So, we are left with the following major asset classes that could provide opportunities for large capital gains: real estate, bonds, commodities, Japanese stocks, emerging markets, US Dollars and other currencies. Now, I wish to emphasise that I am listing here only *major* asset classes. This means that it is entirely possible that *within* the Nasdaq, or *within* the entire US market, some sectors may perform well from time to time, as we saw in 2000-01 in the case of retailers, home builders and small cap stocks. Also, I have little doubt that at some point the extremely depressed telecom sector might rebound rather strongly, because the more companies go out of business or are permanently weakened, the more it strengthens the position of the stronger companies that can capitalise on the situation and expand market share. Moreover, it should also be understood that even if a major investment theme is over, sharp bear market rallies do occur from time to time, providing opportunities for capital gains in the order of 30-50%, and sometimes even more.

However, for the purposes of this book, I am only interested in asset classes with large market value and the potential to rise over the next ten years by as much as Japanese stocks in the 1980s or US equities in the 1990s. (Naturally, we will have to analyse at some point whether it is also possible that such persistent and secular bull markets are a thing of the past.) Thus, I propose in the following to discuss the outlook for several asset classes that, under certain conditions, could provide superior long-term returns. In Chapter 12, I shall also explain why US equities even at their present level (S&P 500 around 800) are not particularly attractive and are, therefore, unlikely to provide the leadership we are looking for in this study.

Can US bonds provide significant capital gains?

There is a growing body of pundits, including most central bankers, who fear that the world is headed into a period of deflation, or at least believe that deflation is the greatest threat to the global economy. This is in stark contrast to the early 1980s, when the main fear was accelerating inflation and a well-known forecaster labelled bonds "certificates of confiscation". It would have been inconceivable then for the Federal Reserve Board to publish an essay entitled "Preventing Deflation; Lessons from Japan's Experience in the 1990s", as it recently did (International Discussion Paper, Number 729, June 2002).

In the early 80s, the American bond market had just completed a bear market lasting more than 30 years, during which the yield on long-term Treasuries had risen from less than 2% to around 15% (see Figure 7). Moreover, because of an inversion in the yield curve, US ten-year government bond yields reached a record of 15.84% on 30 September 1981, while the prime rate rose to above 20% for a brief time. Compare this with today. The Fed fund rate is at a 40-year low, long-term US Treasuries yield less than 5%, and ten-year Treasuries around 4%! At the same time, the inflation fears of the early 1980s that persisted into the 1990s (the inflation psychology has died only very slowly in the last 20 years), have been replaced by complacency and the notion that inflation is dead. I might add that, in the early 1980s, the bond bull market started with great hesitation, because inflationary psychology was so deeply embedded in investors' minds. Thus, as can be seen from Figure 7, the bond market suffered a severe setback from the end of 1983 to the summer of 1984.

Figure 7

FIXED FORTUNES

US Treasury bond futures (nearest futures contract), 1977-2002

Source: CRB.

Just to illustrate how slowly investor psychology changed, *Business Week's* 28 May 1984 cover headline read: "Trouble in the Government

Bond Market". Huge losses had been suffered by some dealers, due to the sharp fall in prices in early 1984. Thomas Strauss, then a managing partner of Salomon Brothers, was quoted as saying, "Investors' psychology is such that no one even wants to hear about bonds. It is a real rout." (The very negative sentiment towards bonds was reflected in the very low bullish consensus figure for Treasury bond futures, which for weeks in May 1984 was around 20%.)

I have mentioned these events at the beginning of a secular bull market in bonds because it is important to understand that when a switch in major investment themes is about to occur, there is a strong disbelief and enormous scepticism in the minds of investors as to the merits of the new theme. Therefore, whatever the next theme might be, sharp corrections and costly setbacks in the prices of the new leadership sector will be more the norm than the exception. I might add that, in the early 1980s, very few market observers believed that a secular bull market in stocks had begun.

Now, it would seem to me that the current environment for bonds is almost a mirror image of the early 1980s. The yield curve is steep (and not inverted, as was the case then); short-term rates are at a record low (not record highs); and the inflationary psychology of the 1980s has given way to complacency or fear of deflation. Moreover, whereas in the early 1980s investors had just gone through the worst period in history for the American bond market - during which long-term bond prices declined by 50% from 1977-81 (see Figure 7) and there was a collapse in the US Dollar (from DM4 to DM1.75 in 1969-80) - today's investors are conditioned by declining commodity prices, low inflation, declining interest rates, an upward-trending bond market and a strong US Dollar.

However, as we shall discuss in Chapter 12, empires (such as the USA now holds itself to be) tend to have accelerating inflation, rising interest rates and a weak currency as they mature. Moreover, if there is one iron law of economics that still applies, it is that excessive monetary stimulus and a rapid expansion of credit will always at some point spill over into real asset markets such as property, commodities and precious metals, which subsequently lead to higher consumer price inflation rates. In fact the Fed paper I mentioned above draws the general lesson from Japan "that when inflation and interest rates have fallen close to zero, and the risk of deflation is high, stimulus - both monetary and fiscal - should go beyond the levels conventionally implied by baseline forecasts of future inflation and economic activity". The report concludes that in the case of Japan, "by reducing debt service burdens and providing support to asset prices, lowering interest rates more rapidly could have alleviated earlier some of the constraints on demand posed by balance sheet problems. Hence, financial fragility did not obviate the potential effectiveness of additional monetary easing in Japan during the 1990s". This paper reflects very much the views that make the rounds at the Fed these days, and have shaped Mr Greenspan's monetary policies over the last 15 years.

If there is a problem somewhere - the Crash of October 1987, the Savings & Loans Crisis of 1990/91, the Mexican Crisis in 1994, the Long-Term Capital Magagement (LTCM) bailout crisis in 1998 and the recent collapse of the Nasdaq - or a perceived problem (Y2K at the end of 1999), the policy response has always been to supply the system with excess liquidity to avoid any economic discomfort *à tout prix*. But that these expansionary monetary policies cannot ensure eternal prosperity ought to be clear. They only alleviate the symptoms of problems that led to the crises, not their causes. Moreover, by interfering in the free-market economy they will inevitably also result in some unintended consequences. On top of the existing maladjustments or excesses that brought along the crises, they will create new maladjustments and new excesses somewhere else, which then bring about an even larger crisis at a later date (see also Chapter 6).

Finally, and this I think is the most important issue associated with a Fed that has increasingly taken on the role of a "central planner", who will always stand ready to bail out the system, is the moral hazard these bailouts bring along. By the late 1990s, investors became increasingly convinced that the Fed would never let the stock market go down and it would always stand ready to support an ongoing bull market in US equities. Thus, people kept investing at ludicrous valuations that had little to do with economic reality. Individuals who still bought the Nasdaq at over 5000 in the spring of 2000 were not even wrong in their assumptions. By aggressively lowering interest rates in 2001, the Fed indeed tried to support the stock market, but where it went wrong was as to where the money would flow. As I have explained above, it can control the money tap, but it cannot control where the money flows. So over the last two years, the Fed's excess money creation no longer found its way into the stock market, but flowed into real estate and boosted that market to what I would now also call a bubbly phase.

The point is that as long as a central bank is willing to supply an endless money stream to an economy, there will always be an inflationary bias somewhere. In some instances, inflation will concentrate in asset classes (bonds and stocks, real estate, collectibles) and in others, it will find its way to wages and consumer prices. Thus, in an environment of preventing deflation *à tout prix* it is unlikely that bonds will perform particularly well, given their already low yields and the fact that they have already enjoyed a 20-year bull market. And while bonds may continue to outperform equities in the US for some time, it is more likely that the secular bull market in bonds is in its terminal phase, or may already have ended, than that bonds will be the next major investment theme.

I concede, however, that in the near future government bonds could continue to perform satisfactorily because the economy is likely to be weaker than consensus holds. I expect American households eventually to reduce spending on housing and consumer goods, which may lead to a temporary further rise in bond prices. Therefore, although we have apprehensions about the bond market in the long term, we feel that, for the near future, government bonds may still hold or even appreciate somewhat. I also think that at some point the purchase of a carefully selected portfolio of distressed or junk bonds could provide very high returns, as they increasingly have an equity character - meaning that their prices will recover when the economy finally improves.

What about real estate?

According to Nationwide, the UK's largest building society, average home prices in the UK soared by 22% over the last 12 months while the figure for the US is 8.8%. According to some close observers, the property bubble may be about to burst in the UK, but the US market is just beginning to show signs of speculative activity and therefore the widely discussed "housing bubble" could last a few years. Personally, however, I doubt it will continue much longer.

As I explained earlier, the money pouring from the giant bowl has since 2000 been leaking into real assets. Thus, in 2002, despite weakness in stocks, residential real estate prices have continued to rise in selected markets - even in Silicon Valley and in the San Francisco Bay area. But in my opinion this rise is rather suspect, since it is being fuelled by artificially low short-term interest rates and indirect subsidies handed out by government-sponsored enterprises such as Fannie Mae, which have continued to support existing home sales and the refinancing of mortgages. However, we should not forget that as soon as interest rates rise, the refinancing boom, which reached a new record in the autumn of 2002, will come to an abrupt end and inevitably lead to consolidation or decline in the housing market. Figure 8, courtesy of Bridgewater Associates, shows very clearly the close correlation between bond yields (inverted in the figure) and the Refinancing Index.

Thus, one could argue that the best environment for the housing market would be a weak economy and a poorly performing stock market that would keep interest rates low or even lead to further declines, whence people would shift money out of poorly performing equities into property. This scenario is a distinct possibility - at least for a while. But eventually a weak economy will take its toll on personal income gains and employment and (via the value of the US Dollar) probably also on interest rates, which might rise even in a weak economic environment (see also Chapter 10). Moreover, it would be the first time I would have experienced an enduring rise in property prices in a bear market for equities. Normally, after a while, property prices join the decline in the stock market.

Figure 8

CLOSE CORRELATION

Mortgage refinancing index vs 10 year bond yield, 1990-2002

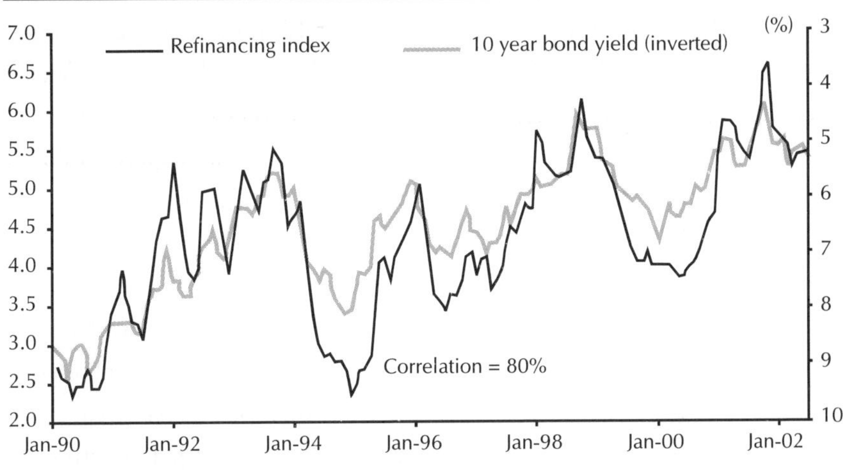

Source: Bridgewater Associates.

Lastly, and most importantly, I would feel far more comfortable with US residential real estate as a major investment theme if house price increases in recent years had not been driven by a worrisome increase in mortgage debt. From Figure 9, courtesy of Ed Yardeni, we can see that home mortgages increased in the 1980s and early 1990s by about US$150 billion annually. Then in 2000 the rate jumped to around US$400 billion and has recently (over the last four quarters) been running at close to US$600 billion - not a trivial amount even for a US$10-trillion economy. In addition, the recent record-breaking existing home sales at a time when new home sales are running below the level of last year should also be viewed with some concern. High turnover in any market is one of the most reliable indicators of speculative activity and serves as a warning flag that the market is overheated (by contrast, markets bottom out amid low volume and turnover - see Chapter 5).

Figure 9

OVERHEATING HOUSING

Home mortgage borrowing

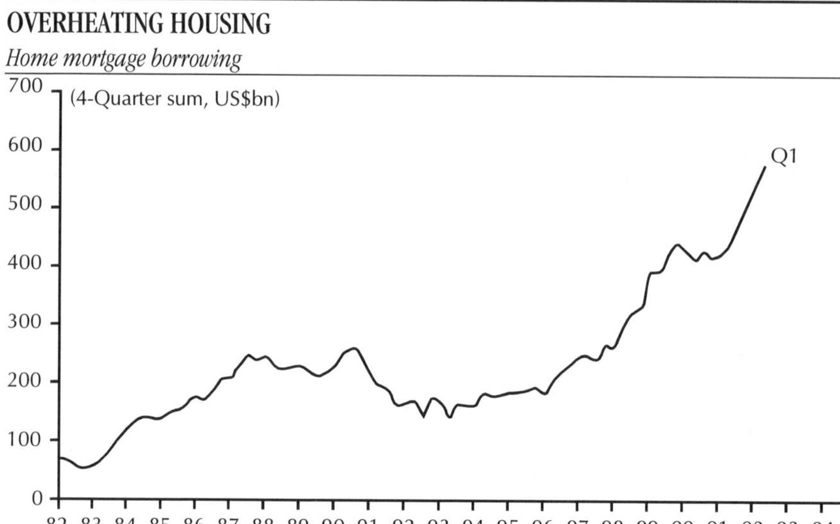

Source: Federal Reserve Board, flow of funds accounts, Ed Yardeni / Prudential Securities (www.prudential.com).

For all the above reasons, I believe US real estate is not overpriced on average compared to US equities and property prices in Europe - but some trophy markets do seem very extended and I doubt US real estate will become a major investment theme for the long term. Any market that is rising because of a colossal increase in credit ought to be viewed with great caution, as we now know all too well from the debacle that befell the telecom sector over the last 18 months!

Real estate in other locations around the world is, however, another matter. In a number of Asian emerging economies, property prices tumbled after the Asian Crisis as a result of collapsing demand, repossessions and currency depreciations. Property prices then stabilised in 1998 and 1999 and, more recently, have begun to rise. Therefore, with prices for luxury condominiums in cities such as Kuala Lumpur, Jakarta, Manila and Bangkok hovering at between US$1,000 and US$1,500 per square meter, the Asian property markets would seem to offer both relatively high current rental yields as well as the potential for future capital gains. Following the collapse of the Argentine Peso, property prices are also once again a bargain in Buenos Aires.

I also believe that, following the breakdown of communism and socialism, the world is experiencing a colossal change in economic geography - a subject I deal with in more detail in Chapter 11. Cities like Shanghai, Beijing, Moscow, Ho Chi Minh, Bangalore and so on are developing very quickly and becoming far more important economically and, therefore, real estate prices will rise there in the long term. Conversely, cities (notably Hong Kong) that thrived as long as China and Russia remained closed societies, because they served as trading and financial intermediaries, will underperform.

In sum, I doubt that US residential real estate will be the next major future investment theme, whereas property prices in some emerging markets, such as in Asia, Eastern Europe, Russia and even Latin America, could yield very high returns in the next five to ten years.

Emerging economies

I discuss the outlook for emerging markets in greater detail in Chapter 9, but I wish to make a few points here to foster my case for overweighting emerging markets - at least for the long term. In the last two years, international investors have purchased a record amount of US assets in the form of direct investment and portfolio flows. Recently, this has subsided somewhat - so money no longer flowing to the US will be invested elsewhere. Undoubtedly, some will find its way into Europe and Japan, but the valuations of equities are so much lower in emerging economies that I am certain some will also flow into this asset class. As can be seen from Figure 10, courtesy of the Bank Credit Analyst's *Weekly Emerging Markets Strategy Bulletin* (www.BCAresearch.com), the relative price/earnings ratios in emerging markets are near an all-time low compared to the US.

And whereas the earnings picture in the US is still very murky, in emerging markets we find an improving corporate earnings cycle, driven less by exports than domestic demand. The latter is fuelled by excess liquidity, accumulated savings now being spent, and the emergence of a rapidly expanding consumer credit market - which, however, does concern me somewhat. Although consumer credit has not yet reached dangerous levels that would cloud the near-term outlook, I am worried that we shall in due course witness a real consumer lending boom that in two or three years could lead to another set of problems.

Figure 10

NEAR ALL-TIME LOW

Relative P/E: emerging markets versus US, 1990-2002

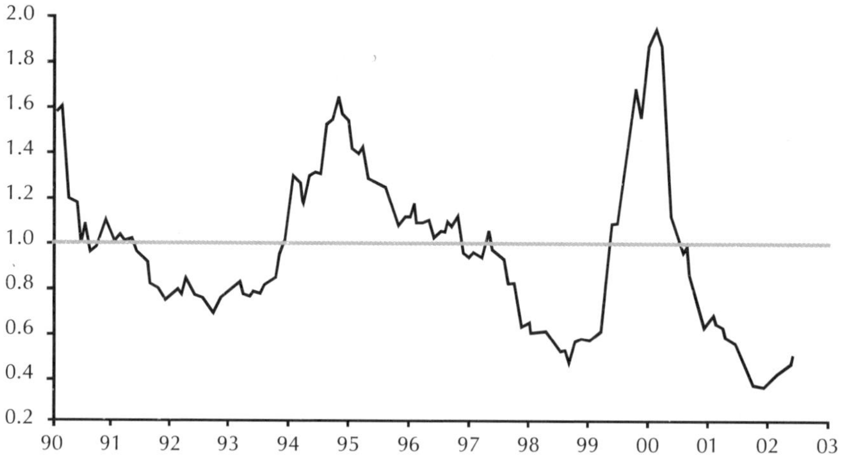

Source: www.BCAresearch.com - emerging market strategy.

Another concern that some strategists have in regard to emerging economies, sluggish exports aside, is the shrinking volume of foreign direct investment (FDI). According to Bridgewater Associates, FDI (ex China) flow to major emerging economies has dwindled from US$95 billion in 1999 to US$59 billion at present. The drop was particularly sharp in Latin America, where, as a percentage of the economy, FDI declined from 4.2% in 1999 to the current 1.9%. (In Asia, by contrast, FDI is rising once again and approaching the 1997 record.) However, I do not consider the overall decline in FDI to be all that relevant for equity investors. More important, in my opinion, are portfolio flows, which in the case of Asia and Eastern Europe are picking up. Moreover, it was partly the high level of FDI that led to the Asian Crisis, as overinvestment led to overcapacity in practically every sector of the economy and then to an earnings collapse.

What Asia and the other emerging economies need right now is a better pricing environment for commodities and commodity-related products - which seems to be underway - and not necessarily more investment. In particular, as a theme for the next few years, we favour emerging economies that will benefit from a pickup in commodity prices, including Russia, Indonesia, Malaysia, Thailand and the Philippines. Moreover, opportunities also exist now in some of the lesser-known markets, such as Sri Lanka and Bangladesh, which have not yet moved up much in price, as well as in the rapidly liberalising Vietnamese economy. Finally, I also believe that at some point great bargains will present themselves in Argentina and Brazil and in peripheral markets such as we find in some African and Middle Eastern countries.

I should like to mention three more points about emerging economies. I would be the first to accept that macroeconomic trends are important, and that in severe global recessions everyone suffers to some extent. Thus, I understand why some investors still hesitate to invest in emerging markets. However, it is important to understand that the emerging economies of today are the lowest-cost producers in practically every sector of the global economy. Oil and gas in the Middle East, minerals in Russia and South Africa, software in India, electronics in China, textiles in Bangladesh, shoes and coffee in Vietnam, steel in Brazil, pulp and paper in Indonesia and healthcare, entertainment, cosmetic surgery, transvestites and golf in Thailand - all can be produced or provided in these countries far cheaper than anywhere else. And while I do not claim that this list is complete or even particularly accurate, the point is that the worse the economic climate might become around the world, the more likely it is that the lowest-cost producers will perform relatively well, as they will be the last to go out of business. The only caveat to this statement is obviously that this will only be true as long as global trade doesn't collapse under newfound American protectionism!

Another point is that if you travelled ten years ago to some of the emerging economies and visited them again this year you would be struck by how much progress there has been. Infrastructure is in place, telephones now work efficiently practically everywhere, modern business methods have proliferated, management has improved and standards of living have in many instances leapt forward. And all of this occurred during a period that was rather miserable for the emerging stock markets, since most of them are still much lower than they were between 1990 and 1994. Compare this phenomenon with the Depression years in the US. Colossal technological progress took place in the 1930s and 40s, and there is no doubt that, by the late 30s, standards of living were higher than in the 20s - and yet the Dow Jones Industrial Index did not exceed its 1929 high until 1954. Economic progress in many emerging economies cannot necessarily be judged by the performance of their stock markets. In fact, official statistics probably significantly understate the size of some of these economies, because they fail to capture a vast number of transactions on the basis of barter or in cash.

My last point, particularly concerning the Asian emerging economies, is that up to now the Asian countries have depended heavily on the US for both exports and FDI. However, I envision an Asia that will be much more integrated into, and dependent on, the Chinese economy. China will become the top consumer of Asian natural resources, send out Asia's largest number of tourists, and invest heavily around the region in joint ventures or take over entire businesses. This coming integration with the Chinese economy will, in my opinion, be rather favourable for the region, as each country will increasingly benefit from its competitive advantages.

To summarise my thoughts, I feel that emerging markets, along with commodities, have the best chance of being the major investment theme for the next five to ten years and of significantly outperforming the stock markets of the Western industrialised countries. However, emerging markets will remain a volatile asset class - so whenever markets, such as Thailand and Indonesia, perform as well as they did in the first six months of 2002, a phase of profit-taking is likely to follow.

Commodities

Since the beginning of 2002, some commodity prices have rallied sharply.

Cotton futures are up 27% from their 30-year price lows, palm oil prices are up 37% since the beginning of the year, grain prices are up 40% from their lows in late 2001, rice futures on the CBOT have rallied from their all-time lows by almost 50%, industrial metals are up by 9% for the year to date and precious metals 13%. Is this the beginning of a major advance in commodity prices? I believe so.

I explained earlier how major investment themes create relative cheapness in other asset classes. This is more so for commodity prices than any other asset class. Never before in the history of capitalism have commodities been as inexpensive compared to the CPI or to financial assets than they are now after a 20 to 30-year bear market. I also explained how eventually the money that pours from the large bowl into major investment themes leaks into other sectors. This process seems to have begun, as some large investors share increasingly serious concerns about the stability of the giant water bowl on top of the real world.

Some readers will, of course, object to this view and argue that commodity prices are low simply because, for many commodities, supply exceeds demand, and therefore they rule out any sustainable price increases. This may be true in some cases, but the fact is that all great commodity bull markets started from a low that was *put in place by oversupply*. The question is whether the present glut of many commodities will one day be replaced by tight supply, or whether a sharply falling US Dollar could lead to a rise in commodity prices. I have earlier described the psychology surrounding the major 1982 stock market lows in the US and argued that the present financial environment is almost a mirror-image of that time. The fear of inflation has been replaced by an almost universal fear of deflation, and financial assets have replaced natural resources as the major investment theme in the minds of almost all investors.

In fact, the current situation reminds me very much of 1969-70 - the eve of one of the greatest commodity booms. Commodity prices were then also very depressed compared to equities, and experts argued that crude oil prices, which then hovered around US$1.70 a barrel, would fall to less than US$1 in the 1970s because the market was so glutted. No one at the time could conceive that oil prices would approach US$50 a barrel on the spot market in 1980, and that gold and silver would rise by more than 20 times over a decade! Nor did anyone think the US Dollar would decline by as much as it eventually did. In those days, investors were still obsessed with "growth stocks", which frequently sold for more than 50 times earnings, and they paid hardly any attention to the relatively low prices for commodities.

But what happened in the 1970s is visible from Table 1. It should serve all investors a reminder that, from time to time, hard assets can outperform financial assets by a wide margin. I might add that the first increases in oil prices by the Organisation of the Petroleum Exporting Countries (OPEC) in the fall of 1973 and on 1 January 1974 to US$11.65 were not taken very seriously. Milton Friedman wrote then that prices would shortly decline again to below US$2 a barrel. In addition, the strength in commodity prices in the early 1970s was remarkable in light of the particularly severe 1973-74 recession. I am not necessarily arguing that we shall experience a repetition of the 1970s, but what I want to show is that investors - who were by no means less sophisticated in the early 1970s than they are today - totally overlooked the next major investment theme.

Moreover, we should realise that commodity prices are today even lower than they were at the beginning of the 1970s - certainly in real terms and in some cases even in absolute terms (see Figure 11). Now, one peculiarity of the 1990s was the lack of synchronised growth in the global economy. In the early 1990s, Europe hardly grew, then throughout the entire 1990s Japan had hardly any economic growth, and in the late 1990s the Asian Crisis led to very weak demand for industrial commodities. So, if there should be, as the optimists claim, a synchronised economic recovery, then in all likelihood commodity prices will increase sharply - particularly for industrial commodities, which are extremely depressed, and for which, in the case of copper, lead, aluminium, tin, zinc and nickel, inventory levels are now rather low.

Table 1

THE 1970S BOOM IN REAL ASSETS

Performance of various investments - June 1970-1980

	Return (%)	Rank
Oil	34.7	1
Gold	31.6	2
US coins	27.7	3
Silver	23.7	4
Stamps	21.8	5
Chinese ceramics	21.6	6
Diamonds	15.3	7
US farmland	14.0	8
Old Masters	13.1	9
Housing	10.2	10
Consumer price index	7.7	11
Treasury bills	7.7	12
Foreign exchange	7.3	13
Bonds	6.6	14
Stocks	6.1	15

Note: Compound annual rates of return. Source: Salomon Inc.

Finally, the US Dollar, which is now almost as overvalued as in the mid-1980s (by some measures, even more), is likely to have started a multi-year bear market (see Figure 12). However, as we shall discuss in Chapter 12, this bear market is unlikely to be as dramatic as the 1970s, when the Dollar fell by almost 70% against European hard currencies, as neither Europe and Japan nor any emerging economy would wish to have their currency appreciate by much more than another 10-15% against the US Dollar. Therefore, the most likely scenario will be that all currencies depreciate against a basket of commodities, including, naturally, gold and silver.

For the individual investor, the question is how best to participate in the coming bull market for commodities. While we think gold and silver prices are at the beginning of a long-term bull market that will end in a couple of years in a speculative frenzy *à la* the Nasdaq in 2000, there may be better intermediate opportunities in commodities that are far more depressed than gold. These include coffee, sugar, rubber, wheat, corn and cotton. Fully realising that it may not be possible for every reader of this book to store ten tons of coffee and five tons of sugar in their kitchen, my advice would be to purchase a basket of commodity futures and roll them over periodically.

Figure 11

TOO DEPRESSED

Adjusted prices of the 17 commodities comprising the CRB index

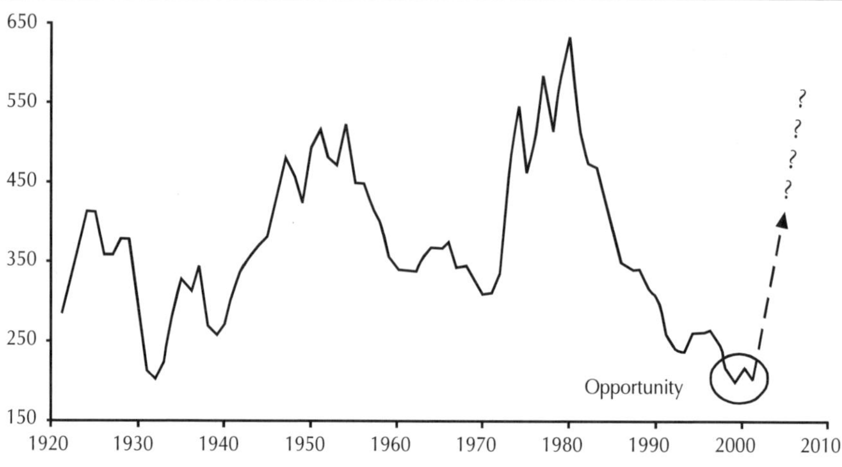

Source: www.ditomassogroup.com.

Figure 12

OVERVALUED

US Dollar real effective exchange rate

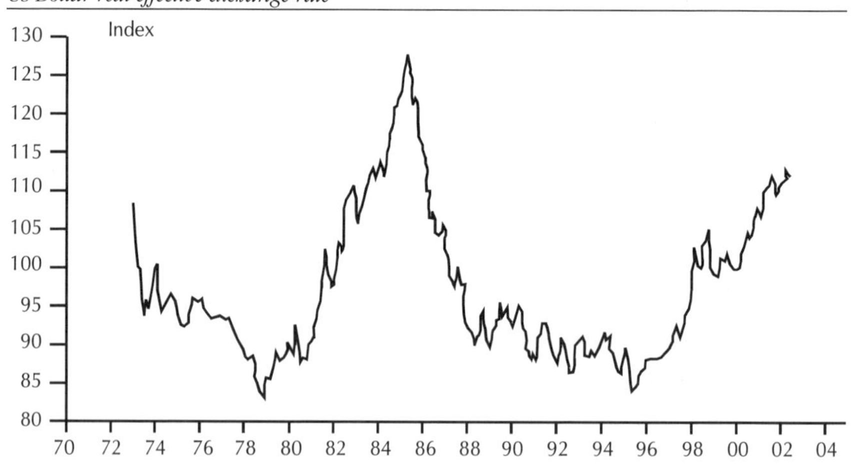

Source: ABN-Amro.

Another way to participate in a commodities bull market is to purchase mining and other resource stocks (pulp, plantations, iron ore, industrial metals, potash, fertilisers, oil, etc) and farmland - ideally in emerging markets that have a heavy exposure to commodities. In fact, if we look at the performance of emerging markets in the past we find a close correlation between the performance of the Commodity Research Bureau (CRB) Index and emerging stock markets. Rising commodity prices have always been favourable for emerging markets, while declining prices have led to economic problems and poor performances. Thus, if commodity prices are at the beginning of a multi-year rise, then investors should overweight emerging markets - particularly the resource rich ones, as pointed out above.

* * *

The aim of this first chapter has been to show that major investment themes always exist but that, from time to time, at major turning points in the investment game and when the rules change, investors cannot see the emergence of a new theme and become frustrated precisely when they should be the most inquisitive about new opportunities. The problem is that, in this phase of the investment environment, investors are still far too used to pursuing the old theme to endorse a new asset class. To some extent, this paralysis of the minds of investors is understandable. As I have shown, when a major theme ends, tremendous undervaluation exists in other sectors, because all the money was flowing during the final, manic stage of the boom into just one major investment theme. Other sectors of the investment universe were thus totally deprived of any investor interest. During the investment mania one will, therefore, frequently hear that the depressed sectors "always go down" and will continue to do so.

I believe the investment environment we are in now is almost a mirror image of the 1981-82 period. Stocks and bonds then entered a secular bull market that lasted until recently. At the same time, commodity prices began their most vicious bear market on record, with the result that they are now, in real terms, lower than at any time in the history of capitalism. However, the emergence of a secular bull market for commodities could be bumpy, especially if, as we believe, the global economy will again weaken in 2003 or 2004. Moreover, don't forget the sharp drop that bonds experienced in 1984. They were already in a powerful secular bull market that had begun in the fall of 1981 and has lasted until now, yet a severe shakeout took place right at the beginning of that bull market. In the present situation, as in 1981-82, there are far too many crosscurrents - so anything can happen, as volatility tends to be very high in this confusing stage of the investment world. So, while I like gold and silver and all other commodities long term, I have no idea how deep a correction we might experience, or whether we could even see new lows for some commodities (however not likely for gold and silver - see Chapter 12).

The emerging markets are similarly depressed when compared to the US and I expect significant outperformance for this asset class over the next few years. Also, as explained, I also like real estate in selected emerging economies, whereas I am very sceptical about the sustainability of the US and UK real estate booms.

Still, I should like to warn investors in the following two chapters to be more realistic about long-term investment returns than they have become accustomed as a result of the powerful bull markets we experienced, in the late 1990s, in the financial markets of the Western industrialised countries.

CHAPTER THREE

A caution about high-return investment expectations

> The art of getting rich consists not in industry, much less in saving, but in a better order, in timeliness, in being at the right spot.
>
> *RALPH WALDO EMERSON (1803-82)*

It is not difficult to show that no asset class or business has done well in the *very* long term. Let us assume that one of our forefathers had put the equivalent of just one US dollar on deposit in the year 1000. Being more modest than today's online trading community and mutual fund investors, who expect their funds to appreciate by more than 15% per annum forever, our ancestor would have wisely opted for a deposit with just 5% annual compound interest and left his capital on deposit up to now. Well, unfortunately, none of us had the good fortune to have such a wise ancestor - since this tiny US dollar would have increased by now to US$1,546 million trillion (a quintillion). If we, today, invested this small fortune at just 6% we would enjoy an annual pre-tax income of US$93 quintillion - three million times the current world GDP.

Since the world's GDP is essentially the cashflow that can be obtained from the value of all the world's assets, it becomes clear from this quick calculation that dreams of very long-term returns of even 5% per annum are totally unrealistic. Otherwise, the world's GDP would not be just about US$30 trillion, but a huge multiple of US$93 quintillion. After all, the combined value of all the world's assets in the year 1,000 were far higher than US$1 (some historians estimate that, in the year 1000, world GDP in today's Dollars stood around US$25 billion).

Obviously, as has repeatedly been the case throughout history, wealth and accumulated savings (investments) were destroyed through natural disasters - earthquakes, floods, droughts, plagues, fire, volcanic eruptions, tornadoes, etc - or wars, revolutions, expropriations, hyperinflation, depression, fraud and obsolescence.

The discovery voyages

This is not to say there were no great investment opportunities over the past 1,000 years. Quite to the contrary, opportunity has always knocked on people's doors. This was particularly true for the period that followed the discovery voyages at the end of the 15th Century, which enlarged the economic sphere of the world dramatically. Equally, the Industrial Revolution at the beginning of the 19th Century brought forth a large number of great investments for early buyers.

But alas, no "great investments" have withstood the test of "the very long term". Consider the following: In the pre-capitalistic age, warfare and the conquest of new territories were an "investment," very much the way a company today acquires additional equipment or takes over a competitor for the purpose of increasing its manufacturing capacity and profit. The conquest of Mexico by the Spanish conquistador Hernando Cortez and of Peru by Francisco Pizarro must be regarded as two of the greatest investments ever. This especially given how few soldiers were needed to secure victory and how much gold and silver subsequently flowed to Spain from the New World. In 1532, Pizarro captured the Inca monarch Atahuallpa (protected by an army of 80,000 men) with only 168 soldiers, held him prisoner, extracted history's largest ransom (a large room filled with gold), then killed him. And within ten years the Spaniards had opened up the silver mine of Potosi (now in Bolivia) from which most of the world's silver originated in the 16th Century. I doubt any investment ever enjoyed the kind of labour productivity Pizarro achieved with his 168 men.

Nevertheless, Spain's returns on its "investments" in the Americas were short lived. Between 1535 and 1560, gold and silver imports increased rapidly and created a tremendous economic boom - the streets of the port city of Cadiz were said to be paved with gold. But, thereafter, shipments levelled off and then declined, which led to several defaults by the Spanish Crown at the end of the 16th Century and a disastrous depression in Spain in the 17th (aggravated by a 25% decline in its population caused by an epidemic).

Nevertheless, the discovery of the Americas radically changed the world's economic geography. Thriving 14th and 15th Century Italian commercial centres such as Venice, Amalfi, Genoa and Florence were thrown into a corner of the world as the centre of commerce switched, first to Lisbon and Cadiz, later to Amsterdam and Antwerp, and then, in the 18th Century, to London.

I am mentioning this here, because we must realise that - as a result of the breakdown of communist and socialist ideology and the end of isolationist policies on the Indian subcontinent - the world's economic sphere was enormously enlarged with close to three billion people joining our free-market, capitalistic system. The importance of adopting capitalism in countries like China, the former Soviet Union, Vietnam and India cannot be underestimated and will again, radically change global economic geography (as we discuss in Chapters 11 and 13).

The Dutch East India Company

Another great investment was the Dutch East India Company, founded in 1602, and empowered to discharge the function of a government in Asia, to engage in warfare with the Spanish and the Portuguese, and to secure a monopoly over the East India trade. Its original capital of 6.4 million florins (equivalent to 64 tons of gold, valued today at about US$640 million) was huge for its time and ten times larger than the capital of the English East India Company formed two years earlier. Right from its start, the Dutch company was very successful. Between 1620 and 1720, it is said to have paid an average annual dividend of almost 20%. But already by the end of the 17th Century, its fortunes began to decline and, after having become insolvent, it was taken over by the Dutch government at the end of the 18th Century.

The Dutch West India Company was less successful. In 1624, it purchased the island of Manhattan from the Canarsees Indians with trinkets and cloth valued at US$24, but New Amsterdam remained a village of less than 1,000 people under the Dutch. In 1667, captured earlier by the English and renamed New York, it became a permanent English possession through the Treaty of Breda, in exchange for the spice-island of Run, then an extremely valuable asset because of its nutmeg.

Even for the British, New York was no great investment. When they evacuated the city in 1783, after a costly military intervention and several disastrous fires, its population was still less than 25,000. Thus, the British missed out on the huge commercial development New York enjoyed over the following 200 years. Much the same can be said of most colonial possessions. Over time, most cost their Western parent nations far more than the imperialists extracted from them. Only very few - such as Haiti for the French and Angola for the Portuguese - provided satisfactory returns and this, as in the case of Peru, for but brief periods.

Investment fads

In the early and mature stages of capitalism, many investment fads have proven to be at least temporary "great investments". The Mississippi Company's stock rose by 40 times between 1719 and 1720, to fail thereafter. Similarly, the South Sea Company's stock rose by eight times in 1720, but then totally collapsed (see Chapter 12). Of the 190 companies founded in England during the South Sea Bubble of 1720, only four have survived! Industrialisation in the 19th Century promised huge profits from inventions, innovations, the opening of new territories and discovery of resources, plantations and new industries, which led to recurring investment manias for companies involved in plank-roads, turnpikes, canals, railroads, mining, real estate, banking, electricity and so on. But again, most investments in new industries created only temporary wealth, because along with the application of inventions and innovations came the process of "creative destruction". Thus, most canals and railroads failed to deliver decent returns and eventually went into receivership or had to be restructured.

To my knowledge, only three canals, the Erie (1825), the Suez (1869) and the Panama (1914) stood the test of time, although much of their profit eluded investors. The Erie Canal Company was initially a great financial success; however, later, it suffered competition from railroads (see also Chapter 4). The first Panama Canal Company went bankrupt and failed to complete its undertaking. The Suez Canal was a financial success, but in 1955, Colonel Nasser nationalised it (at the same time, the Cairo stock market, the fourth largest by market capitalisation in the world prior to the Second World War went to zero). Similarly, most railroad companies in the world, sooner or later failed or were nationalised, and on the whole resulted in huge losses for investors.

The 20th Century brought another wave of great, albeit temporary, investment opportunities in steel, electric utilities, telephone, automobile, chemical, radio, aerospace, airline, office equipment, computer, retailing, consumer goods and, more recently, internet companies. In the 1920s, electric utilities, automobiles and radio companies were growing rapidly and their stocks were almost as hot as hi-tech companies in the late 90s. But, after 1929, they failed to deliver satisfactory returns. Of more than 200 US auto manufacturers in 1910, only three have survived. Not one US radio manufacturer remains. The Dow Jones Utilities Average took until 1965 to exceed its 1929 high, was throughout the 1970s mostly lower than in 1929, and is, today, just 50% higher than at its 1929 peak (admittedly, utilities paid generous dividends until recently). But don't forget that electric utilities were just as revolutionary an industry in the 1920s as the internet today, because for the first time in history they allowed factories to run in any location - not just close to coal or water power sources. This led investors to push their prices up above 30 times earnings and Ben Graham to call their valuations "incredibly absurd". (What would Graham have to say about recent hi-tech valuations?)

In the 1950s and 60s and up to 1972, many great investment opportunities presented themselves in new businesses like bowling, aerospace, discount stores, catalogue retailers, fast food, manufactured homes, etc. Small business investment companies (SBICs) were very popular among investors in the 1960s, partly because they enjoyed tax benefits. Companies like Xerox, Avon, Polaroid, Disney, Levitz Furniture, Kmart, IBM, Burroughs, Digital Equipment, Sperry Rand, NCR, Mohawk Data, Memorex, Addressograph, Bunker Ramo, Dictaphone and University Computing were highly profitable investments for a while. But how many have survived, and if they survived, how well have they done since then? The shares of Avon and Xerox are much lower today than in 1972; Polaroid filed for Chapter XI; and IBM, one of the few survivors of the first batch of computer companies, is up just two times, while the Dow is up more than eightfold even after its recent decline!

Progress and obsolescence

In fact, it seems to me that if there is an "iron law" of very long-term investing, it is that superior returns are only temporary. S&P 500 growth in real earnings - that is, adjusted for inflation - between 1954 and 2001 was only 1.4% per annum. Moreover, between 1951 and 1999 the ratio of US companies with 20% earnings growth per annum was for five years only 10%, for 10 years, just 3% - and no company during this period grew at that rate over 15 years! Competition from imitators or new inventions; government intervention through taxation, nationalisation, price controls and expropriation; and the obsolescence inevitably associated with progress: something will inevitably drive above-average returns down to or below the mean for the whole economy.

The most common feature of all great investments is that in the long run, they start to produce negative returns and eventually vanish from the surface of the earth. And for every successful undertaking or company, there were always many more failures to maintain the shape of the wealth pyramid - with few rich at the top and many poor at the bottom - more or less constant throughout history.

"But what about real estate?" someone might interject. True, there have been some excellent long-term investments there. A family that owned real estate in England at the beginning of the last millennium - property rights having been assured by the passing of the Magna Carta in 1215 - might still hold such property today. But many such holdings have been lost this century under the pressure of estate duties. And what about the real estate once owned by American Indians, Australian Aborigines, Mexican Aztecs and the tribesmen of Africa? Hardly a good investment - since it was taken away by hostile powers through conquest or colonisation. What about Eastern Europe, Russia, China, Vietnam or Burma? In all these countries real estate became worthless in the 20th Century because of the brilliant idea of communism (another "new era" concept that promised prosperity to the masses). So, like other investments, real estate has generally only provided fabulous returns over relatively brief periods. Over the last 1,000 years, most real estate has failed the test of the *very* long investment horizon.

What about art as an investment? Yes, I am sure that if your forebears had acquired the *Book of Kells* (now in Dublin's Trinity College library, well worth a visit) in the year 1000, it would have been a great investment - yet still not worth US$1,546 quintillion (at most, US$100 million). And for every *Book of Kells* or *Gutenberg Bible* that survived, thousands more were destroyed by fire, war, theft, neglect and so on. As in a lottery, the fact that *someone* wins *something* in no way proves the long-term merit and profitability of all investments.

From what we have seen so far, and as depressing as it may sound, it would appear that material goods have seldom provided satisfactory returns for very long. But consider this: Should the merit of an investment be judged solely by the returns it yields to its investors - or should other factors be taken into account? Railroads and canals were hardly great long-term investments, yet the railroad industry allowed entire new territories to be opened up for agriculture, manufacturing and other forms of exploitation, and sped urbanisation throughout the world (on the dark side, it also permitted mass deportations). The Suez and Panama canals had huge impacts on world trade, while the airline industry (collectively unprofitable since its inception despite strong growth) led to an explosion in tourism and overseas manufacturing facilities, to say the least.

Social spinoffs

Therefore, some great innovations and undertakings were poor in terms of investor returns, yet enormously beneficial for progress and global economic development. Thousands of missionary schools throughout the world as well as all colleges and universities would certainly fall into this category. Furthermore, absurd as it may sound, some undertakings and industries that seem, from a "purely economic" point of view, worthless and unproductive, have brought great, enduring benefit to their societies. Just think of the Egyptian pyramids, the 9th-Century Borobudur Temple, the Khmers' Angkor Wat and the Mayans' Copan and Tikal Temples. Economically wasteful structures originally perhaps, they now provide great benefit as tourist attractions. In fact, it is an economic irony that very large structures such as the pyramids - economic white elephants but too big to be destroyed by invaders or stolen by the British or French colonialists - survived well, while productive businesses were eventually all destroyed by competition or obsolescence.

Also, it is surprising that economically unproductive industries such as prostitution and gambling have survived the test of time extremely well. These will continue to thrive, with or without the internet, and never suffer obsolescence! Thus, paradoxical as it may sound, it appears that what has no economic or investment value is the most enduring. There is scant competition for something with no value or little economic use.

This brings me to the only few great and enduring "businesses" that have continued to thrive throughout history: The great "corporations", as one might regard them, of religions such as Judaism, Christianity, Islam, Hinduism and Buddhism. These organisations have survived because their "business" was not related to investment in material goods, but to cater to the soul - the superstitions, faiths, fears and beliefs of people - all human traits never subject to obsolescence. Incidentally, perhaps, Christianity did particularly well in terms of wealth accumulation and preservation. It built its churches, monasteries, schools, universities and cathedrals on prime locations and these were mostly tax exempt. With global population growing and, hence, more and more people dying, it came into the benefit of ever-increasing cashflow. Church education greatly benefited economic development and progress throughout the world. Still, to what extent any religion contributed to the accumulation of wealth among nations is highly debatable - given the continuous havoc the intolerant interpretation of faith has created through endless religious wars, up to this day.

What lessons can we learn from any investments over the last 1,000 years? That economic, social and political *change* would appear to have been the only constant. That great investments at one time turned out to be disastrous at others and failed in the long run. That for every undertaking, colonisation, company, invention, innovation, conquest or merger that succeeded, many more failed. And that even the most successful investments failed to deliver a 5% return in the *very* long term. At all times, therefore, the opportune selection of the "right and undervalued investment theme" was of crucial importance - as was the speedy abandonment of fully valued popular themes that were bound to underperform.

To put it very simply: someone should have owned property in Venice in the 14th and 15th Centuries, then in 16th-Century Lisbon, 17th-Century Amsterdam, 18th-Century London, then 19th-Century East Coast and 20th-Century West Coast USA. Similarly, someone should have switched stock holdings from time to time, over the last 200 years, from one sector to another or from one country to another: German stocks in the 1950s (countries that lose wars usually provide better investment opportunities than countries that conquer - see Chapter 12), US growth stocks in the 60s, oil and mining in the 70s, Japan, Taiwan and South Korea in the 80s and US stocks in the 1990s. In the *very* long term, a buy-and-hold strategy is certainly a losing proposition.

Finally, it strikes me that - as all the great philosophies and religions have argued - material goods are impermanent, whereas human instincts, beliefs, ideas, ethics, senses and emotions hardly change: a fact that accounts for the enduring nature of religious, philosophical and educational institutions, as well as periodically recurring investment manias. Less fortunate of course is that the invariability of human nature has also enabled evil businesses, enterprises and institutions - associated with crime, war, genocide and an almost unimaginable diversity of filth - to survive and thrive.

CHAPTER FOUR

Another warning to emerging market investors!

> Paradoxical as it may seem, the riches of nations can be measured by the violence of the crises they experience.
>
> *CLÉMENT JUGLAR (1819-1905)*

Reading the international financial press of recent years one might think that emerging-markets investment was a phenomenon unique to the 1980s and 90s, recently invented by the likes of WI Carr, Vickers da Costa, Templeton, Morgan Stanley, CLSA and Baring Securities. For a while - impressed by superior performances in the late 80s and early 90s - investors believed that the road to emerging economies was paved with gold. Emerging-market portfolio managers were as popular then as hedge fund managers today, or take-over artists in the mid-80s. In fact, in the early 90s, emerging markets had become so popular that many investors placed more money in Asia than in the US. Ignorance of economic history badly punished them in the late 90s when the Asian Crisis destroyed wealth on a scale unseen since the Second World War.

Personally, I have always been interested in economic and financial history. I have collected first editions of economics tomes for a very long time. Books being bulky, I soon decided to limit my purchases to business-cycle theory - a subject of particular interest. The advantage of old books is the insight one gains on the way contemporaries perceived events, as compared to how we look at them today.

Economics is a young and imperfect science. Before the 18th Century, practically no economic literature was published. But following Adam Smith's *On The Wealth Of Nations* in 1776, numerous economics texts appeared in the United Kingdom and France, dealing principally with such issues as the national debt, taxation, free trade, population growth, land rents and wages. The first major work on business cycles, Clément Juglar's *Des crises commerciales et de leur retour périodique en France, en Angleterre et aux États-Unis* was published in 1860 (and republished with a series of articles in a second edition in 1889). Around the same time, the German economist Max Wirth published *Geschichte der Handelskrisen* and Samuel Benner produced *Benner's Prophesies*, the first book on commodity and stock-market cycles.

The reason books on business cycles began to appear in the latter part of the 19th Century was that although Europe and America had grown very rapidly following the Industrial Revolution, people noted that periods of strong growth were always followed by severe commercial crises. This observation also led early 20th-Century economists such as Wesley C Mitchell, AC Pigou, Nikolai Kondratieff and Joseph Schumpeter to focus on business cycles and their causes, as well as their periodicity.

The emerging states of America

According to Mitchell's *Business Cycles* (1920), American business had passed through a "crisis" on 15 occasions in the preceding 110 years. The list of crisis years (1812, 1818, 1825, 1837, 1847, 1857, 1873, 1884, 1890, 1893, 1903, 1907, 1910, 1913 and 1920) showed that "these cycles differ widely in duration, in intensity, in the relative prominence of their various phenomena, and in the sequence of their phases".

Now you may question what American business cycles in the 19th

Century have to do with today's emerging economies of Asia, the former Soviet Union and Latin America? In my opinion, American business fluctuations of that era provide an excellent historical precedent for today's emerging markets - because America was then the world's largest emerging economy. A study of past American economic cycles and recurring crises may thus provide some insight into the current emerging-market investment environment - and lay to rest the myth about striking it rich in emerging economies, as prevailed in the early 1990s, as well as the current apathy toward emerging economies following their poor relative performance in the second half of the decade.

Emerging economies or emerging industries have always been characterised by violent business cycles of prosperity and depression, so before analysing these cycles in Chapters 6 and 7, let us first have a closer look at the emerging American economy in the 19th Century. The more we research the subject, the more similarities come to light. In particular, the US experienced rapid population growth and underwent a major transformation from a predominantly agrarian producer at the beginning of the 1800s to the world's largest producer of manufactured goods by the end of the 19th Century.

In 1790, the US was a nation of less than four million people dispersed over a huge land area (compared to Europe's 180 million, India's 190 million and China's 320 million). Only seven cities had populations over 5,000, while 12 exceeded 2,500. The remaining 3.7 million people were rural-based. During the first half of the century, the population grew by about 3.5% per annum on average (largely because of immigration), but slowed to around 2% in the decade preceding 1900 (see Table 1).

By 1885, the US - which had hardly any industries at the beginning of the century - now approached 60 million people and led the world in industry, producing 28.9% of global manufactured goods. Britain was second with 26.6% and Germany third with 13.9%. America's rise to global economic dominance is unique from an economic-historical point of view - and today it is the dream of every emerging-market investor to find another 19th-Century American growth story.

Table 1

THE AMERICAN MIRACLE

US population growth, 1790-1900

Census year	Total population	Increase over preceding census (%)
1790	3,929,625	-
1800	5,308,483	35.1
1810	7,239,881	36.4
1820	19,638,453	33.1
1830	12,866,020	33.5
1840	17,069,453	32.7
1850	23,191,876	35.9
1860	31,443,321	35.6
1870	38,558,371	22.6
1880	50,155,783	30.1
1890	62,947,714	25.5
1900	75,994,575	20.7

Source: *A Century of Population in the United States 1790-1900*, US Department of Commerce and Labour, Washington, 1909.

However, and this point we emphasise, America's road from extremely humble beginnings to unprecedented economic dominance and prosperity was *not* smooth and paved with gold (certainly not for foreign investors). Rather, it was strewn with nasty and frequently, even for skilled drivers, unavoidable potholes. Furthermore, the American route to prosperity was often controlled by all manner of banditry and corrupt officialdom, clever at robbing the naive and credulous traveller of his purse.

Economic growth in 19th-Century America was closely linked to the cotton industry (especially in the South), canal and railroad construction throughout the continent (which opened the West), the exploitation of vast natural resources (ie, the gold discoveries in California), the development of new tracts of land and the rise of the steel industry.

In the first half of the 19th Century, the US cotton industry grew very rapidly and the prosperity of the South depended largely on good crops and high prices. Since the invention of the cotton gin by Ely Whitney in 1793, the South had become a highly specialised cotton producing region and the rapidly growing income it received from exports was used to purchase foodstuffs from the West and manufactured goods and services from the Northeast. While the US as a whole had produced hardly any cotton around 1800, by 1860 its plantations supplied five-sixths of world supply (2,300 million pounds). For the South, at least, the industry was then about as important as the oil industry in the Middle East today and certainly far more economically significant than the current agricultural sectors of countries such as New Zealand or Australia.

Just as the South's fortunes were tied to the price of cotton, so too were US manufacturing output, principally in the Northeast, and US imports. In the early 1830s, a cotton boom had favourable impact on the entire economy. Income from the cotton trade rose from US$25 million in 1831 to US$71 million in 1836. But when prices began to fall in 1837, the South's income and ability to consume shrank, which hurt industrial production in the Northeast, as well as imports of luxury goods from Europe. The severe 1837-42 depression was due to some extent to a 70% decline in the price of cotton (see Figure 1). By 1879, cotton prices were no higher than they had been in 1826.

Whenever an economy has high dependence on a single commodity - apart from US cotton, think of Ivory Coast cocoa, Middle East oil and today's gargantuan Western financial markets - the business cycle will correlate very closely to the price movement of that commodity. Rising prices will bring about "excursions into prosperity", while falling prices will inevitably lead to sub-trend growth or "excursions into depression".

But the reason I am discussing the US cotton industry here is that, although it expanded very rapidly, it bankrupted a large number of cotton growers who from time to time overpaid for land when prices were high. The South's reliance on cotton and the cheap slave labour used to grow it also led to the Civil War. Furthermore, cotton fabrics were then as popular for consumers as VCRs, colour TVs, cellular phones and soft drinks are today. Investors in emerging markets and in new, rapidly growing industries or technologies should never overlook this point. That an industry is growing rapidly in the long term does not change the fact that, when the market for its products deteriorates, prices fall - leading to some very painful consequences, not only for the owners, but also for suppliers and especially creditors! Today, every emerging economy wants to grow through the export of manufactured consumer goods, electronic components and semiconductors. But that does not mean that every industry will be successful year after year. Consumer electronics, PCs, cellular phones, Nike shoes, soft drinks and garments are today no different a commodity than cotton was in the 19th Century and are thus, from time to time, vulnerable to periods of overproduction and price falls.

Figure 1

COTTON BOOM (AND BUST)

Prices in New York for middling upland cotton, 1826-1882

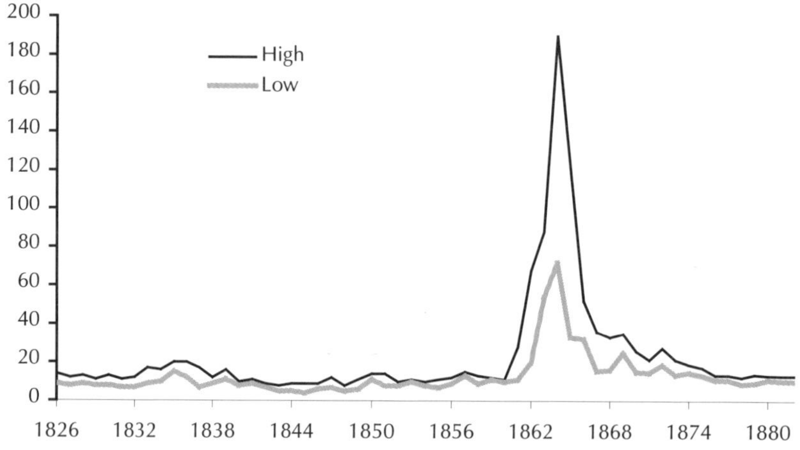

200
180
160
140
120
100
80
60
40
20
0

High
Low

1826 1832 1838 1844 1850 1856 1862 1868 1874 1880

Source: Samuel Benner, *Benner's Prophecies*, Washington, 1884.

But what about investments in infrastructure? In recent years, infrastructure projects have become rather popular among the international investment community, especially in China. However, the story of canal and railroad construction in the US during the 19th Century should dampen some of the prevailing enthusiasm. In the long term, investors lost more money than they gained.

Impetus for the canal boom in the US, which lasted from about 1820 to 1836, was the completion of the 364-mile Erie Canal in 1824. The Erie Canal cut travel time and shipping expenses by 90% on journeys from Detroit, Cleveland and Buffalo to New York. Nine years later, the Welland Canal bypassed Niagara Falls to connect the Great Lakes to the St Lawrence River. The waterways were enormously successful because they enabled grain from the Great Lakes to be brought to New York. They also linked New York to a hinterland of great economic potential and made it the financial and commercial metropolis of the Union (before 1820, Philadelphia had been more populous). The favourable impact on New York also caused a wild canal mania, as every city or state having two or more bodies of water planned or built canals in order to link them, hoping to duplicate the success. The 1820-36 American canal construction boom did not fail to attract the fancy of European emerging-market investors and the demand for American canal bonds and shares was so great that there were not enough issues to satisfy it. When the Morris Canal and Banking Company raised US$1 million, it could have obtained US$20 million, most of which was offered from England. Canals were obviously in those days as popular as internet stocks were in the late 1990s.

Hand in hand with the cotton and canal boom was a wild speculative orgy in real estate and banking shares. Between 1830 and 1837, 347 new banks were licenced, frequently led by men of very questionable background and no banking experience. These banks enabled speculators to purchase land in public sales at inflated prices on credit. Public land sales rose from 4.7 million acres in 1834 to 12.6 million in 1835 and 20 million in 1836 as prices for land in most parts of the East and South more than doubled (admittedly pale by 1990s Hong Kong standards). The Chicago land boom of the early 1830s has been well documented. Until then, Chicago had been relatively unknown with real estate much cheaper than land on the East Coast. However, the planned Illinois-Michigan Canal attracted great speculative interest in Chicago land. Within a few years, prices soared by about 100 times. The canal was to connect the Chicago harbour and Lake Michigan with the Illinois River, which flows into the Mississippi at St Louis. Construction finally began in 1836 at about the same time as Chicago land prices peaked. Following the 1837 crisis, during which stock prices collapsed (see Table 2), Chicago real estate plunged by 90%. It took ten years to complete the canal because construction came to a standstill during the 1837-42 depression as the State of Illinois, burdened by large debts and a poor economy, went into default - as did eight other states. Upon completion of the canal, Chicago did become a major transport hub - but many investors lost their shirts in the bargain.

How the first American boom ended should be of some interest to emerging-market investors: in 1836, British reserves fell by almost 50% as gold flowed to America to purchase American securities. The Bank of England was thus forced to increase the rediscount rate twice, which led to a monetary panic in Britain and the closure of several banks. Higher interest rates in Britain (the call rate in 1837 rose to around 15%) reduced the demand for American securities almost overnight - and this precisely when demand for money in America was at its highest.

Table 2

HOW TABLES TURN

Prices of selected issues, 1837 and 1841

Issue	1837 high	25 November 1841
United States Bank	122	4
Vicksburg Bank	89	5
Kentucky Bank	92	56
North American Trust	95	3
Farmers' Trust	113	30
American Trust	120	0
Illinois State Bank	80	35
Morris Canal	75	0
Patterson R R	75	53
Long Island R R	60	52

Source: Sereno Pratt, *The Work of Wall Street*, and Robert Sobel, *Panic on Wall Street.*

The sudden absence of foreign capital devastated the US. All American banks had to suspend specie payments and between 1837 and 1839 over 1,500 banks failed. The crisis was aggravated by a sharp fall in the price of cotton (see Figure 1), which bankrupted many speculators and led to a sharp fall in Southern demand for consumer goods. By the fall of 1837, nine-tenths of Eastern factories closed. The 1837-41 "Hard Time Depression" was extremely severe. It also had a very negative impact on Europe, especially England, because so much money invested in American canals, banks and real estate had become worthless. Table 2 gives an idea of the gravity of the slump in financial assets that followed the prosperity - a consequence of rising cotton prices, excessive monetary expansion and euphoric purchases of American securities by foreign investors.

While the appetite of foreign investors for US securities had seemed insatiable, following the crisis the *London Times* wrote, "The people of the United States may be fully persuaded that there is a certain class of securities to which no abundance of money, however great, can give value, and that in this class their own securities stand pre-eminent."

From an economic-history point of view, the 1837 crisis and subsequent depression (known in Europe as the "Hungry Forties") are interesting because they were, for the first time, international in scope. The crisis was triggered by an event outside the US (the increase in the rediscount rate in Britain), which reduced the flow of money from Europe to America, leading to the first wave of bankruptcies among American banks. The catalyst for the 1997 Asian Crisis was also a reversal of expectations among foreign investors who no longer were prepared to finance the rising current account deficits of Asian countries (see Chapter 9).

We therefore have here examples of how a sudden reversal of investors' expectations can tilt our gigantic water bowl (Chapter 2) from one side to another - which then leads to a dearth of money in one region or sector, as money flows change. With globalisation we find that, toward the end of a business expansion (that is, usually in the manic phase) foreigners are usually the driving force of the boom. When they, for whatever reason, reduce their demand for the assets they were buying or exit the market altogether, a crisis inevitably follows.

Recovery took place in the mid-1840s and accelerated thereafter, mainly as a result of railroad construction, which played a leading role in the process of economic evolution in the 19th Century and also produced recurring crises. Figure 2 shows that a mini boom took place in 1835 - but in comparison to the canal craze it had little impact on the economy. However, after 1848, railroad construction expanded rapidly and stimulated the economy, bringing about the first railroad mania in the mid-1850s and the crisis that followed in 1857. There were two other factors behind the improving economy and the 1850s boom: cotton prices rose gradually (see Figure 1) and the production of cotton increased from 2.1 million bales in 1850 to 4.5 million in 1859. Also, railroad construction was stimulated by the discovery of gold on Swiss settler Johann Sutter's property in California's lower Sacramento Valley. Table 3 shows how gold production increased after 1847, which helped finance the economic expansion and fuel a terrific land and railroad construction boom in California.

Figure 2

RAILROAD SPIKES

Miles of railroad in the US

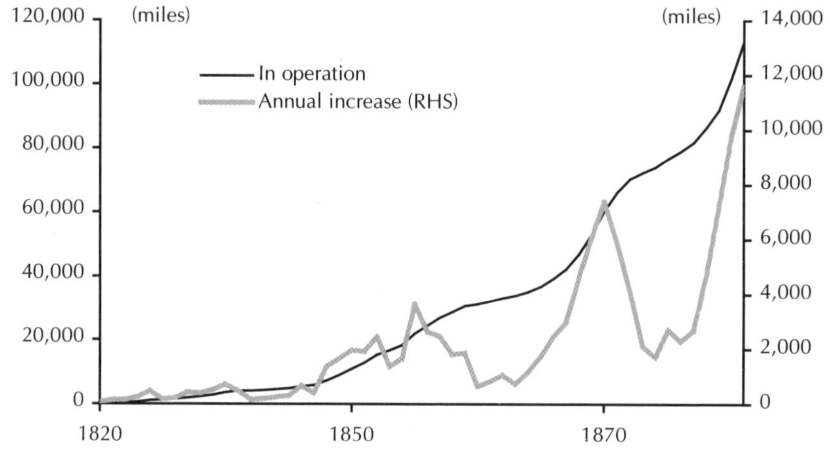

Source: Samuel Benner, *Benner's Prophecies*, Washington, 1884.

Table 3

IN THEM THERE HILLS

Gold production, 1847-1856

Year	Production (1,000 fine troy ounces)
1847	43
1848	484
1849	1935
1850	2419
1851	2661
1852	2902
1853	3144
1854	2902
1855	2661
1856	2661

Source: *Historical Statistics of the United States.*

The railroading of America led to a tenfold increase in the production of pig iron and a doubling of coal production between 1850 and 1856. Foreigners, who after the canal construction debacle of 1837 had left the

US market vowing never to return, were once again eagerly buying US railway securities and, for the first time in American financial history, speculative mining stocks, in order to capitalise on the expected bonanza from the gold discovery. By 1853, 26% of all American railroad bonds were in the hands of foreign investors, who focused particularly on the more speculative issues. One of the interesting aspects of the 1850-57 railway boom was that, for investors, it ended long before the 1857 financial crisis. Table 4 compares the performance of railroad stocks to the completion of railroad miles between 1850 and 1860.

Table 4

DISEMBARKING EARLY

Railroad stock performance vs railroad construction, 1850-1860

Year	All-inclusive index of railroad stocks		Miles of railroad completed
	High	Low	
1850	95	79	1,656
1851	96	87	1,961
1852	110	89	1,926
1853	105	89	2,452
1854	98	74	1,360
1855	80	66	1,654
1856	73	68	3,647
1857	71	39	2,647
1858	61	49	2,465
1859	56	47	1,821
1860	74	48	1,846

Source: Smith, Walter & Cole, Arthur, *Fluctuations in American Business*, 1790-1860.

As can be seen, the railroad index topped out in December 1852. Construction peaked in 1856, largely because capital transfers, which reached a high of US$56 million in 1853, declined to only US$12 million in 1856. The reason for the slowdown in overseas buying was the Crimean War (1854-56) between Great Britain, France and Turkey on the one side, and Russia. The war drained European liquidity, led to rising interest rates and killed Continental demand for American railroad securities - just when the railroads needed to raise a maximum amount of capital to finance their expansion. Simply put, there was a large oversupply of securities in the American capital market which depressed prices, even though business conditions in America remained strong until 1857. In fact, the Crimean War was, on balance, very favourable for America as agricultural product prices rose and industrial production was stimulated. Whatever - the main message for investors is that stock prices can fall long before the economy turns down or well ahead of deteriorating profits, for no other reason than deteriorating monetary conditions, or because the supply of equities exceeds the demand from investors.

The catalyst for the 1857 crisis was the failure of the Ohio Life & Trust Company, which specialised in land and railroad investments and commodity futures. Moreover, sentiment was hurt by the sinking of the steamer *Central America* off Cape Hatteras, with its cargo of US$1.6 million in California gold - because gold shipments from California had always been a confidence booster and had provided some liquidity to the East Coast banks. The panic reached a peak in October 1857 when 1,415 banks and numerous railroads failed (the New York Mining Exchange even closed its doors), and the crisis spread to London and Paris where many American securities were actively traded.

An interesting aspect of the 1857 panic is that it was principally a financial crisis and relatively little damage was done to the economy, particularly with respect to the South. While American cotton worth US$128 million had been exported in 1856, cotton export earnings rose to US$192 million in 1860. The strong economic performance of the cotton growing areas at a time when the financial sector of the Northeast was in a crisis gave the South confidence that, in a conflict, their foes' economy would collapse - a notion that eventually contributed to the outbreak of hostilities and the Civil War. This is another point for investors to remember: a severe financial crisis can occur for a number of reasons (including excessive speculation, which was the case in the 1850s) and not necessarily because of a general and long-lasting downturn in the real economy.

The global crisis of 1873

For emerging-markets investors, the lead-up to the global 1873 crisis and the depression that followed is also of interest. The end of the American

Civil War (1861-65) and the German unification, which was achieved following the Franco-Prussian War (1870-71), gave immense impetus to US and German economic development, enabling them to catch up with Britain and France, previously leaders of the Industrial Revolution era. This was especially true for Germany, whose economy was stimulated by the French War Indemnity. Max Wirth described in *Geschichte der Handelskrisen* (1874) how a new-issue boom swept across Austria, Germany and Prussia from 1869-74, designed to finance railroads, new iron and steel works, real estate companies and banks. In Prussia, 259 companies were established in 1871, and 504 in 1872, as against only 34 in 1870 and 225 since the beginning of the century (1866-73 became known as "the Golden Age of Company Promoters").

People felt extremely confident about the future because the economy in Europe and the US had been expanding rapidly in the late 1860s (between 1866 and 1873 German per-capita consumption of iron more than doubled). Bullish sentiment in Europe was further boosted by the laying of the first transatlantic cable in 1866 (by Cable & Wireless) and by the World Exhibition in Vienna, which was to open in 1873. Hyndman, a contemporary economist, wrote that:

> What made matters even worse was the foundation of all sorts of banking institutions that had little else than stock-jobbing in view. The real object of banks and companies was quite lost sight of, and men were swept into the whirl of speculation without having any other desire than to gamble and to make money in the lottery of the share market. Mortgage banks and building societies gave an undue impetus to building speculations in the great cities, from which Berlin and Vienna still suffer. These building speculations were indeed among the most unsound and ruinous of all the business of the time. The price of land was run up to a purely fictitious level, and loans were made to cover the sites with houses to an extent which, when the crash came, rendered it impossible to recover even a fraction of the principal. The great object was to run up the houses in good, or what were likely to be good, situations, and put a rental upon them which, in nine cases out of ten, was never realised. .... similar follies can be seen in London on a smaller proportional scale, and the speculative builder who, working on a small capital, must live continuously from hand to mouth, borrowing at usurious rates to complete jerry-built structures, is well-known here at home.

HM Hyndman, *Commercial Crises of the Nineteenth Century*, London, 1892

In America, the most important event of the 1860s - apart from the Civil War - was the rapid territorial expansion towards the West Coast, which, aided by the construction of the great transcontinental railways (the first of which was the Union Pacific, completed in 1869), was accomplished in an astonishingly short time. The building of the transcontinental railways led to another speculative mania, largely financed by foreign investors once again. Between 1860 and 1873, railroad miles in operation more than doubled (the largest increase took place from 1870 to 1873; see Figure 2). Foreigners, who held US$51.9 million in railroad securities in 1853, had increased their holdings to over US$260 million by 1872. But this time, the railroad mania was not confined to British or American railroad securities. Austria tripled her rail mileage in eight years and Russia built 12,000 miles in four years. In addition, Latin American borrowers, especially Argentina, raised funds in London and Paris for a number of rail projects (by 1869 British investors held US$200 million worth of South American railroad construction bonds and these investments led eventually to the Baring Crisis in the 1890s). Also, the Suez Canal was completed in 1869, sparking renewed interest in ocean transportation and great optimism with regard to international trade and economic growth.

Reading contemporary comments, one cannot fail to notice how the prevailing optimism then paralleled the upbeat 1990s mood about the prospects of emerging economies such as China, India and Latin America, or the most recent euphoria about our "new economy", which was supposed to be driven by innovations and knowledge! Then, as now, the sky seemed the limit, while risk considerations took a backseat. Everywhere, fraud, stock manipulation, government corruption and all make of illegal or shady scheme were common practice: but no one took much notice because, as McCulloch pointed out:

> In speculation, as in most other things, one individual derives confidence from another. Such a one purchases or sells, not because he has had any really accurate information as to the state of demand and supply, but because someone else has done so before him ...
>
> JR McCulloch, *Principles of Political Economy*, 2nd ed., London 1830

The end to prosperity came in May 1873 when the Vienna Stock Exchange was struck with a devastating financial panic that spread like wildfire to London, Paris, Vienna, Berlin and then to New York.

Although the World Exhibition opened in Vienna in May 1873, stock prices had already begun to drift lower in April and they totally collapsed on 8 and 9 May. Within a month, most bank shares had been sliced in half and, according to a contemporary, "*die Wiener Börse stand förmlich unter der Herrschaft des Schreckens*" [The Vienna Stock Exchange stood under the dominance of fright]. In September 1873, the crisis reached New York. According to a German writer, American bonds could not have been placed in Europe "even if signed by an angel of Heaven". The leading and most prestigious American investment bank, Jay Cooke & Co (the equivalent today would be Goldman Sachs or Morgan Stanley), was forced to close its doors and went out of business. The investment community was stunned and a panic followed that brought the closure of the Exchange for ten days! Unlike in 1857, the 1873 crisis was followed by a deflationary depression that lasted six years (the Wholesale Price Index fell from 133 in 1873 to 91 in 1878). Most railroads under construction went bankrupt and, in the years following the crisis, over 20,000 commercial and industrial failures were recorded in the US alone. America underwent the most severe depression of the 19th Century - a slump almost as bad as the 1929-32 Great Depression.

There were many reasons for the 1873 collapse. The railway boom immobilised capital and strained financial resources, the iron and steel industries overexpanded, there was overtrading in stocks and widespread fraudulence by stock promoters, corrupt government officials and excessive speculation in real estate - all contributed to the panic and ensuing depression, which was felt throughout the world. Reading the works of contemporary economists, one notices that in 1869 some warning signals had become apparent. However, they had been ignored in the whirlwind of speculation as business conditions continued to look promising because so many countries were in the process of industrialising. However, one factor concerning the collapse of the stock market bubble in Vienna,

Berlin, Paris, London and New York should not be forgotten: a flood of new stock and bond issues came to the market between 1871 and 1873. Sooner or later the supply of this paper had to exceed the demand of the investing public and depress prices.

The 19th Century was undoubtedly a period of rapid economic growth in Europe and particularly the United States, then the largest emerging economy. However, in examining historical economic literature, one cannot help being amazed at how much money investors repeatedly lost and how violent the recessionary periods were. Foreign investors, especially, were taken to the cleaners again and again. The most striking characteristic of foreign investors was that they were, throughout the 19th Century, *latecomers* to an investment fad. They invariably bought American canal, railroad and other industrial stocks at or near a peak in the cycle. When prices were low and business conditions depressed, foreign investors were usually absent, having burnt their fingers during the previous boom.

Thus, in the field of emerging-markets investing, nothing has changed, and to my surprise, nobody seems to have learnt from these past experiences that I have tried to document. From time to time, as was the case for emerging economies from 1990-97 and for the TMT sector in the late 1990s, investors seem to become far too optimistic about the prospects of a new region or a new industry about which they usually know very little. As Bertrand Russell remarked, "The degree of one's emotion varies inversely with one's knowledge of the facts - the less you know, the hotter you get."

People who in the 19th Century would have bought American canal and railroad shares (most of which failed), were in the 1990s buying Chinese infrastructure funds and telephone companies in the remotest regions of the world and, later, hi-tech companies about whose business they had no idea. In the late 1980s, investors claimed a recession was impossible in Japan; in the mid 1990s, the same people seemed to believe that Southeast Asia could not experience any business downturns; and, most recently, articles by leading economists claimed that the business cycle was dead and that the US economy would continue to grow forever. However, it should now be clear that investing in rapidly growing emerging economies is much trickier than appears to the casual observer. In turn, as was the case in the 19th Century American economy, great entry points into emerging stock markets do present themselves whenever the foreign investment community is reeling from losses from having overpaid for stocks or real estate investments in emerging economies and is vowing to never again purchase stocks in this asset class.

Geographical shifts

A final point about investing in emerging regions: The centres of economic activity do change over time, as we observed in the preceding chapter. From Table 5, one can see that New England experienced a relative decline in manufacturing in the second half of the 19th Century, while the Great Lakes region grew at above-average rates. Global investors should carefully consider this point. Economic growth could shift from the Western industrial nations to the emerging economies of Asia and the former Soviet Union, and relegate some recent centres of prosperity such as Silicon Valley and Hong Kong to the status of a Buffalo or New Orleans.

So far we have tried to show that making money is not as easy as some academics claim - while writing books about the Dow Jones rising to 36,000 and 100,000 - and that a buy-and-hold strategy not be appropriate at all for the long term may, since the world's economic environment changes continuously. An investor who bought canal or railroad shares in 19th Century America and held them up to this day would not have done well since most canals and railroads went out of business in the 19th Century. In this respect, it is worth looking at the performance of railroad stocks in the 19th and early part of the 20th Century.

Table 5

LABOUR FOLLOWS PROSPERITY

Employment in manufacturing by region as a % of the total US labour market

	1859	1869	1879	1889	1899	1904	1909	1914
New England	29.88	26.76	24.31	20.57	18.91	17.87	17.30	16.83
Middle Atlantic	41.66	39.52	42.04	38.69	37.54	36.99	35.82	35.89
Great Lakes	12.09	18.36	19.19	22.29	22.65	22.29	22.73	23.73
South-East	9.80	8.48	7.57	8.90	11.55	12.87	13.61	13.05
Plains	2.30	4.79	4.46	6.01	5.41	5.37	5.32	5.10
South-West	0.34	0.37	0.44	0.67	0.79	0.97	1.26	1.30
Mountain	0.03	0.17	0.31	0.49	0.71	0.69	0.82	0.82
Far West*	3.90	1.54	1.70	2.37	2.43	2.93	3.14	3.26

*Includes gold mining. Source: *The Cambridge Economic History of Europe*, Cambridge, 1965.

We have seen above that railroad shares reached a first major high in 1852 before bottoming out in the financial panic of 1853. Thereafter, they recovered and made new highs in 1864 and 1869, but most railroad shares failed in the 1860s to exceed their 1852 highs, as railroad construction was just a quarter of what it had been in 1856. After that, according to Benner, the trend for railroad stocks was down until the end of the century, even though miles in operation increased by 14 times between 1852 and 1900 (see Figure 2). It should be noted that the majority of railroad companies failed after the 1873 international stock market crash, and more again, in the severe 1893-96 recession. In 1893, the New York, Lake Erie & Western Railroad went into receivership for the fourth time and the Northern Pacific as well as the Western Railroad followed suit. Five percent of American banks failed during the year, while 30% of rail in operation belonged to companies in receivership. The depression continued until 1896 and led to financial problems for 90% of American railroads. So, it is evident that railroads were not a particularly good investment in the second half of the 19th Century. I have to point out that not all rail issues peaked out at the same time (the composition of the rail index obviously changed over time as new lines started up and old ones went bankrupt) - but some time between 1852 and 1869 most railroad stocks reached their zenith for the century.

Therefore, we have here a good example of a growth industry in the extremely successful and rapidly growing emerging economy of the 19th Century United States whose stock prices performed poorly for half a century and badly underperformed industrial issues in the early part of the next. Figure 4 shows that the Dow Jones Average of 20 railroads peaked out in late 1906 at almost 140, but then declined to less than 70 in 1921.

Figure 3

RAZORBACK

Lowest and highest years for stocks, 1860-1891

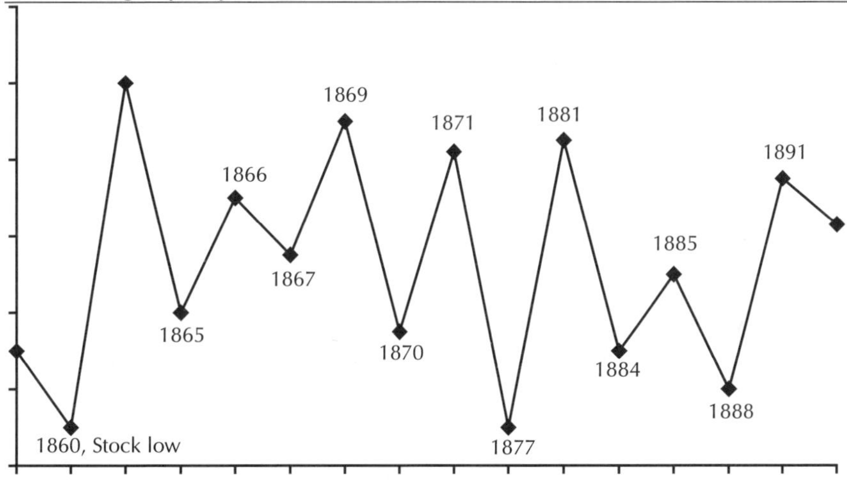

Source: Samuel Benner, *Benner's Prophecies of Future Ups and Downs in Prices* (Cincinnati, 1884)

What had gone wrong for the railroad industry since the middle of the 19th Century? A number of factors accounted for the poor performance. As more and more lines opened, railroads suffered from cutthroat competition and freight rates collapsed. New railroad construction was very capital-intensive and, therefore, a continuous supply of new securities had to be issued, not only for America but also for railroads in Europe, Russia and Latin America. The supply of new scrip was never ending and tended to depress the prices of already outstanding issues. Also, railroads had large bond issues outstanding, which became burdensome in the deflationary environment of the latter part of the 19th Century. But most importantly, the Interstate Commerce Commission was established in 1887, and began to regulate railroads engaged in interstate commerce. In particular, the Hepburn Acts of 1906 and the Mann-Elkins Acts of 1910 gave the commission significant control over rates and had a devastating effect on their companies earnings between 1910 and 1921 as inflation accelerated while rate increases were continually denied. As a result, railroad profits collapsed until 1920. Figure 4 shows how railroad stocks halved in value from their 1906 highs and how they failed to participate in the strong rally of industrial shares between 1918 and 1920.

Figure 4

RUNNING OUT OF STEAM

Dow Jones averages - Railroads vs industrials, 1897-1927

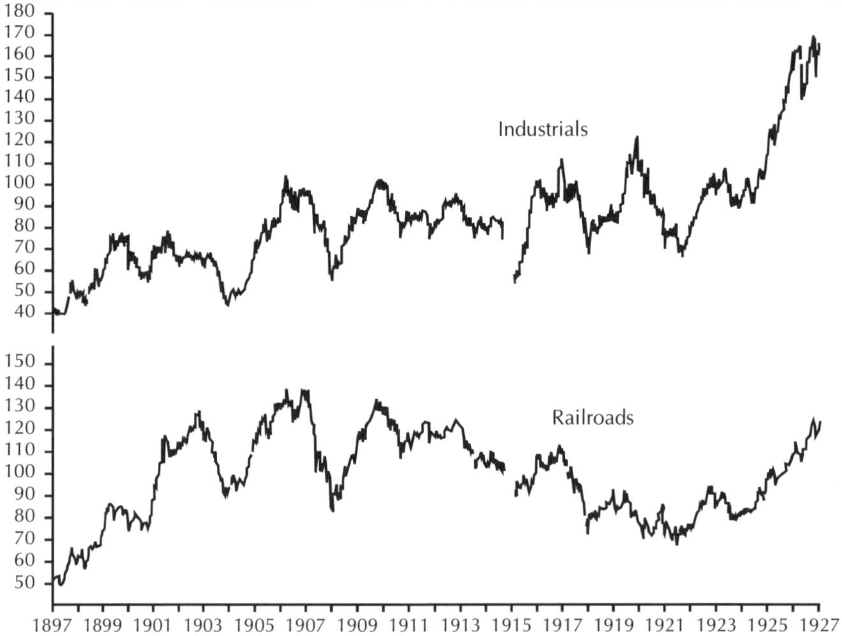

Source: Ralph E. Badger, *Investment Principles and Practices* (New York, 1935).

I have two reasons for discussing the US railroad industry. Firstly, until the early 1920s, it was by far the largest industry in the country. By 1925, in terms of capital, it was still larger than all US public utility companies, more than twice the size of the steel industry, and almost ten times larger than the auto industry. Therefore, it is not unfair to say that the stocks of America's largest industry had performed poorly from the middle of the 19th Century until 1921.

Secondly, given the recent enthusiasm of many contemporary investors for infrastructure projects and telecom companies in emerging markets, the US railroads provide some interesting insights. First of all, we have seen that railroad stocks peaked out already between 1852 and 1869 and failed to perform well until 1920, although the industry continued to grow rapidly, as well as the US economy. Therefore, growth by itself does not necessarily imply higher equity prices. It would appear that the demand and supply for capital, and pricing as well as the regulatory environment within an industry, are more important for stock prices. The capital-hungry railroads had to issue new securities continuously, depleting investor demand at a time when freight rates were falling and hurting profitability (similar to the problems the telecoms face now). As well, in the inflationary environment between 1910 and 1920, rate revisions lagged behind cost increases because of the Interstate Commerce Commission's railroad-unfriendly policies. Politics exacted a toll.

As an emerging-markets investor, I would, therefore, be extremely wary of infrastructure projects. They will absorb an enormous amount of capital and at times competition will depress the rates power or telephone companies will be able to charge. And, when the pricing environment is favourable, or when inflation is high, one can be sure that a number of state or provincial commissions will keep rates down. Their employees - having been educated at American universities and studied with great amusement the history of the growing power of the Interstate Commerce Commission, and being eager to apply what Western capitalism has taught them - will happily cap the return utilities in emerging economies are permitted to earn, in order to keep inflation from getting out of hand: especially if the projects were financed by foreigners. In other words, what I expect for many infrastructure projects in emerging economies is an environment similar to the one the US railroad industry experienced between 1910 and 1920.

As an aside, happier times for railroad stocks came in the 1920s. From 1921 to 1929, the Dow Jones Transportation Average rose from 70 to 189, while the Dow Industrial Average rose from below 70 to a high of 386, indicating once again an underperformance of railroads compared to industrial shares. Although the weighting of railroad shares within the market was no longer as important in the 1920s, it is still interesting to note their total collapse between 1929 and 1932, which brought the Transportation Index down to 13.23 (see Figure 5). At that point, railroad stocks were not only selling at the lowest level ever in the 20th Century, but going back as far as the 1857 panic - at least for the few railroads that had not gone bankrupt in the interim.

Figure 5

TOTAL COLLAPSE

Dow Jones Transportation Average, 1915-1940

Source: The Primary Trend.

I would suggest that investors who believe stocks always go up in the long run think seriously about the dismal performance of American railroad securities between 1850 and 1932, especially in view of the fact that that they were not only by far the largest component of the US market until the end of the 19th Century, but also because they were the most popular group until the early part of the 20th Century.

But the poor performance of railroad stocks up to 1932 was not an isolated case. Between 1929 and 1932, the Dow Jones Industrial Average fell from a high of 386 to 41. At that point, the Dow was lower than it had been at its trough in 1914 when the First World War broke out and at about the same level it had been in 1897! It was also about 50% below its 1920 high (showing again that once a mania comes to and end, the subsequent bear market can take back the entire advance from where the bull move began - and then some).

I may also add that by pursuing a buy-and-hold strategy with railroad securities from 1850 up to this very day an investor would have totally missed on the auto boom of the 1910s, the appliance, radio, movie and utilities booms of the 1920s, missed first the great German stock market boom of the 1950s and the highly rewarding Japanese bull market post Second World War up to 1989 - and failed to participate in the colossal rise of hi-tech companies of the 1990s.

My point, again, is simply this: Every economy, every industry goes through cycles. These cycles are particularly violent in the case of emerging economies, emerging industries and emerging companies, which grow and evolve rapidly and are, therefore, capital-hungry. At the same time, their ability to raise money depends very much on investors' expectations. When investors are confident and optimistic, they will usually not just provide capital, but *too much* capital and, therefore, first bring about a spending boom and an investment mania, but later also cause the inevitable downturn as excess capacity develops because new competitors will enter the booming sector. As a result, new industries and emerging economies are subject to very powerful competitive forces and rapid obsolescence in the early stages of growth. After all, it should be obvious that the pace of innovation and hence obsolescence occurs at a much faster speed in new industries, such as currently the hi-tech sector, than in mature sectors of the economy, such as the paper, steel and chemical industries. Similarly, the speed of change is also far higher in emerging economies - as we have seen in South Korea, Taiwan and Singapore over the last 30 years and in China since 1990 - than in mature economies such as Germany and Switzerland, where the economic landscape has hardly changed over the last quarter of a century.

The consequence of the ever-rapidly-changing economic conditions in the world, where entire new industries are born and new economic centres open up (Texas in the early part of the 19th Century, Silicon Valley in the 1960s, Shanghai and Bangalore in the 1990s), makes a buy-and-hold strategy of any asset a disastrous proposition (see also Chapter 11). The investor must, from time to time rebalance his assets in order to avoid being caught in an industry or country in decline and decay, and continuously keep an open mind to new opportunities that arise in new industries and regions that open up and sprout for a given period of time.

I should like to emphasise that the analysis here is not about "growth investing" as compared to "value investing", but about the fact that if an investor can invest in growth at low valuations the opportunity for achieving substantial capital gains is better than by investing in value situations whose growth prospects are nonexistent. And since we have seen above that emerging industries and countries do grow amid very severe business fluctuations - boom and bust cycles - the opportunity to pick up cheap assets (real estate, shares, bonds, etc) will arise time and again during periods of crisis and economic downturns. Conversely, if investors purchase assets during boom times and during investment manias and hold on to these assets, they will either tend to perform poorly or lose money altogether, because once a boom comes to an end, a bust and then a period of underperformance follows, as the object of the boom and the mania tends to change over time.

In other words, a boom in one sector of the economy is most unlikely to be followed by another boom in the same sector. Far more likely, as we shall later see, is that a boom in one sector *will* be followed by another boom, but that this boom will be in another sector or region of the economy. In the following chapter, I should like to offer a closer analysis of how investors can capitalise on these cycles in emerging economies.

CHAPTER FIVE

The life cycle of emerging markets

> As a general rule, it is foolish to do just what other people are doing, because there are almost sure to be too many people doing the same thing.
>
> *WILLIAM STANLEY JEVONS (1835-82)*

I will now focus on stock market cycles in emerging economies. I fully realise that new industries, driven by revolutionary inventions and innovations, are also "emerging economies" within the macro-economic system. However, since new industries and emerging regions tend to have different drivers, I shall discuss business cycles in Chapter 6 and concentrate here on stock markets in countries in the early stages of economic development. In many ways, economic and market cycles closely resemble the human life cycle. First, economies or stocks are in an embryonic stage. Then, when they reach adolescence, they grow very rapidly (a bullish phase), during which they are accident-prone (experiencing crises and crashes). Later, markets mature, lose some of their energy and volatility, become tired and finally die (decay and bear markets). Fortunately for economies and stock markets, there is usually life after death. A new cycle begins which, like life after reincarnation, is very different in nature from the previous cycle.

Figure 1 shows the various phases emerging markets will move through and Figure 2 compares the trend with the Seoul Composite Index between 1985 and 1998. A word of caution: The phases are not usually clearly recognisable. They tend to be extremely complex and blurred, and most investors, including myself, never really know which phase the market is in. Furthermore, the transition from one phase to another is slow and gradual, and is therefore not as clearly marked as in our figure.

Figure 1

THE LIFE CYCLE OF EMERGING MARKETS

A schematic view

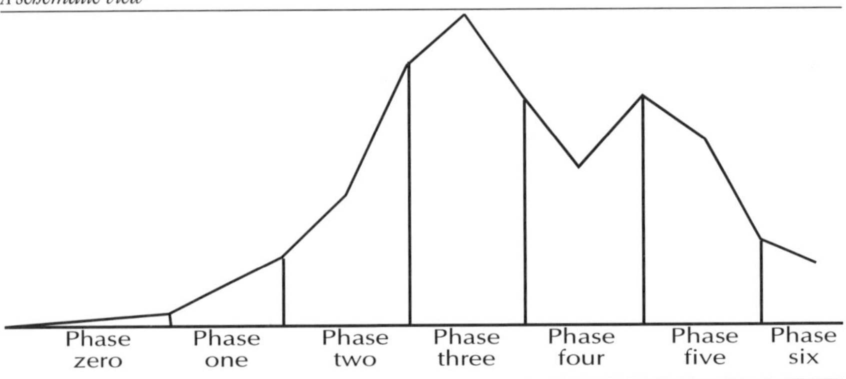

Source: Marc Faber Limited.

Figure 2

A LIVING EXAMPLE

Seoul Composite Index, 1985-1997

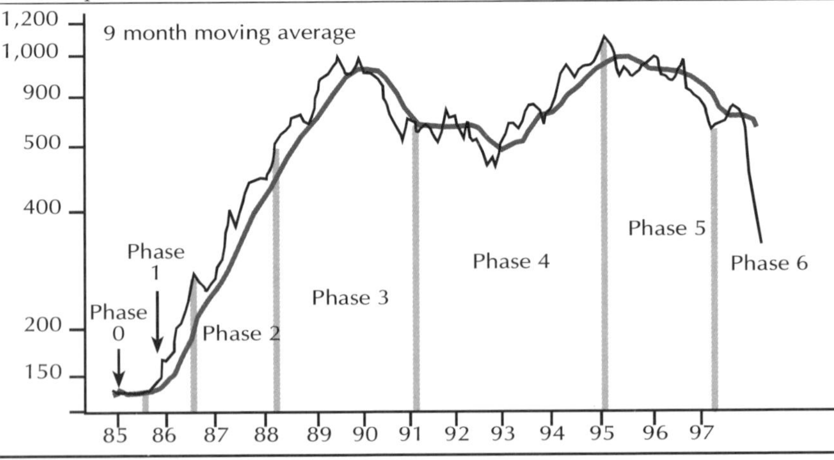

Source: Datastream.

The seven phases of the life cycle

The following discussion focuses on the events that tend to occur and the symptoms that become apparent during the various stages of emerging stock markets. These events and symptoms will show up in varying degrees, depending on each market's peculiarities. Obviously, the more extreme they are, the more likely it is that it will be possible to identify which phase of the cycle the stock market is moving into.

Phase Zero - After a crash

Events

- ❑ Long-lasting economic stagnation or slow contraction in real terms
- ❑ Real per-capita incomes go flat or have been falling for some years
- ❑ High unemployment
- ❑ Little capital spending and international competitive position deteriorates
- ❑ Political and social conditions become unstable (strikes, high inflation, continuous devaluations, terrorism, border conflicts, etc)
- ❑ Corporate profits fall
- ❑ No foreign direct or portfolio investment
- ❑ Capital flight

Symptoms

- ❑ Curfews at night
- ❑ Little tourism (unsafe)
- ❑ Hotel occupancy of just 30% and no new hotels have been built for several years
- ❑ Hotels are run down
- ❑ Extremely low volume on the stock exchange - usually down by about 90% from the previous peak
- ❑ After the a previous boom, the stock market has been moving sideways or moderately down for several years and has built a solid base
- ❑ In real terms and compared to other asset prices around the world, stocks have become ridiculously undervalued. Depressed economic conditions usually coincide with boom conditions somewhere else in the world. As a result, international capital and domestic savings are invested elsewhere and totally neglect the economy in phase zero. Naturally the flow of funds to the boom region will create very low valuations of assets (stocks, currency and real estate) in the phase-zero economy
- ❑ Hardly any foreign fund managers visit the country
- ❑ Headlines in the press are very negative
- ❑ Credit conditions are tight and credit volume is contracting because of a high proportion of bad loans incurred during the previous boom

- Either no foreign brokers have established an office or they are in the process of closing down offices opened during the previous boom. No country funds are launched and no brokerage research reports have been published for a long time
- At investors' conferences the audience has no interest whatsoever in such an economy, sector or asset class (including commodities) and will argue that such a market only goes down
- Investors claim that they lost a lot of money in the past by investing in the phase-zero markets and they are not inclined to reinvest in such a market
- Geneva private bankers exclaim that they would never even consider investing in such a market

Examples

- Latin America and especially Argentina post the petrodollar boom in the 1980s (see Figure 3)
- Middle East prior to the oil boom of the 1970s
- Communist countries after World War Two until the late 1980s
- Most of Asia ex Japan but including among others Thailand, the Philippines, South Korea between 1980 and 1985
- Indonesia, Thailand, the Philippines and Malaysia post 1997 Asian Crisis until recently
- South Africa and the African Continent in general in the last few years

Figure 3

POST-PETRODOLLAR BLUES

Monthly Bolsa index in US Dollar terms

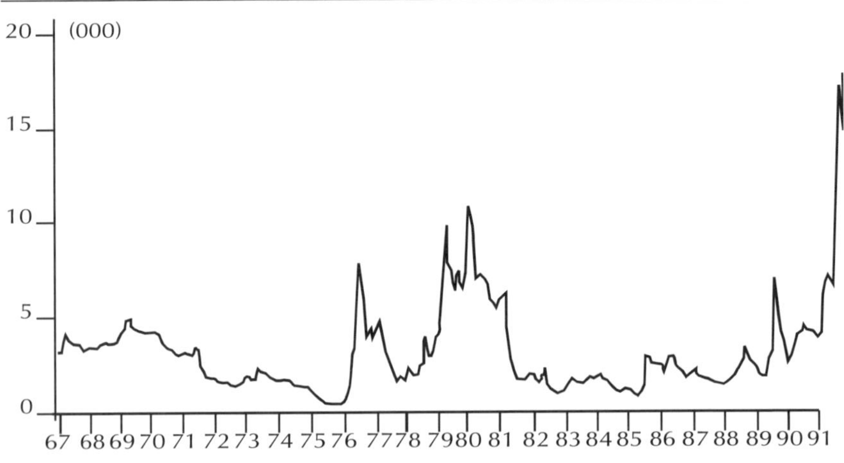

Source: Baring Securities.

It is important to understand that phase-zero is usually found in sectors or economies that first experienced a boom, which was then followed by a serious crisis. After the crisis has run its course, a period of investor aversion follows, because of the severe losses they incurred due their ill-timed purchases during the boom.

The longer phase zero lasts, and the more depressed the economic conditions and financial assets are, the higher the probability of phase one getting under way, provided that some event will spark an improvement in economic and social conditions. What is therefore, important, for phase one to get underway is a *catalyst* that will drive the economy out of its lethargy into an initially slow growth phase.

Phase One - The spark

Catalysts

- Social, political and economic conditions begin to improve (new government, peace treaties, adoption of market economies and capitalistic systems, introduction of property rights, etc)
- New economic policies (tax cuts and preferential treatment of foreign direct investments, removal of capital gain taxes, currency reforms, lifting of foreign exchange controls, the permission for foreigners to acquire 100% of assets including real estate, removal of trade barriers, etc)
- External factors, discoveries of resource deposits, the rise in price of an important commodity, applications of new inventions and innovations
- Improvement in liquidity because of an increase in exports, the repatriation of capital and increasing foreign portfolio flows and direct investments
- The outlook for future profit opportunities improves significantly, as a result of one or several above mentioned factors
- The undertaking of large scale infrastructure projects that improve power supplies, road transportation and port facilities
- The privatisation of entire industries

Symptoms

- Increase in cash balances and wealth
- Consumption, capital spending, corporate profits and stocks begin to rise, as credit conditions are eased
- Stocks suddenly begin to pick up
- Tourism improves
- The unemployment rate begins to decline
- A few far-sighted foreign businessmen become interested in joint ventures and other direct investment
- A few contrarian foreign fund managers begin to invest
- Hotel occupancy rises to 70%
- Curfews are lifted

- A significant improvement in business sentiment and investor confidence
- An increasing number of families buy back shares of their companies or take them private, recognising the low valuations

Examples

- Middle East after 1973
- Mexico after 1984
- Thailand after 1985
- Indonesia after 1987
- China after 1990
- Argentina, Brazil and Peru after 1990
- Russia and Eastern Europe after 1993

Investors must understand that for phase one to begin, a "displacement" - such as a sharp rise in the price of an important commodity, the application of an important new invention, a sudden rise in exports, or changes in tax and investment laws - must take place and act as a catalyst for the economy by stimulating new investment to capitalise on the new profit opportunities. As the brilliant economic historian, Professor Charles Kindleberger, put it:

> ... whatever the source of the displacement, if it is sufficiently large and pervasive, it will alter the economic outlook by changing profit opportunities in at least one important sector of the economy. Displacement brings opportunities for profit in some new or existing lines, and closes out others. As a result, business firms and individuals with savings or credit seek to take advantage of the former and retreat from the latter. If the new opportunities dominate those that lose, investment and production pick up.
>
> Charles P Kindleberger, *Manias, Panics, and Crashes*, New York 1978

Also, I cannot stress enough that a new leadership with a vision for economic growth, political unity and social improvement usually works wonders. Take Singapore. Under the visionary Lee Kwan Yew, this small city-state took a gigantic leap forward in the last 30 years. Or take China under the "revolutionary" Deng Xiaoping, who dared to challenge the conservative forces in the Communist Party and open China to the world. The same may happen now in Russia under Vladimir Putin. When a leader can create a sense of unity and purpose in a country - some sort of benevolent nationalism - the economic climate will automatically improve. (Even if nationalism is not benevolent as was the case for Hitler's

Germany, the economy can temporarily improve.) Finally, large-scale infrastructure projects and the introduction of a well-functioning legal and commercial infrastructure will also move an economy from phase zero to phase one, because both physical and legal infrastructure are necessary conditions for the efficient production of goods and services.

Lastly, if a displacement is accompanied by an extensive expansion of credit (credit inflation), a powerful boom is likely to get underway in phase two and during the early stages of phase three.

Phase Two - The recovery cycle

Events

- Unemployment falls and wages rise
- Capital spending to expand capacity soars, as the improvement in economic conditions is expected to last forever (error of optimism)
- Large inflows of foreign funds propel stocks to overvaluation
- Credit expands rapidly, leading to a sharp rise in real and financial assets
- Real estate prices increase several-fold
- New issues of stocks and bonds reach peak levels
- Foreign brokers and other foreign financial institutions open offices
- Merger and acquisition activity picks up
- Inflation accelerates and interest rates begin to rise
- There are exceptions, however: When countries suffer from hyperinflation and depression at the same time, the recovery, which is usually brought about by a financial reform, will lead to declining inflation and interest rates

Symptoms

- The business capital resembles an enormous construction site
- Hotels are full of foreign businessmen and portfolio managers. Many new hotels are under construction
- Headlines in the international press are now very positive
- A large number of country funds launch. Foreign portfolio flows are picking up
- Foreign brokers publish an avalanche of thick, bullish country research reports
- The thicker the reports, the more offices that have opened up - the more funds launched, the later it is in phase two
- Countries in phase two tend to become favourite travel destinations

Examples

- Houston, Dallas, Denver and Calgary in the late 1970s
- The entire Middle East including Iran between 1978 and 1980
- Japan between 1987 and 1990
- South and North Asia in the late 1980s

- Latin America between 1992 and 1994
- Russia and China at present

The reader may be surprised that I have listed Houston, Dallas, etc as emerging economies. The purpose is to show that we should not be overly dogmatic with the concept of "emerging economies" and only consider less-developed countries to fall into this category. In a modern and well-developed economy there will also always be emerging industrial and service sectors as well as emerging geographical regions that can grow far above the average of the whole nation for a while (but not forever). As a result, I would advise investors to keep an open mind toward the concept of investing in "emerging economies" and to not only include investing in less developed countries but also to consider investments in emerging parts of developed economies (see Chapter 6).

An important aspect of phase two and three is the upbeat mood that permeates the business community. It is common in phase two that when actual economic conditions change for the better, businessmen tend to overestimate the profit expectations and thus make optimistic errors. The economist A.C. Pigou remarked that:

> When an error of optimism has been generated ... it tends to spread and grow, as a result of reactions between different parts of the business community. This comes about through two principal influences. First, experience suggests that, apart altogether from the financial ties by which different businessmen are bound together, there exists among them a certain measure of psychological interdependence. A change of tone in one part of the business world diffuses itself, in a quite unreasoning manner, over other and wholly disconnected parts .... Secondly ... an error of optimism on the part of one group of businessmen creates a justification for improved expectation on the part of other groups.
>
> AC Pigou, *The Economics of Welfare*, London, 1920, page 233

Since it is easier to be optimistic in a crowd, because the crowd is heavily influenced by the principle of imitation, the close contact that exists among businesspeople enables positive sentiment to spread quickly. Modern telecoms, the internet, CNBC, Bloomberg and Reuters terminals, CNN, etc, have facilitated the internationalisation of investor sentiment. Great expectations fuel the boom, which is inevitably characterised by a decline in criticism and an increase in unsound business judgment. As a result, the optimistic error grows! It is common that whatever people ardently wish for, they will soon believe. When they make easy money, they therefore become more and more credulous and careless, and they are also at their happiest.

Phase Three - The boom

Events

- Overinvestment leads to excess capacity in several sectors of the economy
- Infrastructural problems, bottlenecks and an excessive credit expansion lead at times, via rising wages and real estate prices, to strong inflationary pressures
- The inflationary pressures, however, may not take place for consumer prices. In a deflationary environment consumer prices remain steady and wholesale prices frequently decline. In this instance, monetary policies will remain loose, credit will grow far more rapidly than GDP and inflation is evident in asset prices such as stocks and real estate
- The rate of corporate profit growth slows, and in some industries it begins to fall
- Usually, but not always, a shock such as a sharp rise in interest rates, a massive fraud, a business failure, a margin call that cannot be met by a large speculator, or some external unfavourable event leads to a sudden and totally unexpected decline in stock prices
- At times, stock prices begin to decline for no other reason than that they have run far ahead of themselves, and some speculators or insiders - in the know that the boom cannot go on forever and seeing that the profit picture is deteriorating - decide to take profit
- In such cases, it is simply a matter that at some point the supply of equities from the corporate sector and insiders exceeds the demand from the "stupid" and credulous public who, brainwashed by the bullish statements from corporate executives and the press, continue to buy at any price

Symptoms

- Phase three culminates in a once-a-generation investment mania, then in a colossal bust. This is the easiest phase of the cycle to recognise, as speculation gets totally out of hand
- The only problem is that this phase can produce huge gains in a relatively brief period of time before it comes to an end, and is followed by the bust
- Frequently, the currency will collapse along with share prices, due to foreign selling
- The volume of credit explodes and the system becomes highly leveraged
- Many condominium and housing projects, and new hotels, office buildings, and shopping centres are completed. Frequently, one of or the world's tallest and most lavish buildings is about to be completed (see Figure 4)

Figure 4

TOWERS MARKING THE PEAKS

The 18-year New York skyscraper cycle

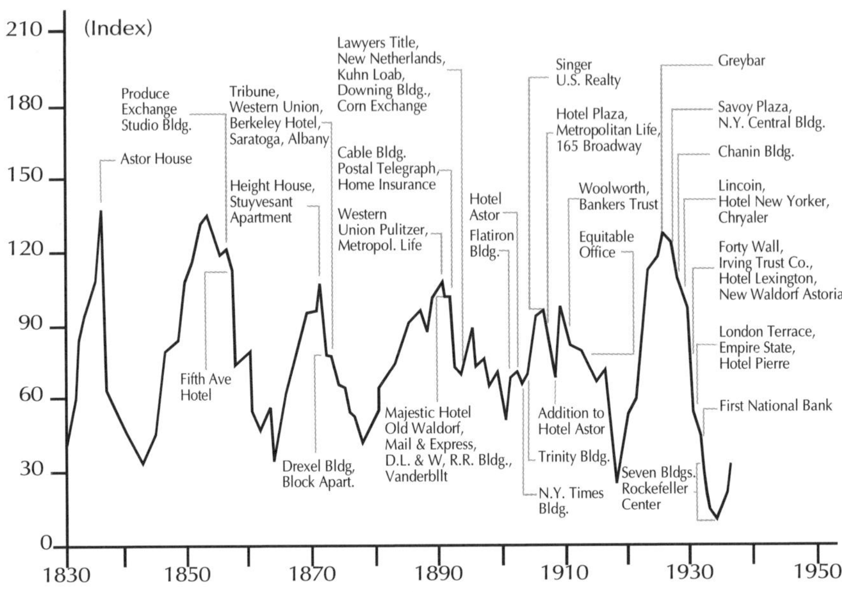

Source: Dewey, Edward, *Cycles - The Science of Predictions*, New York, 1947.

- The business capital resembles a "boom town" - nightclubs packed with speculators and brokers who made their money in the stock or property market. During the day, there is heavy traffic congestion
- Frequently a new airport is inaugurated and a second one is in the planning stages
- "New cities" or industrial zones are planned and developed
- Famous businessmen, real estate and stock market speculators become folk heroes and regularly feature on the first page of magazines. Occasionally magazines will even elevate them to "Man of the Year"
- The stock and real estate markets become a topic of discussion everywhere. The investing crowd finds any number of arguments "why the stock or property market cannot go down" and its ignorance and misplaced confidence is supported by some academics who publish excessively optimistic studies based on some erroneous assumptions. Stock trading is characterised by very active retail and speculative activity, much of it on borrowed money. Volume on the stock market and sales and purchase agreements for properties soar and reach a multiple of what they were in phase one
- Buzzwords such as LBOs, M&A, Red Chips, Tiger Economies, Tiger Cub Economies, New Era, New Economy and so on proliferate and it is common that speculators only know the symbols of the stocks they purchase and not the companies' name, not to mention their line of business

- Housewives become active in the stock market and many people give up their daytime jobs in order to concentrate on "playing" the market. Hairdressers, hookers, 20-something portfolio managers and children of well-to-do families frequently perform better than experienced professional money managers, are regularly interviewed by the press and even write books about their winning formulae
- Corporate executives go on an acquisition spree, usually financed with additional borrowings
- Successful businessmen and speculators begin to invest actively overseas or diversify in other business sectors - usually in sectors and things they have no understanding of and, therefore, overpay for their purchases (art, real estate, stocks, golf courses, etc)
- Foreign money flows reach a very high level, as the boom is well advertised by the record number of foreign brokers who open offices during this phase their offices. Brokerage reports reach the heaviest weight and thickness of the entire emerging market cycle

Examples

- Oil producing regions in 1980
- Hong Kong in 1973, 1980 and 1997
- Thailand from 1992 to 1994
- Singapore in 1980/1981
- Japan in 1989
- Indonesia in 1990
- Taiwan in 1990
- Latin America in 1994
- The TMT sector in 1999/2000

The boom is usually erected on a massive popular delusion. In 1980, investors believed that inflation was about to accelerate further. They thought they were still in phase two. They paid US$850 for an ounce of gold, US$50 for silver and drove energy related shares to lofty levels believing that oil prices would rise to US$80. In 1989, investors began in earnest to believe that the Japanese stock market was no longer subject to market forces and paid 100 times earnings for companies with mediocre growth prospects. They were also caught by the delusion that Japan was suffering from a land shortage and that any price would be paid for real estate. In the early 1990s, Asians began to think that tourism would grow at 30% per annum year-in-year-out and grossly overbuilt hotels and golf courses. And, in 1997, the Hong Kong Chinese began to think in earnest that Hong Kong would greatly benefit from the opening of China, become the hub of Asia (even of the universe) and, therefore, paid ludicrous prices at land auctions. More recently, investors paid fantasy prices for hi-tech, telecom, internet and biotechnology shares.

Happy times and excessive prosperity do not last forever. Something totally unexpected will usually spoil the party. But prices can also begin to fall under their own weight. *A typical feature of phase three is that even after an initial, and usually sharp, shock to prices, the mood remains very optimistic.* The new lower prices are now perceived to be a bargain, and the sharp decline is regarded merely as a correction within a long-term up-trend. The capital losses in this first decline are not serious, because only the capital gains from the final run-up are given back. Therefore, only few people realise that the overall trend has changed from up to down! It is from here onwards that investors will lose serious because they still believe the market to be in phase two and, therefore they average down and will buy on any dip.

Phase Four - Downcycle doubts

Events

- Credit growth slows - unless monetary authorities act irresponsibly and attempt to prolong the mania and keep the economy in a state of a permanent boom
- Corporate profits deteriorate
- Excess capacity becomes a problem in a few industries, but overall the economy continues to do well and the slowdown is perceived to be only temporary
- After an initial sharp fall, stocks recover as foreign investors who missed the stock market's rise in phases one and two pour money into the market and as interest rates begin to fall
- It is not uncommon that foreigners increase their buying of stocks in phase four, since they tend to be latecomers to the investment party
- Some sort of major "hook" keeps investor interest in the market alive. The hook may be an economy that continues to grow, sharply declining interest rates, corporate profits that are still rising, or simply optimistic statements by business leaders and government officials
- The majority of stocks usually fail to reach a new high because a large number of new issues meet demand (the sellers are locals who either know better or are strapped for cash)
- However, it is possible that a stock market index driven by just a few stocks makes a new high (see Figure 2). The advance-decline line and the number of stocks hitting new all time highs will, in such a case, not confirm the new high

Symptoms

- ❑ Some financial stress is evident. Speculators who were heavily geared may be forced to sell out. Banks tighten lending standards in some sectors of the economy. Non-performing loans begin to climb
- ❑ Condominiums have reached prices exceeding the purchasing power of the locals. They are now advertised overseas
- ❑ Office capital values and rentals begin to level off or fall
- ❑ Tourist arrivals slow down and are below expectations. Hotel vacancy rates rise and discounts are offered
- ❑ Brokers continue to publish the most bullish reports, arguing that the decline in stock prices represents a life-time buying opportunity
- ❑ Political and social conditions deteriorate (a coup, a strong opposition leader, strikes, social discontent, increase in crime, etc)

Examples

- ❑ Latin America in the early 1980s
- ❑ Thailand and Malaysia after 1994
- ❑ Hong Kong investors in and after 1997
- ❑ US investors in early 1930, in the fall of 1973 and in 2000/2001

The rebound in phase four (see Figure 1) is very tricky. The economy is still doing well, and the rally is usually powerful enough to seduce even sceptics back into the market. On the other hand, if the fall from the market's phase-three high is very severe, many investors will be convinced that the market has already reached phase six (the ultimate low).

The transition from phase four to phase five tends to be very subtle. Usually there is no panic selling, as occurs frequently in phase three. But prices begin gradually to drift lower and remain in a low-volume downtrend for an extended period.

Phase Five - Realisation

Events

- ❑ Credit becomes tight, bond spreads widen considerably and bankruptcies soar
- ❑ Economic, but even more so social and political, conditions now deteriorate badly. Consumption slows noticeably or falls (car, housing and appliance sales are down)
- ❑ Corporate profits collapse
- ❑ Stocks enter a prolonged and severe downtrend as foreigners begin to exit
- ❑ Real estate prices fall sharply
- ❑ One or several "big players" go bankrupt (usually the ones who made the headlines in phase three)

- Companies are strapped for cash and are often forced to issue shares at distressed prices. This increases the supply of shares and depresses prices even further

Symptoms

- Empty office buildings, high vacancy in hotels
- Discontinued and unfinished construction sites are now common
- The unemployment rate begins to rise
- Budget surpluses, which frequently occur in phase two and three, give way to deficits
- Stockbrokers lay off staff or close down
- Research reports become thinner. Country funds that sold at a premium during phases two and three, now sell at a discount
- The country is no longer a favourite tourist destination, as it frequently becomes unsafe

Examples

- Singapore in 1982 and 1983
- Indonesia, Malaysia, Thailand, the Philippines in 1998
- Argentina in 2002

Phase five feels like a hangover after the financial orgy that took place in phases three and four. Because the boom was built largely upon a major error of judgment (a cause of excessive credit growth), on the day of reckoning speculators suddenly realise their miscalculations and, because their dream of huge profit fails to materialise, the harsh reality sets in. People sober up and begin to realise that they paid far too much for stocks and real estate during the boom phase. At last, investors finally give up. While declines were used as buying opportunities up to this phase, towards the end of phase five and at the beginning of phase six rallies are used to exit the market.

Phase Six - Capitulation and the bottom

Events

- Investors give up on stocks. Volume is down significantly from the peak levels reached in phase three - usually by 90%
- Capital spending falls sharply (error of pessimism)
- Interest rates decline further and reach their lows for the cycle
- Foreign investors lose appetite for new investment and continue to sell
- The currency is weakening or is devalued

Symptoms

- ❑ Headlines turn very negative. The international press depicts countries in phase six very negatively
- ❑ Foreign brokers finally turn bearish and close their offices
- ❑ Assets in equity mutual funds have declined by around 90% as a result of persistent net outflows that can last for several years, and capital losses
- ❑ Flights, hotels and nightclubs are empty
- ❑ Men go out dressed for work, but spend the day in the park
- ❑ Taxi drivers, shopkeepers and nightclub hostesses tell you how much they or their relatives have lost investing in stocks

Examples

- ❑ United States in 1932 and at the end of 1974
- ❑ Hong Kong in 1974 and in 2002
- ❑ Asia after 1997
- ❑ Latin America and especially Argentina in 2002

In many ways, phase six is the mirror image of phase three. Towards the end of phase two and in phase three, people were very optimistic and upbeat. But in phase six, the boom and the atmosphere of greed that were based on an error of optimism give way to a crisis of confidence and fear, the error of pessimism. To quote Pigou again:

> This new error is born, not an infant, but a giant; for an industrial boom has necessarily been a period of strong emotional excitement, and an excited man passes from one form of excitement to another more rapidly than he passes to quiescence.

In phase six, the error of pessimism will depress business and result in a prolonged contraction. It is important to understand that the realisation at some point that the profit opportunity is not as great as was hoped, or that a market cannot go any higher, leads to a "revulsion" of speculators' sentiment and panic selling. Whereas a few years earlier everyone wished to participate in the mania, now everyone wants to get out. It should, however, be noted that stocks have frequently already reached very low prices in phase six. Therefore, as the news deteriorates, prices often no longer decline but begin to build a long-term base for a renewed advance. Base-building process can last, as in the case of Latin America in the 1980s, for several years (see Figure 3).

I believe that time, psychology and trading volume are important factors in determining whether a market is in phase four or six. Phase four will occur 6-18 months after the market's high, while phase six usually occurs much later - frequently after 4-6 years, and sometimes even later - after the market's top. In terms of psychology, there is also a noticeable difference. In phase four, people remain optimistic and confident about the economic prospects. Investors are more concerned with missing the next up-tick than the risk of losing money. Not so in phase six, when pessimism is rampant as a result of total wealth destruction. In phase six, investors no longer want to hear about a market. Moreover - while trading volume is only marginally lower in phase four than in phase three - in phase six trading volume is usually down by 90% from the peak. The US today may still be in phase four or possibly it's already in phase five, while most Asian markets have already passed through phase six and may now be in either phase zero or already in phase one of a new cycle.

Locating the phases

I should like to once again emphasise that we should not be too dogmatic about the different phases I described above. I have found stock market cycles in emerging markets that fit the model perfectly. In other cases, the entire downcycle (phase 4 and 5) is condensed and occurs very quickly. This was the case during the Asian Crisis, when the downcycle took place within just one year. Moreover, although it would now appear that, in the case of Asia, phase six has already ended, we cannot be certain about it because of the uncertainty surrounding the global economy. Thus, we may still be in phase six - during which Asian markets are in the process of building a solid base for the next bull market.

One additional tool for identifying the current phase of a stock market would be to look at market capitalisation as a percentage of GDP (see Figure 5) and at turnover rates (see Figure 6). Stock markets with low market caps as a percentage of GDP, like 1992 Latin America, are more likely to be in phase zero or phase one than markets for which this ratio is extremely high (Hong Kong and Malaysia in Figure 5). A high turnover ratio would suggest that a market is in stage three or four, rather than in phase zero.

Figure 5

LOW MARKET-CAP RATIO, LOW PHASE

Market cap as a % of GDP as of 30 December 1992*

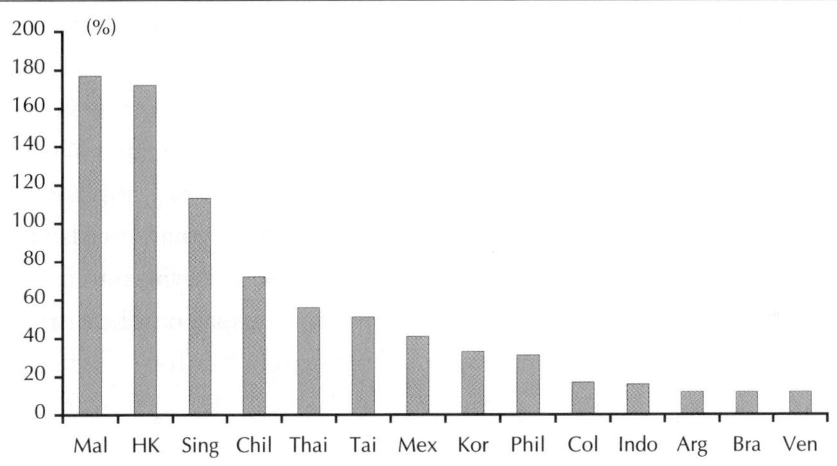

*Estimated 1992 GDP. Source: Baring Securities, Unibanco, Veneconomia, La Nota Economica, Argos.

Figure 6

HIGH TURNOVER RATIO, HIGH PHASE

Value traded as a % of average 1991 market cap

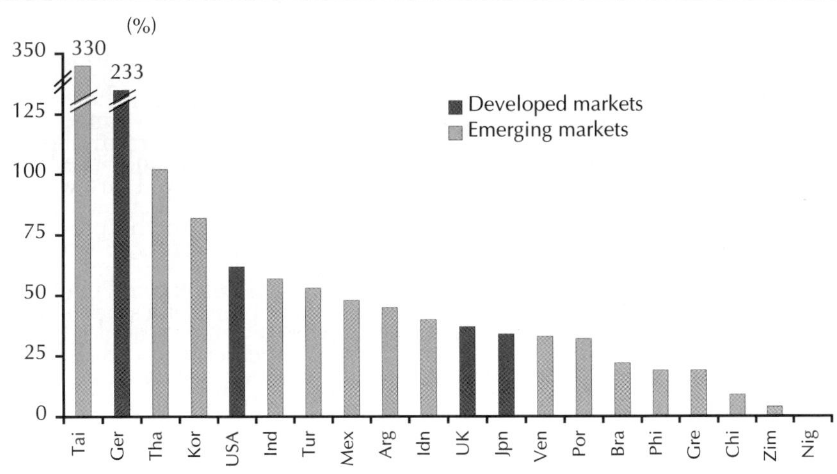

Source: Emerging Stock Markets Factbook.

I do fully recognise the limitations of my life cycle of emerging markets, but I should like to point out that phase three can usually easily be identified even by the layman. In my opinion, one of the central problems of investing is that people focus far too much on the purchase of equities and not enough on selling them. They spend a lot of time analysing companies and looking to buy "value" - that is they want to buy bargains in a market. But little time is spent analysing when to sell "value" - that is when to sell assets for which the risk reward is no longer attractive. Admittedly, it is true that in phase three large gains can be achieved within a short period of time, but the risks are high because, while in phase two almost all stocks rise, in phase three the advance becomes much more narrow as the market's breadth deteriorates. Many stocks begin to decline long before the market's final high! Furthermore, it is impossible to predict when the market will turn down and how sharply it will fall during the initial sell-off (just think of the 1987 crash, the collapse of commodity prices in the early 1980s, the Asian stock market collapse in 1997/98 and the Nasdaq collapse after 2000).

Therefore, given these high risks, the average investor should best leave phase-three markets aside. In fact, I am making this point for both short-sellers and buyers of stocks. In phase three, short sellers can be badly squeezed - as I know only too well from personal experience - because in the manic phase some stocks can rise by five to ten times within just a few months. Therefore, while these stocks eventually tumble by 95% during the bust and even go bankrupt, the short-seller may have to meet very heavy margin calls during the final stage of the mania. Equally, the buyer of such stocks never knows when the bubble will end. The first decline will usually appear to be just a profit-taking phase and investors will tend to hold on to their positions. By the time they realise that the trend may have changed, the market may already be down by 50% or more. Undoubtedly, waves of excessive speculation do not create any macroeconomic benefits and wealth for society but wealth is usually destroyed for the majority of participants on a massive scale.

I have just read an article by a super-bull luminary - who in 2000 predicted the Dow to rise in almost a straight line to 36,000 - in which he establishes a few investment rules. One of his brilliant rules is that you should "always buy a stock with the intention of holding it forever. For one thing, if you don't sell, you don't have to pay capital gains taxes. Also, when you don't sell, you have eliminated two of three difficult decisions: what and when to buy, when to sell and when to buy back."

I totally disagree with this rule and think that you should always buy an asset with a view to selling it one day if its price exceeds its "real" value by a multiple. Naturally, I concede that it is very difficult if not impossible to establish what the "real" value of any asset is. But I can assure the reader that once a market reaches phase three - during which prices soar vertically, speculation becomes rampant and all the symptoms exist that I have listed above - it is highly unlikely that an asset will sell for its "real value". Far more likely it will sell for a "stupid" price - though this situation will never last long.

Thus, for emerging-markets investors, no matter how great the growth prospects of a region, a country, a sector or individual company, timing of purchase and sale remains a crucial consideration. It is in this spirit that I established the different cycles through which emerging markets travel. My intention here and in Chapter 4 was to again highlight some of the pitfalls of emerging-markets investing and to give some guidance on how to identify what phase of the cycle an emerging market is in.

When to jump (on or off)

The ideal entry and exit points will depend to a large extent on an investor's individual strategy. Personally, I like to buy markets during phase zero. Usually, there is no huge price risk during this phase, because prices are already very depressed. The risk instead lies in the fact that markets can build bases for several years, with continuous backing and filling in the market. But the good news is that stocks move from weak hands into strong hands, so when phase one suddenly starts there is little or no supply of shares and stocks can double or more almost overnight. I should like to stress that, percentage wise, during phases one and two, the potential for capital gain is very significant. An individual stock or property can easily rise by 20 to 50 times during these two phases. I usually get out during phase two. This may be premature, but I have always tended to underestimate the ignorance and greed of the investing public and the heights to which speculation (on borrowed money, of course) can push up prices!

In my opinion, there are many pitfalls for investors putting money into emerging markets. Financial markets tend to overshoot both on the upside and the down. As a saying goes, "no price is too high for a bull"! The highs reached during phase three are therefore frequently milestones - often not exceeded for anywhere between eight and 15, and sometimes even more years, although the economy may recover relatively quickly from the slump that occurred in phases four and five. By 1938, US GNP had exceeded the 1929 figure, yet the stock market took until 1955 to beat its 1929 highs.

Purchasing an emerging market in phase three is comparable to buying one stock or an entire industry group at the peak of its popularity. Investors who bought the "nifty fifty" in the US in 1973, oil stocks in 1980 and the Latin American markets in 1980, Japanese stocks in 1990 and Asian stocks in 1994 had to endure miserable performances for many years. How long investors will have to wait until they will see recovery in the shares bought at the top of the Asian markets in the 1990s and the top of the TMT sector mania in 2000, I don't know, but I can only imagine that it will take a very long time. Because of these wide price swings in markets, it is most important for anyone involved in investing in emerging markets to seriously consider and analyse in which phase of the cycle the emerging market finds itself.

In 1991, I attempted to categorise emerging markets according to their level of economic development and prosperity by drawing a "fountain of wealth" (see inside back cover). The idea came from the French economist Richard Cantillon (1680-1734) who noticed that money, like water, always flows downward from a higher level. Applied to our global economy, I felt then that Cantillon's theory simply meant that money had the tendency to flow from countries with a high price level (rich countries) to countries with a low price level (less developed, poor countries). This, I thought at that time, would create in the 1990s an arbitrage effect by raising economic activity in the poor regions and lead to sub par growth in the rich countries. Unfortunately, I was wrong, and in the 1990s the rich industrialised countries of the West raced ahead, while most emerging economies encountered serious economic setbacks (China being the great exception).

But I still maintain that the principle of the fountain of wealth has some validity, as the last will one day be the first and vice versa. Most of the countries at the bottom are clearly still in phase zero but I am pleased that both China and Russia have made a quantum leap in the 1990s and would today be at a higher level than Venezuela, Indonesia, Peru, India, the Philippines and Argentina. And I am sure that in the next ten years or so, we shall see Vietnam making a sharp move upward in the tiers of the fountain - as well as possibly Myanmar, North Korea, Cuba and Mongolia. What these countries really need is to provide the economic and legal infrastructure in order to attract foreign direct investment and lead to a more efficient capitalistic system (as compared to "robber baron" capitalism), which will then act as the phase-one catalyst for new business.

There are several obvious problems when categorizing countries in terms of economic and social development, but it is clear that, say 20 years ago, China, India, Vietnam and the former Soviet Union would have been right at the bottom of the fountain, but today they are climbing the fountain rapidly. Another complication in classifying countries according to their level of development relates to the following. A country such as India may be in many respects backward, but it may have an edge in one or several industries such as in the IT sector and in generic drugs. Therefore, I would also urge investors not to ask too much about which country has the best economic prospects and the most attractive stock market, but which sectors and which companies are the most promising within the emerging universe.

* * *

The purpose of this chapter was to try to impress upon the reader the existence of cycles in emerging stock markets, to show that there is always a time to buy and a time to sell, and to emphasise that a buy-and-hold-forever strategy is in most instances totally inappropriate. What I have not done so far is explain the *causes* of stock-market cycles. Since stock-market cycles and investment manias are closely related to business cycles, the following chapters provide some theoretical knowledge and understanding of the factors that move economies and markets.

CHAPTER SIX

Business cycles - Alive and well!

> For well over a century, business cycles have run an unceasing round. They have persisted through vast economic and social changes; they have withstood countless experiments in industry, agriculture, banking, industrial relations, and public policy; they have confounded forecasters without number, belied repeatedly prophecies of a "new era of prosperity" and outlived repeated forebodings of "chronic depression".
>
> *ARTHUR F BURNS (1904-87)*

During the last bull market, some economists and many public opinion leaders came to question the very existence of traditional business cycles. It was assumed that the Federal Reserve Board and other central banks were in a position to "steer" the global economy on a slow, non-inflationary, 2-3% annual growth path. Under this "perfect world scenario", investors increasingly believed that recessions and bear markets were a thing of the past. But this was a delusion. Business-cycle theory applies - not only to the past but also to the present economic environment.

It is puzzling that - even after the depression in Latin America in the 1980s, the Japanese economic downturn after 1990 and the Asian Crisis - people can still be so naïve as to hold that business fluctuations have been eliminated. By a bunch of ignorant central bankers! But such is the world.

After the longest economic expansion on record in the US, academics were no longer interested in business-cycle theory. It was the same during the prosperous 1920s. Few books on the subject appeared then either. Most of the great works on business cycles came out during the depression of the 1930s, when the subject naturally aroused great interest among hard-bitten investors - then as now.

A simple guide to business cycles

The first record of an economic cycle is found in the Old Testament. In Genesis 41, we read about the Pharaoh's dream, which was interpreted by Jacob's son, Joseph, to mean that there would be seven years of great plenty, followed by seven years of famine. The existence of agricultural cycles was already a fact of life in ancient times. In fact, the entire early business cycle theory focused very much on the influence of the weather on agricultural and economic cycles. The economist William Stanley Jevons, having been intrigued by the periodicity of the great English crises of the 19th Century (1825, 1837, 1847, 1857 and 1866), was convinced that solar cycles were to blame. He believed that the decennial crises of the 19th Century depended on meteorological variations, which in turn depended on cosmic variations, of which he had evidence in the frequency of sunspots, auroras and magnetic perturbations.

The weather's influence on civilisation was also observed by Karl Marx (*Das Kapital,* Hamburg, 1867), who correctly assumed that the necessity for predicting the rise and the fall of the Nile created Egyptian astronomy - and with it the dominion of the priests as directors of agriculture. Ellsworth Huntington extended weather theory by postulating that business cycles depended largely on the mental attitude of people - and that this depended on health, which was largely a function of the weather. Also, since, according to Pigou, the movement of business confidence is the dominant cause of the rhythmic fluctuations that are experienced in industry, climatic changes and their influence on business should not be ignored entirely. (I may add that in recent years some market old-timers, such as Arch Crawford, have made a name for themselves by making predictions about the stock market based on astrology.)

Of course, modern business-cycle theories dismiss the climate hypothesis as hogwash. This may be proper in today's industrial and post-industrial age, but if we consider that, until the end of the 19th Century, agriculture was the dominant sector of an economy (frequently employing about 90% of a country's population), it is clear that pre-industrial economies were heavily dependent on food production which, in turn, depended on the climate. The Chinese believe in a cycle of war and peace, determined by the availability of food (peace) and its scarcity (war). In more recent economic literature, we find underconsumption, undersaving, overproduction, agrarian, psychological, overinvestment (marginal efficiency of capital), monetary, displacement and innovation business-cycle theories. I believe some of them may further our understanding of today's economic trends.

Underconsumption theories

Most underconsumption theories have been dismissed as unfounded, but John A Hobson's *The Economics of Unemployment* (London, 1931) focused on the tendency of production to outgrow the capacity for consumption due to growing income inequality, eventually bringing about a depression. According to Hobson, extreme wealth disparity leads to the paradoxical situation where those at the low end of the income scale would be glad to consume but are unable to - while those at the high end have no desire (underconsumption here could also mean oversaving or overinvestment). In support of his argument, Hobson produced an estimate of savings in relation to incomes in 1910 (see Table 1 - he estimated that about three-quarters of total savings came from the richest classes). It was his view that any "approximation towards equality of incomes would reduce the proportion of income saved to income spent", by which underconsumption and depressions could be avoided.

Table 1

WEALTH BREEDS DEPRESSION

Family spending patterns

Families with	Average income per family	Average spending per family
Over £5,000	£12,100	£7,600
From £700 to £5,000	1,054	690
From £160 to £700	357	329
From £52 to £160	142	138
Under £52	40	40

Source: John A. Hobson, *The Economics of Unemployment*, London, 1931.

Hobson's arguments were confirmed by the movement of output, costs, prices, wages and profits in the US from 1920-30. The findings of PH Douglas (*Controlling Depressions*, New York, 1935) seem to support this: Hourly output in manufacturing industries increased by about 30% between 1922 and 1929. During the same time, hourly earnings of labourers rose by about 8%. The result was an increase in profits of about 84% (although production only increased by 37%), which led to excessive production capacity expansion (bringing about, in turn, an imbalance of production over consumption). According to Douglas, production as a whole increased by 37% between 1922 and 1929, while real incomes of urban lower-salaried groups increased by only 18-20% (and much less for agricultural labourers). Thus, the percentage of salaries and wages of the total value added by manufacturing fell steadily, from 53.4% in 1923 to 47.7% in 1929. Based on this, and on the fact that corporate profits increased by 83% during this period, Douglas concluded that the purchasing power was simply insufficient to absorb the growing supply of consumer goods, leading to the collapse in 1929. AD Gayer (*Monetary Policy and Economic Stabilisation*, New York, 1935) came to similar conclusions and attributed the cause of the depression to the insufficient income of the final consumer to absorb the produced goods. According to him the vast expansion of capacity in durable goods industries were excessive relative to the means of the ultimate consumer.

There are two reasons for discussing the underconsumption theory. According to the dismissive Haberler, underconsumption was used to mean:

> … the process by which purchasing power is in some way lost to the economic

> system, and therefore fails to become income and appear as demand in the market for consumer goods. Money disappears or is hoarded, and the income-velocity of money diminishes. In this sense, underconsumption is just another word for deflation. Deflation is, of course, a possible cause of the breakdown of the boom and the main cause of the depression; but, as such, is covered by the monetary explanation of the business cycle.
>
> Gottfried Haberler, *Prosperity and Depression*, New York, 1946, page 120

I shall leave it to the economics academia to debate the terminology and causal relationship of underconsumption and deflation. For us, it is enough to understand that, in the years to come, the crucial issue facing the global economy may be the possibility of widespread deflation, which, I may add, already exists in China, where the economic environment is characterised by a "deflationary boom". Economists such as Gary Shilling and stock market forecasters such as Robert Prechter share the opinion that deflation is just around the corner. In addition, it is evident that in the 1990s wealth inequality not only increased in the US but also between the rich industrialised countries and the emerging economies. In Western countries the well-to-do increased their income far more rapidly than did labour, because the compensation of CEOs soared as a result of their compensation being tied to options, and also because share ownership is concentrated among high-income groups. At the same time the emerging economies suffered in the late 1990s from sharp currency devaluations with the result that, in US Dollar terms, their per-capita incomes were lower in 2000 than they had been in 1990 (China and Vietnam were probably the exception, but we should not forget that in their rural sectors, where more than half the population lives, per-capita incomes hardly increased in the 1990s and even for the urban workers wage growth in US Dollar terms may not have been that impressive given China's 55% currency devaluation in 1994).

I regard global wealth inequality as one of the central problems of our times. We have a few rich nations with relatively small populations and many poor countries with vast numbers of mouths to feed. The poor of the world would like to consume, but do not have the income to do so. This is certainly a factor in the disappointing growth rates for the world as a whole in the 1990s. From Figure 1, we can see that the rate of economic growth slowed in the 1990s and has been, in 2001, the lowest in more than 30 years (we return to a discussion of wealth inequality in our Epilogue).

However, growing income inequality is not the only factor driving consumption growth down. High debt in the household sector (see Figure 2) and aging populations in most industrialised countries are also going to constrain any significant pickup in demand in the Western world and in Japan.

Now, someone could argue that in a growing economy increased corporate profits will lead to increased capital spending and bring about a rise in employment and wages, thus boosting workers' spending power. Not so, say the underconsumptionists: the corporate profit explosion leads to massive new investment in a first phase and prolongs the prosperity period as it overstimulates the construction of capital goods. But breakdown inevitably follows when the production facilities are completed and consumer goods begin to pour out.

Figure 1

SLOWING DOWN

Global GDP growth in real terms

Source: IMF.

Figure 2

SHOPPING SPREE

Ratio of consumer and mortgage debt to disposable personal income

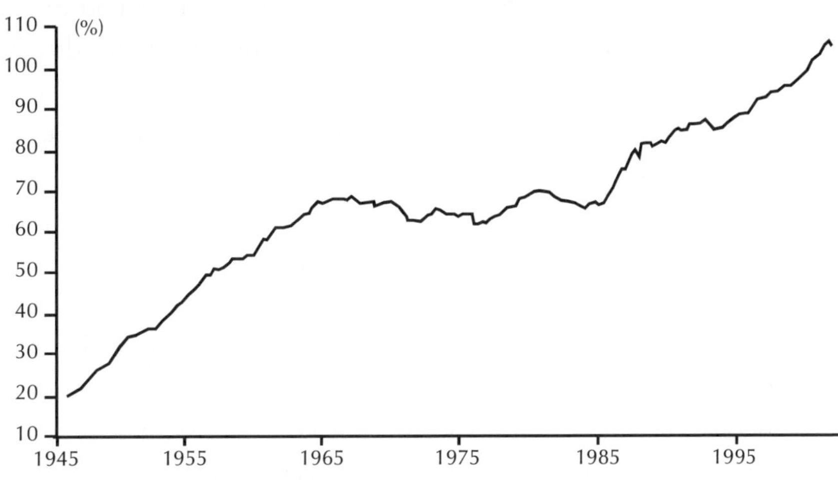

Source: Federal Reserve Flow of Funds, Bridgewater Associates.

Schumpeter also believed that a boom is terminated when the new productive processes are completed and additional finished goods flood the market (see also Albert Aftalion, *Les crises périodiques de surproduction*, Paris, 1913). In other words, sharply rising profits lead to excessive investments, which eventually lead to a collapse of the boom. In this respect, the underconsumption theory has much in common with the overinvestment theory, which stipulates that "credit expansion" is the villain (excessive profits due to the lag in wages are harmful only in so far as they are responsible for inflationary credits that lead to overinvestment). But, regardless of the theory, the proximate cause of the breakdown is insufficient demand when compared with the supply coming to market.

Growing income inequality, high consumer debt, low savings rates and an aging population aside - there are other reasons to be pessimistic about future consumption growth in industrialised countries. A significant proportion of today's capital spending goes into labour-saving investments, which tends to depress wage growth.. Moreover, increasingly, capacity is expanded overseas, particularly in China, where manufacturing is far cheaper. As a result, labour in the US, and even more so in Western

Europe, will only enjoy very modest income gains or possibly even a loss of income in the years to come. Again, one could argue that slowing consumer demand in industrialised countries will be offset (through the multiplier effect) by rising income in emerging economies to which new production facilities are frequently transplanted.

This is certainly a valid point and one I propose to address below. However, I should like to conclude this investigation into the underconsumption theory by reminding our readers how similar US wage and profit trends in the 1990s have been to those in the period immediately preceding the Great Depression. In addition, I should like to stress that, according to the business-cycle literature (regarding both the underconsumption and overinvestment theories), once the boom ends and the contraction period begins, the downturn is accompanied by deflation (of profits, too), because the markets for consumer goods become glutted and because capital spending collapses (due to the acceleration principle).

Psychological and monetary overinvestment theories

According to the French economist Yves Guyot (*Principles of Social Economy*, London, 1884), psychological factors are the driving force of economic fluctuations yet were not sufficiently taken into account in his time - which explained for him why there were so many misleading explanations of commercial crises. In essence, the psychological theory holds that, in a period of growing prosperity and rising corporate profitability, each entrepreneur is likely to overestimate the profits he can obtain as compared to others. As mentioned in Chapter 5, Pigou, the main protagonist of the psychological trade-cycle theory, thought that when an error of optimism has been generated it tends to spread because of the close ties businessmen maintain with each other through the purchase and sale of goods, as a result of psychological ties and through the credit system. As a result there exists among the business community "a certain measure of psychological interdependence". Morover, "... an error of optimism on the part of one group of businessmen itself creates a justification for some improved expectations on the part of other groups". Pigou also observed that:

> ... large errors were especially liable to occur in enterprises in new fields, whose limitations have not been accurately measured by investors, or even by capitalists of proved judgment and experience ... New discoveries and the opening of continents have contributed greatly to these mistakes ...
>
> AC Pigou, *Industrial Fluctuations*, London, 1927, pages 76-9

Lavington had compared businessmen who infect each other with confidence and optimism to skaters on a frozen pond:

> Indeed, the confidence of each skater in his own safety is likely to be reinforced rather than diminished by the presence of numbers of his fellows. .... The rational judgement that the greater their number the greater will be the risk is likely to be submerged by the mere contagion of confidence which persuades him that the greater the numbers the more safely he himself may venture. [However] when, in the order of nature, the sound of a crack is heard and confidence is transformed into apprehension, whose influence on a solitary skater might be small, being reflected from one to another, reinforces itself rapidly and cumulatively, and may, if its natural vent in action be impeded, rise to a panic in the general effort to escape.
>
> F Lavington, *The Trade Cycle*, London, 1922, page 33

Other economists stress the fact that the longer the interval between the investment and the final result, or the greater the uncertainty as to the ultimate usefulness or value of an investment, the greater the possibility of mistakes. Lengthy production processes (Schumpeter talks about the "period of gestation" - the time between the birth of a product to the day when it is ready for delivery) tend to facilitate not only the miscalculation of total demand but, because of competition, each producer is likely to also miscalculate his expected share of the total market (today, every PC manufacturer expects his market share to increase).

New concepts and ideas are particularly prone to errors of optimism. Some of the most pronounced boom-and-bust periods in history were caused by excessive expansion of new industries (canals, railroads, super tankers, radios, autos, PCs, internet sites, cellular phones, etc) or the opening of new territories (the South Seas, America's western territories, Latin America in the second half of the 19th Century, etc). I described in

Chapter 4 the enthusiasm created by the railroads in the 19th Century and their subsequent expansion into new territories, which led to repeated, erroneous forecasts regarding their future profits and later to great losses. In addition, besides overestimating overall demand and their expected share of the market, entrepreneurs are also likely to underestimate their costs (another common error of optimism) and additional supplies by new competitors, which increase very rapidly during a boom.

Psychological theorists maintain that businessmen or speculators exist in a state of great expectation during the expansion and the boom. These expectations being unfounded, they are obviously doomed to disappointment. Thus, the boom and the atmosphere of greed - which was based on an "error of optimism" - gives way to a crisis of confidence and fear (the "error of pessimism").

Other business-cycle theorists argue that, while psychological factors play an important role in reinforcing the expansion and contraction phase (by shifting the demand curve to the right during the upswing and to the left during the depression), they cannot themselves alone be responsible for economic fluctuations. According to the monetary overinvestment theory, every credit expansion must lead first to overinvestment and then to a breakdown. In the words of Wilhelm Röpke:

> ... the credit expansion setting the boom going proceeds by way of the interest rate being 'too low'. The too low interest rate invites a general increase in investment which then leads to the mechanism of the boom drifting on towards its ultimate debacle ... The expansion of credit in the boom expressing itself in the too low interest rate leads to an overexpansion of the economic process and by introducing a general overinvestment disrupts the equilibrium of the economic system. It allows more to be invested than is saved and makes available the necessary increase in money capital from credits which do not originate from savings but are created out of nothing through the banking system ... The demonstration that the credit expansion of the boom leads to overinvestment provides at the same time a proof that the capital formation induced by credit creation, and the extension of production that it sets going, leads to a painful reaction expressing itself in the crisis and depression. This reaction can indeed be postponed by a further increase of the credit supply but only at the price of a corresponding aggravation of the ultimate reaction. An 'eternal boom' is therefore out of the question.
>
> Wilhelm Röpke *Crises and Cycles*, London, 1936

By the interest rate being "too low", Röpke meant that the rate of interest is below the "natural rate" which, according to Knut Wicksell (*Interest and Prices*, London, 1936) is the rate at which the demand for loan capital just equals the supply of savings. Röpke believed that:

> ... a credit inflation can therefore very well arise by the fact that the banks leave their interest rate unchanged or do not raise it far enough at a moment when the equilibrium rate in the economic system - which is only a fictitious figure reflecting roughly the average of profits anticipated from capital investment - has risen. This is, however, exactly what regularly happens in the boom period. If at the commencement of the boom the profit expectations of the economic system rise but the banks maintain their previous rate for credit advances or do not raise it sufficiently, then the automatic consequence is an increase in the demand for credit, owing to the widening of the gap between the rate of interest and the profits on capital.

Röpke further held that it is not only variations in the quantity of money and credit that set the process of booms and depressions in motion, but that the qualitative distribution of the money stream may become a factor of instability. Referring to the late 1920s in the US, Röpke wrote that:

> ... this period which has been followed by the severest crisis in history shows, on the whole, a price level which was slightly sagging rather than rising. How, then, can there have been inflation? ... owing to decreasing costs following on technical progress, prices would have fallen if an amount of additional credit had not been pumped into the economic system. Hence there was inflation, even if only of the relative kind. But it can be perfectly well argued that the quantitative effect of this inflationary credit expansion was considerably aggravated by an abnormal qualitative distribution of credits. One case is the great expansion of instalments credits which gives the impression that the Federal Reserve system was trying to administer the heroin not only *per os* but also *per rectum* ... Another instance is the real estate market which was grossly oversupplied with credits. The worst and most conspicuous case, however, was the stock-market speculation which was the leader on the road to disaster. For purposes of illustration, it may be mentioned that the volume of brokers' loans rose from 1921 to 1929 by about 900 per cent ... We may conclude, then, that the last American boom is a striking example of how the disequilibrating effects of variations in the volume of credit may possibly be greatly aggravated by pecularities in the qualitative composition of the stream.

I should like to point out that, according to the monetary overinvestment theory, it was obvious that the boom in the Japanese economy and its stock market in the late 1980s could not have ended in the soft landing most were expecting. Nor was it ever a question that the hi-tech boom in the late 1990s would continue forever and avoid a colossal bust. But of most interest, with respect to Japan and also the US at present, is what the monetary overinvestment theorists have to say about the ensuing depression period.

Can the recession and the deflationary trend be corrected by massive reflation? According to Röpke, the fact, "that the credit expansion of the boom leads to overinvestment, provides at the same time a proof that the capital formation induced by credit creation, and the extension of production that it sets going, leads to a painful reaction expressing itself in the crisis and the depression." This reaction can indeed be postponed by "a further increase of the credit supply *but only at the price of a corresponding aggravation of the ultimate reaction. An 'eternal boom' is therefore out of the question.*" (ibid, page 118). Referring to the ongoing depression in 1933, Hayek provided the following answer:

> There can, of course, be little doubt that, at the present time, a deflationary process is going on and that an indefinite continuation of that deflation would do inestimable harm. But this does not, by any means, necessarily mean that the deflation is the original cause of our difficulties or that we could overcome these difficulties by compensating for deflationary tendencies, at present operative in our economic system, by forcing more money into circulation. There is no reason to assume that the crisis was started by deliberate deflationary action on the part of the monetary authorities, or that the deflation itself is anything but a secondary phenomenon, a process induced by the maladjustment of industry left over from the boom. If, however, the deflation is not the cause but an effect of the unprofitableness of industry, then it is surely vain to hope that, by reversing the deflationary process, we can regain lasting prosperity. Far from following a deflationary policy, Central Banks, particularly in the United States, have been making earlier and far more far-reaching efforts than have ever been undertaken before to combat the depression by a policy of credit expansion - with the result that the depression has lasted longer and has become more severe than any preceding one. What we need is a readjustment of those elements in the structure of production and of prices which existed before the deflation began and which then made it unprofitable for industry to borrow. But, instead of furthering the inevitable liquidation of the maladjustments brought about by the boom during the last three years, all conceivable means have been used to prevent the readjustment

> from taking place; and one of these means, which has been repeatedly tried though without success, from the earliest to the most recent stages of depression, has been this deliberate policy of credit expansion ... To combat the depression by a forced credit expansion is to attempt to cure the evil by the very means which brought it about; because we are suffering from a misdirection of production, we want to create further misdirection - a procedure which can only lead to much more severe crisis as soon as the credit expansion comes to an end ... We should merely be repeating, on a much larger scale, the course followed by the Federal Reserve system in 1927, an experiment which Mr AC Miller, the only economist on the Federal Reserve Board and, at the same time, its oldest member, has rightly characterised as 'the greatest and boldest operation ever undertaken by the Federal reserve system', an operation which 'resulted in one of the most costly errors committed by it or any other banking system in the last 75 years'. It is probably to this experiment, together with the attempts to prevent liquidation once the crisis had come, that we owe the exceptional severity and duration of the depression. We must not forget that, for the last six or eight years, monetary policy all over the world has followed the advice of the stabilisers. It is high time that their influence, which has already done harm enough, should be overthrown.
>
> Friedrich Hayek, *Monetary Theory and the Trade Cycle*, London, 1933

Obviously the many parallels between what happened prior to the calamity of the 1930s and recent economic and financial trends are striking. Since the economy began to slow in 2000, the Fed has also tried with all its power to engineer a "forced credit expansion in order to "prevent liquidation" with the result that a more serious crisis will likely occur sometime in 2003 or 2004.

Consider, for instance, Röpke's theory that "too low interest rates" lead to a disruption of the economic equilibrium and this is frequently aggravated by an abnormal qualitative change of credits. The 1980s and especially the 90s will be remembered as a time when credit grew at a much faster pace than nominal GDP. As can be seen from Figure 3, debt growth followed nominal GDP growth more or less in tandem in the 1950s and 60s and as a result the US Total Credit Market debt as a percentage of GDP did not change much during this period. But starting with the 1980s, debt growth has far exceeded GDP growth and, therefore, we have today the highest debt to GDP ratio ever.

Please note that in 1929, the debt to GDP ratio was far lower than it is today. The spike of this ratio after 1929 was a result of GDP collapsing, while the debt level remained constant. Or take the year 2001, during which GDP expanded by US$179 billion. At the same time, non-financial credit rose by US$1.1 trillion, and debt in the financial sector increased by US$916 billion - in other words debt grew in 2001 ten times faster than GDP.

Figure 3

HIGHEST EVER

US total credit market debt as a % of annual GDP

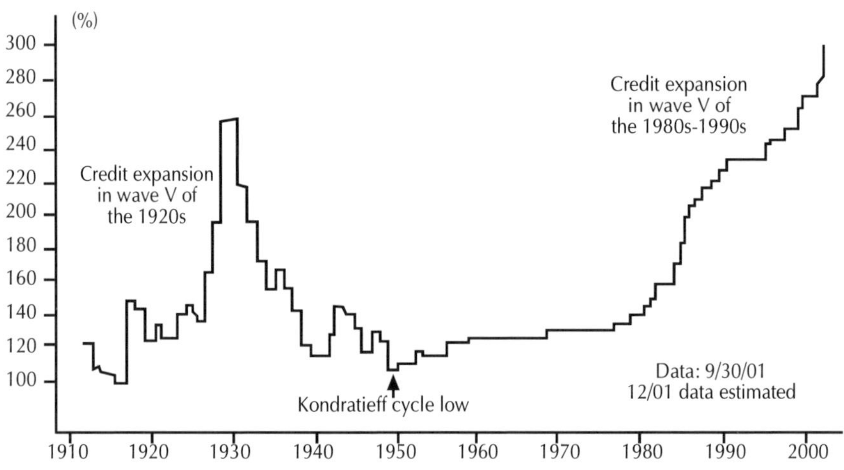

Source: *The Elliott Wave Theorist*, February 2002.

Qualitative failure in the credit system

The last issue I wish to address in this first part of my exposé of the business cycle is Röpke's concern about "the qualitative distribution of the money stream" as an additional source of instability in today's world. As we have seen, in the late 1920s there was an extraordinary expansion of instalment, real estate and stock market-related credits. What about today, given the fact that, in spite of strong credit growth, economic performance in the US (and in other industrialised countries) has been anaemic at best? As was the case in the late 1920s, a shift in money flows has been taking place away from productive investments and into financial assets, as well as government spending (financing of budget deficits) and instalment credits. Mergers and acquisitions hit a new high in 1999/2000, and corporations have been buying back their own shares, frequently with borrowed money.

As a result, we may assume that "the qualitative distribution" of credits has in recent years also deteriorated and is destined to add to the already existing monetary instability at some point in the future.

In the 1980s, rising budget deficits were largely driving debt growth. But in the 1990s, government debt growth slowed because of the budget surpluses in the late 1990s. What increased rapidly was corporate and household debt. Therefore, what is remarkable about the longest economic expansion on record, is that at the end of this expansion we find the quality of corporate and household debt (sub-prime loans) to be of comparatively poor quality, which accounts for the very high yield spreads of corporate bonds compared to treasuries. In addition, in 2002, there were only eight AAA-rated companies left in the US - General Electric, UPS, AIG, ExxonMobil, Johnson & Johnson, Berkshire Hathaway, Pfizer and Merck - compared to 27 in 1990 and 58 in 1979. Also, the first quarter of 2002 was one of the worst-performing quarters on record for corporate bonds. Some 47 issuers defaulted for a total of US$34 billion in bad debt.

As JR Hicks pointed out: "Really catastrophic depression is most unlikely to occur as a result of the simple operation of the real accelerator mechanism; it is likely to occur when there is profound monetary instability - when the rot in the monetary system goes very deep." (*A Contribution to the Theory of the Trade Cycle*, Oxford, 1950, page 163.) According to monetary overinvestment theory, excessive "credit expansion" is the villain. "The expansion of credit in the boom expressing itself in the too-low interest rate leads to an overexpansion of the economic process and by introducing a general overinvestment disrupts the equilibrium of the economic system". The interest rate is "too low" when the market rate is below the "natural rate", which is the rate at which the demand for loan capital just equals the supply of savings. This is now the case in most countries - especially those with large current account deficits.

Monetary overinvestment theory also emphasises the "qualitative distribution of credits". Accordingly, it would appear that, in recent years, as in the late 1920s, too much credit has been diverted towards real estate, and towards instalment credits, the financing of government deficits, and financial markets.

In the psychological business cycle theory, the emphasis is placed on typical reactions, mainly on the part of entrepreneurs and savers. Usually, these psychological factors supplement and accentuate monetary and other economic factors and are not alternative elements of causation. In more recent times, psychological factors have gained more prominence in connection with anticipation and expectations.

Conclusion

It is important to understand that business cycles are very complex phenomena that cannot be explained by just one factor. Thus, most writers on the subject tend to stress that a whole set of factors - and not always in the same combination - produces the periodical alternation between prosperity and depression. But one point is certain: economic fluctuations will always be with us and the failure of the command economies have amply proven that government intervention, whether carried out directly or through the monetary authorities, will never eliminate cyclical fluctuations. In fact, it would seem to me that, as John Stuart Mill wrote almost 200 years ago:

> ... in all the more advanced communities the great majority of things are worse done by intervention of government, than the individuals most interested in the matter would do them, or cause them to be done, if left to themselves.
>
> *Principles of Political Economy*, 7th ed., London, 1871

I have tried to show here that the business cycle is alive and well and will in fact never die, as the economy will always be subject to phases of above-trend-line growth, followed by phases of below-trend growth. How severe a recession will follow the current lull in business will depend on a number of factors, including where we stand in the Kondratieff Wave (see Chapter 7). If, indeed, the long wave has already turned upwards, as some analysts believe, the present recession ought to be already over and we could be looking to a better business climate in 2003 and 2004. If, on the other hand, the contemporary situation resembles that of the late 1920s, when, as Schumpeter explained, a simultaneous occurrence of a downward Kondratieff wave, a downturn in a nine-year Juglar cycle and a Kitchin inventory liquidation led to the slump, then obviously a more serious and longer lasting deflationary recession should be expected sometime in the near future.

So far I have noted that economists hold different views about what causes business fluctuations and their periodicity. Where there is no disagreement among the cycle theorists is on the *existence* of such cycles. Periods of expansion and prosperity are always followed by periods of contraction and depression.

I now propose to discuss long cycles in economic conditions, with the objective of proving their existence and trying to determine at what stage of the long cycle we presently stand. I should like to stress the word *try*. Business cycles are enormously complex phenomena - but it would seem to me that it is for every investor of paramount importance to understand at what stage of the long cycle one might stand because there are some very distinct features to the rising and falling wave that have, in turn, important investment implications.

CHAPTER SEVEN

Long waves in economic conditions

> Our analysis leads us to believe that recovery is sound only if it does come of itself. For any revival which is merely due to artificial stimulus leaves part of the work of depressions undone and adds, to an undigested remnant of maladjustments, new maladjustments of its own.
>
> *JOSEPH A SCHUMPETER (1883-1950)*

Long economic cycles have been traced throughout history. From the Bible, we know of 50-year jubilees during which old debts were forgiven. Every 54 years, the Mayans in Central America held a festival to fend off calamities; and a 54-year cycle in wheat prices can be traced back to the 13th Century. In 1947, Edward Dewey published *Cycles - The Science of Predictions*, which contained a 54-year index of US wholesale prices going back to 1790 and projections for the future (see Figure 1). Most remarkable is that, in 1947, when his book was published, Dewey forecast the next high for wholesale prices would take place in 1979 (the next low is expected in 2006). As a result, many observers posited that the long wave in economic conditions would also follow a 54-year rhythm. This, however, is not the case: the Kondratieff Cycle is much more complex and its authors never suggested a precise periodicity.

Figure 1

LONG WAVES?

US average wholesale prices 1780-1947

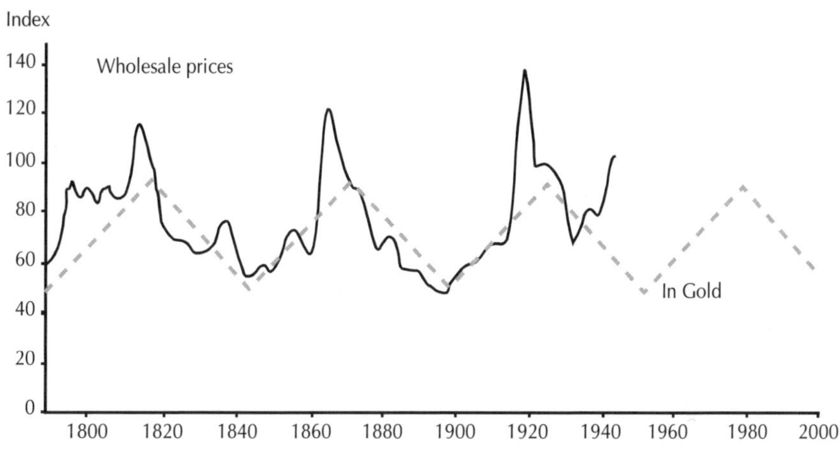

Source: Edward R. Dewey, *Cycles - The Science of Predictions*, New York, 1947.

The Kondratieff wave

In 1925, a relatively unknown Russian economist published an essay entitled "Long Economic Cycles" in which he stated that

> ... the further [my] investigation of recurrent capitalist crises proceeded, the more it became evident that a crisis was only one phase of an entire capitalistic cycle; that the whole cycle usually consisted of three basic phases - upswing, crisis and depression; and that such crises could be understood only by studying all phases of the cycle ... in studying the dynamics of capitalistic society, I came across phenomena that were hard to explain without postulating the existence of long cycles in economic conditions ...
>
> Nikolai Kondratieff, *The Long Wave Cycle*

I have to stress that, unlike other economists (notably Schumpeter), Kondratieff's interest in long waves was empirical and not theoretical. In a 1925 article he stated that he had no intention of laying the foundation for an appropriate theory of long waves, but only of demonstrating their existence empirically. To do this, Kondratieff examined trends of commodity prices, interest rates, wages, foreign trade, production, and consumption of coal, private savings and gold production as well as political events from 1790-1920 and came to the conclusion that the length of the long wave fluctuates between 48 and 60 years.

Figure 2

THE LONG LOOK BACK

The price of grain in Western Europe, 1201-1901

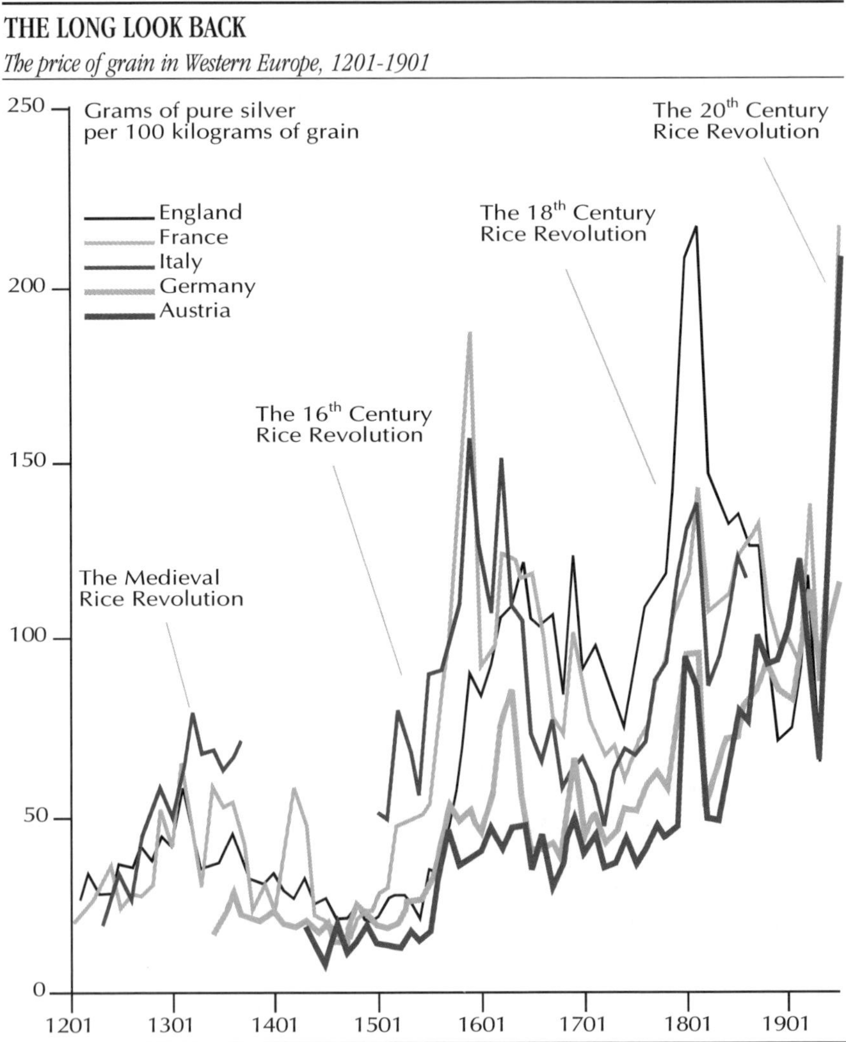

Source: David Hackett Fischer, *The Great Wave.*

Some economists dismiss long waves in economic activity, but the fact remains that the world has always undergone cycles during which prices rose and fell. (From Figure 2, which depicts grain prices in Western Europe between 1200 and 1900, we can see that they rose in the 13th Century, fell until around 1500, rose in the 16th Century, fell until about 1750, rose until the Napoleonic Wars, and fell thereafter until about 1900). Moreover, aside from Kondratieff a number of other notable economists including Parvus (Alexander Helphand), J van Gelderen, Jean Lescure, Albert Aftalion, Arthur Spiethoff, Gustav Cassell, Simon Kuznets, Knut Wicksell and Wilhelm Abel, have also observed long-term cycles - and Schumpeter acknowledged their existence:

> Historical knowledge of what actually happened at any time in the industrial organism, and of the way in which it happened, reveals first the existence of what is often referred to as the 'Long Wave' of a period of between fifty-four and sixty years. Occasionally recognised and even measured before, especially by Spiethoff, it has been worked out in more detail by Kondratieff, and may therefore be called the Kondratieff Cycle.
>
> Joseph Schumpeter, "The Analysis of Economic Change", *The Review of Economic Statistics*, Vol 17, No. 4, May 1935.

Schumpeter further broke down the Kondratieff Wave into a number of cycles of "nine to ten years duration". Named after the father of modern business-cycle theory, "Juglar" cycles have a duration of seven to eleven years. Schumpeter then divided the Juglar into three "Kitchin" cycles of about 40 months each. (Joseph Kitchin, a businessman, published in 1923 a study of British and American cycles, 1890-1922. He distinguished minor cycles of 40 months, major cycles of 7-11 years and trends dependent on the movement of world money supply.)

Kondratieff researched a variety of price and production numbers over a longer period of time and noticed the following trends (among others):

Commodity trends

- In the rising wave of the first cycle (see Figure 3), commodity prices rose from 1789 to 1814 (25 years). The downward wave of the first cycle began in 1814 and ended in 1849 (35 years). The first cycle lasted 60 years.
- The rising wave of the second commodities cycle began in 1849 and ended in 1873 (24 years). The downward wave of the second cycle began in 1873 and ended in 1896 (23 years). The second cycle lasted 47 years.
- The rising wave of the third cycle began in 1896 and ended in 1920 (24 years). According to Kondratieff, the downward wave of the third cycle began in 1920.

Figure 3

RIDING THE CYCLES

Index numbers of commodity prices, 1780-1920

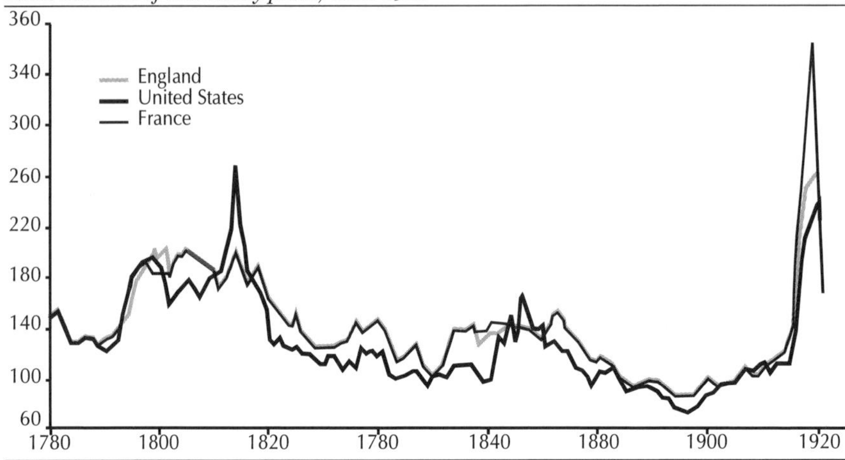

Source: Kondratieff.

Interest rates

Kondratieff studied the price movement of French rents and English consols (bonds). From 1790 to 1813, interest rates rose sharply (English consols fell from 90.04 in 1792 to 58.81 in 1813). After that, interest rates fell until 1844 completing "the first cycle in the movement of interest rates". The downward wave of bond quotations - or the rising wave of interest rates - of the second cycle lasted from the mid-1840s to the early 1870s. From the mid-1870s, interest rates fell again until 1897, but then rose in the upward wave of the third cycle until 1921. "Thus the presence of long cycles in the movement of the interest rate stands out very plainly. The periods of these cycles coincide very closely with the corresponding periods in the movement of commodities." In the US, we can observe a very similar movement in interest rates since 1790 (see Figure 4).

Figure 4

CLIMBING THE PEAKS

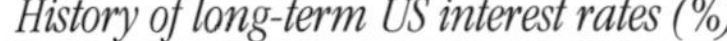

History of long-term US interest rates (%)

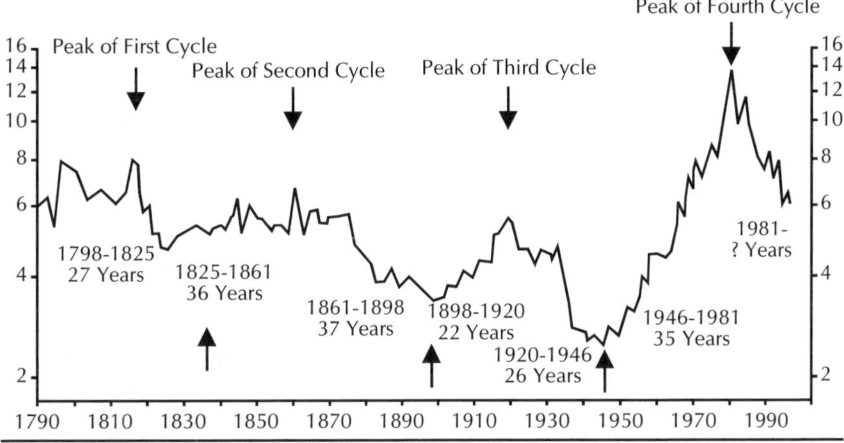

Source: Merrill Lynch.

Wages

Kondratieff observed a rising wage trend from 1790 to a maximum in the period 1805-17, whereby the actual peak probably coincided with the 1812-17 period. After reaching that maximum, the rate of movement slows until the late 1840s and early 1850s, which marks the end of the first cycle for wages. From the late 1840s, wage growth accelerated again until 1873-76, followed by a slowing of the growth rate until 1888-95, which completes the second cycle. Subsequently there was another acceleration in the growth of wages, which according to Kondratieff lasted until 1920-21.

Coal production and consumption

Kondratieff observed that coal consumption in France and England followed price cycles quite closely. Consumption fell in the 1840s but rose sharply until the 1870s. Thereafter, growth slowed until the late 1880s. An upswing in consumption and production resumed in the 1890s. He, therefore, felt that the data of the rate of coal consumption and production provided further evidence of the existence of long waves.

Kondratieff included in his analysis consumption of mineral fuel in

France, production of lead and pig iron in England and loan to deposit ratios in French banks, and concluded:

> I consider it is impossible to determine with absolute accuracy the years of turning points in the development of long cycles, and have taken into account the margin of error in fixing such turning points (from five to seven years), which derives from the very method used in analysing the data, the following limits of those cycles can nonetheless be regarded as the most probable …

Table 1

CATCHING THE WAVES

Kondratieff cycles

First cycle	Second cycle	Third cycle
1. Rising wave: from about 1789 to 1810-17.	1. Rising wave: from 1844-51 to 1870-75.	1. Rising wave: from 1890-96 to 1914-20.
2. Downward wave: from 1810-17 to 1844-51.	2. Downward wave: from 1870-75 to 1890-96.	2. Probable downward wave: beginning 1914-20 (remember, his works appeared in the mid-1920s).

Source: Nikolai Kondratieff, *The Long Waves in Economic Life*, London, 1925, translation Guy Daniels, London, 1984.

Kondratieff then proceeded to examine four empirical patterns discernible within each long cycle:

1. Before and during the beginning of the rising wave of each long cycle, there are profound changes in the conditions of the society's economic life. Those are manifested by significant changes in techniques (which, in turn, are preceded by significant technical discoveries and inventions); in the involvement of new countries in worldwide economic relations; in changes in gold production and monetary circulation.

2. The greatest number of social upheavals (wars and revolutions) occur during the rising wave of each long cycle. Kondratieff rebutted the notion, until then widely accepted, that wars and revolutions caused long economic waves: "Much more probable is the assumption that wars originate in the acceleration of the pace and the increased tension of economic life, in the heightened economic struggle for markets and raw materials, and that social shocks happen most easily under the pressure of new economic forces".

3. The downward waves of each long cycle are accompanied by prolonged and marked depressions in agriculture with falling commodity prices. He also noticed that, during these waves, such as occurred in 1810-

17 and 1844-49, as well as in 1870-75 and 1895-98, the drop in agricultural prices was greater than the slump in industrial prices (the severe depression in agriculture in the 1930s confirmed his observation).

4. During rising waves in the long cycles, the intermediate capitalist cycles are characterised by the brevity of depressions and the intensity of the upswings. During the period of a downward wave in the long cycles, the picture is the opposite.

(We revisit these four points in greater detail below.)

Above, we explained that Schumpeter had broken down the long wave into medium-term Juglar cycles with a duration of 7-11 years and short-term Kitchin cycles of 40 months. Kondratieff also acknowledged the existence of intermediate cycles. He found that during the upswing recessions were relatively brief, while the intermediate cycles occurring during the downward period of a long cycle must be characterised by depressions that are particularly severe and long lasting, and by upturns that are brief and weak. To support this observation, Kondratieff also referred to data compiled by Spiethoff (see Table 2) and which show that during downward waves, years of depression regularly predominate, while during the rising waves, years of upswing take over.

Table 2

BOOM AND GLOOM

Pattern in the long cycles

Periods	Years of upswing	Years of depression
The downward wave of the long cycle of 1822-43	9	12
The rising wave of long cycle of 1843-74	21	10
The downward wave of the long cycle of 1874-95	6	15
The rising wave of the long cycle of 1895-1912	15	4

Source: Nikolai Kondratieff, *The Long Waves in Economic Life*, London, 1925, translation by Guy Daniels, London, 1984.

Kondratieff's theory of the long waves was too closely associated with the approach of socialists - such as Karl Kautsky, J. van Gelderen and Sam De Wolff, who had also published works on long waves - to be acceptable to Bolsheviks like Lenin and Leon Trotzky. The key issue in the famous Trotzky-Kondratieff debate revolved around the question of stability in the capitalist system. Trotsky's view was that "universal crises" do threaten the survival of capitalism, while Kondratieff thought (like Krautsky) that crises were merely a phase within a rather stable capitalistic system. According to Kondratieff's theory, the deepening recession after 1929 was unlikely to be the "final crisis of capitalism" the Marxists were looking for. Thus, in 1930, under Joseph Stalin, Kondratieff was officially repudiated, arrested and sent to a Siberian prison camp, where he died.

The causes of long waves

Although Kondratieff repeatedly stressed that his analysis of the long waves was empirical, he came to the conclusion that the rising wave of the long cycle "is associated with the replacement and expansion of basic capital goods, and with radical regrouping of, and changes in, society's productive forces". Joseph Schumpeter, who resurrected Kondratieff by naming the long wave after him, built a unified theory of the long cycle on the concept of "innovation" and of "leading sectors" of the economy:

> Obviously the face of the earth would look very different if people, besides having their economic life changed by natural events and changing it themselves by extra economic action, had done nothing else except multiply and save. If it looks as it does, this is just as obviously due to the unremitting efforts of people to improve according to their lights upon their productive and commercial methods, ie,, to the changes in technique of production, the conquest of new markets, the insertion of new commodities, and so on. This historic and irreversible change in the way of doing things we call 'innovation' and we define: innovations are changes in production functions which cannot be decomposed into infinitesimal steps. Add as many mail-coaches as you please, you will never get a railroad by so doing.
>
> Joseph Schumpeter, 1935, op. cit.

For Schumpeter, major innovations and new "leading sectors" of the economy supplanted previously dominant industries and produced long upward waves. Each Kondratieff upward wave is thus associated with some major technological innovation. Schumpeter also acknowledged the importance of "credit creation", considered to be the monetary complement of innovation, but stressed that the money market, whilst of deep significance, "becomes the heart, although it never becomes the brain, of the capitalistic organism" (*Business Cycles*, New York, 1939).

Schumpeter, like Kondratieff, considered the period between 1787 and 1842 as the first long-term cycle of our capitalist age. It was, according to him, a period of industrial adaptation to many new inventions: the construction of canals, roads and bridges, and the expansion of banking (the Industrial Revolution - see Figure 5). The second Kondratieff Wave (1842-97) is associated with the age of steam (railroads) and steel, and the third (1898-) with electricity, chemistry, and motors (when Schumpeter published *Business Cycles* in 1939, no ending date was stated).

According to Schumpeter, innovations disturb the economic equilibrium and lead the system into a "prosperity excursion", which is then followed by a "depression excursion" (he distinguishes four phases: prosperity, recession, depression and revival). The depression excursion comes about because the innovation not only increases the output of consumer goods in due course (following the gestation period), but also forces the economy to adapt to a new level of costs and prices and new methods of production installed by the innovators. The innovator is a powerful competitor who displaces old methods of production and forces less-gifted rivals to lose their markets and frequently to suffer economic death. Thus, innovation (with credit creation) leads to a boom, which in turn causes the depression. The depression excursion lasts until painful readjustments brought about by the innovation have taken place. Once the process of adjustment has run its course, the system finds a new equilibrium in which the economy is again at rest.

According to Schumpeter, the decline will continue below the point of equilibrium, and only when the debt structure has been restored to a sound basis will the economy again reach its point of equilibrium. *Thus, the length of the cycle is not measured from one peak to another, or from one trough to another, but from one point of equilibrium to another.* As mentioned, Schumpeter broke the Kondratieff Wave down into Juglar and Kitchin cycles; according to him, their simultaneous downturn in the early 1930s caused the depression (see Figure 6).

Figure 5

HERE COMES THE FIFTH WAVE

Long cycles - Kondratieff waves, 1787-2058

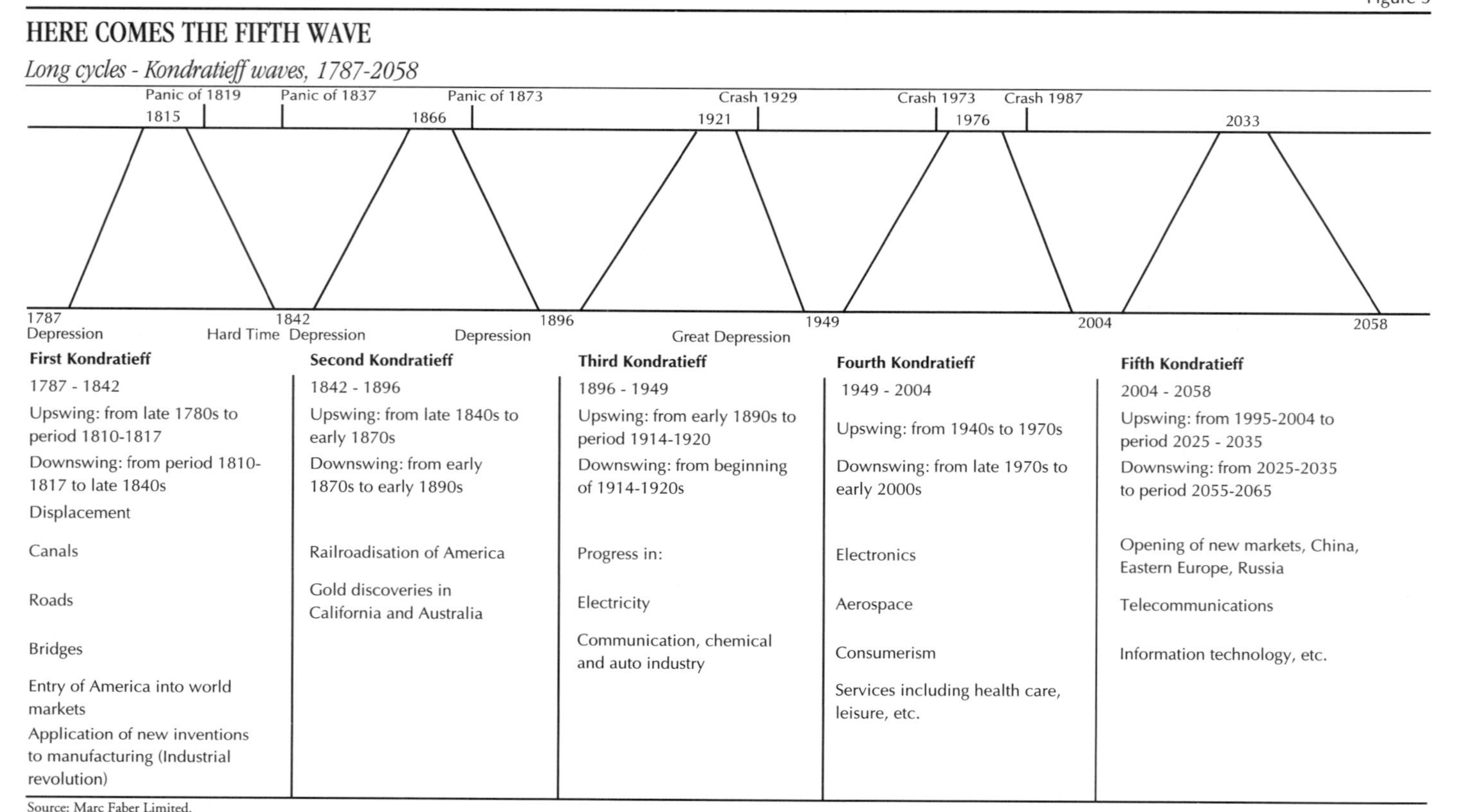

First Kondratieff	Second Kondratieff	Third Kondratieff	Fourth Kondratieff	Fifth Kondratieff
1787 - 1842	1842 - 1896	1896 - 1949	1949 - 2004	2004 - 2058
Upswing: from late 1780s to period 1810-1817	Upswing: from late 1840s to early 1870s	Upswing: from early 1890s to period 1914-1920	Upswing: from 1940s to 1970s	Upswing: from 1995-2004 to period 2025 - 2035
Downswing: from period 1810-1817 to late 1840s	Downswing: from early 1870s to early 1890s	Downswing: from beginning of 1914-1920s	Downswing: from late 1970s to early 2000s	Downswing: from 2025-2035 to period 2055-2065
Displacement				
Canals	Railroadisation of America	Progress in:	Electronics	Opening of new markets, China, Eastern Europe, Russia
Roads	Gold discoveries in California and Australia	Electricity	Aerospace	Telecommunications
Bridges		Communication, chemical and auto industry	Consumerism	Information technology, etc.
Entry of America into world markets			Services including health care, leisure, etc.	
Application of new inventions to manufacturing (Industrial revolution)				

Source: Marc Faber Limited.

Figure 6

GETTING CAUGHT IN THE BREAKERS

Schumpeter's long, intermediate and short cycles

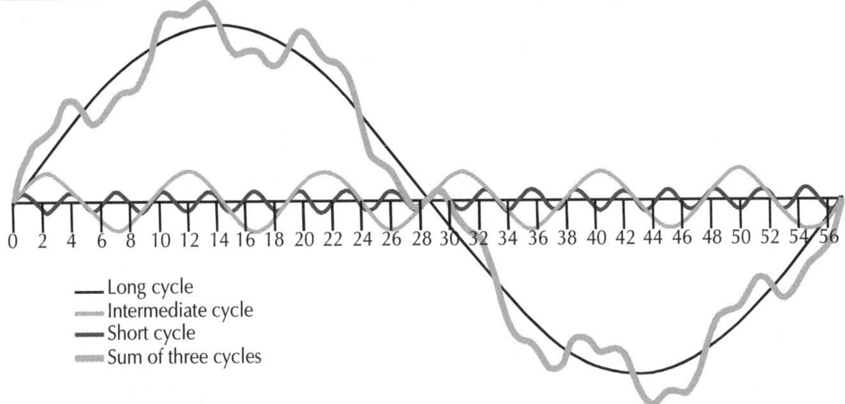

Source: J. Shumpeter, *Business Cycles*, New York, 1939.

Unintentionally, Irving Fisher contributed to the understanding of long waves and business cycles - although not before calling "the business cycle" a myth, comparing its fluctuations to the movement of a sea craft tipped by waves and buffeted by crosswinds:

> Imagine, then, a rocking chair on the deck of a rocking ship, on a rolling sea. The ultimate chair is subjected to so many influences that its motion will not conform to any simple rhythm. The net motion will be made up of many rhythms and non-rhythms, and will, therefore, appear sometimes rhythmic and sometimes completely unrhythmic. At all events, no one would think of referring to it as 'the rocking chair cycle'.
>
> Irving Fisher, *Booms and Depressions*, New York, 1932

Fisher then conceded that the economy is subjected to a vicious spiral of expansion and a vicious spiral of contraction in a cumulative process brought about chiefly by the accumulation and liquidation of debts (debt-deflation theory).

According to Fisher, large debts tend to intensify the deflationary process, because the debt burden becomes heavier with the fall in prices, which then leads to distressed selling and depresses prices further. Also, in some cases, "overindebtedness" may be the cause of the collapse of the boom (by overindebtedness, Fisher meant "that debts are out-of-line, are too big relative to other economic factors"). Overindebtedness is brought about by new opportunities to invest at a big prospective profit such as through new inventions, new industries, development of new resources and the opening of new lands or new markets.

Fisher said "easy money" is the great cause of overborrowing. He then cited a number of examples such as inventions and new discoveries (gold in California), or new business methods (turnpikes, steamboats, farm machines), which "lured" the investor "to go still further into debt, and spend even more than before the loan, relying on the expected return from his investment to repay both his investment and his extravagance. His psychology is not that of the unfortunate. His mood is not fear, gloom or caution. It is enthusiasm and hope" (ibid, page 45). Here Fisher leant very much towards the psychological cycle theory. Referring to the crisis of the early 1830s, he quoted Thomas Tooke (*A History of Prices*, London, 1838), whose observations could have been made with respect to the recent investment mania:

> The possibility of enormous profit by risking a small sum was a bait too tempting to be resisted; all the gambling propensities of human nature were constantly solicited into action; and crowds of individuals of every description - the credulous and the ignorants, princes, nobles, politicians, patriots, lawyers, physicians, divines, philosophers, poets, intermingled with women of all ranks and degrees (spinsters, wives, and widows) - hastened to venture some portion of their property in schemes of which scarcely anything was known except the names.

While acknowledging that other factors played a role in the Depression, Fisher made overindebtedness responsible for the 1929 stampede:

> The depression grew out of a boom, which started in a credit currency boom, which started from a debt boom, which grew out of the World War. The war was responsible not only for the war debts, but largely for the peace debts which followed; and among both the war debts and the peace debts there were international debts of every description, long and short, public and private, the obligations running in every direction, by no means towards America alone; for many Americans were indebted to many foreigners, on short time obligations payable in gold. Every debit in the world has a corresponding credit somewhere in the world, and the world's net indebtedness is always zero; yet if 'A' owes a million to 'B', and 'B' owes a million to 'C', and so on down the line, till we find 'Z' owing a million back to 'A', the failure of 'A' may bankrupt

> 'B', who may then cause the bankruptcy of 'C', and so on to 'Z.' Thus a net debt of zero may bankrupt 26 millionaires, like a row of nine-pins.
>
> Irving Fisher, *Inflation?* London, 1933

The chief culprit of the debt growth in the 1920s was, according to Fisher, the financing of equities with borrowed money, investing abroad and investment bankers' high-pressure salesmen.

> Meanwhile, there was a new trend in corporate finance. From 1921-29, as the boom developed, the new corporate issues took more and more the form of stocks instead of bonds. This policy of reducing the proportion of bonds had one good effect: It left the corporations less encumbered with debt; so that, despite the depression, many corporations kept in a strong position throughout the whole of the depression. This advantage, however, was more than offset by shifting the debt burden from the corporation to the stockholders. That is, in order to buy the stock many persons borrowed, so that, instead of being indebted collectively in the form of a corporation, they became indebted individually ... This preference for investing in equities instead of bonds was fostered by a number of statistical studies that showed that almost always in the past, bonds had produced less income for the investor than had been (or could have been) produced by a diversified assortment of common stocks. The new trend was further intensified by the formation of investment trusts whose express business was to invest the money of their clients in diversified stocks. These trusts began to spring up like mushrooms, and presently became a mania. Many of them operated on borrowed capital, leaving precarious equities .... Meanwhile, the investing and speculating Americans were by no means content with the home market. Foreign countries, European and South American, in the throes of reconstruction and elated like ourselves, were soliciting capital; and Americans furnished much of it - to governments, to municipalities and to private corporations. Already, in the sixty years preceding 1931, according to a member of the British Parliament, British investors had lost 10 billion dollars by such loans. Yet, after the World War, American investors with inadequate experience, marched into this field and took the lead. In this way, America promoted and aggravated abroad the same unhealthy boom which was putting both our neighbours and ourselves in position for a slump. [And, quoting an informed source, Fisher made] American investment banking the chief villain of the piece ... In seeking new issues to feed to a ravenous public, disregard for the debtor's ability to pay, for the possibility of effecting payment by willing and able foreign debtors, and for the existing interests of security holders in concerns to be reorganised or consolidated, mark a high portion of the financing during the period. The governing consideration seems to have been 'can the issue be sold at a handsome profit?'
>
> Irving Fisher, *Booms and Depressions*, op.cit.

Fisher claimed that the "first spectacular evidence that America was in for a depression" was the crash of the New York stock market in 1929, because:

> ... if liquidation, for some reason, gets into a stampede, it wipes out (ie,, deflates) credit currency, which lowers the price level and reduces profits, which forces business into further liquidation, which further lowers the price level and reduces profits, which force business into further liquidation - and so on and on: a tail-spin into depression ... We now come to the paradox that if the debts get big enough, the very act of liquidation puts the world deeper in debt than ever ... Each dollar represented in the unpaid balance grows faster than the number of the dollars is reduced by liquidation. Such is the essential secret of a great depression ... This swelling was caused by deflation of the price level, and the deflation was caused by the liquidation itself. Payments could not catch up with the 'real' indebtedness - the more we paid the more we owed ... the people's real debts are heavier than in 1929, heavier than in March 1932, heavier than ever before in all history. Their interest, rent and taxes are also heavier; and at the same time, their real income and real wealth are less.
>
> Irving Fisher, *Inflation?* op. cit.

I have quoted Irving Fisher extensively, not only because he ranks among the very great economists, but because he was a contemporary of the 1920s boom and the Great Depression who, in his writings and public statements, reflected prevailing sentiment. In 1929, he proclaimed that stocks would continue to rise and that America had reached a new plateau of prosperity. And in *The Stock Market Crash- and After* (written in November 1929, just after the crash), his belief in equities was intact. He felt that in spite "of the tremendous harm that has been done to common stocks" during the crash of 1929, investment trusts had made it safer to invest in common stocks than ever before. The book's last sentence is: "For the immediate future, at least, the outlook is bright."

It was only in 1933 (in *Inflation?*) that Fisher, along with everybody else, realised that the financial excesses, the overinvestment and the debt-accumulation that had taken place in the late 1920s, had led to a full-fledged deflationary depression. Clearly, as I mentioned in Chapter 5, the mood remains very upbeat at the beginning of bear markets and recessions because the economic fundamentals remain quite favourable.

Concerning the Federal Reserve Board's policy in the 1920s, Fisher referred to Paul Warburg (a former member of the Federal Reserve Board) who had pointed out that "had the rate of interest been raised in sympathy with the investment opportunities in America, instead of being lowered in accordance with Federal Reserve easy money policy, the panic might not have occurred". Fisher referred to the stress Warburg laid on the influence of invention on interest rates:

> When a flood of new inventions gives opportunity to make more than the current rate of interest there is always a tendency to go into debt, in order to make money out of inventions, and to the ordinary investor this comes in the form of investing in common stocks. At such time the rate of interest should be high, embracing as it does the opportunity to invest for a high rate of return over cost. If there is a great discrepancy between the rate to be realised to the investor from his investment, and the rate of interest on which he can borrow, he will be inclined to borrow all the more.

Paul Warburg, *The Theory of Interest* New York, 1930, quoted in Fisher, *The Stock Market Crash- and After*, New York, 1930

According to Fisher, after the war the "rate of interest was kept artificially low, which encouraged speculation". He concluded that, "perhaps a once-for-all sharp increase in the rediscount rate two years ago [in 1927] might have hurt business to some extent then, but it might have prevented the market crash later".

I may add that after its low in 1929, the stock market staged an impressive bear market rally (see Figure 7) but after April 1930 the market fell month by month until June 1932. But listen to this: By then most indices had fallen by another 80% from their 13 November 1929 lows. Most investment trusts either went bankrupt or their shares collapsed by 99%. At their peak, many had sold at premiums of more than 100% above their net asset values. A remarkable fact was that the total collapse in equities and in the economy occurred amid continuous optimism and confidence among business leaders and politicians. The Harvard Economic Society, which had made negative forecasts in 1929, but became positive right before the 1929 crash, continued to make bright forecasts throughout 1930 and 1931 (18 January 1930: "There are indications that the severest phase of the recession is over"; 17 May 1930: Business "will turn for the better this month or next, recover vigorously in the third quarter and end the year at levels substantially above normal"; 15 November 1930: "The present depression has about spent its force."). President Hoover stated confidently, in May 1930, that "we have now passed the worst" and that business would return to normal by the fall. So, we can see that Fisher's optimism in late 1929 was not totally out of line with the then prevailing mood. The subsequent depression and catastrophic bear market came as a total surprise to everyone.

Figure 7

WHAT GOES UP . . .

Dow Jones industrial average, 1920-1935

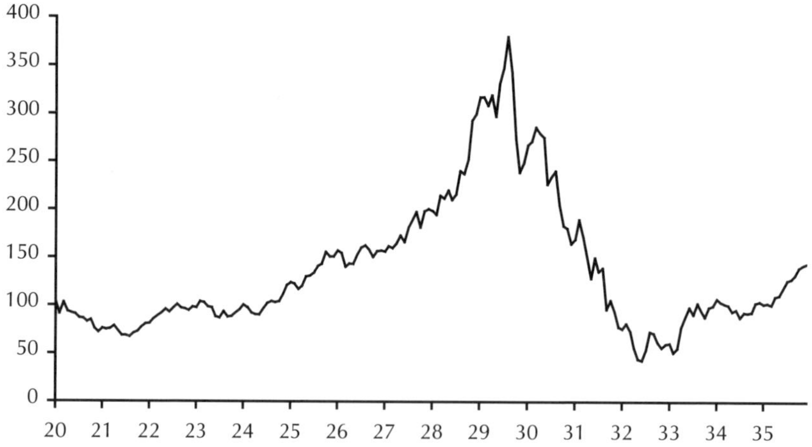

400 350 300 250 200 150 100 50 0

20 21 22 23 24 25 26 27 28 29 30 31 32 33 34 35

Source: Long-term Perspectives.

The similarities between the 1920s and the 1990s are striking: the merger fever, high leverage, easy monetary policies, the presence of foreign funds, downsizing (instead of Fordising), favourable labour conditions, stable prices, declining commodity prices, mutual funds and banks' investment departments (instead of investment trusts), PCs (instead of radios), software (instead of movie companies), the internet (instead of electric utilities), a record number of patent applications, books highlighting the merits of investing in equities, optimistic forecasters, leading Wall Street figures achieving stardom status, politicians' and business leaders' continuously optimistic statements, the belief that the US economy is recovering, and so on.

What phase of the long cycle are we in today?

Before attempting to determine where we may be in the context of the business cycle, I should like to make the following observation: with respect to our history, geography and evolution we may know where we are relative to data available to us. However, we know little about where our planet is located vis-a-vis the rest of the universe, whether our civilisation is the only one that has ever existed, etc. In other words, in terms of the "unknown", we know very little indeed. The same applies to economics. We may know our "economic position" relative to the depression years of the 1930s, the bear market low of 1974, the peak in commodity prices in 1980 and the US stock market peak in 2000. However, we have little knowledge about where we stand with respect to the history of capitalism.

Are we in the early stages of capitalistic development or are we close to the end of the "capitalistic age" as economists such as Ravi Batra are suggesting. (Although academia is not taking Batra very seriously, his social cycle theory, which explains how society moves through different stages - eras of labourers, warriors, intellectuals and acquisitors - is very interesting. After all, based on this theory, he predicted in the late 1970s the breakdown of communism.) Therefore, I should like to emphasise that our attempt to find our present position within long- and medium-term cycles is tentative at best (see Figure 5).

We have seen that, according to Kondratieff and Schumpeter, the peak of the Third Kondratieff occurred in the 1914-20 period. Subsequent events - falling commodity prices, depression in agriculture, falling interest rates and the Great Depression - suggest that a downward wave followed until the late 1930s-early 1940s.

Since commodity prices bottomed out in the 1930s, and interest rates in the mid-1940s (see Figure 4), we have to assume that the upswing of the Fourth Kondratieff began sometime in the 1940s. This would also fit with the idea that the Kondratieff long wave lasts between 48 and 60 years and since the Third Kondratieff began in the mid-1890s, it would have been completed sometime between 1943 and 1955. That the plateau of the Fourth Kondratieff ought to be put around the 1970-80 period is also supported by per-capita income growth figures (see Table 3). So, whereas the world's per-capita GDP grew by 2.9% in the rising wave between 1950 and 1973, it grew by only 1.11% between 1973 and 1995 (and has slowed even further recently with the emerging market crises in Asia and in Latin America, and as a result of the current economic malaise).

Table 3

GROWTH RATES

Capitalist epoch average annual compound growth rate of per capita GDP (%)

	1820-1950	1950-73	1973-95
The West	**1.27**	**3.64**	**1.8**
Western Europe	1.06	3.89	1.72
North America	1.58	2.45	1.54
Japan	0.81	8.01	2.53
The Rest	0.50	2.89	1.38
Other Europe	1.06	3.82	(0.75)
Latin America	1.01	2.50	0.62
China	(0.24)	2.87	5.37
Other Asia	0.32	2.78	2.49
Africa	0.56	2.01	(0.32)
World	**0.88**	**2.90**	**1.11**

Source: A Maddison, *Monitoring the World Economy*, 1995.

I have to point out that several economists have suggested in the last few years that the Kondratieff Cycle has already turned up. J Forrester, of the MIT System Dynamics Group, believed that the peak of the long wave was in the late 1970s and that the low point would come in the mid-1990s, which was going to be characterised by a business downturn that "shakes out the imbalances in our economic system." The June 1995 issue of the *Bank Credit Analyst* also suggested that "the US economy is embarked on its third long-wave expansion of the 20th Century" and Brian Reading of Lombard Street Research talked about the "Great World Boom 1993-2013."

Therefore, one could argue that if the peak of the Fourth Kondratieff took place in the 1970s and if the trough is already behind us, as some economists argue, then strong economic growth around the world should follow.

I have, however, several reasons to question the notion that the Kondratieff wave has already turned up. For one, according to Schumpeter, the decline in the cycle continues - and this is important - *below* the point of equilibrium, and only when the debt structure has been restored to a sound basis will the economy again reach its point of equilibrium. At present, there is nobody who could claim that the debt structure has been restored to a sound equilibrium. In fact, it is getting worse by the day as debt growth exceeds economic growth rates in most industrialised countries and as the US economy is supported by a growing housing and consumer credit pyramid.

Moreover, as we discussed above, one of the factors leading to the depression of the 1930s was the loss of purchasing power of farmers even well before the depression, because in the 1920s agriculture was still the dominant sector in the world's economy. And what the farm population was to the US economy in the 1920s, the developing and emerging economies seem to be to the global economy today. Prices for goods produced by the developing countries seem to be in downtrends, while prices paid by them for products they import from the industrialised countries remain firm or are rising. As a result, many developing countries had rising trade deficits, which led to the Asian currency crisis of 1997 and a significant reduction in these countries' real per-capita incomes. In my opinion, *this growing wealth inequality between rich industrialised countries and the developing world could prolong the present slowdown in global growth and even lead to a severe economic contraction due to underconsumption, overproduction, or a combination thereof* (see the Epilogue). The collapse of real per-capita incomes in Asia after 1997 and more recently in Latin America, continuous structural high unemployment in Europe, recession in Japan and the collapse of the hi-tech sector around the world, which was driving capital spending and economic growth in the last few years, does hardly suggest that we have already embarked on the rising wave of the fifth cycle. More likely, we are still within the Schumpeter downward wave or, at very best, approaching its bottom.

The above economic trends aside, there are other reasons to believe that the global economy is still in a downward wave. Think back to the four empirical patterns Kondratieff discerned within each long cycle.

1. Before the beginning of the rising wave of each long cycle (and sometimes at the very onset), profound changes occur in the conditions of society's economic life. These changes are evident from significant inventions, the involvement of new countries in worldwide economic relations, and changes in gold production and monetary circulation. During the first decades before the beginning of the rising wave, he observed an invigoration in the sphere of technical inventions, which are then applied during the beginning of the rising wave. Major inventions and innovations take place during the downward wave because poor economic conditions stimulate the search for cost cutting. Furthermore, it would seem that major mergers and business consolidations are more likely to take place during a downward wave, as businesses faced with sluggish markets for their products and weak pricing power merge in order to cut costs and become more efficient, and in order to eliminate competition. Obviously, when business conditions are vibrant, such as during the rising wave, costs are less of a consideration than when business is sluggish in the downward wave. Again, the recent record volume of mergers and acquisitions would indicate that the downward wave was still intact.

Equally, many economists and strategists have pointed out that the entry of so many new countries into the global economy, and the opening of numerous new markets following the breakdown of communism, would bring about the rising wave of the fifth cycle. However, in a capitalistic system, new regions are opened up for commerce during periods in which the industrialised countries have a strong desire to exploit new markets. In the 19th Century, new regions were frequently opened up in order to obtain cheap raw materials, while more recently new countries have been opened up for the purpose of capitalising on their cheap labour and untapped market potential. And although I cannot establish a clear pattern, the industrialised countries were always particularly keen to open new markets when they had surplus capacity and required new markets for dumping their products - that is, towards the end of a downward wave when the markets in their own countries were sluggish.

In this context, I doubt that the acceleration of the movement towards globalisation in the 1990s was an accident. The rich countries of the West, faced with sluggish and saturated markets for their consumer goods at home, were particularly eager to find new markets for their surplus products among the developing world and, therefore pushed for the World Trade Organisation (WTO) and to remove import duties in emerging economies. So, while I doubt that the opening of new countries provokes the upswing of a long wave, the benefit from increased global trade - provided it is not set back by recent protectionist measures in the US - may be a factor in contributing to the bottoming process of the downward wave in the years to come.

2. Kondratieff's second empirical observation was that during the rising wave big social upheavals and radical changes in the life of society (wars, revolutions, etc.) are much more frequent than in periods of a downward wave. The entry of new countries into the global economy and their expansion at the expense of older countries (the struggle for political and economic hegemony) leads to an aggravation of international political relations and an increase in the number of military conflicts. At the same time, the rapid growth of new productive forces increases the internal struggle among various classes of society against socioeconomic institutions that have become obsolete and hinder progress and development.

In this respect it is interesting to note that the French Revolution, the Napoleonic Wars, the European revolutions of 1848, the Crimean War, the American Civil War, the Franco-Prussian War, the Russo-Japanese War of 1904, the First World War and the February Revolution in Russia all took place during the rising wave of the long cycle. An exception was the Second World War, which took place right at the end of the downward wave of the third cycle or the very beginning of the fourth cycle. Still, during the rising wave of the fourth cycle (1938-49 to 1973-80), we had the struggles for independence by the colonies, the Korean War, the Vietnam War and, towards the end of the rising wave, the first evidence that communism was in the process of breaking down when China declared its open door policy in 1978.

However, since the downward wave began in 1980, we have had only contained confrontations (such as the wars in the Middle East and Yugoslavia) that did not have a worldwide economic impact. Whether the recent war on terrorism signifies that social tensions and international conflicts are in the process of intensifying, as the downward wave begins to bottom out or once the long wave turns up, sometime early in the next millennium, remains to be seen, but in my view the rise of China as a powerful economic and political force and the potential for a very meaningful recovery of Russian power under Vladimir Putin will lead to increased geopolitical tensions around the world.

3. The third empirical observation Kondratieff made was that the downward wave of each cycle was accompanied by a prolonged and very intense depression in agriculture. In particular, the farm sector seems to suffer immediately after the turning point - that is, right at the very beginning of the downward wave - because, as we have seen above, agricultural prices fall first, while industrial prices hold steady or decline less than farm products. Thus, in the first stage of a downward wave we find that the agrarian sector suffers the most.

But it should be noted that the relative decline in agricultural commodity prices creates a favourable environment for a relative increase in the process of accumulation of banks, industry and trade - also because declining commodity prices allow interest rates to come down. Therefore, booming financial markets in the first phase of the downward wave, as we had in the 1920s and since the early 1980s, are very common.

4. Kondratieff's fourth empirical fact was based on research done by Arthur Spiethoff whose historical analysis of economic, social and political trends made a lasting contribution to the business cycle theory. Intermediate cycles (Juglar cycles of 7-12 years) occur during both the rising and downward waves. However, during the rising wave, the recessions brought about by a downturn in the intermediate cycle are infrequent, brief, and of no great economic significance. Conversely,

intermediate cycles within the downward wave are characterised by depressions that are especially long and deep, and by upturns that are brief and weak. In this respect, we mentioned above that Schumpeter blamed the depression of the 1930s on the simultaneous downturn in the long wave, the Juglar and Kitchin cycles.

Moreover, if we look at the rising wave of the fourth cycle (1938-49 to 1973-80), recessions were relatively brief and infrequent. The first severe recession was actually the 1973/74 recession. However, since then, consistent with the conditions of the downward wave, recessions have been more severe and recoveries comparatively weak. We had, after 1981, a depression in Latin America that lasted until the late 1980s (a depression combined with high inflation), a relatively severe global recession in 1982, the Japanese economic downturn after 1990, which is still in force, the post-communist economic collapse in Eastern Europe and Russia, anaemic growth in Europe following the 1991 recession and, more recently, first the extremely intense economic downturn in Asia, and in 2001, the slowest growth rate for the global economy in 30 years.

So, although all these factors combined with the declining trend in commodity prices and interest rates, and sluggish real wage growth since the early 1980s, would suggest that the long wave is still declining, it may be that in industrial and post-industrial societies, downward waves don't have the same negative economic impact they once had on agrarian societies. So, while the long cycle still appears to be intact, business conditions during the rising and falling waves may no longer mirror the rise and fall in agricultural commodity prices to the same extent. After all Kondratieff, when he made his studies, relied principally on economic statistics and events of the 19th Century, when the world's economy was still largely based on agricultural production and with the rural population far exceeding the urban population throughout the world. He noted then that each new cycle takes place under new historical conditions, and at a new level in the development of productive forces; therefore, it couldn't be a repetition of the preceding cycle.

Consequently, we may have to refine the analysis of the dynamics of capitalistic society to take into account the changes that have occurred in the second half of the 20th Century. So, whereas wheat, corn and cotton were the most important commodities in the 19th Century, crude oil is now by far the most important industrial commodity in value terms and as a cost factor in industrial societies - not to mention its importance in the geopolitical structure of the world. Equally, wages in the 19th Century mirrored agricultural prices very closely, as prosperity in the farming sector led to rapidly rising wages on the farm, while falling agricultural prices had the opposite effect. But in today's industrialised societies, employment in the agricultural sector is insignificant, and, therefore, falling agricultural commodity prices and recessions in the farming sector should have no impact on real wage growth for the economy as a whole. Still, whether by coincidence or not, per-capita incomes around the world have been growing since the 1970s at a slower rate than during the golden age of capitalism from 1950 - 1970 (see Table 3).

Another factor that may diminish the impact of the downward wave on economic activity is the growing role of government expenditure, including transfer payments, deficit financing, etc., in industrialised societies. However, whether the growing involvement of government, because of its inertia and rigidity, will actually prolong and even intensify the downward wave, or lessen it, remains open to debate - but free market economists maintain that government intervention stops the laws of economics working and, therefore, exacerbates business-cycle fluctuations. In Europe, where we have particularly heavy governmental expenditure as a percentage of the economy, unemployment has remained stubbornly high in the 1990s. Also, in Japan, there is also little doubt that the government's economic policies have prolonged the slump. Without the huge deficit-financing policies of Japan in the 1990s, it is likely that the system would be better off. Also, if it were, indeed, true that the public sector acts as a stabiliser during the downward wave, it would also have to reduce the intensity of economic activity during the rising wave.

Lastly it is conceivable, although unlikely, that financial markets have rendered the long cycle largely obsolete. Still, it is interesting and certainly no coincidence that all major stock market booms occurred within a downward wave. The boom in canal and banking shares of 1834-37, in railroad stocks between 1868 and 1873, the 1921-29 and 1982-2000 bull markets all took place during downward waves. In this respect, the recent stock market boom was not particularly unusual, except maybe for its duration and intensity. According to Kondratieff, a relative change in the pricing of agricultural commodities versus industrial products takes place in the downward wave, with the former declining relative to the latter. The benefits of the relative decline in agricultural prices and also other raw materials (particularly oil), and interest rates, combined with sluggish real wage growth, enables corporations initially to boost their profits. Furthermore, with the decline in commodity prices, interest rates tend to fall, which creates a favourable environment for fixed-interest securities and equities. Thus, in past initial phases of downward waves, equity markets frequently experienced a powerful rise as a result of the combination of falling interest rates and rising corporate profits. Moreover, I should like to again point out that during the rising wave bear markets tend to be short-lived and of little or no economic consequences, whereas during the downward wave they are far more severe and have a greater impact on the economy. I am thinking here of the 1873 and 1929-32 crashes, of Japan after 1989 and of Asia recently. To what extent the most recent global bear market will have a negative economic impact will tell us a lot about whether we are still in a Kondratieff downwave, or whether the rising wave is already in place.

Another consideration that would argue against the rising-wave scenario relates to the cycle of speculation. Speculative excesses and bubbles (real estate, commodities, tulips, canals, railroads, stocks, etc) are always associated with peaks in the business cycle, not troughs. Near business cycle peaks, speculation moves very quickly from one market to another (real estate, collectibles, Japanese stocks, emerging markets, the Yen, US equities, etc) and spreads internationally. The opposite is true at long-wave lows, when investors and businessmen are risk averse and commit Pigou's "error of pessimism". Thus, the recent speculative excesses we have seen particularly surrounding the TMT sector on a global scale, the record transaction volumes, the proliferation of leverage and all kinds of new financial instruments, the aversion to risk, the public's participation, new issues jumping to high premiums on the first trading day, etc, are certainly more symptomatic of speculative excesses than Kondratieff troughs in economic activity.

There is another point to consider regarding the long wave theory. Kondratieff based his analysis principally on the movement of commodities at a time when in most countries commodities played a much more important role in the economy than they do today. In 1900, despite the industrialisation in the US during the second half of the 19th Century, agriculture still accounted for over 40% of total employment and was a far larger employer than manufacturing. But today, employment in agriculture makes up just 3% of the total working population in the industrialised countries of the West, while the service sector and government account for over 80%. Thus, in the past, when commodity prices rose, especially agricultural prices, it had a favourable impact on wages and on the economy as a whole. This is clearly no longer the case now in industrialised countries, where employment in agriculture is insignificant and the service sector and government dominate.

But what about the role of agriculture for the world as a whole? I mentioned above that oil has replaced agricultural commodities as the world's most important industrial commodity. This is only partially true, because there are in the developing countries still far more people who depend on the agricultural sector for their livelihood than people employed by the oil industry. In Africa and in Asia, no less than 60% of the population still depends on agriculture as its main source of income and, if I add crude oil, natural gas, timber, rubber, cocoa, coffee, cocaine, opium and mining to the agrarian sector, then I figure that, directly or indirectly, two-thirds of the world's population still benefits from rising commodity prices and is harmed by their fall.

Granted, two-thirds of world GDP goes to the 25% of the global population that is fortunate to live in the industrialised countries - but rapid global economic growth can only be achieved if the poor nation's purchasing power is boosted. That seems not to have been the case in the 1990s, which were very beneficial to the Western multinationals but led to repeated severe currency depreciations in the emerging world. In turn these severe currency depreciations brought about - with the exception of China - only minor or no improvements in the US Dollar per-capita incomes of most emerging economies. Furthermore, whereas in the 19th Century the opening of new territories (facilitated by progress in methods of transportation, such as canals and railroads) put pressure on agricultural prices and led to several severe depressions in the farming sector, today the industrialisation of highly populated countries such as China, India, Brazil and Mexico (again facilitated by modern communications and new methods of transportation, such as the container and the Boeing 747) has increased the supply of manufactured goods to the extent that their prices have been declining as well. And just as falling farm prices had a negative impact on agrarian wages in the 19th Century, today falling prices for manufactured goods have the same effect on the wages of unskilled workers throughout the world.

So, while each long cycle takes place under new social, political and economic conditions and therefore cannot simply be a repetition of the previous cycle, the forces at work during the rising and downward waves of the long cycle appear to have remained in place. In this regard, the severity or mildness of the current global economic downturn and the intensity of the subsequent recovery will be of particular interest to us, as followers of the long wave theory.

The more the world changes, the more it remains the same. Societies rise and fall, new industries come up and then fade. Wealth accumulates, only to be destroyed. People live longer, but their suffering when sick is prolonged. Wars may no longer be fought with huge armies facing each other in trenches but through terrorism and with trade embargoes, holding off supplies from the market (oil cartels), defaults on foreign debts, expropriations, computer viruses, etc. And whereas, in the 19th Century, the Western powers colonised countries with guns, today they do it with

McDonald's, Coca-Cola, Häagen Dazs, Starbucks, Hollywood, CNN, massive capital flows at high interest rates, and by the doctrine that open markets will automatically lead to prosperity. Yet, were the countries that joined the global free-market economic system in the 1990s, with their limited financial resources, ready to compete on global markets?

And while it is possible that economic downturns may be postponed through concerted central bank actions and other economic policy measures, they may not be eliminated altogether. So, while I concede that Kondratieff's (largely agrarian) cycle may have changed somewhat in character, there is little doubt, based on data from the 20th Century, that it is still alive and well.

Financial markets - An end in themselves?

Moreover, if we included all commodities in our analysis, then it should be obvious that the gargantuan global financial market has become the world's dominant commodity in the 1990s. Therefore, if in the 19th Century agriculture - being the then most important economic sector - led long-wave cycles, today the financial markets seem to be far more important for the global economy - especially since growth has in recent years been increasingly financed through credit expansion and rising stock prices. Since financial markets have been growing disproportionately large since the 1980s when compared to the real economy, it is no longer the real economy that drives the markets, but vice versa. In the same way that rising agricultural prices stimulated the economy in the 19th Century, today, rising financial markets benefit the global economy and bring above-trend growth, whereas falling markets lead to economic downturns as we have seen in the case of Japan in the 1990s and more recently in a large number of emerging economies. Thus, it is conceivable that the recent global bear market will have in time - when the effects of easy monetary policies wear off - dire economic consequences.

I may also add that while in the past the intensity of economic downturns was particularly strong around the middle of the downward wave - right after the investment boom brought about by new inventions and by the decline in interest rates and commodity prices ends in a bust - today we may have a situation whereby the economy could be hardest hit towards or at the very end of the long downward wave, as the downturn can be postponed through debt growth and easy monetary policies, as was the case in the 1990s. This hypothesis would certainly be more consistent with the tenets of monetary overinvestment and Irving Fisher's debt-deflation theory, which stipulate that overinvestment and overindebtedness bring about the collapse of the economy.

Earlier we quoted Irving Fisher's criticism of business-cycle theory, with his example of rocking chairs on the deck of a ship tipped by waves and buffeted by crosswinds. As he remarked, sometimes the motion will appear rhythmic, sometimes chaotic. From Schumpeter (see Figure 6), we also learnt that the Great Depression came about as a result of a simultaneous downturn in the long wave, the Juglar and the Kitchin cycles. Therefore, what might have happened over the last 20 years or so is the following: taking the severe 1974 recession as a starting point, we have a Juglar Cycle lasting until the 1982 recession (8 years). Another powerful Juglar upswing gets underway in 1982, which ends with the mild 1990 recession (8 years). This Juglar was largely fuelled by the rising US budget and trade deficits that shifted growth to Japan and emerging economies. Thereafter, we have another Juglar upswing, albeit less vigorous (because of the severe recession in Japan), ending sometime between 2000 and 2003.

The problem, as I see it, could be that the emerging economies that had strong growth in the early 1990s are now, following their post-1997 crises, no longer supportive of global growth, while the US economy with its booming TMT sector, which was in the post-1998 period the driver of global growth, looks increasingly wobbly, having been artificially supported in 2001 and 2002 by strong debt growth. Therefore, we should consider this. The Kitchin cycle clearly turned down sometime in 2001, as massive inventory liquidation got underway. The Juglar cycle is also still in a downtrend, as the hi-tech telecom bubble burst and stock markets have also been very weak since 2000. So, if we are still in a downward wave, a simultaneous occurrence of all these events could then lead to a severe and longer lasting economic contraction, which in turn would be typical of a downswing in the long wave.

I have repeatedly noted that business cycle theory is extremely complex. I certainly do not have all the answers. However, I believe that only the severity and longevity of the present recession will provide a clue as to whether we have already entered a Kondratieff upward wave (in which case the recession will be mild and brief) or whether the downward wave is still in progress (in which case the recession will probably be devastating). Since the economic expansion that began after the 1990 recession has already turned down with quite a bang, I do not think that we will have to wait long to find out!

I should like to stress once again that Kondratieff did not posit a long wave *theory*. He merely observed - through empirical studies of long-term price, wage, production and trade trends - that the existence of long cycles in economic conditions was very probable. And while he provided some explanations for long wave economic fluctuations, he admitted that, the explanation of business cycles encounters "considerable difficulties".

However, it seems wrong to declare, as some economists do, that long waves in economic conditions are obsolete in industrialised and post-industrialised societies. The historian Arnold Toynbee remarked that "The appearance of economic 'long waves' might not be hallucinations but might be economic reflections of political realities that had already been 'a going concern' in the Modern Western World for some three hundred years before the outbreak of the Industrial Revolution in Great Britain". And in explaining the war-and-peace cycle as a consequence of a "Generation Cycle in the transmission of a social heritage", he may have provided the most compelling explanation of recurring long waves in economic conditions as well:

> The survivors of a generation that has been of military age during a bout of war will be shy, for the rest of their lives, of bringing a repetition of this tragic experience either upon themselves or upon their children, and .... therefore the psychological resistance of any move towards the breaking of a peace ... is likely to be prohibitively strong until a new generation ... has had the time to

> grow up and to come into power. On the same showing, a bout of war, once precipitated, is likely to persist until the peace-bred generation that has been lightheartedly run into war has been replaced, in its turn, by a warworn generation.
>
> Arnold Toynbee, *A Study of History*, London, 1954

I suppose that the same "generation cycle" exists in financial markets as well. Investors who lost all they had in the 1929 crash and the subsequent depression probably vowed to never again touch stocks and remained conservative for the rest of their lives and never again borrowed money against the value of their homes. Conversely, the vast majority of today's investors, having never really experienced a severe and long-lasting bear market and the pain of a depression, are much less risk averse.

At present, the question of whether the long wave has already turned up cannot be answered satisfactorily, but as I have tried to explain, a number of economic conditions speak against such a proposition. At the same time, it *is* very likely that it will turn up in the next few years. And once it turns up, it will change the entire rules of investing, because in a rising wave, commodity prices will rise, inflation will accelerate and interest rates will increase. Thus, once the long wave turns up, investors will have to liquidate their bond positions. In a long-wave upturn, equities always outperform bonds as inflation accelerates. Moreover, once the long wave turns up, it will create a totally new investment environment in which equities correlated to commodities, such as in the resource-rich emerging markets, will perform far better than the markets of the Western industrialised countries.

There is a last observation I should like to make about 19th Century price movements and business cycles Kondratieff and Schumpeter observed and analysed. As can be seen from Figure 3, which shows the index numbers of commodity prices and from Figure 4, which shows the trend of interest rates since 1790, the 19th Century was a highly deflationary era. An index of commodities fell from 140 (1910-14=100) in 1800 to 70 in 1896 despite the US population growing from 4 million in 1800 to 80 million in 1900 and the country emerging as the world's largest industrial power - its economy having expanded by about 4% per annum in real terms. The general decline in the price level was also confirmed by the movement of long-term interest rates. Federal Government new issue bond yields fell from 8% in 1800 to 2% in 1900. Price declines in the 19th Century were not only confined to agricultural products. Between 1872 and 1898, Bessemer Steel prices fell almost 80%. Two factors contributed to rapid economic growth amidst falling prices: the opening of the prairies, which increased the supply of farm land several fold, and impressive productivity improvement in both agriculture and industry (as a result of new inventions and innovations), as well as declining transportation costs, which came about from massive railroad construction across North America. For example, between 1850 and 1914, output per man hour in blast furnaces increased by over 30 times.

The "deflationary boom" some observers call the period between 1873 and 1900, during which commodity prices fell particularly hard, wasn't however, a golden era of prosperity for everybody. Grain farmers, particularly in Europe, were in deep trouble, with political consequences that included, the "revolt of the field" in Britain and rural unrest in Europe and Russia, as well as the Populist movement in the US. Returns on agricultural land, both in terms of real estate prices and rents, fell. But on the other hand, real wages rose practically everywhere more rapidly than in the first three-quarters of the 19th Century (see Figure 8), as a result of meaningful productivity improvements in agriculture and manufacturing. Thus, the European landowning class lost out, as they not only faced declining rents and agricultural prices but also rising real wages. However, we should not forget that the economic development of many new regions which led to exports of Mississippi cotton, Argentine beef, Australian wheat, New Zealand mutton, African ore and Canadian timber, combined with declining transportation costs (the Suez Canal opened in 1869), created an integrated global market for commodities, boosted world trade, and brought about large economies of scale. Thus, landowners aside, the deflationary shock that had been brought about by new technologies and inventions, and which permitted the exploitation of the American continent and other new regions and catapulted America into the role of the world's leading industrial power, resembled far more a deflationary boom than a shock! Moreover, while owners of agricultural land in Europe performed poorly, real estate in cities rose again after the 1873-78 crisis, because of the accelerating process of urbanisation. This was particularly true of the US, where real estate in southern California soared in the years preceding 1886. Thus, while real estate may not be particularly attractive in the present deflationary period (certainly not the highly priced property market in financial centres), selected real estate markets such as in Shanghai and Beijing could perform well after the more than 50% capital value decline they have experienced since the end of 1995.

Figure 8

GETTING THE RAISE

The rise of real wages, 1800-1896

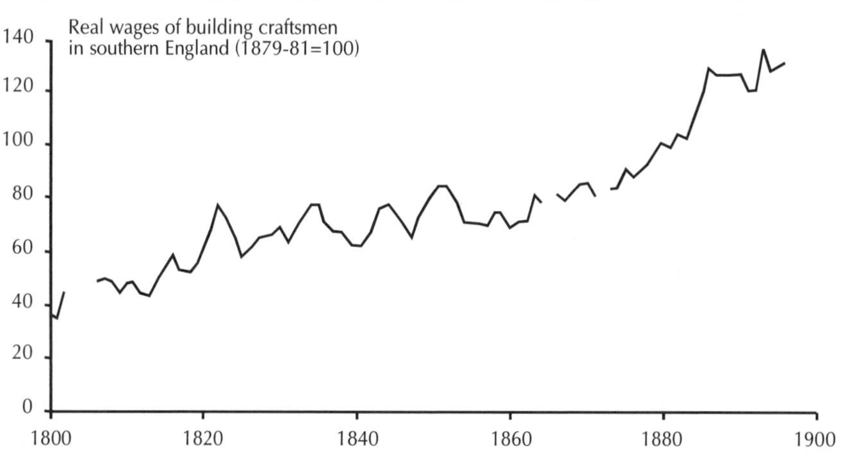

Source: David Hackett Fischer, *The Great Wave.*

The 1873-1900 period was also highly beneficial to holders of fixed interest securities who reaped large gains from deflation. The yield on British consols fell from a high of 3.41% in 1866 to a low of 2.21% in 1897, and in the US the yield on higher-grade railroad bonds declined from 6.49% in 1861 to 3.07% in 1899. Deflation was obviously not particularly favourable for corporate profits, and bonds therefore outperformed equities after 1876.

In sum, I would argue that while the entire 19th Century was characterised by a deflationary trend, it was a century of enormous economic progress accompanied by strong population growth. *Therefore, there is, in principle, nothing to fear from deflation.* The reason so many economists fear deflationary periods is that they only look back at the Depression years of the 1930s, which were truly a deflationary bust. But, instead of analysing the various causes of the bust following 1929, they focus on the devastation the deflationary bust brought about - when, in fact, the Depression was only a consequence of the previous speculative credit-driven boom that led to the excesses of the 1920s.

An analysis of business cycles and long price waves in economic conditions would be incomplete without a discussion of the phenomenon of investment mania. The longer an economic expansion or a rising price trend for an asset class, such as stocks, commodities and real estate does last, the more likely it is that it will culminate in an investment mania whose peculiarities I propose to discuss in the following chapter.

CHAPTER EIGHT

New eras, manias and bubbles

> Speculators may do no harm as bubbles on a steady stream of enterprises. But the position is serious when enterprise becomes the bubble on a whirlpool of speculation. When the capital development of a country becomes a by-product of the activities of a casino, the job is likely to be ill-done.
>
> *JOHN MAYNARD KEYNES (1883-1946)*

I have always been fascinated by the phenomenon of manias. The Crusades, the Inquisition, the witch-hunts, alchemy, mesmerism and McCarthyism - all were manias. In our capitalistic system there have been a series of investment manias that form an integral part and are by far the most exciting phase of the business cycle. And whereas this book is about trying to identify the next big investment theme from which investors could benefit as much as from Japanese shares in the 1980s and US stocks in the 1990s, I also feel that it is important to understand that while the recessions, depressions and crises offer great investment opportunities, manias usually offer once-in-a-lifetime selling opportunities.

Although it would be ideal for investors to participate right to the peak of an investment mania, because the final run up is usually the steepest, it ought to be obvious that all investors will never be able to exit any market right at its peak. However, once an investment mania has begun, the point at which an investor sells is no longer all that important, because I am not familiar with any mania that did not subsequently give back its entire gains over the years leading to the top, and usually some more. So the purpose of what follows below is really to provide some clues as to how manias come about and how any investor can easily identify them and use them as selling opportunities.

As explained earlier, from time to time, a wave of optimism spreads around the world like a bush fire; people believe that they are seeing the dawn of a new era that will bring unimaginable riches and prosperity to all.

A typical characteristic of new-era thinking is that it usually engulfs us not at the beginning of an era of prosperity, but towards the end - and is associated with some sort of a "rush" or investment mania. Well-known examples are the Mississippi Scheme and the South Sea Bubble of 1720, the various canal, railroad and real estate booms of the 19th Century, the Australian and Californian gold discoveries, the late-1920s American stock market run and the Kuwaiti stock and real estate market manias in the late 1970s.

In recent years, a wave of optimism and new-era thinking swept through the investment community. The breakdown of communism, the opening of a large number of new markets, promising new technology, corporate downsizing and layoffs, the lack of any major military threat, low inflation, falling interest rates, globalisation, free trade, etc, were expected to bring about endless profit opportunities. Thus, Wall Street, led by the more speculative Nasdaq Index, displayed a stunning performance between 1990 and 2000. But now we know that the terminal phase of the rise, between 1997 and 2000, was a colossal financial bubble, which only occurs once a generation and which has now come to end the way all previous new-era-based bull markets have ended.

Speculative and non-speculative markets

To understand speculative markets better, let us first consider their opposite. A good example of a non-speculative market was Argentina in the mid- to late 1980s (see Chapter 5, Figure 3). Volume was dismal, stocks sold below book value and replacement cost, there were hardly any initial public offerings (IPO) or rights issues, foreign participation was lacking, stock market capitalisation as a percentage of the economy was low, hardly anyone was interested in becoming a stockbroker or being professionally involved in the financial markets, brokerage offices were very modest, confidence was depressed and the public's expectations about future returns from equities were either extremely low or nonexistent. I may add that the Asian markets in the early 1980s also had all the characteristics of non-speculative markets (see Chapter 2, Figures 2, 3 and 4).

In short, non-speculative markets are depressed and, by traditional yardsticks, undervalued markets. Consider also the US stock market after the Second World War. Market averages were still well below their 1929 highs, volume was depressed, the stock market crash and Depression of the early 1930s were still fresh in people's memories and, although the war had been won, investor expectations were very low. The end of the war did not bring about new-era thinking, but rather apprehension that the US economy would slip back into another depression following the economic war boom. This is evident from comparing stock and bond yields at the time. At their widest spread in 1947, stocks were yielding (dividend yield) over three times more than bonds (reflecting low or no growth expectations), and at the time, not many books were written about the merits of investing in equities or asserting that equities always outperform bonds and cash!

Another example of a non-speculative market is real estate in the 1950s. People bought homes in order to live in them, farmers bought land for farming and investors acquired commercial buildings for their yield and not with the view of achieving capital gains or as a hedge against inflation. Similarly, the commodity markets, especially gold and silver, were non-speculative in the 1950s and 1960s. These markets were then dominated by end-users (insiders), and not by people with nothing to do with metals (outsiders) who participate solely to profit from rising or falling prices.

Lastly, art and collectibles are non-speculative markets as long as paintings and baseball cards are bought by genuine collectors. Take, for instance, the grandmother and great-aunts of one of my school friends who, while studying in Paris in the early 1900s acquired Impressionist paintings with their pocket money. Did they buy these works because they thought about capital gains or because they were contrarian investors and wanted to buy something nobody else liked? No, they bought because they had strange taste and happened to like the pictures (today, my friend's family has one of the largest private Impressionist collections in the world). In fact, the quintessence of a non-speculative market was in van Gogh paintings during his lifetime - only one was ever traded!

Needless to say, a common feature of all non-speculative markets is the almost total absence of leverage. Stocks, bonds, real estate, paintings, gold are bought principally for cash and not on credit. I should, therefore, like to offer the following definition: A non-speculative market is one for which capital gain expectations are low, in which trading volume is comparatively light and dominated by a small group of people (insiders), and in which the public at large does not participate.

So, what are speculative markets? Having felt for some time that financial markets generally have become extremely speculative, I have become more apprehensive about defining excessive speculation. After all, it is easy to say that the 17th Century Dutch tulip mania or trade in the shares of the South Sea Company in 1720, were speculative because both ended in total disaster. But was there really excessive speculation in the American market in 1929 or Hong Kong in 1973? True, following their highs, both fell by 90%, while many companies went broke or never recovered their previous highs, but these markets were not totally *wrong.* Even purchased right at their highs (381 for the Dow Jones in 1929 and 1,700 for the Hang Seng Index in early 1973), these markets would have amply rewarded long-term investors. Equally, real estate purchased in 1836 Chicago, 1886 California and 1926 Florida - right at the peaks of their respective booms - would today be worth much more, even though property prices totally collapsed once these booms ended.

Another difficulty in defining excessive speculation lies in the timing.

Was the Japanese stock market already speculative in 1988? Yes. But that did not prevent stocks from rising another 30% in the 12 months preceding the peak in December 1989. Or take the silver market of the late 1970s. In December 1979, silver had risen to US$18 (having more than doubled in 12 months). The precious metal markets were already extremely speculative, but that did not stop silver from soaring, in a massive short squeeze, to over US$40 within four weeks, before collapsing to US$11 in May 1980 and less than US$4 in 1992! Or take the Nasdaq at the beginning of 1999. It had already risen by four times in the preceding four years, yet it still rose another 2.5 times to its 10 March 2000 peak of 5,132.

Therefore, while the identification of speculative markets, based on some features which I shall discuss below, may be possible, it is almost impossible to know how much longer the investment mania will last and how much higher prices can move before the bubble is punctured. In fact, over the 30-plus years I have been involved in the investment business, I have felt on many occasions like Isaac Newton, who in early 1720 remarked: "I can calculate the motions of heavenly bodies, but not the madness of people". (By selling his shares in the South Sea Company, Newton first made a 100% profit amounting to £7,000, but unfortunately he re-entered the market right at its peak and subsequently lost £20,000.) Still, I shall attempt to describe symptoms of speculative manias and bubbles because, as indicated when describing the life cycle of emerging markets, it is usually better for the average investor to focus on investing in non-speculative markets than to participate in speculative markets.

Symptoms of speculative excesses

Booms, manias and speculative excesses occur in the final upswing of a business or investment cycle. *The longer a market has been in an up-trend, the more likely a mania will follow, as the rising price trend becomes increasingly perceived to be permanent.* We can distinguish between mini manias and major manias. I refer to a mini mania as a speculative bubble which, once burst, does not lead to widespread economic damage.

Following a sharp but brief sell-off, the market up-trend resumes. The 1983 US technology stock mania, the 1987 global stock market bubble and the powerful 1988-90 emerging markets boom can thus be classed as mini manias.

Major manias, on the other hand, are usually once-a-generation affairs that lead to serious economic damage when the bubble bursts. The late-1920s mania was followed by a worldwide depression, the late 1980s Japanese stock market boom led to a lengthy and painful deflationary recession in Japan, and the abrupt end of the commodity bubble in the late 1970s caused serious hardship among the oil-producing regions of the world and a depression in Texas, Mexico and parts of the Middle East (all Texas banks went bust or had to be restructured, as did a great number of oil drilling companies). Lastly, the TMT sector and US stock market's meteoric rise until 2000 should not just be classified as a major mania, but as "the mother of all manias". Major manias occur very infrequently. Once they burst, they shake an entire generation's faith in the object of the speculation.

Therefore, while mini manias may take place every few years (the up-trend leading to the mania may last as little as two to three years), a major mania will represent the final stage, or culmination, of a long-term secular up-trend which may have lasted 10 to 25 years. So, the late-20s bubble came after a decade-long up-trend (the "Roaring Twenties"), and the stock market mania of the late 1960s and early 1970s concluded a secular bull market that had lasted close to 20 years. The late-1980s Japanese stock market boom was the culmination of a fairly uninterrupted up-trend that had begun in 1974, 16 years earlier (see Figure 1). In turn, the US bubble in 2000 concluded a bull market that had taken the Dow from less than 800 in the summer of 1982 to over 12,000. Strictly analysed, one could take 1974 as a starting point for the US bull market, since by 1982 the market had already recovered from the 1974 lows, but if we take inflation and the depreciation of the US Dollar into account, then the 1982 bottom was lower than the 1974 low (see Figure 2). In other words, by the time the bull market ended in March 2000, it was 18 years old.

Figure 1

A LONG ROAD TO RUIN

Tokyo Nikkei 225 stock average

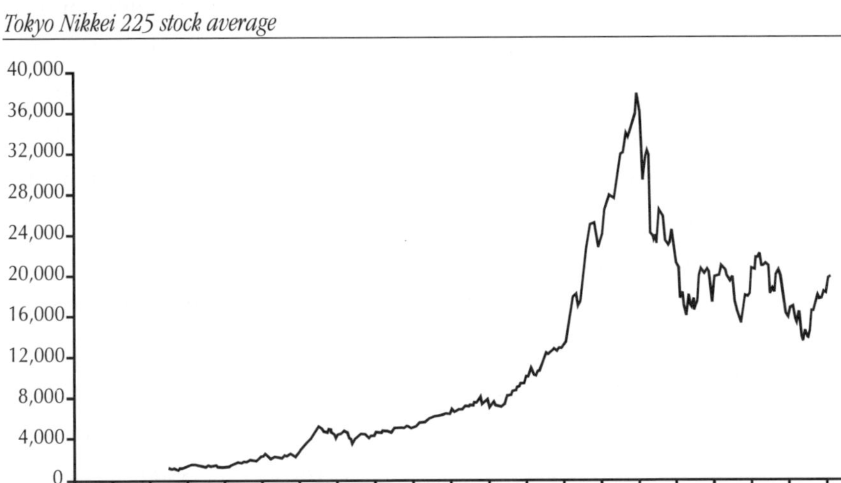

Source: *The Business Picture.*

Figure 2

THE REAL BOTTOM

*Real equity prices**

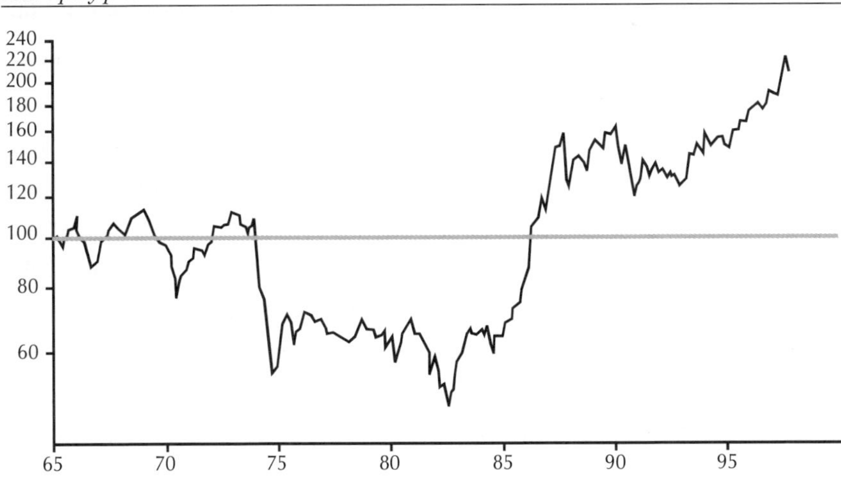

Note: *Morgan Stanley Capital International Index of Developed Markets in US Dollars, deflated by US CPI. Source: *The International Bank Credit Analyst.*

The "time factor" within the stock market cycle captivates my fascination for a number of reasons. First, as just mentioned, it would appear that the longer a bull market has been in place, the more likely it will end in a wild speculative orgy and then be followed by a terrific bust. Therefore, the peak after a 10- to 20-year bull market, that has, in the terminal phase, seen prices accelerate on the upside, usually represents a milestone high. This is important because milestone highs such as occurred in the US in 1929 and most likely in 2000, and in Japan in 1989, are commonly not exceeded for another 10-20 years (in the US, it took until 1954 to exceed the 1929 high while Japan is still down about 70% from its 1989 high - 13 years later).

The bear market that inevitably follows the bubble can take many different shapes. In 1929-32, the US stock market collapsed by close to 90% within just two years and in Hong Kong the stock market fell by more than 90% between 1973 and 1974. In Japan, on the other hand, the market only made a new low after more than 12 years (in early 2000, the market was still above 20,000 and thereafter fell by another 50% or so to its recent low). The steeper the decline, or the longer the decline has lasted, the less risky the purchase of such a stock market becomes, as there comes a point in every market when selling pressure exhausts itself. The same rule may not necessarily apply to an individual sector. Unlike an entire market which is made up of many different sectors and is therefore diversified, even after a 90% decline one single sector may still disappear as a result of obsolescence (mobile paging springs to mind), overleverage and other factors.

Thus, if I look today at the Asian markets, most of which - as I explained in Chapter 2 - peaked in US Dollar terms in 1990 and after major, long-lasting bear markets are today still down by around 70% or more (in US Dollars), I feel reasonably confident that from a "time factor" point of view, we have either already seen major lows or are in the process of building solid technical bases (see Figure 3) from which, in time, powerful bull markets will emerge.

Figure 3

CONSOLIDATION?

Asian stock market performance relative to the United States

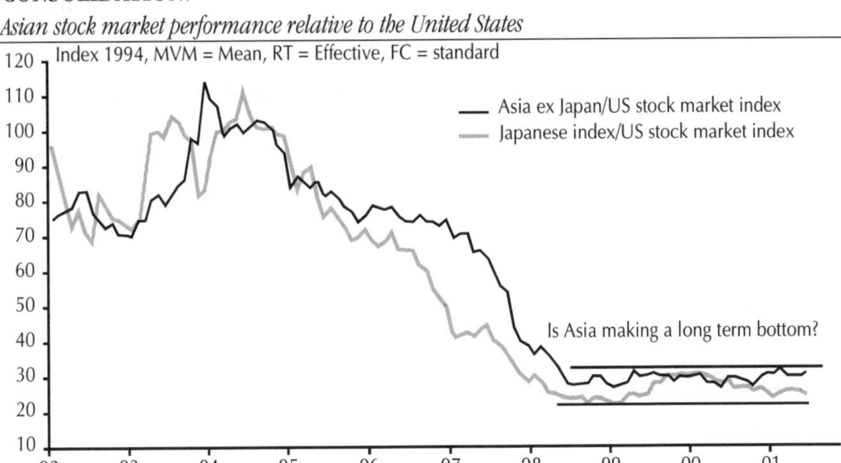

Source: Gaveco.

We have seen that while mini manias may occur at almost any time within the stock market cycle, major manias only come about after a lengthy rise (10 to 20 years' duration) in a market. Thus, although I expect the Asian markets to perform well once the present malaise comes to an end, I doubt we shall soon see the kind of speculative markets we had in the late 1980s and early 1990s, when Taiwan rose by 20 times within just a few years.

Crowd psychology

In the manic phase of a bull market, the mood is euphoric. While investors near bear-market lows want to get out at any price, near manic highs the urge to get in prevails and each minor correction is perceived to be an excellent opportunity, which leads to a renewed buying frenzy. Obviously, the longer the bull market has been in place, the more the up-trend will be regarded as a permanent feature of the new era. Also, towards the final stages of the mania, traditional valuations are thrown out the window.

Since booms involve exciting new concepts, optimism over future "huge profit" opportunities justifies "buying at any price" in investors' minds. The mood is reflected by heavy public participation, risks are largely ignored, the use of credit increases and overconfidence and irrational decision-making become common. A typical feature during manias is crowd behaviour, where the critical faculty of an individual is paralysed. According to Gustave Le Bon, whose excellent book (*The Crowd,* reprinted by Dunwoody) appeared at the end of the 19th Century, "a chain of logical argumentation is totally incomprehensible to crowds, and for this reason it is permissible to say that they do not reason or that they reason falsely and are not to be influenced by reasoning". Similarly, in 1830, JR McCulloch pointed out that speculation is a contagious and herd-like phenomenon. In fact, during the frenzy, demand is always overestimated, while supply is underestimated. Consider that in the oil boom of the late 1970s, it was never seriously considered that rising oil prices would bring additional supplies to the market, while energy conservation would curtail demand.

During the late-1980s US real estate bubble, Japanese demand for US commercial real estate was also grossly overestimated. Similarly, investors overrated demand for Hong Kong property in the late 1990s and never considered that much cheaper alternatives across the border in China would begin to compete. During every manic phase, furthermore, cash is always regarded as a totally unattractive investment alternative. Actually, there is frequently a panic out of cash. In the late 1970s, people seriously believed that money would become worthless because of accelerating inflation. They rushed into gold, silver and resource stocks. Recently, people believed they would not be able to retire on cash returns, so they bought equities. I have to add that easy monetary policies by central banks - which keep interest rates "too low" during the economic expansion and, therefore, are responsible for the boom and the investment mania - are also responsible for people getting sucked into the market at high prices. Take Hong Kong in the years preceding the 1997 top in the property market. Interest rates were low, while property prices and rents were running up at more than 20% per annum. Eventually, people became seriously concerned about how they would be able to pay for future rent increases, which frequently amounted to 50% to 100% within two or three years. Therefore, understandably, many families chose to buy their own apartments. However, because prices had already risen to astronomical levels by 1995, they had to take on larger and larger mortgages. Once the market turned down they ended up with negative home-equity positions - their mortgages exceeding the value of their properties by a wide margin.

So, investment manias have much to do with mass psychology, crowd behaviour and the "herd instinct". Paul Reiwald's fascinating book *The Mind of Crowds* (Vom Geist der Massen, Zurich, 1946), discusses the views and theories of notable biologists, sociologists and psychologists on crowd behaviour and mass psychology. It would appear that all the analysts who have studied the phenomenon of crowd psychology agree that individuals long to be part of a crowd and, once part of a crowd, behave very differently than when alone. The "voice of the herd" has an extremely powerful influence on the actions of humans, and, therefore, humans are subjected to the passion of the pack in the violence of the mob, and the fear of the herd in a panic. In particular, crowds identify themselves closely with leaders and ideas.

According to Sigmund Freud, the leader has a hypnotic impact on the individual; the individual loses himself by identifying with the leader. (In order to establish this association, leaders may display photographs of themselves with children or dogs, which reinforces the belief by the "herd" that the leader is indeed one of them.) In other words, most analysts believe that there is an intimate relationship and close association between a leader and the crowd, and that over time the crowd becomes totally dependent on its leader.

Freud explained, for instance, the difference in the behaviour of the German people in 1918 and 1945 as a consequence of the different intensity in the masses' association with their leaders. In the First World War, Germany capitulated in 1918 under circumstances that were far less hopeless than those prevailing for the German people and the German army in the Second World War as early as 1943. According to Freud, the reason why the German masses endured so many failures and defeats after

1943 was that they associated themselves far more with Hitler and other Nazi leaders in the Second World War than they ever did with the Kaiser and his generals.

It is important also to understand that, because of the intense attachment of the crowd to its leader, the loss of the leader - or the loss of his "prestige" - usually leads to a panic. Freud then went on to explain that ideas can also "lead" a crowd, and the people who represent them become, in such a case, "secondary leaders".

This would seem to be the case during investment manias. The idea of "large profits" is the driving force of the mania, while corporate leaders, successful investors, central bankers, finance ministers and speculators who enjoy great prestige and are written up in magazines and interviewed on television are the "secondary leaders". Thus, the imagination of the crowd is captured by the notion that great wealth can be gained from participating in the boom, as a result of a variety of factors such as instincts, simple reflexes (Pavlov), release impulses, self-perpetuating habits, the suggestive power of the media, association with and imitation of successful investors, emotional excitement, insistence and irrationality, which all tend to override individual judgment and thought. Driven by these impulses, the intelligence of a crowd is always inferior to that of an individual who can remain objective.

According to some analysts, the principal cause of the low level of intellect in crowds is that, for ideas and beliefs to be understood by all members of the crowd, they must be extremely simple. Only then can they appeal to and be adopted by the lowest intelligence within the crowd. This fact was observed earlier by Le Bon when he wrote that 'the reasoning of crowds is always of a very inferior order' and that, "however great or true an idea may have been to begin with, it is deprived of almost all that which constituted its elevation and its greatness by the mere fact that it has come within the intellectual range of crowds and exerts an influence on them". Along similar lines, Carl Gustav Jung wrote that a large group consisting of decent people is, in terms of morality and intelligence, like a large, stupid and violent animal, and that an assembly of a hundred very influential people forms "a blockhead" ("*einen Wasserkopf*").

Sociologists and psychologists have cited examples of crowd actions, such as the witch-hunts, the Crusades, communism, socialism, the Nazi movement, lynchings, revolutions and so on. However, their theories fail to fully explain why a crowd can reverse its expectations, abandon its desires, or panic. Common to crowds is a certain "loss of touch with reality". According to Le Bon, the crowd is "not prepared to admit that anything can come between its desire and the realisation of its desire", while "the notion of impossibility disappears for the individual in a crowd". At the same time, most of these authors agree that, because crowds are under the influence of a wide range of impulses and instincts, they are extremely "mobile". But where I detect some inconsistency is in Le Bon's theory that "a long time is necessary for ideas to establish themselves in the minds of crowds, but just as long a time is needed for them to be eradicated". In other words, we are told that although the mind of crowds is vacillating, it takes a long time for established ideas to be abandoned.

Perhaps the answer to this inconsistency can be found if we assume that the crowd's imagination is captured by an overriding idea that leads to certain reflexes (for example, "because the stock market always goes up in the long run, buy the dips"), but the crowd's mood is also influenced by factors that have an immediate impact (for example, the stock market's short-term movements). Moreover, as in the case of the eradication of ideas, the explanation of the panic is vague at best. Usually it is danger that leads to a panic. In the case of an army, the loss of the leader will lead to panic (since the crowd is closely attached to and identifies itself with the leader), but panics have also occurred without the loss of the leader and when the existing danger was far less than previous dangers the same army had once taken in stride. This led Sigmund Freud to conclude that there is no relationship between the severity of the panic and the impending danger, and that a panic can spread as a result of insignificant events.

Panic can therefore occur under two conditions: Either the danger is really large; or the association and sentimental attachment of the crowd is weak or has been weakened by a leader's loss of "prestige". According to Le

Bon, prestige is a mysterious force that gives "great power" to ideas propagated by affiliation, repetition and contagion. He writes that prestige is a sort of domination exercised on our minds by an individual, a work or an idea, which entirely paralyses our critical faculty and fills our soul with admiration and respect. (I suppose the modern word for prestige would be "charisma".) One of the principal factors in the prestige of a person or an idea is success, but once success is replaced by failure, prestige is called into question. According to Le Bon, "prestige lost by want of success disappears in a brief space of time". He cited the life of Ferdinand de Lesseps, who, having accomplished whatever there was to accomplish:

> ... ceased to believe in obstacles, and wished to begin Suez over again at Panama. But he had aged, and besides, the faith that moves mountains does not move them if they are too lofty. The mountains resisted, and the catastrophe that ensued destroyed the glittering aureole of glory that enveloped the hero [and] after rivalling in greatness the most famous heroes of history, he was lowered by the magistrates of his country to the ranks of the vilest criminals.

Prestige, according to Le Bon, "can also be worn away, but more slowly by being subjected to discussion. This latter power, however, is exceedingly sure. From the moment prestige is called into question it ceases to be prestige. The gods and men who have kept their prestige for long have never tolerated discussion".

The above provides some important insights for our analysis of when investors' optimistic expectations can change and possibly lead to a panic. Investors' faith in equities can be eradicated suddenly if there is a serious danger of capital loss - a situation that may have arisen lately in the US, as stocks have been declining for the last two years - or if there is a sudden and unforeseen severe economic or political development (another recession, the bankruptcy of a major financial institution, war, an act of terrorism, etc). But, according to Freud, the catalyst for a panic can also be an insignificant event. Still, if I look at recent events, it is more likely that the "prestige" the stock market enjoyed as a result of its 18-year bull market (the "success" that Le Bon refers to) has slowly but increasingly been called into question. This is especially so, given the many earnings warnings, earnings disappointments and fraudulent practices that have come to light. Thus, although the TMT sector bubble has already been punctured badly, I expect that it will take quite some time before the idea is rejected that US stocks will always rise and outperform emerging markets like they did in the 1990s. Once it has been rejected, the idea will be out of favour for a very long time, as we know from Japan post-1990 and from other asset bubbles that came to an end (such as gold and silver after 1980). But for as long as the idea that stocks always rise is not totally rejected, markets will remain extremely volatile and the downtrend will be interrupted by recurring but short-lived, sharp bear-market rallies.

The reader might ask himself at this point why the 11 September 2001 terrorist attacks in New York and Washington DC did not lead to a total meltdown of the US financial market. After an initial period of weakness, we saw a very powerful rally into early 2002. There are two explanations in my opinion. When the attacks occurred, the investing community still had great faith in Alan Greenspan's ability to cushion any blow to the financial market and engineer powerful rallies like the one that followed the LTCM bailout in 1998. Moreover, in 2001, investors were still conditioned that every selloff was a buying opportunity - a notion supported by a flurry of articles arguing that the outbreak of war always provided great buying opportunities. The second reason for the sharp recovery was that the market began to discount the strong but brief economic rebound that occurred in the first four months of 2002 - and pundits interpreted that as the end of the 2001 recession and the beginning of a new economic expansion.

Propaganda has long been known to play a very significant role in the formation of crowds and their beliefs - a fact, that leaders such as Lenin, Stalin, Mussolini, Hitler and Mao understood perfectly well. Both Mussolini and Hitler had a low opinion of crowds, believing that they were incapable of achieving anything without strong leadership. Asked in an interview about his relationship with the masses, Mussolini replied that the masses were for him nothing more than a herd of sheep, as long as they weren't organised, and that he had to lead them in order to be able to govern - and the only way to do this was by means of "enthusiasm" and "interest".

What Mussolini meant was that in order to keep the masses in a state of easy manipulation (loss of critical faculty, credulous and receptive) and attached to their leader, they had to be relentlessly bombarded with propaganda. Needless to say, in order to keep the enthusiasm and interest of the masses alive, a tidal wave of lies eventuated. Hitler wrote in *Mein Kampf* that the masses, with their primitive minds, were far more inclined to fall prey to a "big lie" than a "small lie", because it was quite common for people to lie on a small scale, whereas the average person would shy away from big lies. Therefore, the crowd would never even contemplate that anyone might be reckless or bold enough to twist the truth to an extreme degree. (Leaders like Bill Clinton and Tony Blair seem to have recognised this fact as well.) Moreover, even if the truth were to be uncovered subsequently, doubts would remain.

According to Hitler, propaganda had to "forever" target the masses, "forever" repetitive and extremely simple. Also, it had to target the intellect of the least-educated people in the crowd, and the larger the masses were, the lower its quality had to be. There is no doubt in my mind that propaganda machines used to spread "big lies" have kept despots such as Hitler, Mussolini, Stalin, Mao, Saddam Hussein and so on in power for far longer than would otherwise be the case.

In the same way, an investment mania can be kept alive for much longer than one might think possible through clever propaganda which aims to continuously fuel the "enthusiasm" and "interest" of the investing public. This is not difficult to understand - given the widespread vested monetary interest in a never-ending bull market shared by politicians, economic policy-makers, corporate leaders, investment banks and other financial institutions, analysts, strategists, CNBC, CNN, financial websites, venture capitalists and the public itself. Just about everyone gains from rising equity prices, large transaction volumes, mergers and acquisitions, new issues, the launch of new financial products, large numbers of eyeballs or viewers, and so forth. Thus, even once a mania is well past its zenith, propaganda stressing the merits of equities will continue, leading from time to time to powerful bear-market rallies.

Moreover, the whole CNBC phenomenon should now be easier to understand in light of Hitler's views about the intellectual level of propaganda. What CNBC, whose profit depends on the number of viewers it can attract, must do at all costs is to maintain investor enthusiasm for buying and owning equities, and nurture the public's interest in financial markets with all kinds of "good news". That this can only be done for as long as stocks go up and people are making money ought to be clear. And therefore, it should come as no surprise that good news is usually heavily promoted, while bad news is frequently dismissed as irrelevant. If a stock rises by 10%, CNBC commentators will add fuel to the frenzy with enthusiastic comments - never mind that the same stock may have dropped by 98% in the previous five months! And, like the propaganda of the Third Reich, the opinions expressed by commentators (most of whom have an interest in keeping the market from declining) are extremely simple and repetitive in nature - productivity-led growth, no inflation, interest rates declining from their peak, stocks always go up, weakness is a buying opportunity, technology will drive the economy, corporate profits will remain strong, Greenspan (the leader) has already achieved a soft landing, oil prices will fall again, and so on.

I have nothing whatsoever against CNBC, but the problem as I see it is that modern broadcasting, which targets as large an audience as possible, never really analyses any issue critically. It seems that many media companies are only at the top of the viewer tables and lead the masses because they are themselves led by the masses. That such a dependence on the "low intellect" masses can become a danger both to democracy and capitalism ought to be clear. But, as Friedrich von Wieser (*Das Gesetz der Macht*, Wien, 1926) pointed out, the leaders give a movement a goal and a plan but the masses provide the power.

I should like to stress that, during a mania, the mood is not always euphorically optimistic. Investors overpaid for gold and silver (and also for hard currencies) in the late 1970s, not because they were optimistic about the future, but because they felt that the US Dollar would become worthless and that inflation would accelerate. So we can say that hard-asset booms are fuelled as much by pessimism about economic prospects as by optimism about a continuously high appreciation of the commodity in question (gold, silver, hard currency, diamonds, real estate and other perceived inflation hedges). In this sense, commodity booms are characterised by greed based on fear.

In financial manias, on the other hand, the fear element is negligible (the only worry is that your neighbour's investment club or your fellow fund manager is making more money than you in the market), and excessive greed and the desire to speculate is rooted in an optimistic mood about economic prospects, the world and profit opportunities. There is, however, an exception. In some countries, economic and social conditions can deteriorate to such a degree that investors buy shares for lack of alternatives. I am thinking here of countries that experience hyperinflation, but which maintain strict foreign-exchange controls. In such a case there is usually a flight to equities and under certain conditions to property. Also, in countries, where the financial system is about to collapse, investors who no longer trust banks rush to park their liquidity in equities (see Chapter 10).

Another common feature is that, during the boom, the mood is so optimistic and complacent that bad news is either ignored or taken to be the opposite. Take the IMF and US Treasury gold sales in the late 1970s. These sales clearly increased supply and would, therefore, eventually contain the gold market's advance. However, each successful auction was followed by another buying stampede. Or take the US bond market decline in 2001: Some people argued that it was bullish for equities because all the money would flow into equity funds!

I must stress that, in a mania, the optimistic mood is not limited to the public. In the late 1970s, the corporate sector was busy diversifying into oil or taking over natural resource companies at excessive prices. Conoco, Marathon Oil, Santa Fe International, Kennecott, Anaconda, Cyprus Mines, Delhi International, Getty Oil and Superior Oil were all bought right at the peak of the commodities boom. Most of these acquisitions were highly praised, but proved to be disastrous once commodity prices fell. The potential for error in the judgment of corporate management is beautifully illustrated by Standard Oil of California's aborted attempt to take over Amax in 1981 for US$75 per share. Since the shares of Amax fell to US$10 per share in 1985, the management of both companies deserve high marks for their vision: Standard for thinking that Amax was worth US$75, and Amax for telling its shareholders that it was worth even more, thus successfully defending the company's independence (Amax shares subsequently declined by 90%). More recently, the US corporate sector kept on buying its own shares at high prices or took over other companies at what can only be described in retrospect as "crazy" prices - and financed the acquisitions with debt, endangering their financial strength. Another symptom of executives' bullish stance was the technique of selling naked puts against their companies' share prices, which proved an extremely costly exercise once the market fell out of bed after March 2000.

In a mania, the mood of professional investors typically tends to be more cautious than that of the public. But that does not prevent institutional investors from participating in the boom. Near-term performance orientation, indexation and money flows into the best performing funds force them to be in the sectors with the strongest upward moves. In a mania, therefore, the expression one hears again and again is "we can't afford *not* to be" in a market or sector. In the late 1970s, many fund managers felt that oil and resource stocks were overvalued. But since, in 1980, only these shares moved up, funds had to buy them to perform. Similarly, during the Japanese stock market bubble, many foreign fund managers thought stocks were overvalued. But to be out of Japan would have seen them underperforming international indices - so foreigners participated in the mania, albeit reluctantly. More recently, it was evident to many fund managers that hi-tech stocks were priced for perfection. But, since most stocks had not performed after 1998 and only the TMT sector was driving the market higher, fund managers had to be in this sector in order to show performances that would attract new buyers to their funds.

In short, in a buying frenzy there is, through the effect of contagion, a universal drive to participate in the whirlwind of speculation. No one wants to miss out: The public because it sees only profit and no risk, and argues "what else can I invest in - there are no alternatives"; the corporate sector because it overestimates demand for its products or is overly sanguine about future prospects; and professional investors because they cannot afford to be out of a rapidly appreciating market (during the South Sea Bubble of 1720, a banker remarked: "When the world is mad, we must imitate them in some measure"). In this respect, the US stock market boom that lasted until 2000 was interesting. Most of the institutional investors we know were actually quite cautious. But, ironically, they took comfort in the fact that the public (the least informed investors) was pouring money into equity mutual funds. It was, after all, as McCulloch noted - in speculation "one individual derives confidence from another."

International propagation

While minor manias are local events (the rubber boom of the early 1900s, SBICs in the early 1960s, gambling stocks in 1978, US farm land in the late 1970s), major manias have an international character. The South Sea stock bubble and bust of 1720 London coincided with the boom and collapse in France of John Law's Mississippi Scheme, as well as widespread speculation in insurance shares in other Continental European countries (see Chapter 12). British investors flocked to Paris to participate in John Law's companies, while Continental investors (especially from the prosperous Netherlands) bought shares in South Sea stock (as a result, sterling strengthened by more than 10% against the florin in the first half of 1720).

Earlier, I described how in early 1873, a building and stock market boom swept through Europe and the US. But when the crisis erupted in Austria and Germany, it spread to Italy, Holland, Belgium and then to the US, because European investors, having been large buyers of US railroad securities and land in the Western Territories in the early 1870s, were forced to withdraw their capital to repay loans at home.

The international propagation of a boom inevitably leads to a crisis of international character. In the late 1920s, European stock markets also rose sharply, if less spectacularly than the US, and from the 1950s right up to 1973 markets around the world performed well (many European markets, however, had peaked by 1962). Thus, after 1929 and after 1973, all major markets declined. In recent years, the US stock market rise also led to strong performances among the European bourses; and in the years leading up to the March 2000 peak for the Nasdaq, hi-tech loaded indices such as the Neuer Markt in Germany, the Jasdaq and the Kosdaq also soared. Thus, after 1929, 1973 and March 2000 all markets that focused on similar sectors declined in concert.

The financial-asset bull market of the 1980s and 1990s was an equally global phenomenon. Taking the early 1980s as a starting point, stocks were up significantly by the late 1990s in industrialised countries as well as in emerging economies, and new stock and futures exchanges opened for business in many former socialist countries. And never has there been such a proliferation of new financial instruments as over the last 20 years or so. Since I began working on Wall Street in 1970, I have seen the introduction of listed options, interest rate, currency and index futures (and options on these futures), a wide variety of derivative products, swaps, etc - and not just in industrialised countries but practically everywhere in the world. Thanks to modern communication, media that broadcast financial news into every corner of the world, and sophisticated banking and custodial facilities, as well as the removal of most foreign exchange restrictions, financial markets really have moved into a "new era". As capital can now easily flow from one country, stock exchange and investment theme to another, the financial markets have become very closely interrelated. This connectivity can lead from a boom in one country to another boom somewhere else. Similarly, an investment mania in one place is transmitted across borders through "psychological infection" or "contagion" of investors and speculators. Investors argue, "if such and such a market soared last year, why can't our market do the same this year", or "if Japan sold in 1989 for over 70 times earnings, why can't ours sell for 100 times?"

The result of this international propagation of speculative excesses resembles volcanic eruptions - violent booms spring up, quite unpredictably, in different regions and sectors at different times. We seemed to have been - and still are to some extent - in a rolling financial orgy, which similar to a rising tide lifts all boats, but at different times and with different intensity. As we have seen, a tidal wave of speculation raised the Japanese stock market in the late 1980s, then moved on to the emerging markets in 1993 and then culminated in the Nasdaq bubble in the US.

The role of foreigners in investment booms

Because of the proliferation of a truly global capital market, foreign capital flows are an increasingly important source of demand (and supply) for national markets, currencies and even individual stocks. Foreign investors, however, do not exhibit counter-cyclical behaviour, but tend to behave like lemmings. Foreigners usually do not enter markets near their lows, or for that matter, proceed with direct investment, when economic conditions are depressed, as was the case in the mid-1980s in Latin America or in China following the Tiananmen massacre of 1989, or more recently in Asia. Their buying usually occurs when everything looks bright, that is, near the market peaks or in the period just following a peak in the belief that the first phase of a bear market is just another correction in a rising market.

Thus, foreign investors are frequently responsible for the final spike in a market in two different ways. Directly, by increasing their purchases in the final phase of an investment mania. Indirectly, as follows: the locals become accustomed to rising foreign capital inflows and, therefore, are more and more convinced that these flows will continue to grow in perpetuity. Consequently, the locals, expecting foreign capital to boost prices ad infinitum, continue to buy themselves or do not sell in the hope of realising even greater capital gains.

I have never seen a boom during which investors did not ardently believe that foreigners would drive prices higher. During the gold boom of the late 1970s, everybody focused on the seemingly insatiable appetite of Middle Eastern investors for gold. In the mid-1980s, Americans thought Japanese purchases of US real estate would never end. During the Japanese stock market bubble, foreigners were expected to come in because they were underweighted in Japan, and in the 1993/94 emerging-markets boom, all emerging countries were expecting continuously rising foreign portfolio flows. In my experience, foreign demand is usually grossly overestimated during investment booms. In the last few years, Americans have taken for granted that foreigners will forever finance their current account deficit by making direct investments through massive portfolio flows into US bonds and equities (see Figure 4). Whether, as some pundits believe, this time will be different because of a lack of alternatives, remains to be seen - but in my opinion, there will come the day when foreigners will become net sellers of US assets.

Figure 4

FEEDING THE FIRE

US capital inflows, 1980-2002

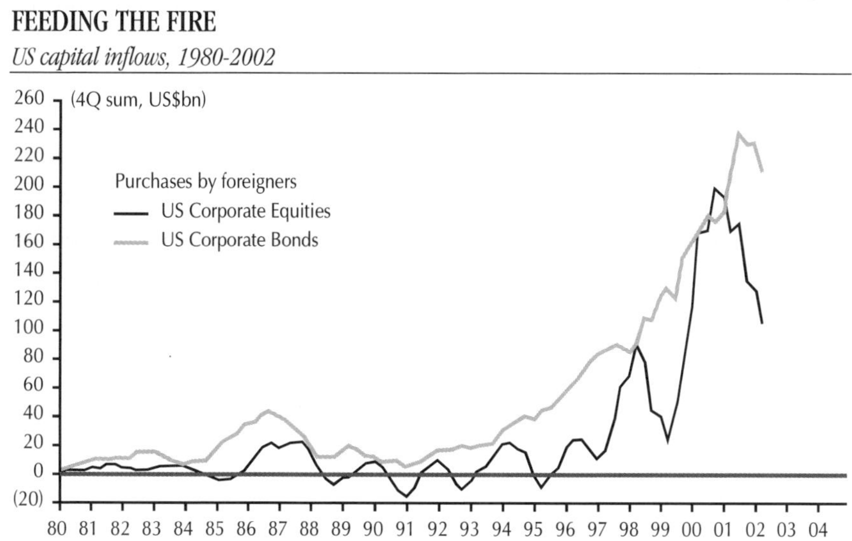

Source: Federal Reserve Board, Flow of Funds Accounts, Ed Yardeni / Prudential Securities (www.prudential.com).

Investment pools and new issues

Characteristic of every investment mania is the formation of investment pools and a rising number of new issues flooding the market. The first public companies - such as the Dutch East India Company of 1604, or the South Sea Company and John Law's Mississippi Company in the 1720s - were more like investment pools than companies with a specific business purpose.

This is evident from a new issue launched during the South Sea Bubble, described as: "A company for carrying on an undertaking of great advantage, but nobody is to know what it is." But the first major wave in the formation of investment trusts took place in the late 1920s (see Figure 5). This was followed by a wave of mutual funds in the late 1960s. More recently, as we all know, another wave of mutual fund formation has taken place and this time on a global scale.

Economics cannot satisfactorily explain the phenomenon of the proliferation of a large number of investment companies coinciding with major market peaks. Economic theory suggests that demand increases when prices decline, and falls as prices rise. But in the case of speculative markets, the opposite seems to be true. When stock prices were low in the 1930s and in the 1970s, hardly any new investment companies arose. But, in recent years, with equities richly priced, new investment companies have sprung up like mushrooms (Japanese Zaitech and Tokkin funds became popular near the market's high, see Figure 6). In America, since investment clubs are easier to form and dissolve than investment companies, their manic activity amplifies this "anomaly". According to Robert Prechter (the Elliott Wave theorist), investment clubs in the US did not start forming as fast as they dissolved from 1975-76 until 1987, when 987 clubs were formed. The annual total of investment club formation did not exceed 1,000 until 1992 but in the late 1990s, interest among investors in pooling their funds soared (partly stimulated by the Beardstown Ladies' apparent success which was documented in a bestselling book, but eventually proved to be another hoax) and thousands and thousands of investment clubs were formed every day.

Figure 5

MONEY POOLS . . .

Equity funds and the stock market - United States, 1925-1955

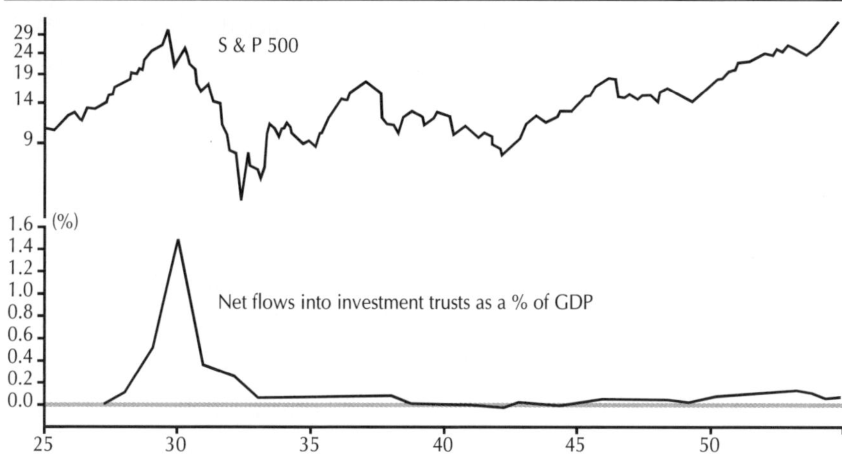

Source: *The Bank Credit Analyst.*

Figure 6

. . . ON BOTH SIDES OF THE PACIFIC

Equity funds and the stock market - Japan, 1982-1996

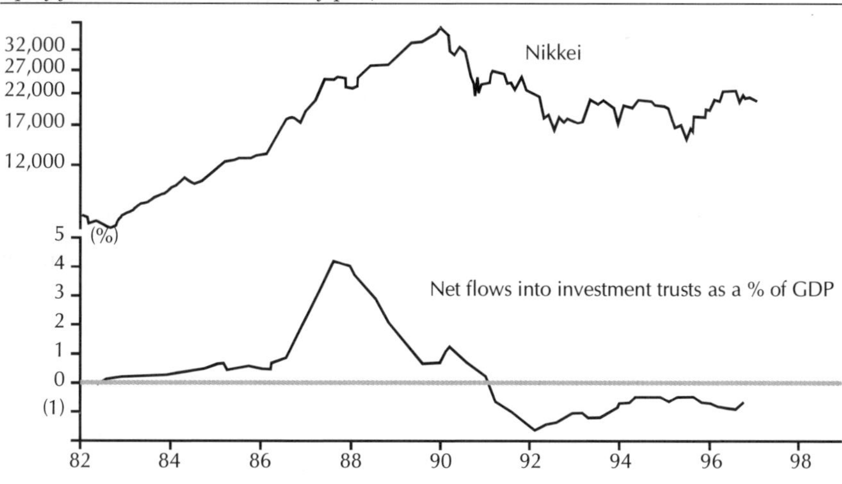

Source: *The Bank Credit Analyst.*

With regard to net inflows to the US mutual fund industry it is interesting to note that remarkable shifts in composition have occurred from time to time. Whereas the bulk of money went into bond funds (77% in March 1987), by 1993, net inflows were about evenly distributed between bond and equity funds. However, in the late 1990s and in 2000, almost all the money was allocated to equity funds - particularly to hi-tech and growth funds (see also Chapter 2, Figure 1). More recently, however, the flows into bond funds have picked up again. Now, considering that bonds made an important high (about 80%) in 1986, which was not exceeded until 1993 - the heavy allocation of money to hi-tech funds in the late 1990s is another indication that the US stock market is likely to fail to exceed its March-2000 high for several years.

Investment booms not only lead to the formation of a large quantity of investment pools, but to an avalanche of new issues. Each canal, land and railroad boom of the 19th Century did so. The new-issue calendar was heavy in the late 1920s and late 1960s and in emerging markets in late 1993. During the oil and natural resources boom of the late 1970s, energy and mining shares were floated. During the 1983 mini technology mania, those stocks dominated the new-issue calendar. Then came junk bonds in the mid-1980s. In the late 1990s, it was first the turn of China-related stocks (Beijing Investment's IPO in 1997 was 400 times oversubscribed) and then of all kinds of hi-tech and internet shares. Excessive speculation is particularly evident when IPOs are grossly oversubscribed (remember some Chinese H and B shares in 1996 and 1997, and internet-related shares in the late 1990s) and when they jump to huge premiums on issue day. Furthermore, the larger the number of new issues concentrated in one industry (river boat gaming, biotechnology, real estate investment trusts, country funds, hi-tech and internet companies, etc), the more likely it is that such an industry is approaching a longer-term or cyclical high.

Towards the end of a new-issue boom, offering prices tend to become excessive and the quality of companies going public also deteriorates. Still, as is the case with so many other mania syndromes, the ultimate degree of the "madness" is difficult to predict.

Price movements and volume during the boom

Non-speculative markets may trade with low volume in a narrow trading range for many years (the oil, gold and silver market in the 1950s and 1960s, the Taiwan stock exchange between 1975 and 1985, etc). In speculative markets, however, prices tend to rise parabolically and sometimes even vertically at the very end of the boom. During the manic phase, volume is also unusually high, and daily price swings are wide and erratic. Also, while non-speculative markets can move sideways for a considerable time (sometimes 20 or more years) and repeatedly test their lows, speculative markets usually end in a blow-off. The spike price peaks are then immediately followed by sharp falls and subsequently the highs are never reached again or, at least, not for a very long time (10, 20, or more years). In the speculative blow-off phase of a stock market, the leadership becomes very narrow. Usually, only a handful of stocks soar and continue to lift the index while the broad market becomes lethargic (the new high list contracts). Although the American stock market reached its final high in the summer of 1929, most stocks had already peaked out in 1928.

Similarly, the US market made its high in January 1973, led by the "nifty fifty". But the broad market had already performed poorly in 1972. In 1979 and 1980, the broad market did not move much, but oil, drilling and mining stocks soared and led the market to its late-1980/early-1981 high. In Japan, banks and other financial issues pushed the market up to its final high at the end of 1989. More recently, most stocks performed poorly after 1998, but the TMT sector became red hot all over the world. Thus, one of the most reliable symptoms of a stock market mania coming to an end is that speculation becomes extremely concentrated among a few issues, usually in just one sector. Also, frequently the last speculative up move is accompanied by a surge in low-quality stocks or companies, which change their line of business (or sometimes even just the name) and suddenly focus on the hot sector. In Australia, in the late 1990s, a number of mining companies became dot.com companies with the sole purpose of boosting their share prices.

The US stock market of the last few years exhibited all these symptoms.

While most stocks no longer rose or even fell after 1998, hi-tech, media and telecommunication shares and along with them the Nasdaq went ballistic. The rise of the index up to its peak in March 2000 (see Figure 7) reminded me of the Tokyo market in the late 1980s. In fact in the five years leading to its high in March 2000 the Nasdaq significantly outperformed the Nikkei between 1985 and its 1989 top. I might add that, when comparing the peak valuations of previous new-era stock bubbles, such as took place in 1929, 1969, 1973 and 1983, with the recent US stock market mania, we note that stocks were in 2000 more expensive than ever before.

Figure 7

THE PRICIEST PARTY EVER

Nasdaq, 1992-2002

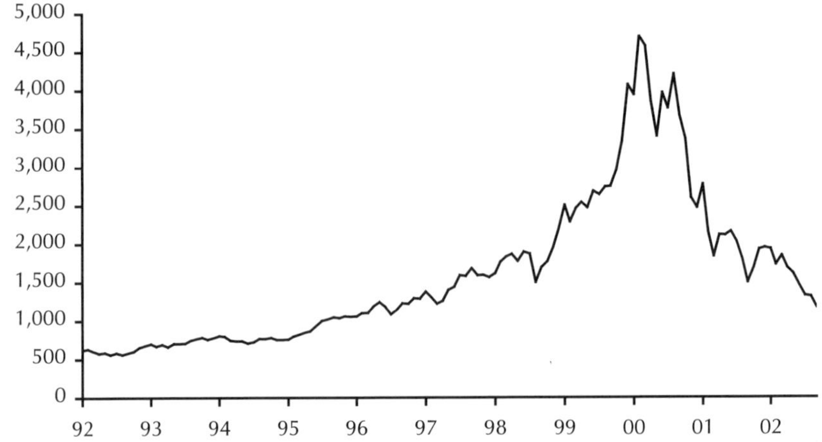

Source: Datastream.

We explained above that, in a bubble, huge volume is concentrated among one group of stocks. In 2000 and even up to recently, the most actively traded issues have been technology stocks. Moreover there were frequently IPOs whose first-day volume exceeded their issue size. Nasdaq volume has also regularly exceeded New York Stock Exchange volume - another sign of a "truly" new era or mania.

Boomtime literature, media and conferences

According to Irving Fisher, many books were published in the late 1920s to show that stocks provide higher returns than fixed-interest securities. In August 1929, John Raskop, then chairman of the Democratic National Committee wrote an article in *Ladies Home Journal* entitled, "Everybody Ought to Be Rich", in which he urged readers to save US$15 per month and put it into the stock market via an "Equities Security Company" (yet to be formed). The late 1920s also witnessed the emergence of many stock-picking letters and investment magazines (*Business Week* was first published in 1929).

In the late 1970s, a large number of books emerged stressing the merits of investing in high-P/E growth stocks. Winthrop Knowlton's famous book, *Shaking the Money Tree*, came out in 1972, just ahead of the 1973/74 bear market, which devastated growth stocks. Then, in the late 1970s, a flurry of new releases dealt with *Crisis Investing* (1979), *New Profits from the Monetary Crisis* (1978) and *How to Prosper During the Coming Bad Years* (1979). All argued that the US Dollar would become worthless (the US Dollar index bottomed out in late 1979 and almost doubled by 1985) and that hyperinflation, which would push precious metal prices into the sky, was around the corner (gold and silver topped out in January 1980). Investment conferences and newsletters focused principally on gold, silver and oil- and energy-related stocks. It was a time when the "gold bugs" enjoyed huge popularity and drew massive crowds to their seminars all over the world. Headlines and magazine front covers regularly featured oil, OPEC, gold, the Hunt brothers, SaudiArabian billionaires, the Shah of Iran, Texas, Denver, farmland, diamonds, the weak US Dollar, stocks like Schlumberger, Halliburton, Dome Petroleum, Tom Brown and the flow and power of petrodollars. On TV, one either watched Dallas, then the most popular show, or followed the results of OPEC meetings and the whims of Sheikh Yamani and King Saud. Needless to say, Wall Street's oil analysts commanded a huge following as well, and most research (thick reports) focused on energy-related stocks.

Shortly before the crash of 1987, business books focused on mergers and acquisitions and famous takeover artists, arbitrageurs, and their financiers - people such as T. Boon Pickens, Ivan Boesky, and Michael Milken featured regularly in the press. Later, just before the end of the Japanese stock and real estate bubble, it was the time of "Japan Inc", when books documented the superiority of the Japanese system and numerous research reports justified Japan's high stock valuations.

In recent years a flurry of books described successful investment strategies, famous stock investors, and how the Dow would rise to anywhere between 36,000 and 100,000. High technology or the internet featured on the front page of magazines as often as oil and gold in the late 1970s, and new investment letters, business magazines, and business news channels were springing up like mushrooms all over the world. Particularly popular were books about how novice investors such as the Beardstown Ladies could make a fortune in the stock market. In *Main Street Beats Wall Street* one was taught "How The Top Investment Clubs Are Outperforming The Top Investment Pros". This is not surprising, because small investors could easily identify with the Beardstown Ladies and follow their investment strategies (in the 1960s, *How I Made US$2,000,000 in the Stock Market* by the famous dancer Nicolas Darwas was a bestseller).

Another sign of a mania is when bookshops allocate disproportionate shelf-space to business books and books about the market in which the mania is taking place. In the late 1990s, the selection of books about the stock market and successful hi-tech entrepreneurs became awesome.

When and how does an investment mania end?

Unfortunately there is no precise answer to this question. But consider this: Manias frequently end when the pros and the insiders become cautious or outright bearish, while the public rushes into the market. In the late 1920s, contrary to popular belief, many professional stock traders were bearish. In the late 1970s, many pros shorted gold and silver as well as oil stocks (Dome Petroleum had a big short position). During the 1983 hi-tech mini mania, Commodore and other stocks had huge short positions and most foreign hedge fund managers had already shorted Japan in 1988 and early 1989. Similarly, large professional foreign exchange speculators got badly burnt by being short the Yen too soon in 1994 and early 1995.

At the end of an investment mania, corporate insiders also step up sales of their company's shares, recognising their overvaluations, or in anticipation of less favourable business conditions. It is not uncommon to find chief executive officers who make very bullish comments at investor conferences, but then proceed to sell their shares. At a number of hi-tech companies, the executives cashed out in the late 1990s, but continued to make glowing comments to the investment community about the prospects of their companies.

Another characteristic of a bubble is the emergence of swindles. However, and this is important to understand, the revelation of fraud usually only comes after the bubble has burst, because for as long as the boom went on and share prices rose, nobody cared about dubious practices and fraudulent behaviour. But once the bubble has burst, investors become more critical, ask questions and look for scapegoats. Moreover, while during the boom overleveraged positions and all sorts of accounting gimmicks boosted earnings artificially, once the bubble has burst, extraordinary profits turn quickly into extraordinary losses. In *Manias, Panics, and Crashes*, Kindleberger devoted an entire chapter to "The Emergence of Swindles". He wrote: "The propensities to swindle and be swindled run parallel to the propensity to speculate during the boom." Kindleberger said swindling is demand-determined, because "in a boom, fortunes are made, individuals wax greedy, and swindlers come forward to exploit that greed". Moreover, he argued, that fraud "increases further in financial distress from a taut credit system and prices that stop rising and begin to decline".

Among other dubious and illegal activities, Kindleberger cited the systematic embezzlement from the Royal African Company, the East India Company, and the Union Pacific by insiders who skimmed off profits due to stockholders through contracts with companies they themselves controlled. He cited contemporaries who referred to the 1920s as "the greatest era of crooked high finance the world has ever known". According to Kindleberger, the revelation of the swindle, fraud or defalcation:

> ... makes known to the world that things have not been as they should have been, that it is time to stop and see how they truly are. The making known of malfeasance, whether by the arrest or surrender of the miscreant, or by one of those other forms of confession, flight or suicide, is important as a signal that the euphoria has been overdone. The stage of overtrading may well come to an end. The curtain rises on revulsion, and perhaps discredit.

In fact, every mania involves some sort of Ponzi scheme. Carlo Ponzi was a swindler who, in 1920, devised something akin to a chain letter, whereby early investors were paid out of money invested by late buyers. Ponzi promised to pay 50% interest for the use of 45 days' deposits, based on a strategy to arbitrage International Postal Union coupons bought with depreciated exchange rates abroad and to exchange them at higher fixed exchange rates for US stamps (for which the coupons could be redeemed) in the US. The scheme was purely fictitious. Ponzi took in close to US$8 million, but had only US$61 worth of stamps in his office when arrested. His "pyramid" scheme, the success of which depended on attracting new depositors at an ever-accelerating rate, collapsed when a number of depositors began to suspect that they wouldn't get their money back and attempted to withdraw their funds.

Ponzi schemes resurface from time to time in emerging economies where a sufficiently large number of naive people can be found who believe that 50% returns on short-term deposits can be achieved. However, it is a fact that for most investments, sooner or later, early buyers will be paid out by late buyers. This would seem to be particularly true in the case of investment booms and manias, which require a large number of participants to fuel and maintain the upward price momentum. The boom ends when the amount of money flowing into the popular investment theme starts to decelerate, as buyers become suspicious about the sustainability of positive returns, or when the supply eventually exceeds the demand. Thus, the early buyers of US stocks in the 1920s, 1960s and 1990s did well, while the latecomers were badly burnt by the subsequent market declines. The same was true of the gold and silver booms, and of the Japanese stock market bubble in the 1980s.

In fact, I would argue that one of the principal features of an investment bubble is the existence of a giant Ponzi scheme. Entrepreneurs no longer start businesses with the objective of achieving recurring profits from their investments, but rather seek to set up ventures in order to flog them off to speculators through IPOs and secondary offerings. At the same time, investors almost totally abandon the concept of investing according to strict value criteria and real economic merit. Instead they purchase stocks solely because they figure that, as more and more people join the investment party, someone - "the greater fool" - will be willing to pay an even higher price than they did for their stocks.

Ponzi schemes raise some fascinating questions. Why are so many people repeatedly fooled by them? And why did Carlo Ponzi's scheme fail in less than a year, while other similar schemes have lasted so much longer? Investors get caught again and again in Ponzi-type chains because of the very high returns they promise. Had Carlo Ponzi promised to pay a return of only 2% for a 45 days' deposit (102% annually), no one would have bothered to invest with him. But with the promise to pay 50% for such a deposit (162,450% annually), he was able to attract quite a sum, considering that he was operating only in Boston. His main problem was the regional scope of his scheme. Had he been able to operate globally with the support of CNBC, CNN, internet chat-rooms and a variety of questionable stock advisory services, his operation could have flourished for much longer. The money flows that financed his operation would have continued for as long as the incoming funds were sufficient to pay out the redeeming depositors. And the longer this had continued, the more confident the investing crowd would have become in the merits of his financing skills, possibly to the extent of attracting even central banks to invest their reserves with him. Moreover, Ponzi's promised returns were such that even if interest rates had risen to 20% per annum, they wouldn't have jeopardised his scheme. It was his inability to raise money fast enough and the loss of investors' confidence that brought him down.

Now suppose that Ponzi had reinvented himself. Instead of a questionable character operating regionally in Boston and promising to pay

50% for 45 days' deposits, we have the credible and proven capitalistic system and Alan Greenspan as well as the US Treasury guaranteeing that every time there is a crisis there will be a bail-out - as was the case with Mexico, Asia, LTCM and most recently Brazil. Thus, the system and Alan Greenspan, and not Carlo Ponzi, were vested by the global investing public with the power to underwrite a 20% per annum return for the US stock market, as was the case from 1982 to 2000. Even better, the system and Greenspan, supported and cheered on by the media, were believed to guarantee an almost 100% annual gain from investing in a basket of technology stocks, which was the return of the Nasdaq 100 over a few years leading up to March 2000 (up nine times in five years and almost four times from 1998 to 2000).

A Ponzi scheme may not fly with a 20% guaranteed annual return, but a sure 100% return is a tempting proposition for any investor. So, for as long as the Nasdaq could sustain these returns, ebullient investors reallocated more and more money from conservative investments such as short-dated bonds, money market funds, CDs, and even value stocks, into the high-tech sector. Even rising interest rates cannot derail this process, because the returns promised by a Ponzi scheme are so much higher than interest rates.

The breaking point, however, is reached when insufficient new money flows into the market, or the supply of equities begins to exceed the demand, and investors start to experience significant capital losses. Only when this happens do investors lose confidence and scramble for the exit, bringing about a meltdown. This was apparent in the US when, in 1999, a total of 555 companies went public (an all-time record) and raised US$73.6 billion. But that US$73.6 billion represented only 27% of the issuing companies' market caps. In 2000, however, the lock-up period for most of these issues expired and, in addition to the then prevailing heavy new-issue calendar (in early 2000, there were weeks when new issues raised over US$8 billion), insiders were able to sell more than US$200 billion of previously locked-up shares.

Also symptomatic of investment manias are pros who turn bearish too early, sell short, and get very badly squeezed first (I speak here from personal experience). This is so because the most overvalued and questionable stocks tend to have the biggest short positions. Therefore, at the end of an investment mania, we frequently have a massive short squeeze in the most speculative sector of the market, as the momentum players target stocks with large short positions in order to force the shorts to cover.

Towards the tail end of the mania, some divergences or inconsistencies in the market become evident. As mentioned above, the leadership becomes extremely narrow. The broad market no longer performs, but one sector continues to roar ahead. In 1980, driven by energy stocks, the S&P peaked out in November. But the American Stock Exchange Index, which contained the more speculative oil stocks, continued to rise until August 1981 (thereafter, this index tumbled within nine months by close to 40%). In 2000, the Dow Jones Industrial Average peaked out in early January, but the Nasdaq and the S&P powered ahead until March.

Lastly, at the end of the mania, some cracks begin to appear. Now and then, corporate results disappoint and individual stocks react with freefalls. Sometimes, the results are still very good, but since the market has already discounted "better than expected" earnings, stocks also fall. Sometimes, as in 1929, the economic news deteriorates; sometimes, political or social conditions worsen.

In the late 1990s and in 2000, all the excesses that typically accompany a major mania were evident. In addition, signs that the final stage - the blow-off - was taking place were also obvious, as the Nasdaq rose almost vertically while "old economy" stocks performed poorly.

The difference between whether one is dealing with a mini mania or a major mania is that in a minor mania, such as in 1961 and 1983, only the most popular sectors, which attracted most media attention and speculation, totally collapse. Following the mini bubble in the early 1960s, SBICs, electronic, and bowling stocks collapsed by over 85% and following the 1983 tech stock mania, issues like Apple, Datapoint, Oak Industries, Micron Technology, TeleVideo, Wang, Computervision and Commodore collapsed on average by more than 80%. Most of the best-performing stocks of the mini mania and the vast majority of new issues that came out in the boom phase either vanish completely, go into oblivion, or fail to reach their manic phase highs for a very long time. However, after the busts, the indices recovered and made new highs.

The bust of a mini mania is, at the very least, always followed by a major change in leadership. *Conversely, the bust of a major mania is not only followed by a change in leadership, but also by a change in direction for the entire market, with the major stock market indices and the majority of issues not making new highs for a very long time (generally 10 to 25 years and sometimes never).* I should like to again stress the point of changing leadership, because so many investors around the world still believe that hi-tech will lead the next market advance. I have earlier explained that in the 1920s the hot sectors were appliances, radios, movies and electric utilities. From Figure 8, it is, however, clearly visible that after the 1929 to 1932 crash electric utilities did not lead the market. In fact, whereas the Dow Jones Industrial made its low in 1932, it took the Dow Jones Utilities until 1941 to bottom out. Moreover, while the Industrial made a new high in 1954 (25 years after its 1929 high) it took the Utilities until 1965 to better its 1929 high. So, the bursting of a bubble always leads to a change in leadership - another reason why I doubt the US stock market will lead the next major advance (see also Chapter 12).

When we say that no mania is recognised until it is too late, this is especially the case for major manias, which are always justified by academics and experts on the grounds that the fundamentals have taken a quantum leap for the better and therefore justify the lofty valuations. After the October 1929 crash, most investors, including the bears, thought that the market decline had gone as far as it could. The same happened in Japan in late 1990, when the index had fallen to around 24,000, in the gold market in 1980 when the specie had fallen within two months from its high of US$850 to US$450, and more recently in the US where most strategists remained very positive throughout the 2000-01. The tricky part of manias, after all, is that one underestimates both the upswing and the subsequent collapse. Consequently, very few people survive an investment mania unscathed. The bears are either mildly hurt because they underperform on the upside or badly damaged because they go short too early while the bulls are eventually devastated because they "overstay" by remaining too optimistic too long.

Figure 8

LONG CLIMB BACK

Dow Jones Utility Average, 1929-1989

250
200
150
100
50
0

1929 1935 1941 1947 1953 1959 1965 1971 1977 1983 1989

Source: Arnold Investment Counsel, Inc.

Lastly, we must understand this: In a bubble, many people realise that there is excessive speculation and that the bubble will burst one day. But the lure of large profits tempts even the most sophisticated investors to participate in the late stage of an investment mania because, in the terminal blow-off, during which prices rise almost vertically, profit opportunities with leveraged positions are vast. In addition, these sophisticated people believe that by following all kinds of economic and technical indicators they will be able to correctly anticipate the timing of the bust and get out in time. The problem in a major mania, however, is not to be found in the real economy. The problem really is the mania itself, which can fizzle at any time and then, because of its disproportionate size in comparison to the real economy, threatens the whole system.

This is what happened in the late 1980s in Japan and prior to 1997 in Asia. There were at the time few excesses in the real economy, but the problem was the grossly inflated stock and real estate markets. Thus, once these bubbles burst the entire economy suffered badly, a topic I propose to address in the following chapter.

CHAPTER NINE

Opportunities in Asia

> The art of progress is to preserve order amid change and to preserve change amid order.
>
> *ALFRED NORTH WHITEHEAD (1861-1947)*

In the preceding chapters, I have written extensively about business cycles and investment manias because emerging economies, due to their relative smallness and rapid economic growth rates experience very pronounced swings in business conditions and in their financial markets. The same way small cap growth stocks tend to be more volatile than well-established blue chips, emerging stock markets tend to be more volatile than the enormous stock markets of the Western industrialised countries.

Early days in Asia

When I moved to Hong Kong in 1973, Asia was still a poor region and, with the exception of Japan, price levels were extremely low compared to the industrialised world. In Hong Kong, one could rent a luxury flat for about US$800 per month (current rent is approximately US$7,000), the initial fare in a taxi cost less than US20 cents, the harbour ferries cost next to nothing and the Cross Harbour Tunnel was still yet to open. The place was so cheap that, when shopping, I frequently asked whether quoted prices were in Hong Kong or US Dollars (at the time the exchange rate was US$1/HK$5). South Korea was so poor that local banks had problems raising money in the Eurodollar market and in Taiwan, where strict foreign exchange controls prevailed, confidence was so low that US Dollars sold for a 20% premium on the black market. Taiwanese people were then still obsessed with the threat of communist China.

Asian cities like Seoul, Taipei and also Singapore were real dumps with hardly any modern buildings. In those days, Taipei was, however, well known as a nightlife paradise. Rich Chinese from all over Asia would go there over the weekend, stay in the most luxurious President Hotel with its renowned Champagne Room nightclub, and patronise "Asia's most beautiful girls" at the famous "Singapore Ballroom", where an orchestra would play Tangos, Waltzes and the Cha Cha. Indonesia had no stock market and the entire market caps of Hong Kong and Singapore were only about US$2 billion and US$1 billion respectively.

There were no fax machines or cellular phones, listed options were in the future, the word "derivatives" did not exist, *The Asian Wall Street Journal* was not yet in circulation - and in Jakarta and Manila a working telephone was a rare thing indeed! Furthermore, Asia was not yet littered with foreign brokers. There were just a few American brokers, such as Merrill Lynch, EF Hutton, Bache & Co and White Weld (where I worked) - and a small number of British brokers with small offices: WI Carr, James Capel and Vickers da Costa. And while the British firms were placing Asian stocks with British institutions, American brokers focused exclusively on the sale of US stocks to Asian investors. In the seventies and early 1980s American portfolio investors had practically no investments in Asia, a few Japanese stocks aside.

Between 1973 and 1978, I spent a lot of time in Japan and was immensely impressed by its economy and hard-working people. I also regularly visited Taiwan and South Korea and felt that they had economic potential similar to Japan, only starting from a much lower base. I invested some savings with a South Korean and Taiwanese broker. When people asked me how I would ever get my money out of these countries (both had strict forex controls), I replied that I intended to leave my money in these promising economies until their strength would give them confidence to remove any form of currency restriction.

The popular investment themes in the early 1970s were steel mills, ships and shipyards. Every country wanted to have its own steel mills, equipped with the latest technology - the larger the better. Meanwhile, well-to-do families became aware of the potential of the shipping industry because shipping magnates such as YK Pao, CY Tung (father of Hong Kong's present chief) and the mysterious Indonesian Robin Lo had become Asia's richest and most respected businessmen, regularly featured on the covers of business magazines. Every wealthy family wanted to own some ships. This mania was facilitated by the zeal to get into the ship-lending business by local and international banks and the finance companies they established for this purpose. Shipping loans were considered to be as profitable as mortgage-backed securities are today, regarded as totally risk-free. This ship-owning investment boom led to huge orders for new ships, from which the shipyards in countries like Japan and South Korea benefited temporarily.

The 1970s, however, were not easy: The oil crisis and the 1974 recession hit most Asian countries hard. Many steel mills became white elephants and tanker charter rates began to fall, bringing huge losses for ship owners and their lenders. But recovery followed - with resource-rich countries such as Indonesia and Malaysia (oil) experiencing mini booms in the late 1970s. Ironically, the greatest oil-stock boom took place in the Philippines, alas a country with no oil! But as we, now, all know - following the massive fraud at BRE-X Minerals - Philippine geologists' findings have to be taken with a grain of salt. Mining and oil stocks aside, Asian investors were, however, not particularly interested in equities in the 1970s. Their attention focused on copper, gold and silver and in "bucket shops" all over Asia gold was traded day and night. During the gold mania of the late seventies, I was running Drexel Burnham Lambert's Hong Kong operation, and, at night, our office resembled a casino. Crowds of gamblers would come to our premises to trade the precious-metal markets ferociously - naturally on high leverage, which led to huge losses for all Hong Kong-based commodity brokers when the market collapsed in early 1980.

Nobody in those days paid attention to "initial jobless claims", "consumer confidence" gauges or "change in nonfarm payrolls" statistics. What everybody anxiously awaited were the results of the US Treasury and IMF gold sales to see how much of the gold had been taken up by Middle Eastern investors and central banks. I may add that in the late 70s commodity brokers and gold dealers made fortunes. In Hong Kong everybody wanted to become a commodities futures broker - whereas a career as fund manager, research analyst, equity strategist or bond or stock salesman was hardly considered. In fact there were then no Asian equity strategists and just a handful of fund managers, such as Wardley, Jardine Fleming and Schroeders.

Boom years

During the 1982 global recession, a number of Asian countries suffered badly as petrodollar flows dried up and real estate markets including Hong Kong and Singapore collapsed. But, then, led by strong US consumption growth, which brought about an explosion in the volume of Asian exports, the region really took off. Between 1985 and 1990, Asia was truly firing on all cylinders. The Japanese economic miracle was at its height and seemed unstoppable. Because Asian export growth averaged around 25% per annum, the region was flush with liquidity from rapidly growing trade and current account surpluses. Not surprisingly, Asian stock markets went through the roof - with Taiwan, South Korea, the Philippines and Thailand all rising by approximately ten times between 1985 and 1990 while Taiwan shot up by more than 20 times (see Chapter 2, Figure 2).

In fact, if ever there was a "best of all possible worlds," we had it in Asia in the late-1980s. The liquidity-driven Japanese boom had spilled over to Southeast Asia, whose exports did not yet feel competition from China, Mexico or Latin America in the lucrative and fast-growing US consumer market. At the same time, and this is important to remember, Southeast Asia came into the benefit of rapidly rising foreign direct investment, as there was practically no competition from other emerging regions. The Iron Curtain still existed, and poor infrastructure made it difficult for foreign manufacturers to capitalise on China's low labour costs. Neither country had capital markets. There was still very little interest in Latin America, as this continent was just coming out of depression and hyperinflation. Portfolio investors who wished to invest in emerging economies had practically no choice but Southeast Asia. In short, in the late 1980s, Asia (ex-China) went through a period of once-in-a-lifetime prosperity as its exports met the consumer demand of the rapidly expanding industrialised Americas, Western Europe and Japan - and this, practically without any competitors. The export led growth in those years brought Asia a period of unprecedented prosperity, but at the same time numerous seeds were sown for problems that emerged in the late 1990s. How so?

The seeds of destruction

During the 1985-90 boom, Asian exports were growing at about 25% per annum - far above the long-term trend. Clearly, this was unsustainable. Export growth had to slow for a variety of reasons.

The 1990/91 recession in Europe and the US brought Western consumption growth to a standstill and, in the post-1990 recovery phase, to far more moderate rates of growth as demographic trends deteriorated and because consumers remained burdened with large debts accumulated in the 1980s. Also, after 1990, Japan went into long-lasting recession and, therefore, reduced its imports of Asian natural resources (lumber, plywood, base metals, etc).

In the meantime, a number of other developing nations - especially China - went through structural economic and political reforms, opened up, and their exports began to compete in the large Western consumer markets. This had an impact because, in the 1990s, Asia's price levels (especially wages and real estate) had increased to the point where many traditional exporters - such as South Korea, Taiwan, Hong Kong and Thailand - had become far less competitive in world markets.

But even without the new competition, Asian export growth would likely have slowed as its export volume had grown from US$400 billion in 1985 to US$1.4 trillion in 1996. Clearly, it was easier to grow exports at 30% per annum when Asia's exports made up less than 20% of total global exports, as was the case until the mid 1980s, than in the early 1990s when they, including Japan, accounted for close to 30% of global exports.

In addition, just as exports began to slow, imports started to swell. With rising prosperity, Asia's *nouveaux riches* developed an insatiable appetite for foreign brands. The successful Asian businessmen wanted Ferragamo shoes, Cardin suits, Gucci belts, Hermès ties and Ralph Lauren shirts. His female companion also wanted to distinguish herself from the masses with a cornucopia of imported dresses, shoes and jewellery (in the process resembling a grotesque, kitsch, overloaded Christmas tree). Asia's *jeunesse doree* wanted Mercedes, BMW, Harley Davidson - and to furbish their flats with Italian furniture and Japanese consumer electronics. First they drank lots of Hennessy XO and later switched to expensive French wines and Tequila, smoked Cuban cigars, and travelled and shopped more and more overseas. Thus, as Asian consumption rose, imports of consumer goods soared.

At the same time, imports of capital goods also increased at a torrid pace. By the early 90s, companies had become accustomed to the 25-30% export growth rates of the late 80s and perceived the boom to be a permanent fixture. Manufacturing capacity was added everywhere in order to meet the West's "inexhaustible" consumer demand (a typical "error of optimism"). Foreign companies now increased their direct investment in Asia to capitalise on the promising domestic markets. But, while FDI had a favourable multiplier effect on economic growth in Asia, it also led to further deterioration of the trade accounts. Practically all capital goods had to be imported (usually at inflated prices, in order to get even with the local partner or for tax purposes) and, once the factories were operational, higher-value assembly parts such as car engines had to be purchased from foreign suppliers (principally Japan). So, at the end of the 1980s, import growth rates began to exceed export growth rates, which led to a gradual but visible deterioration in Asian trade surpluses.

During the late-80s global prosperity, we also saw inbound tourism increasing at about 20% per annum, which provided Asian hotel owners with very high rates of return. For Asian families flush with cash, to own a hotel - or, even better, a golf course - became glamorous (in the case of Thailand, hotels were also a convenient way to launder money) and, in the expectation that tourism would continue to grow at 20% per annum, hotels popped up everywhere. Alas, with the Iraq war, tourism slumped and, thereafter, grew only slowly as Japan's outbound traffic suffered from recession. Additionally, new tourist destinations such as Eastern Europe, China, Vietnam and Latin America opened up and competed with established Asian resorts. As a result, many Asian cities (notably Bangkok) became glutted with hotel rooms, which subsequently led to low occupancy rates - particularly after the Asian Crisis in 1998 and 1999. In the meantime, just as inbound travel was slowing, Asians began increasingly to travel to Europe, Australia and the US. East Asia's travel surplus now started to dwindle and led, along with worsening trade balances, to further deterioration in current account balances.

During the late-80s boom, excess liquidity badly inflated Asia's price level. As we noted above, this initially found its way into stock and real-estate markets. Property prices also benefited from rapidly progressing urbanisation as people flocked to the cities on whose outskirts new export-oriented factories mushroomed. In turn this rapid industrialisation led to strong employment gains and wage increases. In the meantime, foreign companies opened offices and built factories in and around Asian urban centres, and staffed them with well-paid expatriates, which increased the demand for real estate even more. Thus, residential and commercial property prices in urban agglomerations rose several-fold (see Figure 1). Again, people forgot that in the 70s and early-80s Asian real estate prices had been steady or even falling - relentlessly rising real estate prices on the back of strong domestic and foreign demand became regarded as a permanent feature, and an unprecedented construction boom swept across Asia - leading to glutted property markets practically everywhere as early as 1990.

In most Asian countries, the real and financial-asset inflation in the period 1985-90 and, following a respite between 1990-91 (see Figure 1), again after 1993 far exceeded median real wage gains. Income and wealth disparity went up. Families who owned property became immensely rich while workers and pensioners who rented their homes were impoverished, as they had to pay higher and higher rents or were forced to borrow heavily to buy homes at inflated prices. Naturally, at some point, this widening wealth inequality had to bring about a slowdown in consumption (see Chapter 6).

In summary, then, we note that the late-1980s economic boom in Asia created a set of conditions that had to lead to serious problems sooner or later. What surprised me was that the problems occurred later than expected. But several factors contributed to this delay, which, in fact, aggravated the severity of the downturn after 1997.

Figure 1

INFLATING THE BALLOON

Hong Kong office capital value index, 1984-1994

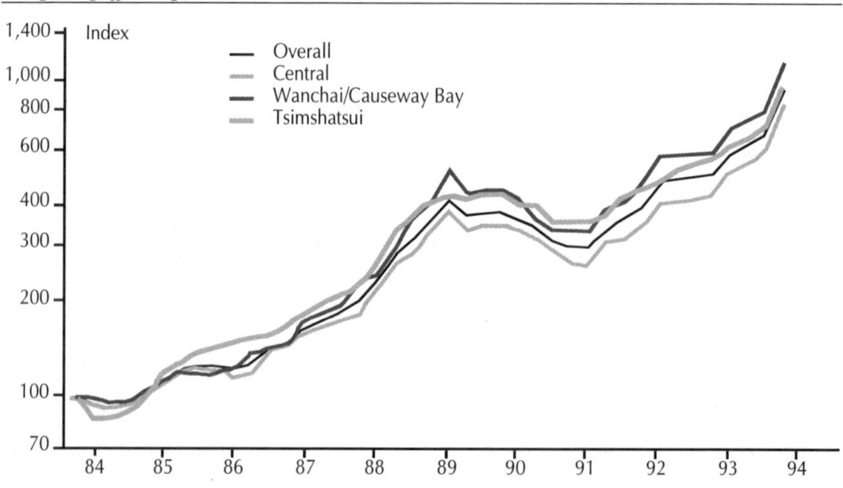

Source: Jones Lang Wootton.

The 1987 global stock market crash did not have a long-lasting impact on Asian stock markets. South Korea's even rose on the day following the New York crash of 19 October, as did Sri Lanka - presumably because nobody had heard of the previous day's events in New York. By 1988, most Asian markets had already exceeded their 1987 highs, while the New York market was still well below its 1987 peak. Remarkably, at their 1989/90 peaks, the Taiwan and South Korean stock markets had risen from their pre-crash tops by 300% and 250% respectively (see Figure 2).

Indonesia, whose market had remained totally inactive and depressed until 1987, shot up by almost six times by 1990 (see Figure 3) and in Japan the Nikkei soared from a pre-crash high of 26,646 to 38,915 in late 1989. This sensational recovery in Asian stocks boosted investor confidence in the merits of equities and reinforced their belief that Asia was really something special and any setback in share prices simply created a buying opportunity.

Figure 2

OBLIVIOUS . . .

South Korea Composite Index, 1980-1996

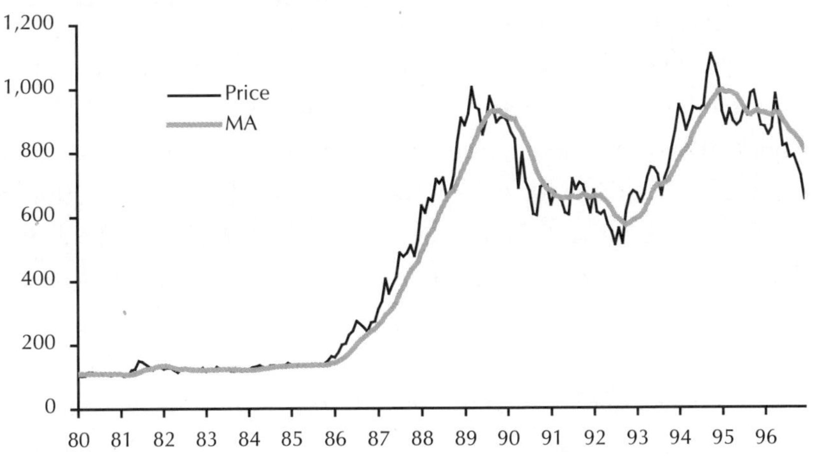

Source: Baring Securities.

Figure 3

. . . TO THE 1987 CRASH

Indonesia Jakarta Composite Index, 1983-1996

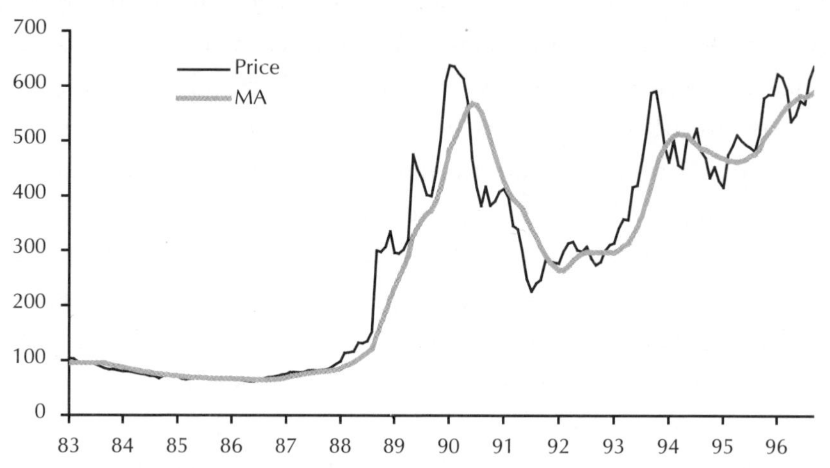

Source: Baring Securities.

The Japanese recession after 1990 and easy monetary policies in the US had a profound effect on East Asia. Since many Asian currencies were closely linked to the US Dollar, exchange-rate risks were perceived to be minimal. This led investors to invest more and more of their savings into higher-yielding Asian currency deposits. Furthermore, when Japanese interest rates collapsed and the Yen began to weaken after 1995, the famous Yen carry trade continued to finance Asia's growing current account deficits. I may add that, at the time, Asian leaders never criticised foreigners for borrowing Yen or US Dollars and purchasing Thai Baht, Malaysian Ringgit or Indonesian Rupiah certificates of deposits. Quite on the contrary, foreigners were encouraged to invest in these currencies because of these countries' fixed exchange-rate policies.

Then came the Mexican crisis in early 1995, which raised confidence in the infallibility of the Asian economies even further. Asia's incorrigibly optimistic pundits argued: "See, Mexico and Latin America have a financial crisis because they depended largely on portfolio flows. We in Asia, however, are recipients of far larger foreign direct investment than portfolio flows. And since foreign direct investment flows are far more stable than portfolio flows, which can leave a country overnight, Asia will never experience similar problems." Needless to say, no Asian strategist then predicted that - after the Mexican Peso collapse in 1995 and as a result of the North American Free Trade Agreement (Nafta) - Mexican exports would become extremely competitive and displace some of Asia's exports (notably textiles and garments). Growing trade deficits were dismissed as irrelevant because they were - so one argued - due to imports of capital goods, which were designed to produce consumer products for export. The problem, however, was that the imported capital goods increasingly produced consumer goods for the *domestic* market, which further worsened the trade account.

The Asian hangover might have struck when emerging stock markets fell sharply in 1994. It was, however, postponed by the Mexican bailout and, so, made worse. After the global bond market rout in 1994, bond prices around the world rallied strongly with spreads between lower quality bonds and US treasuries falling continuously after the 1995 Mexican bailout. Therefore, performance-oriented and yield-hungry investors, disregarding any risk, were only too eager to invest in domestic and foreign-currency-denominated fixed-interest securities of emerging economies as they could profit from both falling interest rates and narrowing yield spreads. In addition, in the US stocks continued to rally strongly in 1996 and 1997 and as a result, money continued to pour into emerging economies. These money flows, which increased in the two manic years preceding the 1997 Crisis (see Chapter 2, Figure 4), kept Asian markets buoyant and allowed its companies to issue shares and foreign-currency bonds and convertible securities in the international capital markets.

The mania

By the early 90s Asia had become crowded with local and foreign brokers, investment bankers, portfolio managers and battalions of private bankers - whose role in the Asian boom-and-bust cycle must be mentioned too.

Having lived in Asia since 1973, I have yet to meet a Thai, Philippine, Malay or Indonesian broker who was not consistently bullish about his respective market. These brokers travelled the world with the sole purpose of getting foreign investors to purchase securities in their own capital markets. Excessive confidence, rising nationalism and self-awareness in Asia also had an impact. A Thai broker negative on Thailand would have been akin to a traitor, a national disgrace. In Hong Kong, after the 1997 Crisis, the head of the monetary authority vowed not to place any funds with foreign fund managers who were believed to have sold the Hong Kong Dollar short. And in Singapore, a foreign-based analyst uttering unflattering remarks about the island's economy could cost his employer valuable government-related investment business - and lead to his dismissal. Such facts do not shed a particularly favourable light on the quality of Asian leaders and government officials - although recent practices we find in the US do not seem to be any better!

In the 1990s, as the size of the Asian capital markets expanded rapidly, there was for a brief period a shortage of portfolio managers. A group of very inexperienced people joined the financial industry and we had Asian portfolio managers with an average age in the mid-20s and average investment experience of less than two years. Most of them focused only on what they perceived to be the "Asian Miracle". They had no idea what a map of Latin America or Eastern Europe looked like - nor the slightest knowledge about capital markets outside Asia or the importance of international capital flows. Their knowledge of economics was no better. When China began to open up in earnest in the 1990s and grow exports at a frantic pace, not once did we hear that this would gradually displace other Asian countries' exports or attract a shift of FDI flows from Thailand, Malaysia and Indonesia. Also, since their livelihood depended solely on raising as much money as possible for their Asian funds, they engaged, in the years preceding the Asian Crisis, in a massive campaign of totally discrediting any sceptic of Asia's economic miracle.

When Paul Krugman - admittedly an economist of controversial reputation - published a critical article about Asian growth prospects, numerous Asian fund managers and strategists basically said he did not know what he was talking about. One article, by a noted Asian economist, published in the *Asian Wall Street Journal* on 6 November 1996, concluded: "For the time being, the tigers' structure looks firm. They will sooner or later ride out their present cyclical problems." To be fair, I have to mention that several Asian economists - including Paul Schulte, David Shairp, David Scott and Jim Walker - had become concerned. However, their comments were frequently guarded or carefully worded as they drew strong protests.

Not to forget, either, was the role international investment banks and private bankers played in this game of self-denial and disinforming foreign investors. Having just undertaken costly expansions in the region, their principal concern was to place stocks and bonds of Asian issuers in the international capital markets. So, when one of their analysts was negative about a company or a country, he was silenced in order not to jeopardise that investment bank's chances of getting a corporate finance mandate or to participate in an underwriting syndicate. Similarly, many largely inexperienced private bankers told their private clients of the risk-free returns that could be obtained from borrowing foreign currencies and investing in Thai Baht or Indonesian Rupiah deposits using high leverage.

However, to blame the investment community solely for providing overly optimistic forecasts about the Asian economies would be wrong. After all, in 1993-96 numerous books were published with titles like Jim Rohwer's *Asia Rising* (resonant of the bullish "Japan Inc" books of the late 1980s) while "Asian Tigers" roared on business magazine front pages. The platitudes in books (strongly endorsed by the media) and newspaper articles were soon exceeded by academic papers on "Asian Values" (guess who paid the academics) - and how superior such values were for economic growth and capitalism. Needless to say, many Asian leaders strongly endorsed the extremely far-east-fetched views. Investor optimism about Asian stock markets was fuelled with buzzwords like "Asia's Consumer Boom", "The Rise of the East", "Asian Tigers" and "Paradigm Shifts".

Just to give the reader an idea of the irrational exuberance common in

Asia in the years preceding the Crisis, I reprint below some comments published in those days, which, incidentally, were almost to the word duplicated in the last phase of the US bull market in 1999 and 2000. In its 16 November 1995 issue, the *Far Eastern Economic Review* asserted that:

> What is happening in Asia is by far the most important development in the world. Nothing else comes close, not only for Asians but the entire planet. The modernisation of Asia will forever reshape the world as we move toward the next millennium. In the 1990s Asia came of age. As we move toward the year 2000, Asia will become the dominant region of the world: economically, politically and culturally. We are on the threshold of the Asian Renaissance.

Another Asian super-bull was John Naisbitt. In *Megatrends* (London 1993) he wrote that, "Asia was once the centre of the world and now the centre is again returning to Asia". He followed up in the *Global Paradox* (London 1994) by emphasising that, "Growth in the Asia Pacific region is as close as we can get to a textbook example of the global paradox - the bigger the world economy, the more powerful its smallest players." In the meantime, *Business Week* mused in its November 1993 issue that, "the region's banks have some of the most solid capital ratios in the world, averaging 6% to 9%. And its developers, airlines and utilities have remarkable little debt, typically no more than 20% of equity... Governments and business have avoided the borrowing that has left others in trouble".

I do not dispute that some of these claims are apt for Asia's very long-term prospects. But what happened prior to the 1997 Crisis was in essence the hyperbole we have recently experienced in the US. Businessmen, brokers, government officials, investment managers and economists - with very few exceptions - put self-interest ahead of objective reportage. Even to a layman it should have been quite obvious that the fundamental positions of many Asian economies were showing signs of stress - not just prior to the Crisis but since the early 1990s.

The bust

As explained above, Asian economies had run into overcapacity problems in the early 1990s. From Figure 4, compiled by Jones Lang Wootton in September 1994, it was obvious that there was already an oversupply problem in the Thai property market. And after global interest rates rose in 1994 and the outbreak of the Tequila Crisis in early 1995, Asian stocks declined sharply. Table 1 shows how Thai property stocks tanked between 1994 and early 1995. As mentioned, the Mexican bailout granted a new lease of life to the Asian bubble. Stock markets recovered in the second half of 1995 and then moved in a trading range, in Thailand until late 1996 and in some other markets until the spring of 1997. But once the Asian Crisis hit, the trading ranges gave way to unforgettably violent moves on the downside, accompanied by a collapse in currencies (see Figure 5). All the Thai property stocks listed in Table 1 - which, with the exception of Land & Houses, had all already declined by around 80% from their highs by the spring of 1995 - approached or hit zero in 1998. The Crisis spread like wildfire, first to the rest of Asia and then, in 1998, to Russia.

Figure 4

FOR RENT . . . ANYONE?

Thailand office supply and vacancy (Grade A)

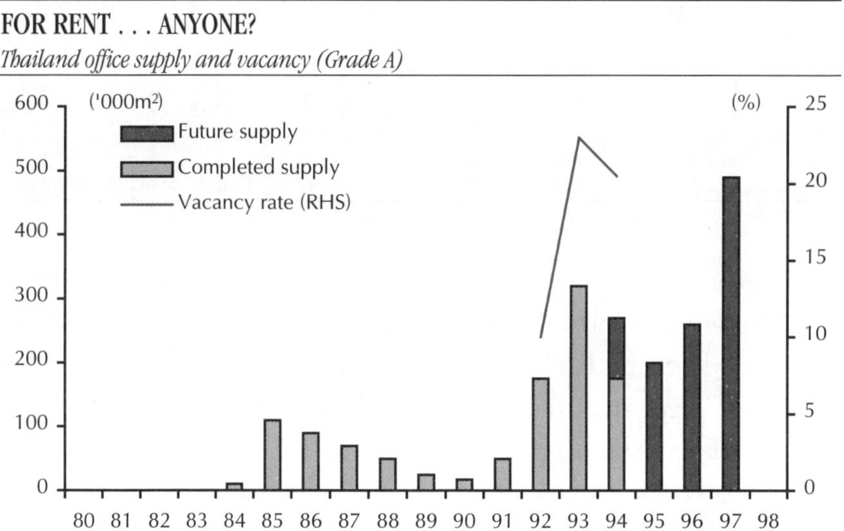

Note: 1994 figures are as at September. Source: JLW Research.

Figure 5

FALLING OFF A CLIFF

Jakarta Composite Index (US$ terms), 1995-1999

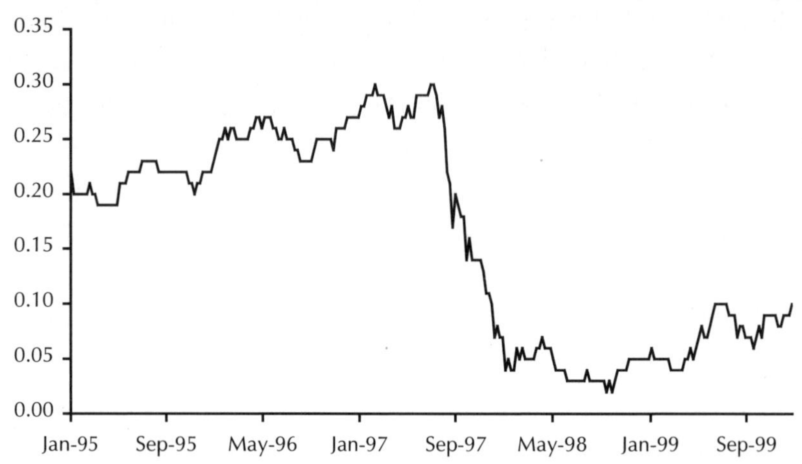

Source: CLSA Asia-Pacific Markets.

Table 1

BURNING BAHT

Performance of selected Thai property stocks from January 1994 to April 1995

Name	Ticker	Price 4/1/94 (Bt)	Price 21/4/95 (Bt)	Price performance (%)
Hemaraj Land & Development	HEMRAJ	352.00	56.00	(84.09)
Supalai	SUPALI	300.53	47.74	(84.11)
Somprasong Land	SOMPR	280.00	42.75	(84.73)
Raimon Land	RAIMON	151.24	33.25	(78.02)
Bangkok Land	B-LAND	170.00	31.00	(81.76)
M.D.X.	MDX	195.00	38.50	(80.26)
Tanayong	TYONG	119.00	31.00	(73.95)
Rattana Real Estate	RR	56.00	15.50	(72.32)
Land & Houses	LH	716.00	362.00	(49.44)

Source: Marc Faber Limited.

Markets frequently trade in a range for several years after reaching a "milestone" high and only then totally collapse - as was the case for the Asian markets after 1997, the oil market after 1985 and Japan after 2000. But what aggravated the Asian Crisis was, as indicated above, that a combination of unusual conditions prolonged the boom, which led local and foreign companies to continue to invest and expand their businesses in Asia in the 1990s. In turn, their overinvestment, and the Asian consumer boom which led to growing trade and current account deficits, were financed by complacent, happy and credulous foreign investors at a time when the region's fundamentals were actually deteriorating. Thus, it is fair to reiterate that foreign capital flows, which were encouraged by the Mexican bailout, enabled the Asian boom to last much longer than would have been the case had Mexico not been rescued, and consequently the pain or hangover after the Crisis was also far more serious than initially perceived.

To be sure, the severity of the Asian Crisis left even me - then a great sceptic of the boom - shell-shocked. Having always been interested in economic history, I had some knowledge of booms and busts in emerging economies, of investment and financial manias and their inevitable painful outcomes, and of massive wealth destruction as a result of wars, expropriations and deflationary depressions. I had also experienced first-hand the 1973/74 global bear market and recession, the depressions which followed the oil boom in the oil producing regions of the world, the Japanese contraction and, in 1993/94, the slump in Russia on the demise of the communist order. *But, I had never read about, or seen, the kind of total economic breakdown and wealth destruction - on such a massive scale, in such a short period of time, and against all expectations - as we saw in Asia in the six months following the onset of the Crisis.*

Just think of it. Had anyone predicted that the Thai Baht would fall from 25 to 54 against the US Dollar and the Indonesian Rupiah would collapse from 2,500 to less than 15,000? Asians would have loudly mocked such a forecaster and sent him by ambulance to the asylum. Even I, a sceptic, found a bearish October forecast by Condor Advisers hard to believe (see Table 2). But by November 1997 their predicted slide in exchange rates one year out was already exceeded by the Rupiah and the Baht, and their six-month target for the Philippine Peso and the Malaysian Ringgit was reached in December 1997.

Table 2

A PRESCIENT BEAR

Condor's Asian foreign exchange and index forecasts, 31 October 1997

	Current	3 months	6 months	1 year
Baht/US Dollar	40	43	46	50
Ringgit/US Dollar	3.40	3.90	4.50	4.75
Rupiah/US Dollar	3,600	4,200	4,800	5,000
Peso/US Dollar	34.70	40.00	45.90	48.00
SET equity index (Thailand)	445	400	360	325
KLSE comp index (Malaysia)	662	530	420	400
PSE comp index (Philippines)	1,813	1,540	1,300	1,200
JSE comp index (Indonesia)	503	430	360	325

Source: Condor Advisors LLC.

But, I was not only shell-shocked by the violence, intensity and self-feeding momentum of the Asian Crisis - I was also deeply concerned about the global economy and our ability to understand the much-discussed "new era" phenomenon. It really seemed to me that the world economic equilibrium that existed prior to the breakdown of communism and the globalisation drive had been punctuated and we were moving into uncharted waters. There was then simply no way to know how the world would look in two or three years. Would the Asian Crisis pass and be quickly forgotten like Mexico in 1995, or was it the opening salvo to a 1930s-type global deflationary depression - or, like Latin America in the 1980s, would some countries or even the whole world experience hyperinflation?

The Crisis gave me at the time an impetus to study the economic and financial trends carefully because I also realised that the type of crisis Asia experienced would also provide some outstanding investment opportunities. As we have seen before, according to Kondratieff, a crisis is only one of three basic phases in an entire capitalistic cycle - *upswing, crisis* and *depression.* Thus, following the Crisis a depression was likely to occur, but at the same time the basis for an upswing would also be laid, which stocks would obviously discount well in advance.

As I have explained before, Asia's rapid economic expansion came from strong export growth, brought about by strong consumption growth in the US at the time of Reagan's expansionary economic policies (rising budget deficit) beginning in the mid 1980s. This "displacement" in Asia - brought about by spectacular export growth in the late 1980s - was, when export growth slowed in the 1990s, replaced by an extensive expansion of credit (debt-inflation according to Irving Fisher) and led to an overexpansion of the economic process. By introducing general overinvestment and an abnormal qualitative distribution of credits (largely into real estate and hotels) it disrupted the economic system (see Chapter 6 for Röpke's overinvestment theory).

In this respect the economic upswing and the boom in Asia was no different to any other boom. As had been the case for canals, railroads and the opening of new markets in the 19th Century, the "new era" expansion in the US in the 1920s and the Texas oil boom in the late seventies - the lure of enormous profits led businessmen and governments to go deeper and deeper into debt. Remember Irving Fisher: overindebtedness is brought about by "new investment opportunities" and "easy money is the great cause of overborrowing".

A unique crisis?

However, what was different in the case of Asia and also other emerging economies in the 1990s was that corporate debts were largely accumulated in foreign currencies because foreign-currency loans and bonds carried lower interest rates than domestic instruments. Another important difference to other emerging-economy booms (Latin America in the late 19th Century and late 1970s, Russia between 1895 and 1915, etc) was that, in the 1990s, corporate and government bonds as well as equities replaced syndicated and government-to-government loans as a prime source of finance. Thus, whereas in 1980 international institutions (the World Bank, the Asian Development Bank, etc), governments and commercial banks had supplied 80% of the capital that flowed into emerging economies, these institutions combined accounted for less than 25% of the money flows into emerging economies in the 1990s, while over 75% of the money came from non-bank private creditors and equity investors.

Simply put, emerging economies in the 1990s were financed not by banks - which traditionally held their loans to maturity and had in the past not marked them to market on a daily basis - but by performance-oriented mutual funds, hedge funds and other institutional investors. The private sector and governments in emerging economies that thereto had depended largely on bank loans, gained access to the open global equity and credit markets in the 1990s. How this shift came about is not entirely clear, but the reluctance of banks to extend credit following the Latin American crisis in the early 1980s, the process of securitisation of financial assets (Brady bonds), the global financial bull market driven by excessive liquidity, increasing risk-taking on the part of the investing public, massive privatisations, the removal of foreign exchange controls, the opening of new economies, modern technology, information and communication systems, and the belief that free and largely unregulated markets would allocate resources most efficiently - all contributed to this structural change in global finance.

Another change in the financial structure concerned the use of leverage. Most financial institutions, including banks, and even individuals became in the 1990s leveraged hedge fund type operations - borrowing short term and investing in longer term high yielding bonds or borrowing in a low-interest-rate currency (Yen) and investing in higher-yielding currencies (Thai Baht, Indonesian Rupiah, etc). And while there was hardly anything wrong with these structural changes in global finance, it is easy to see that they brought along far higher volatility. Performance-oriented institutional investors and their managers who were compensated based on their results tended to invest in rising market momentum - thus prolonging and exacerbating the boom - but ran for the door once prices began to slip.

In this respect, the Asian Crisis was rather unique. The American financial and economic crises of the 19th Century were principally caused by tightening monetary conditions in Europe, which reduced capital flows to the US - then an emerging economy. But our Crisis was not caused by tighter monetary conditions elsewhere. Instead, a sudden loss of confidence spread like a bushfire throughout the region and led to collapsing currencies, financial asset prices and real estate values.

Discussing the onset of a crisis, Kindleberger (in *Manias, Panics, and Crashes*) refers to *causa remota* and *causa proxima* that precipitate a crisis. In the case of Asia, the remote causes were rising trade and current account deficits (Figure 6 shows the sharp deterioration of South Korea's current account position in the years before the crisis), reckless real estate speculation, excessive capacity expansion in industries, fraudulent practices, the opening of China and collateral market-share losses on export markets, etc. The immediate cause was *a reversal of expectations* among a few foreign financial institutions (hedge funds, banks, etc) and some local well-to-do families - and this must be stressed, since foreigners were later accused of causing the crisis. At some point in early 1997, some foreign investors but also some "smart" local money chose to unload their Thai Baht holdings and this got the ball rolling (I may add that contributing to the Baring Crisis of 1890 were German investors who stopped buying Argentine paper in 1888 and sold the country's bonds).

Figure 6

CRISIS *CAUSA REMOTA*

South Korea: Current account balance

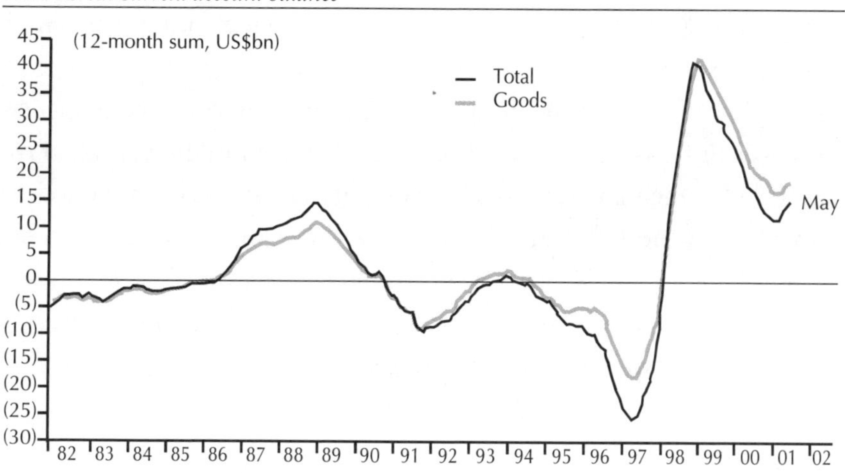

Source: CLSA Asia-Pacific Markets.

In addition, I must point out that only "a few" foreign institutions contributed to the onset of the 1997 Crisis, since the majority of foreigners were still happily investing in the Asian region right up to the crisis.

Besides massive corporate debt in foreign currencies - which led to an unfortunate mismatch of assets and liabilities, and far reaching changes in the structure of global finance, which brought about increased volatility - there was a third important difference between 1997 and previous crises. Consider in this respect the predominantly agrarian economy of the 19th Century, when financial markets were small compared to the real economy. The rural population was self-reliant and much trade was transacted through barter or for cash. By the late 1990s this had all changed. Financial markets - including equities, bonds, sovereign loans, mortgages, instalment credit, credit cards, derivatives, leverage, etc - had become disproportionately large compared to the real economy.

When discussing Kondratieff Waves, we stressed that cyclical fluctuations in the 19th Century were largely agrarian. When farm prices rose, the economy expanded and when they fell, recession followed. Similarly, the Texan and Middle Eastern economies of the late 1970s were driven by oil prices. Rising oil prices brought an unprecedented boom to Dallas and Houston, and to the oil producing countries of the Middle East, but, when oil stopped going up and then collapsed in 1985, depression followed with practically all Texan banks going out of business and Arab nations experiencing severe slumps. Thus we see that an economy depends largely on price movements in its largest or dominant sector. Since, however, financial markets had become so dominant in the *new era* of the late 1990s - the same way rising commodity prices had led to periods of prosperity in the 19th Century and falling prices to recessions, in recent years - *more so than ever before, rising financial markets themselves provided the fuel for an economic expansion while falling financial markets would inevitably lead to recession.*

Aftermath

When the Asian Crisis occurred, some economists took comfort from the fact that a number of Asian countries immediately began to run current account surpluses and that, therefore, the predicament was about to be defused (see Figure 6). But since the economies of Indonesia, Malaysia, Thailand, South Korea and the Philippines had contracted by over 50% in US Dollar terms, a quick recovery to the pre-Crisis level of economic activity was almost out of the question. In December 1997, car sales in Thailand had plunged by 73.9% year on year and were down for the full year by 38%. In Indonesia, the situation was even worse. GDP per capita collapsed by approximately 70% in US Dollars because of the Rupiah's free fall. Clearly, a devastating impact on sales had to follow (see Figure 7). From their highs in May-August 1997, car sales were down by 50% in December - at a time when the Rupiah was still trading at around 5,000 to the US Dollar. But in January 1998, PT Astra, Indonesia's largest car assembler, had to increase its prices by about 40-45% because of the cars' import content. Then as the Rupiah slid beyond 15,000, prices had to more than double just to break even.

In fact, what Asian countries faced when their currencies collapsed was a typical debt-deflation crisis, during which the real price level (expressed in US Dollars) collapses and reduces corporate profits and GDP while the real debt burden (the external debt denominated in US Dollars, Yen, etc) soars (see Figure 8). As a result of the devaluations the real debt burden in Asia rose even more than during the Depression years when the price level in the US fell by "only" 30%. In addition, we should be aware that when an emerging country devalues its currency in order to become more competitive, a heavy external debt burden usually makes such a policy quite ineffective, as the servicing and repayment of the external debt becomes more expensive in local-currency terms.

In addition to a rising debt burden because of a collapse in Asian currencies, two engines of Asian growth - exports and foreign direct investment - also suffered right away. While the sharp currency declines improved Asia's competitiveness somewhat, due to a high content of US-Dollar-denominated imported parts and raw materials, the impact of devaluation was muted. Furthermore, manufacturing cost advantages were initially offset by higher financing costs, especially if exporters had borrowed in US Dollars. Also, in many cases in the months following the Crisis, finance could not be obtained at any cost, thus production and exports slumped. So, the only reason for the abovementioned meaningful improvement in some Asian countries' trade and current account balances was less a function of rapidly rising exports and more because of a total freefall in the domestic economies - which led to a collapse in imports. Similarly, whenever the US economy goes into a serious recession, its trade and current account deficits also improve.

Collapsing imports in Asia in late 1997 also took a toll on Japanese exports to the region: In November 1997, orders for industrial machinery fell by 56% (72% of such exports go to Asia). Thus, even if Japan had been successful at reflating its economy in 1998, weaker exports would have offset any improvement at home. The Asian countries were unable to boost their exports to Japan, whose economy thus failed as an engine of growth for the region.

Figure 7

TAKING THE PAIN

Indonesian domestic automobile sales, 1995-1999

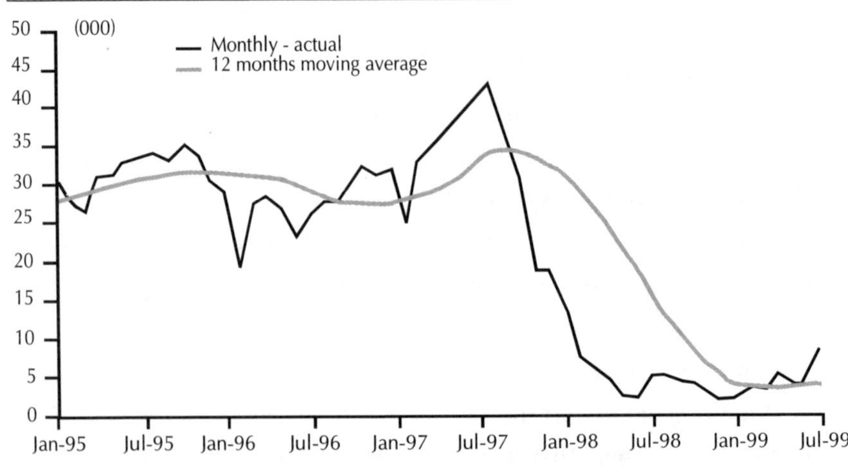

Source: Baring Securities.

Figure 8

DEVALUATION EFFECTS

Indonesian foreign debt, 1988-1998

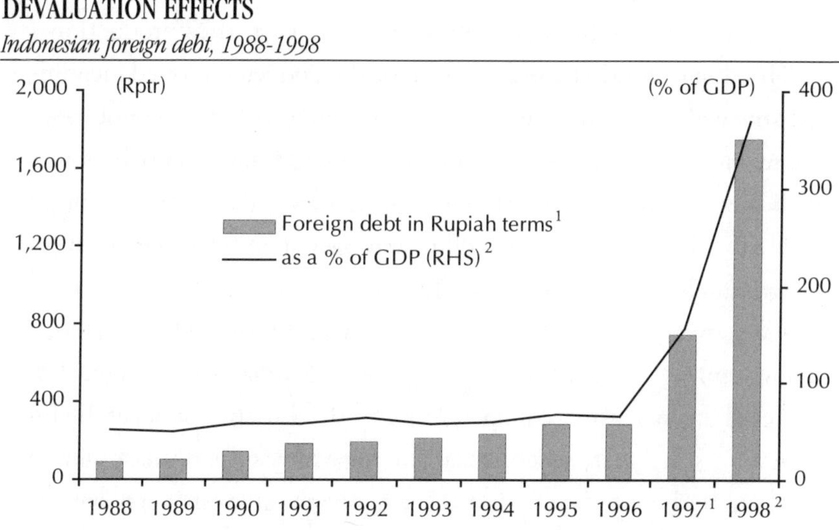

[1] Based on Rp6,000/US$. [2] Based on Rp13,000/US$. Source: World Bank, Indonesia, Bank for International Settlements, Reuters, Peregrine Estimates.

But then a fortunate event for Asia occurred in the autumn of 1998, when the Russian and LTCM crises led Mr Greenspan to ease monetary conditions aggressively, which led to the hi-tech boom of 1999 and early 2000. Consumption then picked up in the US (doubling the US trade deficit), which created a recovery in Asian exports (see Figure 9). In addition, domestic consumption stabilised relatively quickly and also provided some stimulus for an economic recovery in late 1998 and 1999. But whereas foreign direct investment did not recover as much as economists had expected, it did not remain totally depressed. Whereas some foreign companies decided to take advantage of devaluation-depressed prices, they no longer came to Asia to build car assembly plants, hotels and manufacturing facilities - due to existing overcapacity. Instead, they came to acquire existing facilities and companies. This boosted the value of existing assets, which had sold at deep discounts to replacement cost, and also saved several local companies - but it did not have the same stimulative multiplier effect on the economy as the undertaking of new projects. In addition, because of a lack of funding and the inability to access the international capital market, badly needed infrastructure projects were postponed or abandoned.

There was another reason for the muted recovery of foreign direct investment in Asia. We have seen earlier that in the 1990s, the economic environment for most Asian countries changed as China had become a mighty competitor on export markets and was squeezing many countries that had relied on rising exports for economic growth (see Figure 10). But unfortunately for its neighbours, Chinese competition was not confined to exports. Increasingly in the 1990s, because of its highly competitive manufacturing position and high-potential domestic market, China attracted an increasing volume of FDI at the expense of other emerging economies. In fact, even local manufacturing companies in Asia increasingly invested in China to take advantage of its very low labour costs and much-improved infrastructure.

Figure 9

FEEDING AN ASIAN EXPORT RECOVERY

US merchandise trade balance

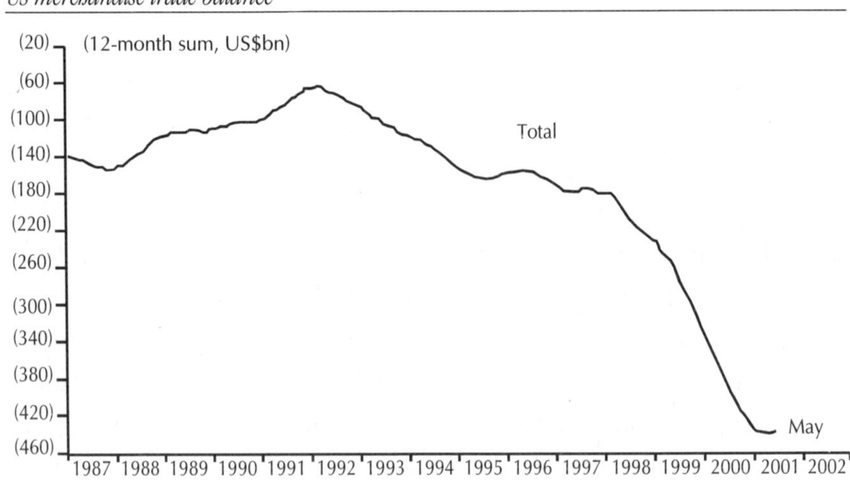

Source: Ed Yardeni / Prudential Securities (www.prudential.com).

Figure 10

SQUEEZING OUT THE NEIGHBOURS

Share of US imports

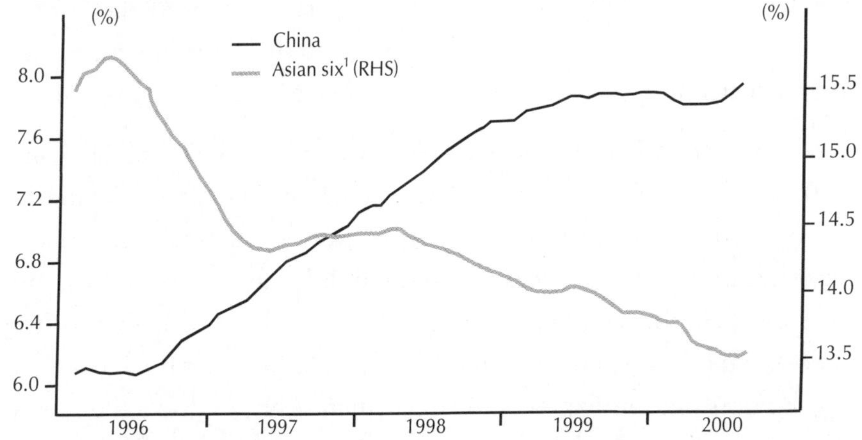

[1] Includes South Korea, Singapore, Malaysia, Thailand, the Philippines and Indonesia. Source: *Bank Credit Analyst.*

Thus, the Asian economies entered a difficult period. Exports recovered until 2000, but when the US hi-tech boom fizzled and its economy slowed they contracted once again. What did stabilise, particularly in resource-rich Asian economies, was a robust rural sector. As we have seen, in many Asian economies a larger portion of the population still lives in the rural sectors than in the urban centres, where manufacturing tends to be concentrated. The rural sector in all emerging economies depends largely on commodity prices. Among others, rising palm oil, coffee, cocoa and rubber prices boost rural sector incomes, whereas falling prices depress them - as was the case in the 19th Century US economy. Now, what happened during the 1997/98 Crisis, is very interesting. As we have seen in the case of Indonesia, the Rupiah fell from around 2,500 against the US Dollar to over 15,000. However, since the rural sector produces commodities, priced off the world's markets in US Dollars, agricultural commodities - although weak at the time - appreciated in Rupiah terms. In other words, while leveraged domestic assets were hard-hit - in particular real estate and the manufacturing sector - there was a relative improvement of the rural sector compared to the urban centres. Despite sagging exports, most Asian economies enjoyed in 2001-02 a modest "domestic led economic recovery".

A silver lining

And while the Asian Crisis took on historic proportions in terms of wealth destruction it also brought about some outstanding investment opportunities. Every financial crisis creates unusual investment opportunities because prices fall precipitously and overshoot on the downside, but then, like a ping-pong ball, inevitably rebound sharply (the so-called dead cat bounce). Still, I have to point out that the rebound in stock prices frequently proves to be only temporary, as prices then retest the lows or even exceed them. Moreover, it is important to understand that price falls for stocks, real estate and other assets can occur in different ways. A typical direct asset-price deflation occurred during the depression of the 1930s, when stocks fell by close to 90% from their 1929 highs. Another example would be the recent collapse of the Nasdaq. But frequently, asset prices decline only moderately in local currency terms, while they totally collapse relative to real (US Dollar) values as a result of significant currency depreciation.

This was the case during the German hyperinflation period of 1919-23, in Latin America after 1980, in Russia in 93/94, Mexico in 95 and Asia in 97/98. Particularly sharp falls in real price levels usually occur immediately for financial assets immediately in a crisis, because currency depreciations are normally accompanied by price declines for equities and bonds, since these are the only assets that can be liquidated quickly in a crisis of confidence. Take as an example the Indonesian tobacco company, HM Sampoerna, which in the spring of 1997 commanded a market cap of over US$6 billion. Following the Crisis, it collapsed to around US$120 million in early 1998.

In the meantime its business remained healthy, because the Crisis had not affected the rural sector (the stock subsequently recovered sharply, reaching a market cap of more than US$16 billion by the end of 1999).

Similarly, in the case of the German hyperinflation, equity prices (indexed in gold) collapsed by almost 90% in 1919, because of the fall in the German Mark. In Latin America following the petrodollar crisis in 1980/81 and more recently again in Brazil and Argentina, sharp price declines brought about by currency depreciations were very common.

In fact, the opportunities for investment are so compelling when countries experience meaningful and often prolonged currency depreciations that I analyse the economics of hyperinflation in more detail in the following chapter.

How long to repair the damage?

We have seen that many Asian countries' export growth suffered following the Mexican Peso devaluation in 1995 and because of China gaining a larger share of total Asian exports - especially after this country's 55% devaluation in 1994 (since 1987, China's share of total Asian exports to the US has risen from 6% to 26%). Thus, to some extent, recent devaluations in Asia should improve some countries' competitive positions. However, the effect of the 1997/98 devaluations should not be overestimated. Mexican and Chinese labour is still cheaper than that in Thailand, Malaysia, Indonesia and the Philippines. Mexico continues to enjoy the advantage of proximity to the US and lower US import tariffs as a member of Nafta. And China is becoming more competitive by the day as its unit labour costs decline with productivity gains.

In particular, China has lately been able to boost production and exports of electronic products. At present, such products are foremost in a number of Asian countries as a percentage of total exports (see Table 3). But, after having become a dominant manufacturer of textiles, garments, footwear and toys, I would expect China to also become the world's largest manufacturer of electronic components, communication equipment and semiconductors.

Already we can see that as a percentage of total exports, Chinese electronics are growing rapidly (see Figure 11). And given the current overcapacity in the electronics industry, it is likely that China will over time wreak havoc for other Asian manufacturers once its capacity comes into full production. Therefore, even in a global economic recovery we should not expect Asia's manufacturing sector outside China to do particularly well. On the other hand, as we shall analyse in Chapter 13, China will increasingly become the biggest customer for some sectors of the Asian economies.

Table 3

COUNTING ON GREENBACKS

Asian GDP exposure to US slowdown

	Exports as % of GDP 2000	Exports to US as % of exports	IT exports as % of US exports
India	10	39	30
Japan	10	31	31
China	23	40	30
Korea	37	23	55
Taiwan	48	27	55
Singapore	85	24	73

Source: CEIC/JP Morgan.

Figure 11

MORE AND MORE WIRED

Chinese electronics exports as % of total exports, 1996-2000

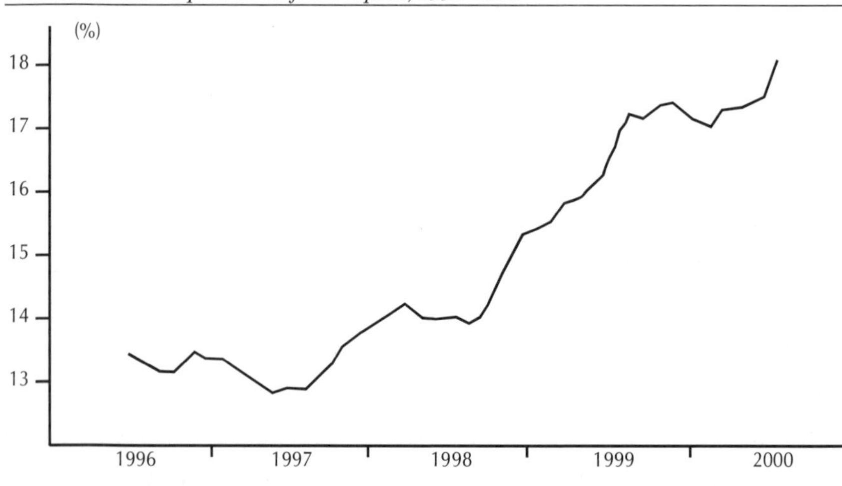

Source: BCA Research.

Are there any lessons to be learnt from the fall-out of Asian stock markets? Yes. The business cycle is alive and well and has not been tamed, as was claimed in recent years by some economists. Furthermore, investors should always be wary of countries that depend on large foreign capital flows to sustain their excessive spending - a fact that will certainly one day come to haunt the USA.

CHAPTER TEN

The economics of inflation

> The first panacea for a mismanaged nation is inflation of the currency; the second is war. Both bring a temporary prosperity; both bring permanent ruin.
>
> *ERNEST HEMINGWAY (1899-1961)*

About 20 years ago, my friend Gilbert de Botton, who founded GAM, suggested I read *The Economics of Inflation*, a 1931 book by Professor Costantino Bresciani-Turroni, an Italian economist and member of the German Reparation Commission during the Weimar hyperinflation years. We highly recommend this book to anyone interested in investing because it is the most comprehensive analysis of the causes and effects of inflation on the prices of goods, assets, commodities and foreign exchange, as well as on economic activity, the budget, foreign trade and society's social structure.

Most investors believe that inflation is bad for financial assets and good for real assets such as gold, silver, diamonds and real estate. However, what is usually overlooked is the fact that, in very high inflation economies, at some point, stocks become ridiculously undervalued in real terms and therefore provide outstanding buying opportunities. I call this phenomenon *"the paradox of inflation"*: instead of producing high price levels, hyperinflation tends to create extremely low prices as currency depreciation (due to massive capital flight) overcompensates for domestic inflation.

I can recall several instances when stocks in high-inflation economies became dirt-cheap: The Philippines in 1985/86, Argentina in 1989 and Peru and Brazil in 1990. In the Philippines during the early 80s, high inflation and poor economic, social and political conditions under the Marcos regime had driven down stock prices and the value of the Peso. By 1985, the Commercial Stock Index was down by 76% in US Dollar terms from its all-time high of 1980. The Mining Index had declined by 94% and the Oil Index by 97%. The combined market capitalisation of the six largest companies (at the time Benguet, San Miguel, PLDT, Atlas, Philex and Ayala) had fallen to only US$340 million and the entire Philippine stock market amounted to less than US$500 million (today, even after the 1997 Crisis, it is around US$25 billion). PLDT was selling for less than US$40 million and at 1.7 times earnings. San Miguel had a market cap of only US$60 million - less than the value of its 75%-owned Hong Kong-listed subsidiary. By its peak in the late 1990s PLDT exceeded US$4 billion, while San Miguel reached over US$4.5 billion. So, if strategists want you to believe that US stocks are looking cheap, just remember the valuation of Philippine shares in 1985!

Latin America in the 1980s

Being interested in high-inflation/low-price economies, we visited Argentina in 1988 and Peru and Brazil in 1990. In the 80s, all these economies had suffered from economic depression, social strife, hyperinflation, lack of foreign direct investment, capital flight on a large scale and a collapse in their currencies. The result was an extremely low valuation of assets in these countries. In fact, a comparison of Argentina during the hyperinflation years of the 80s with Argentina following the convertability plan in the 90s again illustrates the paradox of inflation. Table 1 compares the rate of inflation from 1977-87 with the US Dollar market cap of Argentina's 16 leading issues. As can be seen, the best buying opportunities occurred when inflation was at its worst.

Table 1

THE PARADOX OF INFLATION

Argentina stock market cap of 16 leading issues versus inflation, 1977-1987

	US$ million	Inflation rate
1977	292.056	160.4
1978	771.334	169.8
1979	2,010.622	139.7
1980	1,801.148	87.6
1981	674.855	131.3
1982	349.867	209.7
1983	722.715	433.7
1984	567.346	688.0
1985	1,092.563	385.4
1986	637.550	81.9
1987	584.728	131.3

Source: Consultores de Inversiones Bursatiles Y Francieras, Buenos Aires.

When I visited Argentina in 1988, I was truly amazed: total market capitalisation was only around US$750 million and daily volume on the Buenos Aires stock exchange averaged less than US$1 million. A high quality baby-beefsteak cost only US$5, a luxury apartment US$70,000 and an entire office block in a prime location US$1 million! That was when inflation stood at about 600% per annum. But what was the situation a few years later, in 1994, when Argentina's inflation had been curbed to less than 10%? Everything had become dear and Buenos Aires was once again - as it had been in the 70s - one of the world's most expensive cities.

Argentina's stock market had also soared. Molinos, which could have been bought in 1987 for as little as US$20 million, was worth US$515 million in 1994; and Picardo, which sold for a mere US$12 million in 1986, had reached US$213 million (the total capitalisation of the market had in the meantime grown to US$34 billion, although obviously part of the increase was due to privatisation of state assets). Over the same period, prices of Argentina's debt had also risen significantly: the yield on Bonex issues, which in the late 80s had hovered around 20%, fell to around 9% by 1994, and Argentina's foreign loans, which traded as low as 12 in 1989, had risen to above 80.

Between 1991 and 1994, under President Alberto Fujimori, Peru experienced a similar turnaround. Inflation fell from over 1,000% per annum to less than 10%, its market capitalisation rose from around US$600 million to US$5 billion, and its foreign debt appreciated from three cents to the Dollar to above 70! (It is important to realise that, both in developed and emerging economies, distressed bonds and country loans sometimes offer great investment opportunities. At present I would look to invest in country loans of Cuba and North Korea.) One of the reasons I recall Peru is that in 1990-91 the country was on the brink of civil war and was not a very safe place to visit. Yet at night, the country showed distinct energy! Obviously, hyperinflation combined with a poor political and social environment creates fantastic buying and entertainment opportunities.

Russia in the early 1990s and German hyperinflation

In 1993-94, a similar situation developed in Russia and a number of pundits then compared the political and economic landscape to the hyperinflation years that followed the establishment of the Weimar Constitution on 19 August 1919. Whether such a comparison was appropriate is debatable, because the catastrophic German hyperinflation years of 1919-23 were followed by a period of prosperity in the late 1920s, which has not been mirrored in Russia.

Figure 1, by Bresciani-Turroni, shows how real prices in Germany moved between 1913 and 1924. It is clearly visible how wholesale prices, cost of living, real wages and stock prices all fell dramatically until 1922 - and note the sharp rises in 1923. *The paradox of inflation* is clearly recognisable in Figure 1 and was also well documented by economists in Germany at the time (Bresciani-Turroni for instance). In late 1922, the German cost of living index had fallen to around 40 against an index of world prices that stood at 150 (basis: 1913 = 100 expressed in gold). The German economist, Richard Gaettens, wrote in his book *Inflationen* of a Dutch businessman travelling in Germany in 1923 who noticed that a necktie cost only 20% of the price in Holland. He purchased the shop's entire inventory of 4,000 ties and resold them at a considerable profit back home. Gaettens also points out how foreigners acquired German real estate and stocks at fire-sale prices. Figure 1 and Table 2 show how cheap stocks had become, adjusted for the depreciation of the Mark. (Please note that on Table 2, the first column shows the German share price index in local currency. The second column shows the share index adjusted for the depreciation of the Mark.)

Figure 1

WEIMAR DEFLATION 1

German prices 1913-1923

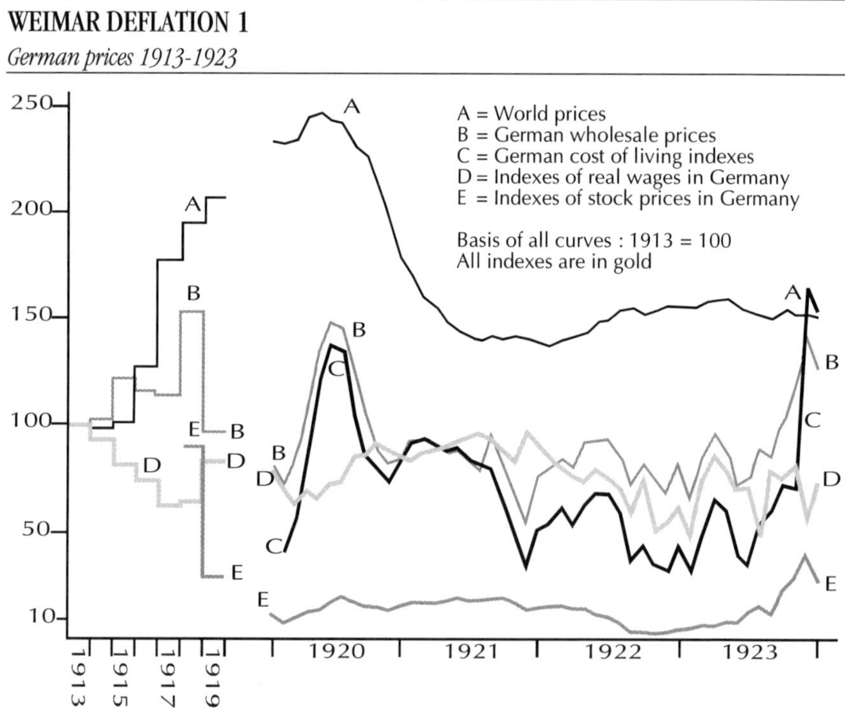

Source: Bresciani-Turroni.

Table 2

WEIMAR DEFLATION 2

Index numbers of the prices of German shares (1913=100)

	1918		1919		1920		1921		1922		1923	
	In paper marks	**Adjusted according to the exchange rate of the Dollar**	**In paper marks**	**Adjusted according to the exchange rate of the Dollar**	**In paper marks**	**Adjusted according to the exchange rate of the Dollar**	**In paper marks**	**Adjusted according to the exchange rate of the Dollar**	**In paper marks**	**Adjusted according to the exchange rate of the Dollar**	**In paper marks**	**Adjusted according to the exchange rate of the Dollar**
January	126	101.55	97	49.68	166	10.73	278	18	743	16.27	21,400	5.24
February	131	104.32	98	45.57	200	8.47	260	17.82	841	16.98	45,200	6.79
March	132	106.48	97	39.2	196	9.82	265	17.84	986	14.57	33,600	6.66
April	133	109.23	96	31.99	184	12.93	275	18.17	1018	14.69	50,200	8.61
May	138	112.75	91	29.74	160	14.45	277	18.71	873	12.63	95,100	8.38
June	137	107.36	96	28.77	167	17.93	299	18.12	823	10.89	352,000	13.44
July	137	99.34	100	27.85	187	19.92	337	18.45	897	7.63	1,349,400	16.03
August	143	98.53	99	22.08	204	17.98	389	19.36	1156	4.28	12,474,300	11.33
September	135	86.03	112	19.56	220	15.94	492	19.69	1262	3.61	531,300,000	22.56
October	109	69.28	124	19.41	245	15.06	644	18	2062	2.72	171,322[1]	28.47
November	95	53.72	125	13.7	260	14.12	936	14.94	5070	2.96	23,680,000[1]	39.36
December	88	44.63	127	11.4	274	15.79	731	15.99	8981	4.97	26,890,000[1]	26.8

[1] Millions. Source: *The Economics of Inflation*, Costantino Bresciani-Turroni.

The first great buying opportunity occurred in February 1920 when the US Dollar index of German shares sold for as little as 8.47 (1913 = 100). Within five months, the index doubled in Dollar terms, largely because the Mark appreciated briefly but sharply. From the summer of 1920 until February 1922, the US Dollar index maintained its value, but thereafter plunged rapidly as currency depreciation exceeded the rise in local-currency stock prices by a wide margin. According to Bresciani-Turroni, at the beginning of November 1922 (when the Dollar index had fallen as low as 2.72), the domestic prices of stocks had increased 89 times compared with 1914, while the value of the Dollar had increased 1,525 times, the price of coal 1,250 times, bar iron 2,000 times and the index number of wholesale prices 945 times.

The enormous relative drop in share prices (down over 97% in Dollar terms) created some odd situations. Daimler, one of Germany's largest and most profitable companies, had share capital of less than 980 million paper marks. Since one of its cars cost three million marks on average at that time, the stock market valued the entire Daimler Company at the equivalent of only 327 cars. Similarly, the market capitalisation of the sixteen great Tietz shops equalled the price of just 16,000 suits.

The final months of 1922 provided an outstanding buying opportunity for German shares (see Table 2). From a low of 2.72 in October 1922, the Dollar index soared to 39.36 in November 1923 - a gain of almost 15 times in 13 months! In other words, by November 1923, anyone who had purchased German shares after March 1919 was making money, even in Dollar terms. The 1923 rise in share prices was quite extraordinary in view of the French occupation of the Ruhr and rising unemployment in Germany. However, what must be understood is that throughout the period of hyperinflation, a speculative fury characterised the German stock market. The public believed that the paper Mark could no longer fulfil the function of "the store of value" and therefore the purchase of shares was not only considered a form of investment for surplus capital and savings, but a temporary use for liquid resources which would preserve working capital, which was throughout 1919-23 threatened by the continuous monetary depreciation.

Frequently, in fact, the worse conditions grew, the more the stock market would rally. This paradoxical situation was described in a July 1923 article in *Plutus*, then a leading financial paper: "There have been extraordinary rises in the quotations for all shares, the chief cause being the catastrophic change in the economic situation". I may add that in 2001-02, the Zimbabwe stock market rose very sharply in local-currency terms. Because of this country's catastrophic economic and financial conditions, people with cash in Zimbabwe rushed to buy stocks because they were the only practical store of value given this country's hyperinflation, currency depreciation and the expropriation of white settlers' farms.

The Weimar hyperinflation came to an end in late 1923 when, by the decree of 15 October 1923, the German government introduced the Rentenmark, whose maximum issue was fixed at 2,400 million, of which 1,200 million was put at the disposal of the government. To everyone's surprise, the financial reform worked and became known as "the miracle of the Rentenmark". Immediately, consumption and production began to improve. The consumption of meat, which before World War One had reached 52kg per capita and had fallen to 22kg in 1923, rose again to 41kg in 1924. Beer consumption, which had collapsed by more than 50% between 1921 and 1923, doubled in 1924. Following a powerful economic recovery in 1924, a "stabilisation crisis" occurred in 1925 because of a lack of working capital for business - a consequence of the hyperinflation period, during which time capital had been immobilised. (The immobilisation of capital takes place during an inflationary period because the most advantageous ratio between "fixed capital" and "circulating capital" is moved in the direction of the former.) In 1925, money grew very tight and stocks declined quite sharply (but not to 1923 lows). The stabilisation crisis, however, proved beneficial from a longer point of view. It forced a dramatic rationalisation of German industry, thus freeing up funds, and mobilised individual savings and attracted foreign investment because of high domestic real interest rates. Thus, a vigorous economic expansion followed, which lasted from 1926 until the onset of depression in the 1930s.

The Weimar inflation, the 1923 financial reform, the stabilisation crisis and the subsequent strong economic recovery is a period of enormous economic complexity, and its careful study is a must for any student of economics. However, for our purpose - which is to show that in hyperinflation countries or in countries that experience a severe currency devaluation, such as in Asia in 1997/98, stocks become ridiculously "cheap" - the following should be remembered: German stock prices bottomed out in October 1922 - one year before the Rentenmark, by which time they had already risen by more than ten times (see Table 2). After the Rentenmark, stocks performed poorly until 1926, when strong economic growth resumed. Furthermore, while US stocks fell well below their early 1920s level during the 1930s depression, German shares held well above the 1922 lows. Clearly, the best time to have purchased German equities in the century was in the midst of the Weimar inflation when economic, social and political conditions looked horrendous (see Figure 2 - please also note that German shares made a high in 1962 and that it took until 1984 to exceed this high - 24 years later).

Figure 2

OPPORTUNITY IN INSTABILITY

German share price index 1919-1986

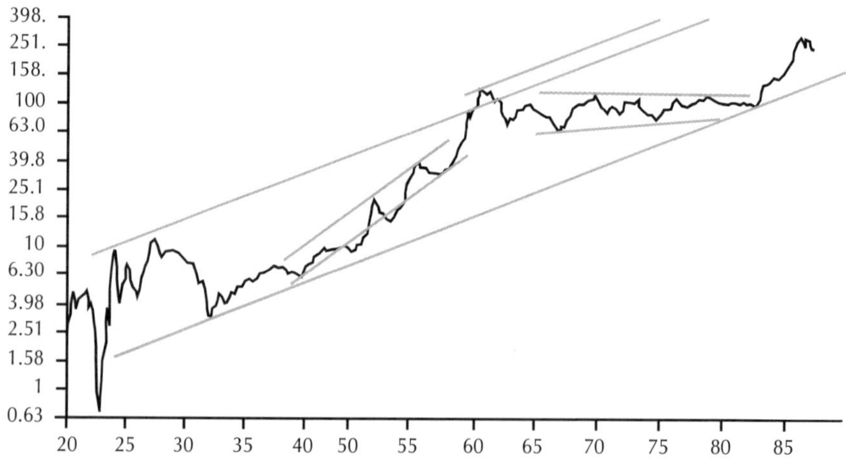

Source: Rolf Bertschi, Credit Suisse Private Banking, 1987, Zurich.

I had two purposes in mind when discussing *the paradox of inflation* in detail. For one I wanted to show that when, for whatever reasons, a sharp currency depreciation takes place, stocks usually become extremely undervalued. This was the case in the US in the 1970s (when the Dollar depreciated by around 70% against hard European currencies), in Latin America in the 1980s, in Russia in the early 1990s and in Asia after the 1997 Crisis. I may add that currency depreciations always occur because of inflationary pressures (not vice versa). In Germany in the early 1920s, in Latin America in the 1980s and in Russia after communism it was hyperinflation that caused the collapse in the currency and led to a low price level.

In the case of Asia, however, it was not hyperinflation that led to overvalued currencies and then the collapse in their value but overvalued asset prices - in particular real estate and equities. Moreover, as I have pointed out in Chapter 9, the mismatch of local assets, which provided an income stream in local currency and liabilities denominated in foreign currencies, exacerbated the problem. I may add that if high-inflation periods lead to low equity valuations, low-inflation countries usually have a high price level and also high equity valuations. This was the case in Japan in the late 1980s and in Western financial markets in the late 1990s.

My other purpose for discussing the impact of inflation on equity prices is that in Russia in the early 1990s a lifetime buying opportunity presented itself, similar to the case during the German hyperinflation in the 1920s - and that although since then equity valuations have risen, by international standards they are *still* extremely low - so the opportunity still exists. Following the breakdown of communism, the former Soviet Union experienced a terrific economic meltdown. From Table 3, we can see that the Russian economy contracted by about 50% from 1989 to 1994.

I must, however, point out that these official statistics may have made the economic performance look worse than it actually was because under the planned economy and the totalitarian political system, the former Soviet Union strictly controlled all economic activity. There was very little smuggling, black market activity was extremely limited, and since a strict output quota system existed, the state knew exactly how much was produced by the agricultural sector and by the Russian industrial complex. After the collapse of the communist system this all changed. Law and order broke down as state institutions lost their power. Additionally, an economic jungle replaced the inefficient yet highly regulated former planned economy, because the legal and commercial infrastructure necessary for capitalism was not yet in place (absence of property rights, commercial law, an equitable taxation system and high accounting standards). The result of this "wild west" lawlessness was a dramatic fall in official output and a simultaneous explosive increase in the grey economy, which simply did not appear in government statistics. This unofficial economic activity was usually associated with the Mafia, but if no well-defined commercial laws were in place, or if laws did exist but were not enforced by a government that had lost its power and authority and which was totally discredited among the Russian people - who was to say what was legal and what was not?

Table 3

CUT IN HALF

Eastern Europe economic performance (GDP growth, %)

	1989	1990	1991	1992	1993	1994
Russia	3.0	(2.0)	(12.9)	(18.5)	(15.0)	(9.0)
Ukraine	4.1	(2.6)	(11.2)	(14.0)	(15.0)	(10.0)
Kazakhstan	-	-	(12.0)	(13.0)	(15.0)	(10.0)
Poland	0.3	(11.6)	(7.6)	1.0	4.0	4.0
Czech Republic	1.4	(1.2)	(14.2)	(7.1)	0.0	3.0
Slovak Republic	1.0	(2.5)	(11.2)	(7.0)	(7.0)	(2.0)
Hungary	0.1	(3.3)	(11.9)	(4.5)	(3.0)	1.0
Bulgaria	(0.6)	(9.1)	(11.7)	(7.7)	(5.0)	0.5
Romania	(5.8)	(7.4)	(13.7)	(15.4)	(6.0)	1.0

Sources: Vienna Institute for Comparative Economic Studies, Commerzbank Estimates for 1993 and 94.

I should mention that in most emerging economies the statistics do understate GDP, since official statistics fail to capture a large portion of the economy. Moreover, because a large portion of the rural economy still functions as a household type of economy where barter is common, I would estimate GDP in predominantly rural economies to be about 20-25% higher than official statistics indicate. Conversely, in highly developed economies, which have replaced transactions that were traditionally carried out by the household (washing, ironing, cooking, sawing, etc) by outsourcing all these functions to the service industry (laundry shops, fast food, catering services, tailors, etc), GDP would appear to overstate true economic activity.

What occurred in the early 1990s in Russia was total economic anarchy, a time probably similar to the "robber baron" days of America in the 19th Century. What must be understood also is that the rise of an entrepreneurial class did not begin after the breakdown of communism in 1989, but long before. The 29 June 1981 edition of *Fortune* carried a detailed article entitled "Russia's Underground Millionaires - How to succeed in business where business is a crime". Many of the successful families in the early 1990s were, therefore, extremely well versed in the methods of conducting business according to their own rules. What people then referred to as the Mafia was, therefore, frequently not organised crime, but very sharp entrepreneurs who operated in an organised and well-structured fashion in a chaotic economic environment.

I first went to Russia in 1981 and have returned several times. In my opinion, there was simply no doubt that people in the early 1990s, despite the severe decline in GDP according to the official statistics, were much better off than during my initial visit. Because the inefficient official economy had been contracting, while the underground economy had been expanding very rapidly, some people with good connections and flexible wits became rich very quickly while others like pensioners lost out badly. But this was more a consequence of the hyperinflation that gripped Russia in the early 90s than a contraction in the real economy. In fact, I have observed this very rapid polarisation of society in most transitional economies. In China, Vietnam and Eastern Europe, members of the government, the police, army and secret service and their relatives, as well as people with connections to these people, became fabulously rich in the years following the breakdown of communism, while the working class and the pensioners lost out (they were probably absolutely better off after the breakdown of communism but compared to the well-to-do they became poorer as wealth inequality increased).

In fact, one of the problems Russia faced was that it had - unlike China - moved very fast and radically in its effort to privatise the state sector by starting, already in 1992, its Mass Privatisation Programme. The "people's privatisation" stipulated that the greater part (40-51%) of the property to be privatised should belong to the workers and the management of the respective companies. The rest was to be transferred to State Property Funds, which were legally obliged to sell at least 29% of the equity in these companies through voucher auctions. Vouchers were distributed to every Russian citizen for a nominal fee and were the only means of paying at the auctions (a voucher was thus a state-property privatisation check). Already by the end of 1993, 144 million Russian citizens, or 96% of the total population, had received privatisation vouchers with a nominal value of 10,000 roubles (worth about US$25 in June 1992). Since the vouchers were valued in roubles they were immediately tradable, which quickly led to the formation of officially licenced voucher funds, the Russian equivalent of mutual funds (in 1993, about 550 voucher funds had acquired some 17% of all vouchers issued). While practically everything else has gone bad in Russia since the breakdown of communism, the Mass Privatisation Programme was actually extremely successful and far-reaching, given the difficulties involved in such a novel scheme and implementing it in a country as vast as Russia. Thus, by the end of 1993, over 7,000 medium and large enterprises and in excess of 90,000 small companies had been privatised.

Since their issuance, vouchers were actively traded and their prices fluctuated between US$3 and US$26. A secondary, albeit then still illiquid, market for shares of privatised companies had also developed with most of the trades occurring off-market between workers, managers, strategic investors, voucher funds, speculators and a few foreigners. When the privatisation took place, valuations were extremely low. By June 1993, approximately 15% of Russian industry had been sold through the voucher auction system. Of these privatised companies, about 20% of the equity had gone to outsiders (as opposed to workers and managers who, as we saw earlier, kept a majority interest in their companies). In other words, by June

1993 about 3% of Russia's industry had been purchased by outsiders who tendered approximately 15 million vouchers. Assuming that, on average, these vouchers were worth about US$8 when they were tendered, 3% of Russian equity was thus valued at about US$120 million. In 1994, the privatisation vouchers were priced around US$12, which valued the entire Russian industry at only about US$5-6 billion!

Considering that Russia ranked first in the world in the production of many mineral and energy resources, including manganese, titanium, nickel, crude oil and natural gas, second in the production of aluminium, vanadium and platinum, and fourth in the production of gold and coal, and that it had a relatively well-educated population (Russia was in no way a third world country), Russian assets were ridiculously cheap. Table 4 provides an idea of the natural resource wealth Russia possessed.

Table 4

VAST RESOURCES

Resource reserves of the Former Soviet Republics

Resource	Estimated reserves	Market value (US$ billion)
Oil	57 billion barrels	1,268.00
Manganese	500 million short tons	192.50
Gold	8,710 metric tons	103.60
Nickel	8.1 million short tons	57.51
Vanadium	4 million metric tons	30.05
Platinum	6 million kilograms	23.40
Silver	50,000 metric tons	7.04
Chromite	129 million metric tons	6.45
TOTAL		1,689.00

Source: *International Energy Annual*, Energy Information Administration.

The incredible undervaluation of Russian assets in 1993/94 also becomes evident if we look at the market caps of individual companies in 1994: Surgutneftegaz (the largest oil company in Russia), which produces about 2% of world oil output, was privatised through the voucher process in 1993 and had in early 1994 a market cap of only US$170 million! Uralmash and Permsky Motors, each of which employed over 30,000 people, were valued at US$7 million and US$4 million respectively. Gum Department Stores, a leading retailer in Moscow (its main store, which it leases, is right next to the Kremlin, but it owns freehold another 15 stores in Moscow), was valued at about US$24 million.

Apart from the paradox of inflation, there were other reasons why Russian assets were so undervalued. When the Mass Privatisation Programme began, the book values of all the companies to be privatised were fixed as of 1 July 1992. But after that the rouble fell by almost 80%, which explains the low privatisation prices at the voucher auctions in 1993. Another reason related to the fact that the management and the workers of the companies to be privatised were, right from the start, major buyers of their company's shares (usually 51%). Since the prices they could acquire the shares at were based on book values (as of 1 July 1992), they had a vested interest in grossly understating the assets of their companies.

In the case of Russia, there is no doubt that much went wrong after communism failed. However, the Mass Privatisation Programme was remarkably successful. No other post-communist economy transferred so many assets so rapidly into the private sector as Russia did in the early 1990s. Not only were thousands of companies privatised, from small enterprises to very large companies, but apartments were also sold to their tenants at nominal prices. So most Russian people relatively quickly owned some assets, which ensured that Russia would not move back to the inefficient planned economy. In fact, in the early 1990s, Russians became fed up with government and the bureaucrats. Consequently they no longer cared about government regulations and laws. The only thing they cared about was how to make as much money as quickly as possible in the unofficial economy. And while this jungle capitalism and extreme economic Darwinism had numerous problems, it also created a very dynamic private sector, which led, following the 1998 crisis, to strong economic growth (this was also very much the case in China).

Russia is a huge country with vast natural resources. Should commodity prices rise in the next ten years, as we expect, it would be a prime beneficiary (along with Argentina, Brazil, Indonesia, Malaysia, Thailand, Vietnam and the oil producing nations).

Russian financial assets were extremely depressed in the early 1990s and, although there were some risks involved, it was clear that they were unlikely to fall much from these rock-bottom prices because wealthy

Russians were likely to continue accumulating shares to build controlling interests. As mentioned above, all Russian assets were valued at year-end 1993 at about US$5-6 billion whereas the Hong Kong stock market by then exceeded US$300 billion.

But, there is another reason I have discussed in detail the economics of inflation and the low valuations hyperinflation countries create. Since 1980, we have had (as we saw in Chapter 7) declining commodity prices and declining inflation rates. This has led to complacency about inflation and even fear of deflation in the Western industrialised countries. True, at present, manufactured goods seem to be deflating, as China can produce just about anything at a lower cost than the West - and therefore, China is exporting deflation. But, easy monetary policies by Western central banks could lead at some point in the future to renewed severe inflationary pressures which, given the shaky state of the global economy, may not be countered by tightening monetary policies.

Therefore, I would expect in years to come to increasingly see inflation erupting in one or other sector of the global economy or one or other country. I, therefore, find that investors should at least be familiar with the opportunity such inflationary bouts provide in the equity markets.

Moreover, in 2002, US government and government agency bonds have become the favourite asset class. But having rallied since September 1981 and their yields being at the lowest level in over 40 years, such bonds have become vulnerable to future inflation, which would exceed investor expectations. Rising inflation, such as we had from the mid 1940s to 1981 and such as we find in hyperinflation countries, is a total disaster for bondholders. In the environment of rising inflation I expect some time in the next few years, investors should be far better off owning equities or real assets - provided they can be acquired at reasonable prices, as is now the case in most emerging economies.

Concerning emerging economies, there is one more point to consider. Over time the economic geography of the world has changed very significantly as a result of wars, more efficient trading routes, discoveries, new industries and new inventions, etc. The breakdown of socialist and communist ideology released around three billion people into the market economy and the capitalistic system. This occurred at a time of great technological progress (in particular instant and wireless information and communication) - and will, in my opinion, lead to an almost unimaginable and rapid shift in the world's clusters of production, commerce and finance, as I try to explain in the following chapter.

CHAPTER ELEVEN

The rise and fall of centres of prosperity

> The cities that were formerly great, have most of them become insignificant; and such as are at present powerful, were weak in olden times. I shall, therefore, discourse equally of both, convinced that human happiness never continues long in one stay.
>
> *HERODOTUS (5th Century BC)*

There are a number of reasons why the rise and fall of cities and changes in economic geography have always captivated me. One of the more remarkable aspects of economics is how unevenly progress and development evolve. Since ancient days, a great number of cities, countries and civilisations have flourished and withered - but at very different times and in different regions of the world. One characteristic of economic growth is continuous change, with some regions growing and developing faster than others for a while, before experiencing their own declines.

In order to understand this "mutation in centres of prosperity", we need look no further than the composition of America's ten largest cities since 1850 (see Table 1). Of the ten largest American centres in the second half of the 19th Century, only three are still on the list today. Baltimore, New Orleans, Cincinnati, St Louis, Pittsburgh, Buffalo and Cleveland have been replaced by "newcomers" Los Angeles, Chicago, San Francisco, Detroit,

Houston and Dallas. The rise of Los Angeles is remarkable: Counting only 50,000 inhabitants in 1890, it is America's second largest city today. So, while some cities and regions have outperformed overall economic growth over the last 100 years or so, others have sustained relative and sometimes even absolute declines.

Table 1

JOCKEYING FOR THOSE BIG-TEN SLOTS

America's ten largest cities 1850-1986 (population, '000)

1850		1900		1930		1950		1986	
New York	516	New York	3,437	New York	6,930	New York	7,892	New York	17,807
Philadelphia	340	Chicago	1,699	Chicago	3,376	Chicago	4,921	Los Angeles	12,373
Baltimore	169	Philadelphia	1,294	Philadelphia	1,951	Los Angeles	3,997	Chicago	8,035
Boston	137	St Louis	575	Detroit	1,569	Philadelphia	2,922	Philadelphia	5,755
New Orleans	116	Boston	561	Los Angeles	1,238	Detroit	2,659	San Francisco	5,685
Cincinnati	115	Baltimore	509	Cleveland	900	Boston	2,233	Detroit	4,577
St Louis	78	Cleveland	382	St Louis	822	San Francisco	2,022	Boston	4,027
Pittsburgh	47	Buffalo	352	Baltimore	805	Pittsburgh	1,533	Houston	3,566
Buffalo	42	Cincinnati	326	Boston	781	St Louis	1,400	Washington	3,429
Washington	40	San Francisco	343	Pittsburgh	670	Cleveland	1,384	Dallas	3,348

Notes: 1) Philadelphia, the second largest city in 1850, had dropped to number four by 1950. 2) Baltimore, New Orleans, Cincinnati, St Louis, Pittsburgh, Buffalo and Cleveland, all among the ten largest cities in the 19th Century had disappeared from the list by the second half of the 20th century. 3) Los Angeles, not on the list until 1930 is now America's second largest city. 4) Detroit and Cleveland, the most prosperous industrial cities in the twenties experienced a relative decline thereafter. 5) Before 1800, America's largest cities were: Boston, Philadelphia, New York, Baltimore, Salem, Charleston, Newport, Providence, New Haven, New London and Norwich. Source: Marc Faber Limited.

We have earlier repeatedly emphasised that the world is undergoing changes today that are comparable in scope to the period of global discovery at the end of the 15th Century, or to the second half of the 19th Century when huge technological progress was achieved (especially in transportation, through canals and railroads, as well as in manufacturing) and as a result of America's entry into the global economy. The dramatic changes in these two periods led to the economic ascent of entirely new cities and regions and decline or absolute decay of then well-established centres of prosperity. Similarly, the current ongoing rapid integration of so many new regions into the global free market economy - following the breakdown of communist and socialist ideology - will lead to the rise of entirely new centres of economic strength, while others will inevitably lose out.

Having lived in Hong Kong since 1973, I have had the good fortune to see the meteoric economic development of many Asian cities and countries. Twenty-five years ago, Taiwan, South Korea, Singapore and Malaysia were still relatively poor. Today, they are rich and their capitals are large, modern cities with infrastructures one could not have foreseen two or three decades ago. We may similarly underestimate how quickly cities in formerly closed societies, such as China, Vietnam, the Soviet Union and Eastern Europe, may develop, and in some cases, displace present centres of prosperity. I am thinking of Hong Kong in particular. Could the opening of China affect Hong Kong just as the opening of the sea route to Asia under the Portuguese in the 16th Century affected the then thriving cities along the silk trade route, such as Turfan, Khotan, Kashgar, Samarkand and Bactria? What about the political issue? Can the reunification of Hong Kong with China in 1997 be in any way compared to the integration of the Spanish Moorish capital of Cordoba into the Berber Almoravid Empire in the 11th Century; an event which precipitated Cordoba's decline? Will its fate be similar to Salzburg's after it was absorbed by Austria in 1803? Or will Hong Kong continue to thrive under Chinese sovereignty, as Alexandria thrived under Roman dominance and Constantinople flourished under the Ottoman Empire? Founded by Alexander the Great in 332 BC, Alexandria was under Ptolemaic rule until Cleopatra's suicide in 30 BC, upon which Egypt became a Roman Prefecture. Under Rome's rule, Alexandria became the Empire's most important economic centre and its second largest city (see below).

Some studies show that stocks always go up in the long term. If this theory was correct, any investment in the ancient centres of wealth, such as Tyrus, Sidon, or Carthage, thanks to a comfortable head start of more than 2,000 years, would be worth substantially more than any investment in the US or Japan (at 3% compound, one dollar invested in each of these cities would now be worth over 142 billion trillion dollars). But this is fantasy, because in the course of history, from time to time, things go badly wrong and economic equilibrium is thrown upside down.

What I propose to do is look at a number of cities and regions that became powerful, influential and rich, and then lost out as a result of social, economic, or political change. While it is impossible to write about all former great cities in this chapter, the history of at least a few might give some food for thought.

But what criteria should one use to define a city as being powerful, influential and rich? Using population statistics, one can compile a list of power centres, political, economic or both (see Table 2). But at the same time, as a result of commerce, unusual resources (mines, oil, agriculture), or industries, many smaller cities became rich whose GDP per capita may have exceeded the per-capita income of the largest centres.

Table 2

FORMER GLORY

Cities that have been largest

City	Year	City	Year
Memphis	from 3100 BC	Cordoba	935 AD
Akkad	2240	Kaifeng	1013
Lagash	2075	Constantinople	1127
Ur	2030	Merv	1145
Thebes	1980	Constantinople	1153
Babylon	1770	Fez	1170
Avaris	1670	Hangzhou	1180
Memphis	1557	Cairo	1315
Thebes	1400	Hangzhou	1348
Nineveh	668	Nanjing	1358
Babylon	612 (first over 200,000)	Beijing	1425
Alexandria	320	Constantinople	1650
Patna	300	Beijing	1710
Chang'an	195	London	1825 (first over 5,000,000)
Rome	25	New York	1925 (first over 10,000,000)
Constantinople	340 AD	Tokyo	1965 (first over 20,000,000)
Ctesiphone	570		
Chang'an	637		
Baghdad	775 (first over 1,000,000)		

Source: Tertius Chandler, *Four Thousand Years of Urban Growth*, New York 1987.

Wealth in ancient times

In early history, the world's largest cities were all located in the Nile Valley or in Mesopotamia (ancient Iraq) and were either capitals of the Egyptian, Sumer, Babylonian or Assyrian empires. These became rich principally because of agricultural production, mining and, in some instances, a very favourable geographical location which, as in the case of Babylon, led to active foreign trade and commercial activity (near Babylon, where there is only a narrow strip of land between the Euphrates and Tigris rivers, a number of connecting canals and an elaborate irrigation system were built). In addition, as the capitals of their respective dynasties, they benefited from treasures acquired through warfare with neighbouring societies. Equally, the fall of these cities resulted largely from losing wars, and ensuing internal decay frequently played a role.

The first Babylonian dynasty, which had flourished under Hammurabi, fell at the hands of the Hittites around 1600 BC. Under the Hittites, then Kassites and Assyrians, Babylon's fortunes declined and the city became a temporary wasteland following its total destruction by the Assyrian King Sennacherib (689 BC). His successor, King Ashurbanipal, totally subdued Egypt and destroyed its largest city, Thebes (664 BC), at about the time of the zenith of the Assyrian Empire (whose capital, Nineveh, then became the world's largest city; see Table 2). Assyrian rule in West Asia (a territory encompassing Greater Mesopotamia and Egypt) did not last long and was overthrown by the Babylonian King Nabopolassar (Nineveh was destroyed in 612 BC, upon which Assyria ceased to exist) and his son, Nebuchadnezzar, who conquered Egypt and Jerusalem (which led to the Babylonian deportation of the Jews). Under Nebuchadnezzar, the Neo-Babylonian Empire reached its peak (the famous ziggurat of Babylon, better known as the Tower of Babel, was completed then).

Babylon was rebuilt and flourished once again thanks to its favourable location as a trading centre - first, under Babylonian rule, and later, as part of the great Persian Empire founded by Cyrus the Great (550 BC), who also captured the proverbially wealthy Croesus, last king of Lydia (according to some historical sources, Croesus was burnt alive in olive oil). And although Persepolis and, later, Susa were the capital cities of Persia during most of the Achaemenian period, their locations prevented them from ever becoming important trading centres. Thus, even while it decayed, Babylon remained the world's largest city for almost 300 years before Alexander the Great's (356-323 BC) conquest of the entire Achaemenian Empire.

Babylon is interesting because of its rise, fall and restoration. Cities such as Berlin, Shanghai, Ho Chi Minh, St Petersburg, Prague, Budapest, Havana and Moscow - which prospered in the first half of the 20th Century, but were economically devastated by the communists - could also bounce back and exceed their earlier prosperity!

Whereas the cities of Mesopotamia and the Nile valley had prospered thanks to agriculture, mines, extortion (ie, tribute payments) and warfare (certainly true in the case of the Assyrians), the Phoenician cities of Byblos, Sidon and Tyre grew wealthy as trading centres from the 15th Century BC. The Phoenicians were great shipbuilders and navigators (they are credited with the discovery of the Pole Star), and they founded the first global trading empire by eventually establishing hundreds of trading settlements, the most famous of which were Carthage, Utica and Gades (Cadiz). In fact, with the rise of the Phoenician trading empire and the spread of Hellenistic influence, we note a shift in the centres of power and wealth towards the Mediterranean Sea, where Carthage may have briefly become the most prosperous trading city, its population numbering over 700,000 at its peak. Tyre was eventually destroyed by Alexander and when he founded Alexandria (in 332 BC) the east-west trade shifted to this new city on the Nile delta.

Alexandria rose to splendour under Ptolemaic rule and, later under Roman jurisdiction. Benefiting from its privileged situation, the city was able to take advantage of the Romans' rapidly expanding east-west trade. It not only became a wealthy city of over 500,000 inhabitants (including slaves, the population may have exceeded one million), but was the centre of Hellenism and Semitism (the Septuagint, the earliest Greek translation of the Old Testament from the original Hebrew, was written there). The Roman Emperor Hadrian praised Alexandria's pace of life and commercial activity, where "even the blind people work", and where "money is their God, worshipped by Jews, Christians and all other religions." Alexandria's gigantic Pharos lighthouse could be seen from 40 miles away and its library attracted doctors, astronomers, philosophers and other scholars from all over the known world.

There are several reasons for Alexandria's economic success. Under

Ptolemaic rule, trading routes to India and the Far East had already begun to shift. Greek and then Roman ships called on ports in India and brought back goods through the Red Sea to Egypt (Marcus Aurelius sent a mission by sea to China in 166 AD). A canal between the Nile and the Red Sea had been built, though its neglect required goods to be brought from the Gulf of Suez to Alexandria on camelback. By Roman times, the importance of the Silk Road had already begun to diminish, as more and more trade was conducted by sea - for two reasons. The Romans discovered the monsoon winds, which considerably reduced sailing time to India and, in addition, continuous warfare with the Parthians and their final uprising made the Silk Road permanently unsafe and even closed it from time to time. This shift may have contributed to Tyre's failure to fully recover after its destruction by Alexander the Great. Alexandria's decline began with its partial destruction by Marcus Aurelius; later the process accelerated with the breakdown of the Roman Empire. Finally, the fate of what was possibly the greatest centre of commerce of all time, based on its locational advantages for sea trade, was ironically sealed by the discovery of a better sea route in 1497 - around the Cape of Good Hope (see below).

A similar scenario befell Petra, and later Antioch, which under Roman rule had become an important cultural and trading centre. Petra had for some time enjoyed a monopoly of the spice trade. But when trade routes were diverted, the city totally disintegrated (this once flourishing trade centre disappeared from the map, until it was found inhabited by nomadic tribes in 1812 by the Swiss explorer JL Burckhardt). In the case of Antioch it was not a shift in trade routes that destroyed the city but war. In 260 AD, Antioch, then a city of at least 300,000, was sacked by the Persian King Shapur I, who had previously captured the Roman Emperor Valerian (Valerian died in captivity; whenever Shapur mounted his horse, he used the Roman's neck as a footstool). I may add that Antioch was destroyed in 1401 by the great Timur of Samarkand and years later it was reported that it had only 300 inhabited houses. So ended one of the greatest cities of the Near East!

There is no doubt that the huge Roman Empire was extremely

beneficial to the growth of trade. By the standards of its time, the empire was huge. Its might rested solely on military and political power and on civil engineering skills, which were not exceeded until the 19th Century. Its very sophisticated legal system incorporated property and hereditary rights, commercial, naval and civil laws, and was applied throughout its empire. Rome was the first power to build an extensive and high-quality road network, with miraculous bridges and tunnels. It also established the first efficient postal and communications system, and news travelled in record time (probably faster than at any time until railroads were built in the 19th Century). Its coins were accepted throughout the empire. Lastly, at the time of the *Pax Romana* (which did not last for long; see Chapter 12), the empire was relatively safe, as highway robbers and pirates had been largely exterminated and shipping and roads were well controlled.

The beneficial impact of all these factors on trade is not difficult to understand, especially since Rome was not a meaningful producer of any goods. What Rome produced was brainpower, military skills, law and order, a well-functioning capital market and an administrative system, which, in spite of its shortcomings, was far better than the other major powers ever achieved! Because of this lack of self sufficiency, practically all goods had to be imported from its territories or from neighbouring countries: gold, wild animals, ivory and corn came from Africa; iron, wool, fruits and silver from Spain; garments, pearls and textiles from Persia; sulphur, wines and cedar wood from Syria; perfumes from Egypt and Arabia; silk and porcelains from China; and precious stones and spices from India. With the rise of Rome's population (at its peak, this figure comfortably exceeded 500,000) and its increasingly insatiable appetite for luxury goods, the heart of the empire became the world's biggest consumer market - comparable, to some extent, to modern-day America. It also had a huge trade deficit, which eventually led to hyperinflation, currency depreciation (the silver content of its coins was successively reduced; see Chapter 12), decay and loss of power.

The decay of Rome was well underway in the 3rd Century AD. But the first serious blow was Constantine the Great's decision to take residence in

Byzantium (330 AD), rebuild it and adorn it with splendid churches, and rename it Constantinople (he had converted to Christianity and claimed to have created the new city "by the command of God"). Henceforth, the Roman Empire had two heads - one in Rome and one in Constantinople, and the population of the latter was soon superior. Rome suffered further blows in the 5th Century when it was sacked by the Visigoths, Ostrogoths and Vandals. In 455, the Vandal king Genseric plundered the city for 14 days: it never recovered. In 600 AD, it was home to 50,000; this figure bottomed out around 30,000 in 1300, down from over 500,000 at its peak in the 1st Century - just think what this 90% decline in population did to property prices.

Constantinople, due to its privileged geographical situation at the mouth of the Black Sea, proved to be one of the most enduring of the great cities. As part of successive empires, it remained among the world's ten largest cities until the 19th Century (except for a few years following its capture by the Ottoman Turks in 1453, when its population declined from more than 500,000 to less than 50,000).

The 500 years following the breakdown of the Roman Empire were characterised by wars, a cultural breakdown and economic misery in Western Europe. By contrast, the death of the prophet Mohammed at Medina in 632 gave rise to a powerful Islamic empire under the caliphate. Within 150 years, the caliphs and their largely Arab followers established an empire that included Mesopotamia, Syria, the entire Middle East, North Africa and a large part of Spain. In 750, Al-Mansur established the caliphate in Iraq and built Madinat al-Salaam (the City of Peace) on the site of a small Sasanian village called Baghdad, with stones taken from the deserted ruins of Ctesiphone, which, until its capture by the Arabs in 637, was the largest city in the world! It is hard to believe that the world's biggest centre could completely vanish within less than 120 years. The equivalent today would be the total disappearance of a city like Tokyo, New York or London!

Baghdad rapidly grew into a cultural and commercial centre, with a peak population of 900,000 inhabitants in the mid-9th Century (when it was the world's largest city). Its fortunes, however soon declined as a result of civil war. By the year 1000, its population had already dropped to around 150,000, and in 1258 the Mongol Helagu Khan overran Mesopotamia and killed Baghdad's entire population.

The caliphs conquered North Africa in the 7th Century and in 710, the Berber Tarik made the crossing to Spain to defeat the Visigoth King Roderick (the Visigoths had occupied Spain since the 5th Century AD). Tarik conquered the greater part of the Spanish Peninsula (including Toledo). Under the Omayyad caliphs, Cordoba became the capital of Moorish Spain. The city flourished in the 10th Century, becoming briefly the centre of the Islamic world because of its religious tolerance, attracting merchants, scientists and poets, of all races and religions, who lived together in considerable harmony (in Spanish, *convivencia*). According to some contemporaries, Andalusia had never been so mildly, justly and wisely governed as by her Arab conquerors, and by the year 1000, Cordoba was the world's largest city and Moorish Spain the most populous nation in Europe.

Cordoba's success did not last long, for conflict between Berbers, Arabs, Jews, slave officials, Christians and Spanish converts to Islam weakened the city. Already long past its glory, Cordoba was retaken in 1236 by the Spanish King Ferdinand III of Castile, an event that accelerated its decline (by 1300, the population had shrunk by 90% from over 450,000 in the year 1000). In those days there were no stock bear markets, just bear markets in the population of cities).

So, while Cordoba's prosperity began to wane in the 11th Century, Marrakesh and Fez - under Berber rule on into the next century - became important centres of commerce and civilisation.

We have already remarked that, by 361 AD, Constantinople had grown larger than Rome. And as Rome's decline accelerated in the 5th Century, Constantinople became Western civilisation's most important centre, as capital of the Byzantine or East Roman empire. From the 5th to the 15th Century (when it fell to the Ottoman Turks), Constantinople remained the world's greatest market and shipping centre - replacing Rome in terms of power and Alexandria in terms of trading. Because of the Roman Empire's continuous hostilities with Persia, under Byzantine rule, ports had been established in the Black Sea and trade routes had shifted to that area, then north of the Caspian and Arral seas to Sogdiana (a region in today's Uzbekistan), to Samarkand, Kashgar and China (the so-called Northern Silk Road). The Byzantine Empire probably reached its peak at the time of Justinian the Great (527-565), when it included the Balearic Islands, Sardinia, Corsica, the Balkans as far as Venice and the Danube in the north, Asia Minor, North Africa, Egypt and Syria.

Byzantium had a highly developed banking system and an indication of its prosperity is the level of Byzantine interest rates, which were lower than anywhere else in the world. Justinian fixed the maximum rates at 4% for loans to peasants, 6% on private loans secured by collateral, 8% on commercial loans and 12% on maritime investments. However, Constantinople's prosperity began to wane soon after Justinian's death, as his successors had to deal with internal discord and, on every side, external attacks: Avars and Slavs had crossed the Danube and were conquering imperial territory and towns, Persians had temporarily gained control of most of Western Asia, and, later, Islamic forces invaded most of Syria, Egypt and all of North Africa.

By the 11th Century, the Byzantine Empire seemed near collapse. However, through clever diplomacy, Emperor Alexius Comnenus I was able to rally the European powers against Islam (the Seljuk Turks had taken Jerusalem in 1076) and unleash the Holy Wars (the eight Crusades), which first gave a lease of life to Constantinople, but eventually caused its destruction. While the first Crusades strengthened the Byzantines' position by repelling the Seljuk Turks and establishing the Kingdom of Jerusalem, the fourth Crusade turned out to be a watershed for Constantinople, because in order to pay for supplies and ships the Crusaders, led by the Venetians, mercilessly pillaged Constantinople (in 1204), a disaster from which the city never fully recovered (and which goes to show that your allies can never be fully trusted!). Constantinople fell in 1453 and, under Islamic rule, became Istanbul, capital of the Ottoman Empire.

I have spent some time discussing the early centres of civilisation for two principal reasons. First, it is remarkable that none of these early centres retains today any strong cultural, economic or political significance. In addition, we hear so much about first-mover advantage when new industries emerge or a company invents a new product. But the fact that most of the great cradles of civilisation have either disappeared or mostly decayed does not suggest that such an advantage exists, or certainly not for very long.

The Renaissance - West and North

The emergence of Italian trading cities, such as Genoa, Amalfi, Florence, Pisa and Venice, as major economic centres from the 11th to the 16th Century was due to a number of factors. Following the breakdown of the Roman Empire, east-west trade had slumped, but began to revive with the rise of urban centres in France and northern Europe in the 9th and 10th centuries. On the back of regional trade, some industry and mining, the north and west had developed prosperity, and along with it, an appetite for luxury goods and spices from Asia. The coastal cities of Amalfi, Genoa and Venice took advantage of this demand and their ships called on ports in Egypt, Palestine, North Africa and Constantinople to load cargo for transport across the Alps to northern European cities or to the six fairs held annually in Champagne and Brie.

One great advantage for their trading empires was the sophisticated banking, insurance and accounting systems these cities had developed (double-entry bookkeeping was used for the first time, and in 1157 Venice issued the first government bonds). The Florentines, in particular, excelled in banking. A catalyst to Genoa and Venice's wealth came from the Holy Wars, which began with the first Crusade at the initiative of Pope Urban II in 1096. The crusaders needed regular supplies, and ships for the transport of these goods and troops were provided and often financed by the Italian trading cities, which, in return, obtained access to the seaports in Palestine. At its peak, Venice controlled the islands of Crete, Rhodes,

Negraponte, Lemnos and Cyprus, with its thriving port city of Famagusta, as well as the long-distance sea trade between the port cities of the Near East and the Adriatic. The economic might of Venice is also evident from its size: after Paris, it boasted Europe's second largest population, averaging about 110,000 inhabitants between 1300 and 1500 - larger than Constantinople, which shrank to less than 50,000 in 1450 (down from a high of 400,000 in 500 AD and 300,000 in 1000).

I may add that following the outbreak of the Black Death in the trading city of Caffa on the Crimea in 1346 (after a Mongol prince had laid siege to the city), the plague rapidly spread through Europe and reduced its population between 1346 and the middle of the 15th Century by about one third.

Of particular importance to the trade at Venice was the rise of the Hanseatic League in northern Europe, which had as its centre Lübeck, and at its peak included over 100 cities in northern Germany and *Kontore* (counters administering their own German law) in cities such as London, Bruges, Bergen and Novgorod. Under the Hanseatic League, Bruges became by far the most prosperous city of the period (the Venice of northern Europe). Bruges capitalised on the fact that, since 1200, it had been included in the circuit of Flemish fairs, as a result of which the city was already receiving foreign merchants, who brought wool for the rapidly expanding cloth-making towns of Flanders, grain from Normandy and Bordeaux wines. At the end of the 13th Century and in the early 14th Century, Genoese and Venetian ships also began to call on Bruges, bringing spices and pepper and buying textiles from Flanders. In time, rich Italian merchants settled there, bringing capital and modern financial techniques.

In 1309, the famous Bourse was created; this became the centre of a sophisticated money market. But Bruges' commercial hegemony of the north did not last. In the second half of the 15th Century, the silting-up of the Zwyne estuary harmed its trade activity and Damme became the main port. Flemish industry and German traders decamped for Antwerp, which replaced Bruges as northern Europe's leading port and financial and commercial centre (the Antwerp Bourse was founded in 1460; see below). In the meantime, the German cities of Nürnberg and Augsburg, had become in the 15th Century, along with Cologne, Germany's largest and most prominent cities (Nürnberg was an important trading city located on the Venice-Bruges axis). Augsburg made a name for itself as the home of famous 15th and 16th Century merchant banking families, such as the Fuggers, the Meutlings, the Welsers, the Hochstetters and the Manlichs, who later all set up businesses in Antwerp, as the economic centre of Europe moved from Venice to the north.

The rise of the north-European cities greatly expanded Venice's commercial importance temporary because, until the 16th Century, the merchants there had to purchase goods from India and the Far East almost exclusively from Venice. However, it also laid the foundation for its demise, as we shall see, because the 16th Century punctuated the world's economic equilibrium and in the process damaged the commercial dominance of Bruges and of the Italian trading cities.

The 16th Century was dominated by the struggle between the great powers of Spain, France, England and the Ottoman Empire for supremacy. In this century, new trade routes were opened up to Asia and to the Americas. It was also a period of powerful monarchs, such as François I and Henri IV of France, Charles V, Holy Roman Emperor and King of Spain, Henry VIII and Elizabeth I of England, Philip II of Spain and Suleiman the Magnificent, Sultan of the Ottoman Empire (who in 1529 was forced to abandon the siege of Vienna, but whose colossal empire stretched from Tangier to Baghdad and included North Africa, Egypt, Asia Minor, Palestine, Syria, the Balkans and Hungary).

According to A Blanqui (*L'Histoire du Commerce*, Paris, 1826: the shortest and one of the best-ever economic history books), the circumnavigation of the Cape of Good Hope and the opening of a new trade route to the Orient by Vasco da Gama in 1498 hit Venice like lightning. This may be something of an exaggeration, since Venice remained an important trading city for most of the 15th Century, but the long-term impact was, as Montesquieu remarked, to throw Venice into a corner of the world, where it has remained. Of equal importance in the decline of Venice were extremely costly wars against the Turks, which essentially impoverished the city.

The circumnavigation of the Cape of Good Hope was the crowning achievement of the Portuguese expansion along the West African coast, a process that had started at the beginning of the 15th Century. All-water trade routes to the Orient meant far lower transportation costs between the northern European cities and Asia than could be provided via the troublesome land route across the Alps to Venice, by ship to Alexandria or other Mediterranean ports in the Near East, and then along the Silk Road to Asia or by ship to India.

The Portuguese did not waste any time with the expansion of their Oriental trading empire. Through military action and diplomacy, they established settlements at Hormuz, Goa, Diu (on India's west coast), Cochin, Malacca, Macau, the Spice Islands of Indonesia, Limpiao (Ningbo), Nagasaki, Ceylon and Mozambique. The impact of the new Portuguese trading empire was felt almost immediately in Venice. Its merchants found it increasingly difficult to purchase pepper in India due to the competition from the Portuguese. Because of lower shipping costs pepper subsequently sold for about 50% less in Lisbon than in Venice, which naturally attracted northern European traders to buy from the Portuguese capital.

The rise of Western empires

Around 1550, we encounter a global economy that bears little resemblance to that of the 15th Century. The Portuguese hold almost a monopoly over the Oriental spice trade. Goa (then a very wealthy city) is their centre in Asia and the chief port of western India. Through Malacca (probably the richest city in the region before they arrived) they control the passage from the Indian Ocean to the South China Sea. Through Ormuz, they control the Persian Gulf and trade routes to Central Asia; through Aden, trade in the Arabian Peninsula; while a number of forts along the west and east

African coasts secure them the route around the Cape. From Macau, the Portuguese trade actively with Japan, and at the same time, their settlements in the Moluccas ensure control over the supply of spices. The only other European nation with a presence in Asia is Spain, which had laid claim to the Philippines after Magellan's landing in Cebu in 1521 (Manila became Spain's administrative centre in 1571).

In the West, Lisbon was now the most important commercial centre in the south, while Antwerp had taken over that role for northern Europe from Bruges. In fact, according to Braudel (*Civilisation & Capitalism 15th-18th Century*, New York 1982), Antwerp in the "age of the Fuggers" became the centre of the entire international economy, dethroning Venice and edging out Lisbon, mainly because the Portuguese decided to ship their pepper to Antwerp and load there the copper and silver from German mines to pay for the spices, rather than trading at Bruges. Initially, this prosperity rested on the pepper trade with Lisbon. Later, Antwerp's strength was due to the trade of silver, exchanged at Antwerp with the Spanish city of Seville for linen, timber, household goods, tar, ships, wheat and rye, partly for Spain's own use and partly for trans-shipment to the Americas. But, even more importantly, silver had to be shipped to Antwerp to pay the interest on the huge Spanish war debts.

In the second half of the 16th Century, Antwerp's economy came under pressure from a series of unfortunate events, which included the Spanish state bankruptcy of 1557 (followed by further Spanish defaults in 1575, 1596, 1607, 1627 and 1647) and the sacking of Antwerp by unpaid Spanish mercenaries; as well as internal disturbances because of religious wars. After the city's recapture by Spain, in 1585, many Jewish and Protestant families chose to move to Amsterdam, at the time a city within the jurisdiction of the Independent United Provinces, where in 1672, as Sir William Temple wrote, no man had "any reason to complain of oppression in Conscience" (*Observations upon the Provinces of the United Netherlands*, 1720).

There were other reasons for Antwerp's decline and Amsterdam's emergence as northern Europe's leading commercial centre. By the mid-

16th Century, Amsterdam had, to the detriment of Antwerp, become the principal grain market in northern Europe, which inevitably attracted merchants and bankers. France's revocation of the Edict de Nantes in 1685 also had a significant impact on the population and economy of free cities such as Amsterdam, Geneva, London, etc. A stream of mostly skilled and educated refugees (French Huguenots, Sephardic Jews, Antwerpers, German merchants, English, etc) chose to live in Amsterdam because of greater religious freedom and tolerance than in Spanish-controlled Antwerp.

The prosperity of Lisbon did not last much longer than that of Antwerp. The turning point was the unification of Spain and Portugal under King Philip II in 1580 (Portugal became independent again in 1640). Since the Dutch had been involved in a bitter struggle for independence from Spain, unification turned them into enemies of Portugal as well. As a result, they were no longer permitted to load cargo, which originated from the East, at Lisbon. This loss of business forced the Dutch to explore the East for themselves. In search of silk and spices they travelled to the Far East and eventually destroyed Portugal's lucrative East Asia trade monopoly. Therefore, Portugal experienced following its boom period, the most horrible poverty, as Blanqui remarked, because during the trading boom it had totally neglected its agriculture.

In 1596, the Dutch landed in the Spice Islands. Right from the start, Dutch policy in the East revolved around eroding the power base of the Portuguese. A particularly fortunate event had been the crushing defeat of the Spanish Armada by England in 1588, ending Spain's naval supremacy. In 1602, the Dutch East India Company was founded and empowered to discharge the function of a government in Asia, to engage in warfare with the Spanish and the Portuguese, and to secure a monopoly over the East India trade. The Dutch East India Company was extremely well capitalised and powerful (see Chapter 3).

After 1600, the Dutch were, thus, competing actively with the Portuguese in the East and managed to gradually undermine their rivals' position. In 1640, the Dutch dealt the Portuguese a fatal blow with the capture of Malacca, strategically the most important port city in the East. At about the same time, they also took possession of Ceylon from the Portuguese and established themselves at Nagasaki, following the expulsion of the Portuguese by Japan on religious grounds.

By the mid-17th Century, then, there was an important change in the economic centres of Asia. Under the Portuguese, Goa had been the focus of all westbound trade (mostly spices). Now, with the Dutch controlling most of the Far Eastern region, Batavia became the focal point. All goods shipped to the West had first to be sent to Batavia for clearance - a practice that became terribly inefficient as the amount of trade increased. The instructions from the Dutch government had been to monopolise the trade with the East Indies, and by 1680, the Dutch were in full control of the Far Eastern trade. Batavia was the East's most important centre, while Amsterdam had replaced Lisbon as Europe's commercial and financial nexus. For the first time in history, capitalism began to flourish. Amsterdam opened the first active stock exchange. This allowed the very high risks associated with overseas trade to be spread and thus fostered its expansion enormously.

The Portuguese had lost their Far East trade monopoly to the Dutch, and the English were not yet important players. The Dutch East India Company flourished, and at its peak had about 150 trading ships, 40 war ships and some 8,000 employees. However, Dutch hegemony didn't last much longer than the Portuguese. Continuous wars in Europe, decadence in the colonies, mismanagement and corruption all had a negative influence on the country's economic power base, rendering it vulnerable. Towards the end of the 17th Century, the Dutch East India's Company's fortunes began to decline, and this provided an opportunity for England to break its monopoly.

Britannia and the Far East

The English sailed to the Far East in 1600 and established factories at Bantam in Java; they landed in Japan and China in 1637. But the efforts of the British East India Company were focused on India, where it established several settlements. In 1765, it took possession of large territories in India and the company's headquarters moved to Calcutta, which became the centre of the British Eastern Empire and the capital of India.

In the 18th Century, England also developed an active and highly profitable trade with China, and gradually eroded the Netherlands' strong economic position in the East because of a change in demand for various commodities. Until around 1700, spices, silk, cotton and foodstuffs were the main exports to Europe. In the 18th Century, tea and coffee became the most important export commodities. At the time, tea originated exclusively in China, while the Dutch East Indies produced coffee. The problem with the China trade was that, while England was buying increasing quantities of Chinese silk and tea, China bought little from the English merchants apart from some cotton, woollen goods and furs. So there was a constant balance of trade deficit, with silver flowing out of England.

In an attempt to correct this situation, the English began to ship opium from Calcutta to their "factories" in Canton (now Guangzhou), where it was sold to the Chinese. The English were not the first foreigners to sell opium to the Chinese. The Portuguese had done so for centuries, and American merchants had begun to supply Turkish opium to China. But it was the English who were able to supply large quantities cheaply, because the drug came mainly from Bengal, which enjoyed favourable growing conditions and was under British rule.

At the start of the 19th Century, the English were shipping around 2,000 chests (of 150 pounds each) of opium to China. By 1836, the annual trade in the drug had reached 26,000 chests. A consequence of this sharp rise was a swing in the trade balance with China in favour of England. For the British Eastern Empire and its capital, Calcutta, the opium trade became a huge, highly profitable business, which strengthened the position of the English in Asia. By the 1840s, about 25% of India's revenue was derived from opium sales. But China was now losing silver, and the opium trade began to be of great concern to its government.

Another event, which badly damaged the Dutch, was the Napoleonic Wars in Europe. When Holland was annexed by Napoleon, the Dutch East Indies became French. But following the defeat of the French navy in the Battle of Trafalgar, the English captured Batavia and annexed the island of Java. However, after the Battle of Waterloo, in 1815, the British returned Malacca and the East Indies to the Dutch in return for the Dutch recognition of Stamford Raffles new city Singapore, whose strategic location at the narrow Straits of Malacca was of vital importance for the Calcutta-Canton trade. The gateway to China was now secure.

In 1825, the situation in Asia was as follows: the metropolis of commerce was Calcutta, which was also the capital of the British Eastern Empire. The Dutch had suffered seriously as a result of Amsterdam's economic decline (which began around 1750) and the country's annexation by France during the Napoleonic War. Amsterdam had for some time been replaced by London as the commercial and financial centre of Europe. London was England's dominant city; in 1700 it was home to over 550,000 (10% of the country's population) and was Western Europe's largest city.

London's size and commercial importance in the 18th and 19th centuries was remarkable, considering that, in the 18th Century, the total population of the British Isles was less than half that of France or Spain. The reason for London's dominance was that, as the country's capital, it was the political centre, the royal court was there, it was Britain's main port (handling three-quarters of England's foreign trade), it was high society's playground, and the locus of international finance, commerce and culture. In Asia, trading between Canton and Calcutta had become the main business. Previously important cities, such as Malacca and Penang, were losing out to Singapore, which had become a significant port of call for English ships sailing through the Straits of Malacca. New Holland (Australia) had received its first shipments of English convicts, who were largely dependent on food supplies shipped from England. Much of Asia was still unexplored (the Borobudur temple in Java was only discovered by westerners in 1814).

In 1839, Chinese troops surrounded the foreign factories in Canton and demanded that all stocks of opium be handed over to them. All together, 20,283 chests were surrendered and promptly destroyed. This incident provoked the First Opium War and, after the defeat, China agreed to cede the island of Hong Kong to Britain and open five ports for trade. These so-called treaty ports were Canton, Amoy, Fuzhou, Ningbo and Shanghai. Following the second Anglo-Chinese War (1856-58), China also ceded the south tip of the Kowloon Peninsula to the British, and in 1898, the mainland leased the New Territories to Britain for 99 years. Hong Kong's population grew from around 30,000 in 1851 to 880,000 in 1931. When Japan occupied Manchuria in 1937 and Canton fell to the Japanese in 1938, there was a massive influx of refugees to Hong Kong. At the start of the Second World War, Hong Kong's population was estimated to be 1.6 million. In 1941, the Japanese occupied Hong Kong and evicted large numbers of the Chinese residents. By the end of the war, the population had fallen to around 600,000. However, the rise to power of the communists in China led to a tremendous influx to the city, and by 1950 around 2.2 million people lived in the colony.

Asian developments

The opening of the treaty ports was very beneficial to commerce, and the concession system in Shanghai was equally favourable for that city's economic development. By 1930, Shanghai accounted for over 54% of all of China's foreign trade, and it was one of the largest and economically most important cities in the world, comparable to London, New York, Berlin and Chicago.

By the time the Second World War began to loom, the balance of economic power in Asia had altered significantly. Shanghai was the Paris of the East and the most important city in Southeast Asia. Burma had been opened up and had grown rich in the process. The capital, Rangoon, was much more important that Bangkok, in economic terms. The French had conquered Vietnam, and Calcutta's heyday was over. When China concluded an agreement with India in 1907 to sharply reduce the opium trade, Calcutta's main source of revenue dried up. The city's economic and political decline accelerated when Delhi became the new capital of India in 1911.

Japan had emerged as a powerful military force, having defeated China in the Sino-Japanese War of 1895 and Russia in the Russo-Japanese War of 1905. The country's military and economic achievements were particularly impressive, given that Japan had had very little contact with the Western world before the mid-19th Century, when Commodore Perry forced the Japanese to sign a treaty with the United States which called for the opening of several ports to American ships. The treaty port system developed in China was later established in Japan, with the most-favoured nation clause extending US landing rights and benefits to other Western powers as well. The opening of Japan to Western influence led to the Meiji Restoration, which transformed the formerly highly decentralised, archaic, feudal system into a modern state.

Taiwan, occupied since 1895 by the Japanese, was still an agricultural country, and Korea had been annexed by Japan following the Russo-Japanese War. The port cities of Hong Kong and Singapore were thriving, but they looked like villages in comparison with the industrial colossus of Shanghai. Manila was growing in importance. In 1898, following the Spanish-American War, the Philippines had been ceded by Spain to the United States, along with Puerto Rico and Guam. In the 16th and 17th centuries, Manila had been a rather rich and economically important city in Asia because of its role as an entrepot for the silver trade. Silver mined at Potosi (Bolivia) was shipped from Acapulco to Manila, where it was exchanged for Chinese porcelain, pearls, precious stones and luxury cottons from India. Shortly before the Second World War, Manila was probably the third most important city in Asia, after Shanghai and Tokyo, since the Philippines was an American protectorate.

In China, civilisation developed early. There, we find a large number of cities, which, under different dynasties, became the capital (see Table 3).

Since China was for great periods a rather centralised society, dependent on the emperor and his political power, the political capital was usually also the county's largest, most prosperous city. In the Tang dynasty, under the emperor Taizong (627-650 AD), the country became quite wealthy and its capital, Chang'an became a showpiece of elegance and riches. Silk, then selling in Europe for its weight in gold, was common dress for half of Chang'an and fur coats were worn by many. Under the Sung dynasty, the capital moved first to Kaifeng (some estimates place its population at 1,200,000 in the 11th Century), but when invading Mongols destroyed it, the capital was relocated south of the Yangze River to Hangzhou.

Table 3

LEADING THE PACK

Largest cities of China

City	Population ('000)	Year
Ao (Cheng Chow)	32	1360 BC
Anyang	30	1200 BC
Loyang	50	800 BC
Lintzu	80	650 BC
Yenhsiatu	180	430 BC
Chang'an[1]	400	200 BC
Loyang	420	100 AD
Nanjing	150	361
Loyang	200	200
Chang'an	400	622
Chang'an	600	800
Chang'an	500	900
Kaifeng	400	1000
Keifeng[1]	442	1150
Hangzhou	255	1200
Nanjing	482	1400
Beijing[1]	672	1500
Beijing	650	1700
Beijing	1,100	1900
Shanghai	1,500	1925
Shanghai	5,000	1980

[1] Then also the world's largest city. Source: Chandler, *Four Thousand Years of Urban Growth*, New York, 1987.

Hangzhou had been an important commercial centre since the Tang dynasty, and the city gained importance following the construction of the Grand Canal connecting it to Beijing (its splendour and effective administration is well documented by Marco Polo, who stayed there at the court of Kublai Khan: "the streets are all paved with stone and bricks - there is an abundant quantity of game of all kinds - the number of bridges amount to 12,000 - in other streets are the quarters of the courtesans, who are here in such numbers as I dare not venture to report". Under Mongol rule (Yuan dynasty, 1271-1368), Beijing became the capital, but thanks to the issuance of paper money on a grand scale, industry and cities, like Guangzhou, Ningbo, Shanghai, Wenzhou and as mentioned above, Hangzhou, developed rapidly.

Still, in spite of the fact that, from time to time, important merchant cities developed, key economic areas shifted, principally depending on the empire's irrigation systems and the construction of water control works to increase agricultural productivity and facilitate grain transportation. Since antiquity, an elaborate system of irrigation canals, surface tanks, drainage, flood control works and artificial waterways were built as public works and, therefore, were linked very closely to politics. All these waterworks were used as crucial political tools by the various dynasties and their purpose and development were decided by the political objectives of the ruling class. In each period of Chinese history, there were favoured regions that received more attention at the expense of others (the shifts in the irrigation policies are reflected in the history of Chinese peasant rebellion).

So, whereas in Europe the shift in financial centres occurred more for economic (trade) reasons, different regions in China seem to have flourished at different times based on the state's waterworks policies. If I may make one general observation about the history of China's largest cities (and the capitals of the empire), which were also commercially more important, it is that none of these cities were located further south than Hangzhou; a fact that may have some relevance for making projections about the future regions of wealth in China. But the pattern in Chinese civilisation was overall much the same: over time, cities and regions rose and then fell depending on political, economic and social changes.

For our purposes, this brief description of some of history's great cities should be sufficient to permit us to formulate some thoughts on factors, which contributed to their rise and decay.

Reasons for the rise and decay of cities

Location

In looking at the fortunes of prominent cities, we cannot say that one particular factor was always dominant, but clearly location was important. Cities grew in regions that were fertile, or where irrigation systems (proximity to waterways) facilitated the exploitation of land. Very early civilisations developed in Mesopotamia between the Euphrates and the Tigris rivers, in China along the Yellow River and in Egypt along the Nile. This is natural, since the early civilisations were almost entirely agrarian. But it would appear that, up to this day, location has remained important to the prosperity of regions and cities. When commerce developed, cities that were located along the trade routes flourished (Turfan, Khotan, Samarkand, Bukhara, Bactria, Petra, Merv, Kashgar, Texila, Mathura, Pataliputra, Babylon, Seleucia, etc). Later, when the sea trade became more important, port cities emerged as great commercial centres (Tyre, Tripoli, Sidon, Carthage, Gades, Athens, Marseilles, Syracuse, Rhodes, Alexandria, Odessa, Aden, Ormuz; later, Venice, Famagusta, Genoa, Constantinople, Kaffa, Lisbon, Bordeaux, Bruges, Lübeck, Bremen, Danzig, Riga, Hamburg, Antwerp, Cadiz, Barcelona, Seville, etc).

Access to a port was also significant following the discoveries. This was the case in the Caribbean for Havana (the Spanish gateway to Latin America) and in South America for the coastal cities of Cartagena, Salvador de Bahia, Rio de Janeiro and Acapulco; and in Asia for Malacca, Goa, Batavia, Surat, Hangzhou, Canton, Shanghai, Amoy (Xiamen), Fuzhou and Nagasaki. Port cities also became North America's first important centres (Salem, Boston, Baltimore, New York - especially because of its inland waterways - Newport, New Orleans, Quebec and Montreal). In Africa, flourishing cities developed along the coast at Zanzibar, Mombassa, Mozambique, Luanda, Cape Town, Tangier, Algiers and Tunis. Location has remained important to date: during the Industrial Revolution, proximity to resources and waterways was crucial, and there is little doubt that access to the sea contributed to the economic development of the American western seaboard states (Long Beach is the largest seaport in the US today).

But are ports by themselves all that important? Or do they depend largely on trade flows? We have seen that the discovery of the trade routes around the Cape lessened the importance of the Mediterranean port cities. Equally, much later, the opening of the Suez Canal had a devastating impact on the transit port island of St Helena. And why did the port cities on the American West Coast begin to thrive? Obviously, because trade between the US and Asia gradually rose. Yet, had there been a huge desert between California and Asia, instead of water, which allowed for cheap transport, trade between the two would never have taken off. Thus, port cities, at least up to the present day, seem to have both stimulated and depended on trade. Cause and effect are not entirely discernible.

Prosperous cities also developed around resource-rich regions. We have seen that, at the beginning of the 17th Century, Potosi was South America's largest city. In the US, gold mining areas led to boomtowns. Much later, cities like Houston and Dallas became some of the nation's largest and economically most prominent centres on the back of their proximity to oil. So, throughout history, location has been important. Whether it will remain as significant in the future as it has been in the past, may be debatable. It is possible that seaports will lose importance as more and more high value cargo is shipped by air. Thus, the favourable location of airport hubs may become more of a factor. Or it may be that proximity to main markets will be more vital, because of the shortening life cycle of products through technological obsolescence (something which has certainly benefited Mexico in recent years, thanks to its closeness to the US). Maybe cities will thrive that are close to higher learning institutes (universities, technical colleges, research institutes). In any event, location is likely to remain of significance, although it will naturally be influenced by different issues, than in earlier times, when agriculture, resource wealth and trade routes contributed to the creation of rich cities.

I would add that a favourable location has also led to some very enduring centres of commerce. Since the dawn of history, there has always been an important city near the Nile delta: first Memphis, then Thebes, Alexandria and Cairo. Constantinople, as Istanbul, has remained relatively important thanks to its location straddling the Mediterranean and Black seas. There has always been an important city at the Straits of Malacca: Malacca, followed by Penang and Singapore. Similarly, in northern China, important cities always developed on the coast between Ningbo and Tianjin. Therefore, a favourable geographical situation is clearly a long-term positive factor for a city's economy.

Civic infrastructure and tolerance

Just as a company's long-term success depends largely on the quality of its management, cities with good administrations became rich. But what is a good administration? Is it the Singapore model, with strong economic management by the government, or is it the Hong Kong laissez-faire system? In my opinion, this is not the crucial issue. Both types of economic administration can succeed, as long as there is a *system* - as opposed to chaos. It must be fair to all market participants: with clear civil and commercial laws (well-defined accounting standards, property rights, well-regulated but free markets for goods, services and labour, an efficient financial market, bankruptcy laws, fair taxation, etc) strictly enforced and administered in an impartial way. One of the reasons for the rise of Rome and London was their sophisticated legal systems, which, certainly in the case of London, was completely impartial towards foreign merchants. Judiciary equality and independence may actually be more important to a city's success than is generally credited.

Successful cities not only had a good legal infrastructure, but other institutions and policies that fostered economic development. In former times, roads, bridges, ports and access to fresh water through aqueducts and canals, as well as to fresh food were particularly important (Rome dominated the world at least partly because of its unbelievable infrastructure and its rapid communication network). Today, a cost-efficient and technologically advanced communication system, uninterrupted power supply, convenient airport access, entertainment facilities, good living conditions and a pleasant climate may be factors to consider. Law and order is another component. Since people, especially minority groups, want to feel safe, efficient and incorruptible police and fire forces are relevant.

The devising of laws and their strict, impartial administration helped cities prosper; of equal importance was tolerance. Earlier, religious tolerance was an issue. Cordoba, under relatively relaxed Muslim rule, became rich, but disintegrated under the Spanish Inquisition. Throughout history, all great merchant cities, including Alexandria, Venice, Genoa, Lisbon, Antwerp (initially), Amsterdam, London, Hong Kong and Singapore, offered minority groups (admittedly, more or less) a level playing field. But religious matters or race were not the only areas in which tolerance had an impact. A dynamic society arises where there is also intellectual tolerance, freedom of conscience, social mobility, freedom of ideas, and their expression, even when hostile to established beliefs or to the government. When intellectuals, scientists and philosophers were persecuted and imprisoned (or tortured and murdered), they fled, taking with them their know-how; and it is this knowledge on which progress depends (after 1685, many of the French Huguenots, and their watch-making skills, moved to Switzerland). It is no accident that the calibre of teachers and pupils in higher learning institutes depends on the tolerance of the political system. I suppose that intellectual tolerance and religious freedom are important issues when we compare the economic success of relatively resource-poor North America in the 16th to 19th Century with resource-rich Spanish South America, or the wealth of market-based Western economies versus the poverty of totalitarian communist regimes in the 20th Century (it is interesting to note that, Japan aside, Asia has no world-class universities so far).

Still, I wish to repeat one caveat with regard to the abovementioned factors: causes and effects are not always clear-cut. Do cities and regions become rich because they have a good administration, a fair legal system, tolerance, free markets, higher learning institutes - or could it be that when cities become prosperous, there is a tendency toward better organisation (better administration), with the ruling class wishing to introduce laws to protect their property (ie, for their children's sake, they wish to replace the arbitrary system, under which they may have thrived, with the rule of law), with minorities becoming more acceptable and society generally growing more tolerant? Just consider the pirate Henry Morgan, who later in his life became an honourable man and was knighted! Or think of all the great gangsters, drug dealers and smugglers who send their children to American business schools to turn them into decent citizens! Obviously, with wealth comes the desire to preserve, and laws are introduced to protect one's property. So, again, causes and effects seem to continuously interact and reinforce themselves. In this respect, I am relatively optimistic that in time the nouveaux riches of Russia and China will wish to have a more structured commercial legal and commercial infrastructure in order to protect their earlier - frequently ill-acquired wealth.

Another caveat: When looking at factors that were conducive to the creation of wealth, we cannot be overly dogmatic. Whereas well-established property rights are favourable in the long term, the absence of such may have occasionally led to fantastic growth and development in the short term (mining cities, privateer centres, etc). I am also thinking of Shanghai's recent explosive growth. Had well-defined property rights been in place, it would never have been possible to develop so much new infrastructure in such a short period of time. Equally, I believe that, under the rule of law and with established property rights, Shanghai would not have decayed as much as it did under communist rule. So, a well-defined legal structure may be desirable in the long run, but it may have some growth-constraining effects in the short run. Yet, it should never be forgotten that, whereas the introduction of a good legal infrastructure usually has some beneficent effect on an economy, the removal of good legal practices in a system has always had a devastating impact on confidence and economic development!

In connection with tolerance, we should also consider whether religious beliefs, philosophies and ideologies were factors that led cities and societies to prosperity. Sociologist Max Weber thought that Protestant ethics were conducive to capitalistic behaviour by stressing strong work practices such as thrift, punctuality, austerity and dependability - a moral background he thought was absent elsewhere (Max Weber, *Protestant Ethic and the Spirit of Capitalism*, New York, 1930). But does Weber's theory hold? Could it not be, as a friend of mine maintains, that Protestantism was, at least in his native Germany, largely a movement against the economic power of the monasteries and the numerous religious holidays which prevented the labourers from working seven days a week: after all, Protestantism was happily supported by the feudal landlords, who wanted to make their labourers work harder. Equally, for years, books were published explaining why a capitalistic system never developed in China because of Confucianism, as opposed to feudal Japan, where the system took off. But in more recent years, scholars and political-freedom-averse politicians have been lauding the beneficial effect of Confucianism on economic development. In the context of China, I find this argument rather far-fetched, since China has remained relatively poor and because in the Chinese hierarchy, merchants (the pillars of capitalism and free markets, in our society) always belonged to the lowest class. So, what is the answer? Based on my observations, I strongly believe that a moral background, which encourages thrift, education, hard work, austerity, dependability, punctuality (all attributes also encouraged by Catholicism and Islam) - in short, discipline - is important. However, zealous excesses and fanaticism at the expense of freedom and tolerance are obviously destructive for economic development, as the Inquisition and communism have amply demonstrated.

Military and political power

Are military and political power factors in the creation of wealth? We have seen that the Assyrians, the Romans and the Mongols became rich largely because they invented an early and pre-capitalistic technique of takeovers, management buyouts, asset stripping (taking an entire population into slavery), downsizing (I am thinking of how influenza brought by the Spanish to the New World decimated the native population) and restructuring (the Romans spread their efficient management skills - good administration and legal system - throughout their entire empire) by means of military warfare. Was Timur the early version of a hedge fund manager? Smart and educated, with tremendous courage and a will to win (killer instinct), he rode throughout the world, sacking one city after another and making his own Samarkand a rich and glorious city.

But we have also seen that the Phoenicians, the Italian trading cities, and the Hanseatic towns became prosperous due to commerce and some industry - and without any military or political ambitions (the same applies to Switzerland, Australia, New Zealand, Singapore and Hong Kong). What is the answer? There are several points to consider: some people developed superior military skills and, for a while at least, had momentum and a "nothing to lose mentality". For momentum, we may consider the psychological elation of victory, which in warfare, may certainly lead to more victories (a winning streak). For "nothing to lose mentality", we may read a poor and oppressed people, with little or no economic opportunities (this phenomenon leads also to terrorism). One or other of these factors was certainly of some importance in the case of the Huns, the Tartars, the Mongols and the Romans, as well as Hellenistic Greece under Alexander the Great, France under Napoleon and Germany under Hitler. But raw power does not seem to have created lasting wealth. Initially, the purely military power - let us call it the parasite - was successful because it fed on an ageing society, the rich and helpless carrier. But, sooner or later, the parasite grew too big and itself became the carrier, which attracted other parasites to feed on it.

Also, to be fair to the Romans, we must understand that they did not become a highly developed society by military warfare. Rather, it was because of technological superiority (engineering skills), education (common sense, courage, nationalism, etc) and discipline (frugality, punctuality, reliability, accountability, etc) that they established an effective civilian defence force, which eventually became an aggressor and expanded the empire. Similarly, Venice also became a military power, but it did so because it had to protect its wealth. In the case of the Venetians, we can say with unquestionable certainty that their wealth did not derive from military power; rather, it was the other way around. The same is true of the Americans: Unlike Timur, they did not become rich through military aggression. They became the dominant military power in the world because they had technology, organisation skills, a strong sense of unity (patriotism) and could afford to maintain a large army.

So, while military power can lead to temporary wealth, lasting prosperity, such as we find in ancient Rome (an empire that lasted a surprisingly long time), and in modern times in the cases of the British Empire and the US, depends on other factors. However, there is no question that, in the past, military power did prolong prosperity - up to a certain point and with many qualifications, as I shall explain in Chapter 12. Still, we should not forget that, without military power, Constantinople or Venice would have been gobbled up by the attacking Turks. But would that have been so bad? After all, Constantinople regained its glory under Suleiman the Magnificent.

Is innovation necessary for a city's rise? In ancient times, innovations were the sail, the wheel, the war chariot, irrigation systems and, later, Roman infrastructure (roads, bridges and aqueducts), law and order. During the Dark Ages, Islamic societies advanced civilisation greatly with their mathematical skills (including accounting). The Italian city-states were great innovators of commercial and financial techniques. British and American cities became rich because of the industrial application of so many new inventions. Clearly innovation - that is, the application of innovation - is a powerful factor in the creation of rich cities. But innovations and inventions alone may not be sufficient. China excelled in both early in its existence, but what seemed to be lacking was an environment conducive to the commercial exploitation of its inventions. Compare this with 19th Century America: freedom, a capitalistic mentality, free markets and the drive and desire to succeed that the immigrants (released from conventions) brought to their new home, combined with abundant resources, created a very favourable environment for unprecedented economic development and progress.

Sheer size?

What about size? Do small cities have a better chance to become rich than large cities? Rich centres frequently grew into large ones (Babylon, Alexandria, Rome, Constantinople, Cordoba, London, Hangzhou, New York, etc). But, many small cities became immensely prosperous despite their lack of scale (Amalfi, Cadiz, Goa, Batavia, Geneva, Abu Dhabi, Monaco, etc). I am not sure there is an answer to this question. Which perform better: large or small companies? Recent experience would suggest large companies, but obviously there are times when small companies do better. Similarly, there may be times when large cities are more successful, while in some circumstances small cities may have an edge. Consider warfare as an issue. Since conquering armies always target the political capital of a country, such cities, which are also economic centres (London, Paris, Tokyo) may be more vulnerable. Conversely, capital cities that rely mainly on politics (Brasilia, Canberra, Beijing), would not seem particularly vulnerable - although the 11 September terrorists attacked both the economic and political meccas of America. A generalisation about the size factor may not be possible. However, one point would seem to be relevant. Take a small city-state or city with a high degree of autonomy at the edge of or in the middle of a huge empire (Venice, Bruges, Goa, Tangier, Antwerp in their early days, Genoa, Hong Kong until July 1997, Singapore for the foreseeable future). In such cases, because of its autonomy, the small city can obviously benefit greatly from such a favourable position.

Why great cities fall

What do we mean by the fall of a city? In some cases, it is obvious: Pompeii was totally destroyed by the violent eruption of Vesuvius in 79 AD. Nineveh, Babylon, Seleucia, Carthage, Rome, Pagan and Angkor also experienced categorical declines. But the decline of Venice in the 16th and 17th Centuries was not so absolute. After all, until the 18th Century, it remained quite prosperous, though its commercial importance had definitely diminished. So, when we talk about cities' rise and fall, we must consider that the rise of most lasted for a long time and was always accompanied by cycles of rapid growth and interruption by recessions. Conversely, their decline (aside from destruction through war or natural disaster) also took time, sometimes up to several hundred years, and was interrupted by periods of recovery.

Cities that became rich through warfare (most ancient cities) also generally lost their wealth through war. War is, therefore, an important factor in the loss of a city or country's wealth. However, this is a superficial explanation of a system's decline. For why does a city that became rich from warfare suddenly begin to lose conflicts? There must be underlying factors at work, which lead to this loss of military competitiveness, which indicates that the loss of wealth through war is a symptom, and not the actual cause. After all, in our capitalistic age, when a company goes bankrupt, competition is not the cause of the collapse. What caused the bankruptcy was the company's failure to take adequate measures (reserves, low gearing, innovation, new markets, new products, cost cutting, etc) to beat the competition. Thus, when discussing reasons for the fall of great cities, we must be careful to distinguish between symptoms and causes.

Do success and wealth sow the seeds of failure? Cities and countries that became rich and powerful inevitably grew arrogant, overconfident and complacent, and they tended to overspend. Internal strife inevitably followed the accumulation of wealth and power. Prosperous cities and countries tended to concentrate on the business that made them rich and neglect diversification of their interests. Wealthy cities and countries also always had surplus funds to invest: this excess liquidity led to a high domestic price level (loss of competitive position) and, as time went by, these funds were invested in less profitable ventures. Consequently, profit margins fell. Rich cities also always invested in foreign countries and so became more vulnerable to outside shocks. And, lastly, whereas hardship and outside pressure have a unifying effect and bind a society together, wealth leads to internal struggle and factional division.

Wherever we live, whatever we do and whomever we socialise with, it is quite obvious to us all that with success a certain arrogance, self righteousness, overconfidence and complacency arise. Very successful societies, and all the cities I have mentioned in this chapter were at some point the Xeroxes of the urban universe, and suffered the consequences. Having enjoyed incredible success, they adopted a "nothing can go wrong" attitude and committed gross errors of optimism. In some cases, they overspent and overinvested.

Lack of diversification also instigated the decline of cities. Most cities became rich as a result of one product or one industrial or service sector. They were trading, manufacturing or financial centres, or had built their wealth on conquests. However, the reliance on one product also made them vulnerable to changes in the demand for their product. Markets for all goods, including conquests, become saturated. Furthermore, competition in one or other form inevitably comes up and lowers profit margins. Worst of all, the demand for a product can disappear - for whatever reason. The rounding of the Cape by the Portuguese led to decreased demand for Venice's trading services and profit margins deteriorated. Venice's profit margins also came under pressure because the city tried to protect its trading monopoly through costly warfare. Incidentally, the lack of diversification is a problem endemic to all boomtowns. Potosi and Manaus completely failed to diversify, and when the demand for their products or the supply shrank (depleted mines), they subsided into oblivion.

Every wealthy city had to cope with the problem of rising prices, which led to a loss of competitiveness. Rome and Spain suffered from high inflation. The armies of these empires consequently became more expensive than their competitors' (enemies).

Social strife was also endemic to wealthy cities. I presume (because statistics are lacking) that this discord arose because of an unequal distribution of wealth or because of economic downturns. Class struggles always proved costly and weakened the city's *esprit de corps*. By no longer pulling together, the members of rich societies became less resilient to foreign intruders or outside shocks. And whenever something went wrong, someone had to be blamed for the social, political or economic disturbance. Naturally, this was reserved for the minorities. At worst, these groups (Jews,

Huguenots, Indians, Armenians, foreigners generally) were expelled (as happened in Spain in 1492 and in many other European cities during the Middle Ages, as well as in the 1970s in Uganda) or their security was threatened to the point that they left voluntarily.

One should not forget the fact that the merchant class and banking families frequently belong to minority groups. Because of their social structure and the international nature of their businesses, minorities can be extremely mobile. When business or social climates deteriorated, they simply packed their bags and left (this was particularly true of the Jews in the Middle Ages, since they were frequently prevented from owning property, which made them even more mobile). In this respect, it will be interesting to see what the Chinese reaction will be if conditions in Hong Kong deteriorate badly one day. Guess who might be blamed for the problems.

Looking at the history of cities and empires, it strikes me that some rose very rapidly and then fell with similar speed, while others were actually extremely resilient and endured for a surprisingly long time. Whereas the Huns, Tartars and Mongols enjoyed a brief place in the sun, the Roman and British empires survived for centuries. Their endurance was largely due to their discipline, education, patriotism, legal and commercial infrastructure, strong administrative skills, and military power. Conversely, where societies only developed informal structures with arbitrary governments, their success depended entirely on the genius of their leaders. Therefore, when Alexander, Attila, Genghis Khan, Timur, Akbar and Kublai Khan died, their empires and cities expired with them.

What of the future?

We have seen that centres of prosperity do change over time - and we can expect much of the same in the future. The difference may be that change could, in fact, accelerate. Consider that, at the time of the Portuguese expansion in the Orient, a return sea voyage to the Moluccas took up to three years. At the start of the 18th Century, return sea voyages to China took about two years. Even in the 1850s, ships still took over four months to sail from London to Shanghai. But after the opening of the Suez Canal in 1869, travel times to Hong Kong and Shanghai fell to just 40 and 43 days, respectively. Today, ships can cover this distance in about 25 days and jumbo jets do it in less than 13 hours. In the meantime, electronic communication has become instantaneous and almost negligible in cost terms.

So, change in the economic landscape of the world will occur at an increasing pace. Now, think of America in 1850 (see Table 1) and in 1950. In 1850, urban real estate prices on the East Coast were maybe 100 times higher than in the West Coast (which was barely settled). A century later, this price differential no longer existed because the American economic geography had changed radically. In just 100 years, entirely new cities had sprung up and taken positions as important commercial and industrial centres - the Midwest and Texas too. I believe that, because of the *acceleration in the pace of change we are currently experiencing*, countries that began to open up after the breakdown of communism can industrialise and become prominent economic centres in less than 20 years.

Compare the industrialisation of the American continent with recent development in Asia. It took America about a hundred years to industrialise, and by 1900, agriculture and mining were still more important than manufacturing. Japan, Taiwan and South Korea industrialised in about 40 years and now China has essentially done it in a little more than 20! Or consider the development of China's equity markets. Stock trading started in the late 1980s and by 1990 the market cap reached about US$1 billion. By 1997 it was US$172 billion and it now exceeds US$500 billion - after Japan, the largest market in Asia. By comparison, the US markets in 1950, more than 100 years after trading began, amounted to only US$86 billion and only rose above US$500 billion in the mid 1960s. Japan's market cap exceeded US$50 billion for the first time in 1971, and Hong Kong's in 1986.

No other country in the world has ever developed, in such a short space of time, such a large financial market as China. Moreover, a few years ago, real estate prices in Hong Kong were still eight to ten times higher than in Beijing and Shanghai. The difference has quickly narrowed as prices rise in China and fall in Hong Kong. I believe that, in the next ten to twenty years, we are going to see mind-boggling change in terms of new centres of wealth. Shanghai property values might easily exceed Hong Kong's and possibly even New York's. Bangalore in India, never a topic of discussion ten years ago, may one day displace Silicon Valley. After all, American manufacturing centres also displaced Manchester, Birmingham and Lancaster (in 1835, Lancashire had more industrial machines installed than the rest of the world combined).

Therefore, I would not rule out that, just as Lancashire was the workshop of the world in the early 19th Century, China will one day assume the mantle and produce, with its 1.2 billion people, more manufactured goods than the rest of the world combined. Why not? After all, its population as a percentage of world population is far larger than that of Lancashire ever was! Also, if you look at China's economic geography before the communist takeover in 1946, it is evident that Shanghai and Manchuria were the dominant economic centres (see Tables 4 and 5). When China shut its doors to the outside world in 1949, it created opportunity for Hong Kong, Taiwan and South Korea to develop very quickly. But now with China opening up at breakneck speed, I believe the economic geography will once again change radically - with the Ningbo-Shanghai-Tianjin corridor becoming the principal cluster of economic activity.

Table 4

WHO WAS WHERE

Geographical distribution of foreign direct investment in China in 1931

	Great Britain	Japan	Russia	USA	Total (US$m)	% of total
Shanghai	737.4	215.0	-	97.5	1,049.9	46.0
Manchuria	-	550.2	261.8	-	812.0	36.0
Rest of China (incl. Hong Kong)	226.0	108.9	11.4	52.7	399.0	17.6
Total	963.4	874.1	273.2	150.2	2,260.9	100.0

Table 5

BRITISH FOCUS

British business investment in China, 1929

	Pounds	US$	% of total
Shanghai	151,527,500	737,408,000	76.6
Hong Kong	18,455,300	89,812,000	9.3π
Rest of China	27,979,000	136,160,000	14.1
Total	197,961,800	963,380,000	100.0

Note: Hong Kong even though it was a British colony only received 9.3% of Britain's investments in China! Source: Remer, C. F., *Foreign Investments in China*, New York, 1933.

The point of this chapter is really that if investors sit and think that the world's economic geography will still look the same in ten, twenty or fifty years time, they are in for some financially unpleasant surprises. The breakdown of communist and socialist regimes and the end of Indian self-reliance and isolationism will enlarge the world's economic sphere as much as the discovery voyages of the 15th Century. We have seen how, after the discovery of the Americas and the trade route around the Cape of Good Hope, the established order altered totally. The entire economic centre of the world, until then concentrated around the Mediterranean, moved to the Atlantic coast to capitalise on the rising movement of goods and people to the Americas and the Far East. Similarly, the rise of China, India and the rest of Asia, with their three billion people, will undoubtedly have a very profound effect on the global economic, social and geopolitical balance. The same will be true of the rise of Russia and the former countries of the Soviet Union.

I, therefore, argue that the richest cities of the present day are most unlikely to remain so in the future and that investors should not be complacent and underestimate the rapidity with which changes are taking place right now! A young adventurer in Asia today would be wise to look at cities like Shanghai, Ho Chi Minh, Yangon or Ulan Bator - and possibly even Pyongyang.

In Chapter 2, I explained how money will always pour from the large water bowl on to the earth, but that from time to time there will be changes as into which sector of the economy or regions around the world money would flow to. In the late 1990s, the world's surplus funds found their way to the US and financed its rising trade and current account deficits. But, for reasons I shall explain in the following chapter, I doubt that the world's monetary surpluses will continue to finance the imbalances of the US *ad infinitum* and that a major shift in the movement of international capital flows is already underway.

CHAPTER TWELVE

Why the US is unlikely to provide the next leadership

> The most important thing about money is to maintain its stability ... You have to choose (as a voter) between trusting to the natural stability of gold and the natural stability and intelligence of the members of the Government. And, with due respect to these gentlemen, I advise you, as long as the Capitalistic system lasts, to vote for gold.
>
> *GEORGE BERNARD SHAW (1856-1950)*

I am always amazed when people talk about a new era being so much different from the past, when in fact human nature and people's behaviour has changed so little in the course of history. Recently, I read Virginia Cowles' entertaining *The Great Swindle - The Story of the South Sea Bubble* (Collins, 1960). The book deals with the rise and fall of the South Sea Company and John Law's Mississippi Company in the early 18th Century. As I read, I became fascinated by the many parallels between this early period of speculation in our capitalistic age and today's financial environment. In particular, I was astounded by the similar role that paper money, excessive credit creation and highly questionable practices - by governments as well as businesses - played in fuelling the financial excesses of both periods. I was initially hesitant about discussing this unusual period at the dawn of capitalism, but when I stumbled across a figure showing the movement of the Argentine Peso per ounce of gold (see Figure 1), I knew that what happened in recent years was not much different from what happened with John Law's first experiment with pure paper money (of which, more follows below).

Figure 1

UP IN SMOKE

Argentine Pesos per ounce of gold, 2000-2002

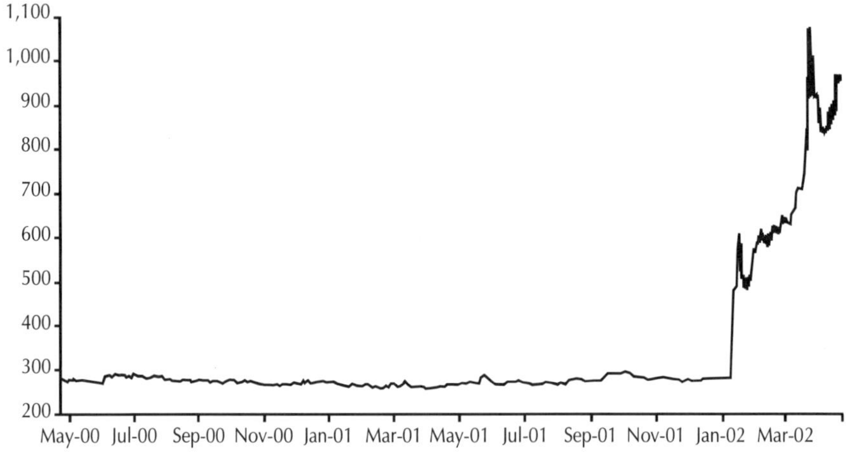

Source: Prof. Werner Antweiler, University of British Columbia, Vancouver.

What also caught my attention in early 2002 was the rallying cry by a number of US academics and opinion leaders that the US should not only behave like a superpower but also like an empire. This change in attitude was most likely a consequence of the 11 September attacks and deserves some discussion in the second part of this chapter.

As we saw in Chapter 8, from time to time, waves of optimism spread around the world like bushfire. People believe that they are seeing the dawn of a new era that will bring unimaginable riches and prosperity to all - and investment manias flourish. New-era thinking has been associated with discoveries (the Americas, new gold deposits), the opening up of new territories (the American West, China in recent years), new inventions (canals, railroads, the automobile, radio, PCs, the internet, wireless devices, etc), rising commodity prices (rubber in the early 20th Century, oil in the 1970s), peace treaties (the breakdown of communism), or strong economic performances in hitherto unconsidered countries.

The 1990s entailed all these factors. We had, with the breakdown of communism, a colossal enlargement of the global economic sphere, whereby many countries opened up and close to three billion people joined the capitalistic system. We also experienced the application and vast improvement of many new electronic inventions, which led to a boom in the hi-tech and communications sector. There was, also thanks to the breakdown of communism, a peace dividend in as far as Western defence budgets could be reduced. Then, we had the move towards globalisation, which led to a significant pickup in world trade as countries removed or reduced import restrictions, tariffs and foreign exchange controls. Lastly, for the first time in history we had a truly global financial market, which enabled capital to move from one corner of the world to another and finance all kinds of investments, which led - at least temporarily - to strong economic growth in some parts of the world.

The South Sea Bubble and the Mississippi Scheme

A typical feature of new-era thinking is that it usually engulfs a country or the world not at the beginning of an era of prosperity, but towards the end, and is associated with some sort of a "rush" or investment mania. Two of the best examples of this phenomenon are John Law's Mississippi Scheme and the South Sea Bubble, which occurred almost simultaneously in the early 1700s and have some relevance with respect to the current monetary environment.

In 1711, Robert Harley, Earl of Oxford, established the South Sea Company to take over £10 million of government debt, which was converted into shares of the company. In exchange, it received annual interest payments from the government and a monopoly to trade with the Spanish subjects in South America. In addition, a year later, the company obtained exclusive rights to sell slaves in South America. Right from the start, it enjoyed great prestige, but profits were elusive. The Spanish King Philip V refused to let it send more than one cargo of merchandise per year to South America - and even from this slim venture, insisted on a share of the profit. Moreover, the *Assiento*, the permission to transport black slaves to the South American plantations, was fraught with high risks, since many died on the way and the unarmed ships were frequently attacked by buccaneers or were driven away by Spanish coast guards, who sided with competing privateers and pirates.

On top of these difficulties, in 1715 the company lost two of its founders, Lord Bolingbroke and Lord Oxford, both of whom were accused of treason. At this point, the directors thought it wise to interest King George I in their affairs in the hope that he might secure them more advantageous terms with Spain. Since the Hanoverian king had no wish to embroil himself in English business matters, the directors enrolled the services of his two mistresses, Madams Schulenburg and Kielmansegge, both of whom were extremely greedy (and ugly), but held considerable influence over George. As a result, the company eventually managed - through political manoeuvring, bribes to the two mistresses (in the form of shares in the company), and intrigue - to get him to accept an invitation to act as Governor of the South Sea Company.

In the meantime, John Law a Scottish adventurer, understanding the laws of probability, had made a fortune as a professional gambler. Law had been exiled from Britain for killing a man in a duel and was later also banished from France for holding the view that paper money was superior to gold and silver. "When blood does not circulate through the body," he said "the body languishes; the same when money does not circulate." But in 1713, after the War of the Spanish Succession, he returned to France where, following the death of Louis XIV in 1715, he was successful in convincing the regent, the Duc d'Orleans, of the advantages of paper money and credit. In 1716, Orleans gave him royal permission to open Banque Générale, which issued paper money on the guarantee that it would always be redeemable in gold coins of a fixed weight (in principle, a private gold standard). The bank's capital comprised of one-quarter in coin and three-quarters in government billets. With the help of the regent, the bank became an immediate success. Its notes were very convenient, since the government accepted them for tax payments. (In 1718, the government even guaranteed the bank's obligations.)

In 1717, Law convinced the regent to grant his new Mississippi Company a monopoly over all commerce between France and its territories in North America - which included the present states of Louisiana, Mississippi, Arkansas, Missouri, Illinois, Iowa, Wisconsin and Minnesota - in return for accepting outstanding notes of the French government as payment for the Mississippi shares. This amounted to a partial conversion of France's government debt into shares of the Mississippi Company.

The operations of the company did not prove profitable. In part, this was because, when it issued shares, instead of cash it received only government debt. It was also due partly to the fact that very few French wanted to emigrate to the American territories. In desperation, Law devised a scheme whereby imprisoned women and men were released on condition that they marry and emigrate. Such couples were paraded through Paris in chains - which, it appears, were less a symbol of marriage than a means to prevent the newlyweds from 'eloping'.

Nevertheless, by 1719, the Mississippi Company's shares had declined to 300 livres, down significantly from the issue price of 500 livres. At this point, Law had a great idea: he announced that, in six months' time, he would pay 500 livres for a certain number of shares in the company. The public immediately thought that if the promoter was willing to pay almost twice the prevailing stock price, it must be because he knew of some favourable developments. Investors assumed that future capital gains were assured and so gradually pushed up the price of the stock.

Following his announcement, the highly regarded Law - as great a talker and promoter as some of today's high-tech executives - announced that the company had engaged in a series of new ventures and acquisitions with the support of the regent. In 1718, he had bought the monopoly on the tobacco trade, and in 1719 he purchased the French East India and China companies and acquired the coinage monopoly, the tax farms and the national Banque Royale - all in return for taking over the entire French national debt, which then amounted to 1.5 billion livres.

The scheme was brilliant. The Mississippi Company would pay the government 1.5 billion livres; in turn, the government would repay its creditors - who would then invest the money they received in shares of the company, which Law offered them at a discount. The government was to pay only 3% interest on its debt to the Mississippi Company, whereas it had paid its public creditors 4%.

The scheme worked perfectly well for a while, as each time the company announced some new venture, additional shares would be issued at higher and higher prices, which attracted a larger and larger number of speculators to participate in, what became, a mania. In particular, public enthusiasm was fuelled by the government, which had begun to run its money-printing presses around the clock. By then, the regent had taken over Banque Générale (presumably given by Law in exchange for all those privileges), which now became the Banque Royale in December 1718. But, whereas Law had always maintained a small gold reserve to back the paper money the bank issued, he now advised the regent that the public had gained sufficient confidence in paper money and that, therefore, gold reserves in the bank's vault were no longer necessary. (This rings a bell when one considers the recent gold sales by central banks.)

As a result, in 1719, the government increased the money supply dramatically and lowered interest rates by lending money for as little as 1% or 2%. In addition, it became common practice to buy the company's shares on instalment, spread over 12 monthly payments (an early margin account). The aim of this measure was clearly to manipulate the shares to higher and higher prices. Indeed, a wave of unprecedented speculation spread through France, and people came from all over Europe to speculate in Mississippi Company shares in rue Quincampoix, where even common people made fortunes. (The word "millionaire" was coined at this time. From the latin *mille*, it originally referred to someone possessing a *thousand* livres.) When aristocrats complained that their cooks had thus become millionaires and left their employment, Law wrote: "The gates of wealth are now open to all the world. It is that which distinguishes the fortune of the old administration from those of the present" (typical new-era rhetoric). In fact, Law was very generous to the aristocracy, on whose goodwill his scheme depended to some extent. He always reserved shares for important people.

The vast increase in the supply of paper money, combined with the ability to purchase shares in the Mississippi Company on credit, led not only to the share price rocketing above 20,000 livres towards the end of 1719 (from 300 at the beginning of the year). Alas, it also saw rapid price increases across France. The cost of bread, milk and meat rose sixfold, while cloth was up by 300%.

The result of this horrendous inflation made the holders of Mississippi shares and paper money nervous, and in January 1720, just two weeks after Law had been appointed Comptroller General of Finance, a number of large speculators decided to cash out and into "real assets" such as property, commodities and gold. This drove down the price of the shares, and since the speculators could only pay for real assets with banknotes, as confidence in paper money quickly waned, the price of land and gold soared. This forced Law, who at the time still enjoyed the backing of the regent, to take extraordinary measures. Two things had to be done: people had to be prevented from reverting to gold (since by then Banque Royale had only 2% of its assets in gold); and the share price of the Mississippi Company had to be stabilised. Thus, Law proclaimed that, henceforth, only banknotes were legal tender: Payments in gold and silver above 100 francs were prohibited, and ownership of gold exceeding 500 livres was declared illegal. He even abolished the use of gold and silver as specie (from May 1720, gold and silver would no longer be coined), and proclaimed that they could no longer be used to pay any form of debt, including foreign ones.

Severe penalties were imposed on people who hoarded gold. To enforce this most blatant expropriation, Law handed out large rewards to those who assisted in the discovery of gold, which was then confiscated. He then implemented another even more desperate measure. Altogether, the Mississippi Company had issued 624,000 shares. Given a share price of about 10,000 livres, the market cap was therefore around six billion livres (or about £300 million), a colossal amount at that time. The only way such a large market cap could be maintained would be to pay a dividend. But the company didn't have sufficient income to pay even a 1% dividend and was therefore in a precarious position.

So Law merged Banque Royale and the Mississippi Company and announced that the price of the Mississippi stock would be fixed at 9,000 livres/share. He opened a bureau of conversion where the shares of the Mississippi Company could be bought and sold in exchange for banknotes. With this measure, he hoped that speculators would hold on to their shares until development of the American continent could produce a large profit for the shareholders. However, by then speculators had completely lost faith in the shares and selling pressure continued (in fact, instead of putting a stop to the selling, the fixed price acted as an inducement to sell), which led the bank once again to increase the money supply by an enormous quantity. The result was another round of sharply escalating prices. In four years, the supply of circulating medium had trebled.

Law suddenly realised that his main problem was no longer his battle against gold, which he had sought to debase (as today's central bankers are trying to do); his real enemy was inflation. He issued an edict by which banknotes and the shares of the Mississippi stock would gradually be devalued by 50%. As one can imagine, the public reacted to this edict with fury, and Law was soon 'asked' to leave the country. In the meantime, gold was again accepted as the basis of the currency, and individuals could own as much of it as they desired. Alas, as a contemporary noted, the permission came at a time when no one had any gold left, as the government had confiscated most of it.

The initial success of John Law's financial dealings hadn't gone unnoticed in England. Inspired by his scheme, John Blunt, a shady character who was dominant on the board of the South Sea Company, obtained rights to convert a large portion of government debt into shares of his company in return for a promise to pay the government £7.5 million. Blunt had beaten the Bank of England's proposal, which was similar in nature, because of the South Sea Company's excellent connections to influential politicians. The king and his entourage were all richly rewarded (bribed) for their support. (Unlike the Mississippi Company, the South Sea Company was a fraud right from the start.)

Blunt had spotted an opportunity to make a lot of money by having permission to issue £100 of South Sea stock for every £100 of debt it converted. At the time when a parliamentary act granted permission for the conversion, the price of the his stock stood at £128. But assuming it could be driven to £300, then, if an individual owning £1,200 of government debt wanted to convert, the company would have the right to issue 12 shares, but give the creditor only four. The company could then sell the remaining eight in the open market and book the proceeds as profit. In fact, when the Commons passed the South Sea Bill, only the conversion price of the government's redeemable debt was fixed; the conversion of irredeemable debts or annuities was left open.

The success of this scheme obviously depended entirely on the shares rising in value. Fortunately for Blunt, everyone stood to gain from an appreciating share price. For the company, the higher it rose, the fewer shares it had to exchange for annuities. The government and key politicians had an interest in a rising share price because, without it, the South Sea Company wouldn't have the £7.5 million it agreed to pay the government. Moreover, the company had secretly allocated shares to the Chancellor of the Exchequer, John Aislabie, the Postmaster James Craggs, the Secretary to the Treasury Charles Stanhope, and the king's two mistresses. These were issued at a small premium to market price, but the recipients didn't have to put up any funds and were therefore as interested in the company's share price going up as are today's executives, whose options incentive plans give them a vested interest in pushing up the stock.

In April 1720, at about the time the Mississippi Scheme was already in deep trouble, the South Sea Company placed two very successful issues of shares - first at £300 and then at £400. However, unlike John Law, it didn't have the power to increase the money supply in order to push up its share price. The unscrupulous Blunt soon found another way: He announced that the company would grant loans to stockholders, and that only a 10% down-payment was required for the purchase of a third issue of shares at £1,000, in June 1720. Since the shares had risen from around £100 at the beginning of the year to almost £1,000, the public went wild. In the process, they bid up the prices of other rather suspect companies seeking funds "for insuring marriages against divorce", "for a wheel of perpetual motion", "for planting of mulberry trees and breeding silk-worms in Chelsea Park" and "for carrying on an undertaking of Great Advantage but no one to know what it is". Aside from these highly dubious undertakings, some companies, such as a "Company of London Adventures for the carrying on a trade to settling colonies in Terra Australis" and "Puckle's Machine Gun", were floated which had a vision but were ahead of their times, since Australia was only discovered by Captain James Cook about half a century later and the machine gun did not finally appear until the 19th Century.

The problem with this flood of new "bubble companies", most of which were fraudulent, was that it endangered the South Sea Company, which depended entirely on a steady flow of new money to boost its share price and keep the party going. Therefore, in an attempt to reduce the competition for speculators' money, John Blunt issued writs against a number of companies, which he claimed were operating illegally. The Lord Justices ruled that, indeed, a few had been operating illegally, and the "outlawed" stocks collapsed. However, as this happened, it triggered margin calls, since everyone had been investing on credit, and consequently dragged down other stocks, including the South Sea Company. Once the mood among the speculators had changed, nothing could protect the South Sea shares from a vicious collapse. Having sold for around £1,000 in July, they tumbled to £190 by the end of September (see Figure 2).

Blunt, who had already cashed out (so, what is new in the US?), had meanwhile tried to arrange for an emergency loan from the Bank of England to stabilise the South Sea share price at £400, but the bank backed out at the last minute, because of a further fall in the stock. An inquiry was launched, as the public and the gentry, having suffered colossal losses, sought a scapegoat. In the end, the directors had to return most of the profit they had gained from the company's highly questionable practices. When called upon to testify, Blunt claimed he didn't remember a thing. The company treasurer skipped town. After Blunt was promised leniency, he finally testified, and at that point it became evident that the company had engaged in all sorts of schemes to defraud its shareholders to the benefit of close associates and directors. The company was eventually wound up, with shareholders receiving £33 per share.

Figure 2

SOUTHERN FURY

South Sea Company's share price, 1719-1722

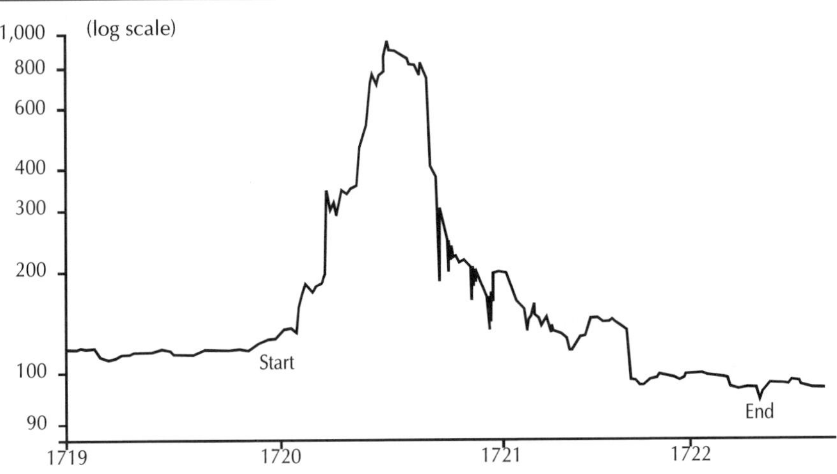

Source: Elliott Wave International.

Over the following 300 or so years the stage sets of investment manias have repeatedly changed - but the script, the props, and the nature of the actors participating in the bubble have largely remained the same.

The "bubble" model always involves a "displacement", which leads to extraordinary profit opportunities, overtrading, overborrowing, speculative excesses, and swindles and catchpenny schemes, followed by a crisis during which fraud on a massive scale comes to light. Then, in the closing act, the outraged public calls for the culprits to be taken to account. In each case, excessive monetary stimulus and the use of credit fuels the flames of irrational speculation and public participation, which involves a larger and larger group of people seeking to become rich without any understanding of the object of speculation.

The saga of the Mississippi Scheme and the South Sea Company is relevant to us because it contains all the major features of subsequent manias: shady characters, corruption, fraud, dubious practices, the creation of money and the extension of risky loans in order to keep the speculative orgy going, the catalyst, which leads to the initial collapse - usually the revelation of fraud, the inability of a large speculator to come up with the money to meet a margin call, the revelation that insiders cashed out, or some adverse economic or political news - and then the panic during which greed and euphoria are replaced by fear and the speculators' desire to get out at any price. In fact, the events of the last ten years, particularly in the US, are redolent of the Mississippi scheme - including the privatisation wave we had, which John Law also seems to have promoted in his time by convincing the regent to sell him the tobacco monopoly and other state assets.

What is also important to understand is that both the South Sea promoters and John Law attempted to support the market at any cost - but at some point market forces proved to be far more powerful than any price-supporting measures. In particular, Law's antics echo today in central bank policies, the aim of which is to solve any problem the same way he did - simply by increasing the money supply. That such monetary policies will lead to the same price increases that destroyed people's faith in paper money, ought to be clear. Whether, at that point, current central bankers and government officials will conspire to expropriate investors' gold possessions, as Law did, remains to be seen, but we should not forget that in 1933, in the midst of the Depression, the US government declared the possession of gold by individuals to be illegal.

I should also like to mention that during the Mississippi and the South Sea booms, there were critics, but no one wanted to pay attention to the party spoilers. The British ambassador to France, the Earl of Stair, resisted the temptation to invest in the Mississippi shares and, in a heated argument with Law, contended that his crazy scheme would more likely ruin France than enhance its power. But the cold relationship between Stair and Law, which was well known in London, brought him down. All over Europe, Law enjoyed enormous prestige as the most successful minister of finance (similar to Alan Greenspan nowadays), and he was also greatly admired in England. Therefore, the rift between Stair and Law became an embarrassment to the British government, which decided to call him back. In the case of the South Sea Company, the prominent member of Parliament, Archebald Hutcheson, published a series of pamphlets maintaining that people who bought the shares at an elevated price must be "deprived of all common sense and understanding"- since the company had no real business, they would be giving money to the original shareholders and the annuitants.

Similarly, the Irish-born French economist Richard Cantillon (known as the first true monetarist) thought that South Sea Company shares could be held up for a number of years, but that there was "a melancholy prospect for those who shall stay last". But, as is usually the case during investment manias, the speculators paid no attention to the rare voices of scepticism. Cantillon had a full understanding of how a rise in money supply could, on occasion, produce short-term increases in output and employment, but would in due course also haul up the prices for commodities. He had made a huge fortune in Mississippi Company shares, because he had sold out near the peak in early 1720 and had the foresight to leave France that year for Holland. (Upon his return to Paris ten years later, several parties who had incurred losses took him to court. The suits, however, had no merit and were all dismissed.)

But in the case of the South Sea Company, even Cantillon - one of the most brilliant financiers and economists of his time - underestimated the forces of gravity, since the share price collapsed soon after his comment that "those who would stay last" would incur losses. Cantillon was murdered in London in 1734 and his house, with all his writings, set on fire - a crime assumedly committed by his cook, whom he had dismissed a week earlier. The only surviving work by this brilliant economist is *The Essay on the Nature of Trade in General*, which contains an analysis of banks, bank credit, coinage and the automatic mechanism that distributes the monetary metals internationally. Schumpeter, in his *History of Economic Analysis*, regarded *The Essay* to be almost "faultless", saying that it stood "in most respects unsurpassed for about a century".

Lessons to be learnt

John Law's Mississippi Scheme, despite (or because of) its eventual failure, is an important event in economic history since it represents an attempt to introduce paper money on a large scale. The Banque Générale was primarily a deposit taker and not a lending bank, and it proved to be a great success for a while. With a limited note issue, which was backed by gold, and several branches in the provinces, it facilitated means of payment away from the financial centres of Paris and Lyons. It, therefore, had a beneficial effect on trade and industry. The problem occurred when the regent took over the bank (it became the Banque Royale) and began to issue notes without limit. That having been said, we must realise that there is, of course, always a limit to the quantity of money being issued, and this limit comes from the market mechanism. At some point, as we heard, the French public began to distrust the Banque Royale and then - despite all Law's efforts as finance minister - no one wanted paper money anymore. The banknotes depreciated rapidly against real assets.

We see, therefore, that a financial system based on paper money depends almost entirely on the confidence of the public in the currency issued by the monetary authorities - and if confidence is badly shaken, painful consequences are inevitable. The reader should ask how much longer foreign investors, who are financing the US trade and current account deficit, will be willing buyers and holders of American stocks, bonds and the Dollar? Surely, there will come a time when the "chain letter" type of fiat money operation practiced by the US Federal Reserve Board longer works and there is a sharp depreciation of the US Dollar. The other possibility, of course, is that the Dollar begins to depreciate, not compared to foreign currencies, but against commodities and real assets. As I explained above, the excessive money supply created by the Banque Royale led to soaring prices for commodities and real estate, as the French public realised that the banknotes were depreciating in value.

Concerning real estate, it is very common for prices to keep rising for some time after a stock market bubble has burst, for two reasons. Once speculators realise stocks have hit a peak, they shift their funds to another object of speculation. When the world is engulfed in a wave of speculation, the wave doesn't end abruptly, but tends to carry on for a while and spreads to assets other than equities, such as real estate, commodities, art, etc. Furthermore, towards the end of a speculative stock market bubble, the smart investors and (especially in the case of the recent high-tech bubble) corporate insiders realise that prices have shot up too much and bear little resemblance to the underlying fundamentals. Therefore, they shift and diversify part or all of their funds into assets that did not participate in the whirlwind of speculation and are consequently absolutely, or at least relatively, "cheap". Thus, as can be seen from Figure 3, real estate prices continued to rise in Japan throughout 1990 although the stock market had already topped out on 29 December 1989. And in the case of Australia, real estate prices continued to rise for another two years after the stock market peaked in 1987 (see Figure 4).

It is therefore not abnormal that the US real estate market has stayed buoyant over the last 18 months even though the stock market has performed poorly. But although real estate prices can stay strong for some time after a bubble bursts, as money shifts from liquid assets into real assets, in due course some kind of a bubble also occurs in real estate because the property market becomes - in the absence of a strong stock market - kind of the only game in town. As a result, real estate prices eventually also succumb to the forces of demand and supply, and then follow the declining trend of equity prices. The timing of the peak of property prices after a stock market top is difficult to determine, but it should occur any time between six months and two years after a stock market top.

Figure 3

CARRY ON REGARDLESS

Japanese house prices, 1986-1994

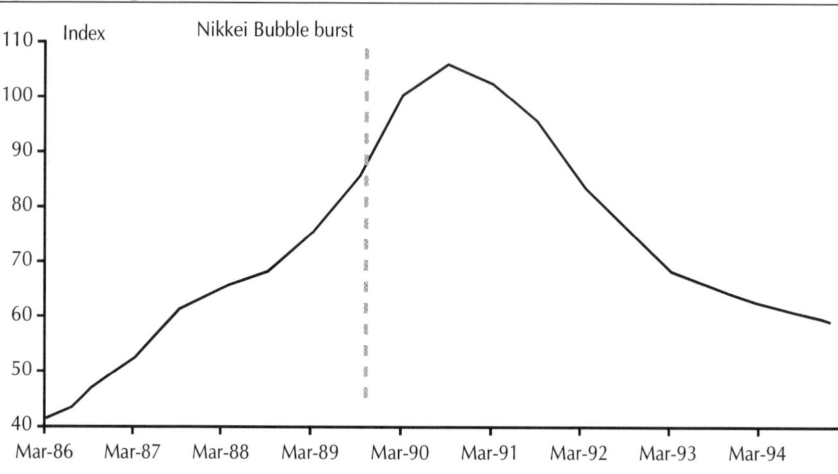

Source: HSBC.

Figure 4

THE RISE AFTER THE FALL

Sydney house prices, 1986-1989

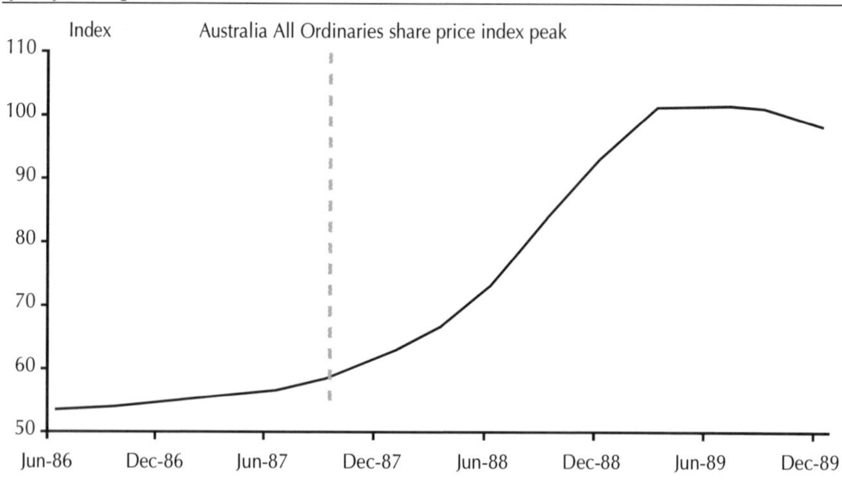

Source: HSBC.

The Mississippi Scheme and South Sea Bubble are also interesting from another point of view. The wave of speculation in 1717-20 spread across the entire European continent and the subsequent crisis was international in scope. The Mississippi Company's initial success attracted investors from all over Europe and Britain to Paris, where they speculated in the company's shares. Many investors from the Continent also bought shares in the South Sea Company and other hot new issues in London. (The conservative Swiss canton of Bern speculated in London with £200,000 of public funds and sold out at a profit of £2 million.) In fact, in early 1720, a "bizarre" reallocation of assets seems to have taken place among international investors. As we saw, Mississippi shares began to collapse in January 1720, but in London the South Sea Company only really took off at that time. In other words, British and international investors were in no way perturbed by the collapse of Law's scheme. In fact, in London the view was that the scheme had collapsed because of a political conspiracy against Law, since he was of Scottish origin. In the summer of 1720, just about as the South Sea stock peaked out, speculators moved funds from England to Holland and Hamburg to speculate on Continental European insurance companies. I mention this because once excess liquidity has been created, money will flow from one sector or country to another very quickly and can therefore lead to a series of new bubbles somewhere else.

When Cantillon kept his wealth intact by moving to Holland and staying out of the speculative 1720 South Sea stock boom, he perhaps inadvertently followed an important investment wisdom, which states that once an investment mania comes to an end, usually the best course of action is to exit altogether the country or sector in which the mania took place, and move to an asset class and/or a country that has little or no correlation to the object of the previous investment boom.

I have described above how commodity prices began to rise in France because of the excessive issuance of banknotes after 1718. In future, a bull market in commodities, which could exceed investors' expectations, is a distinct possibility, especially if the US economy weakens again as a result of consumers having to cut their spending habits. I have no doubt that the Federal Reserve Board would once again flush the system with liquidity, which at some point could spill over into the commodities markets, in the same way that the excessive liquidity created at the time of the Mississippi Scheme, and also in the late 1960s, led to a sharp rise in commodity and real asset prices.

In particular, I want to emphasise once again that commodity prices can increase sharply under any economic scenario provided that there is excessive money and credit creation and investor confidence in financial assets is shaken. Take the early 1970s, when commodities soared, even as the global economy headed for the worst recession since the 1930s (see Figure 5). Even more impressive than the rise in the CRB Index was the performance of agricultural commodity prices. From their lows in 1968/69 to their highs in 1973/74, wheat rose by 465%, soybean oil 638%, cotton 317%, corn 295% and sugar by 1,290%. Or take the deflationary depression years of the 1930s. As can be seen from Figure 6, the price of silver had been in a bear market since 1919, but made a first bottom at US$0.2575 on 16 February 1931 and a marginal new low on 29 December 1932 at US$0.2425. From there, however, silver prices advanced to US$0.81 in 1935 for a gain of more than three times their lows. In addition, if an investor bought silver in 1929 instead of the Dow, which was then above 300, by 1980, when silver hit US$50, he would have realised a profit of close to 200 times, whereas by 1980 the Dow was up less than three times above its 1929 peak. (Admittedly, the performance of the Dow was far better if dividends were included; also we have to take into account that the 1980 peak in silver prices was similar in nature to the March 2000 Nasdaq peak at over 5,000 - in other words, a once-a-generation bubble peak.)

I might add that gold shares performed superbly in the Depression years. From a low of US$65 in 1929, Homestake Mining rose to a high of US$544 in 1936. Also, from 1929 to 1936, Homestake paid a total of US$171 in dividends, which was more than twice the price of its stock in 1929. (Dome Mines rose from US$6 in 1929 to US$61 in 1936.)

I am mentioning commodities here once again for several reasons. First, the most dramatic commodity bull markets all originated after extended bear markets, such as we have had since 1980 and which accelerated on the downside following the Asian Crisis and again in 2001, when it became clear that the global economy was in trouble. Take, as an example, coffee, which peaked out in 1976 and has since been in a bear market - although interrupted by strong rallies such as in 1997 (see Figure 7). The price of coffee bottomed out at US42.75 cents in October 2002 and has since rallied to more than US60 cents. Now, if we assume that the US42 cents level was the bottom for the coffee price in this cycle and take the average price appreciation following coffee's low in 1903, 1909, 1915, 1921, 1931, 1940, 1963, 1969, 1975, 1981, 1992 and 1996, which averaged 88% within a period of less than 12 months, then we shouldn't be surprised to see further strong gains for coffee in the next 12 months. But that's not necessarily the point here; at issue is the fact that off their lows - whenever these lows occurred - commodity prices had dramatic upward moves (see also Figure 5) within a brief period of time. I may add that recently grain prices had sharp upward moves, signalling that their long-term bear market has most likely ended. Moreover, the CRB Index is up by more than 25% over the last twelve months, which is remarkable considering the weakness in share prices!

Figure 5

DRAMATIC HEIGHTS

CRB commodity index, 1968-1974

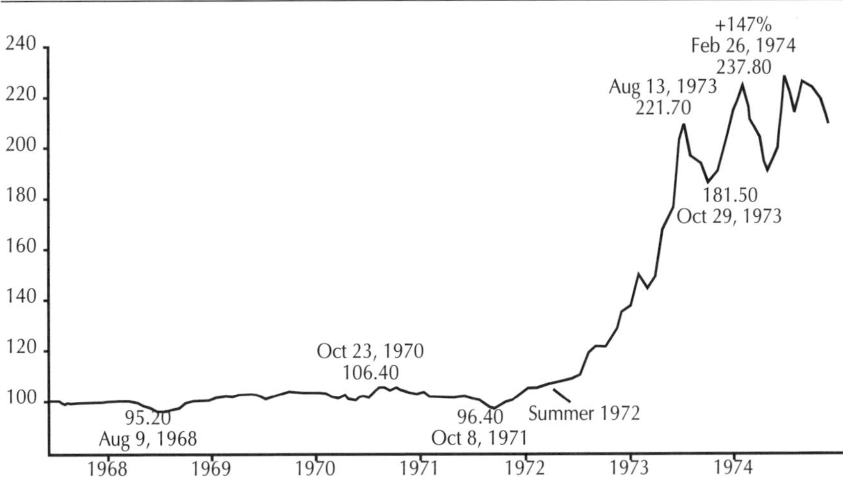

Source: National Institute of Investment Research.

Figure 6

LOOKING FOR THE SHINE

Silver, 1915-1948

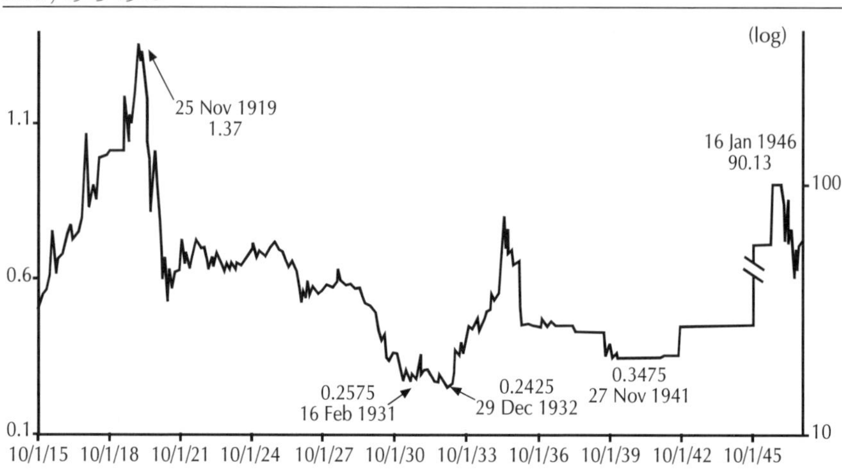

Source: National Institute of Investment Research.

Figure 7

READY FOR A HIT?

Coffee weekly nearest futures, 1996-2002

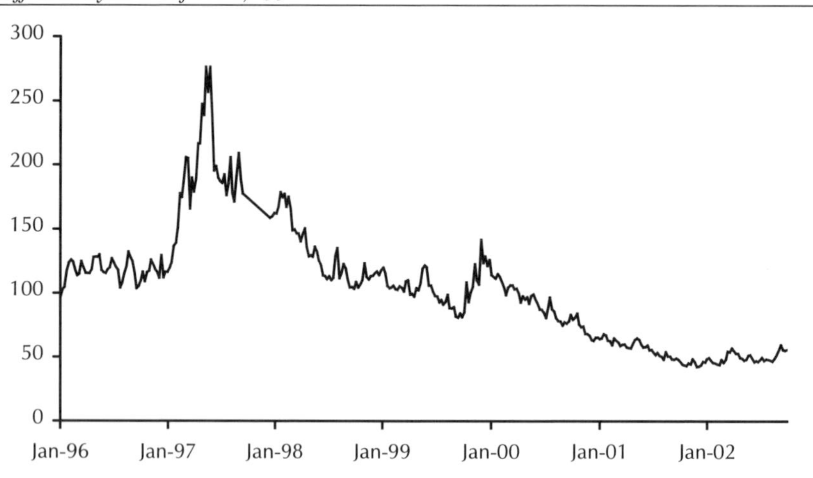

Source: Super Charts and National Institute of Investment Research.

Also, while I have serious doubts about the widely held belief that the recession is over, I would argue that if, indeed, it *is* over, commodity prices will strengthen considerably as global demand for resources picks up. And if the global economy doesn't recover, it is likely that commodity prices will be boosted because of further liquidity injections by the monetary authorities as well as expansionary fiscal policies. (At present, US government expenditure is rising at an alarming rate.) Moreover, if the US economy and the investment climate for financial assets in the US do not improve, it is likely that the US Dollar will weaken much more.

Now consider this: investors have little faith in either the Euro or the Yen. Therefore, if, in future, international investors lose confidence in US$ assets, where will they go with their liquidity? Take as an example the Asian central banks whose assets are concentrated in US Dollars and who only hold about 3% of their reserves in gold (down from 30% in 1980). If the day should come when their faith in the US Dollar is shaken, will they pile into Euros or the Yen? Possibly - but it is also conceivable that, given the less than stellar fundamentals for these currencies, a diversification into gold will be considered.

I have also emphasised the potential for commodities to rise significantly because there is a close correlation between the performance of commodities and emerging markets (see Figure 8). So, if an investor believes, as I do, that one day, commodity prices will rise dramatically, an overweight exposure to resource rich emerging markets is advisable.

Figure 8

FEEDING OFF COMMODITIES

Emerging markets versus commodities, 1988-2000

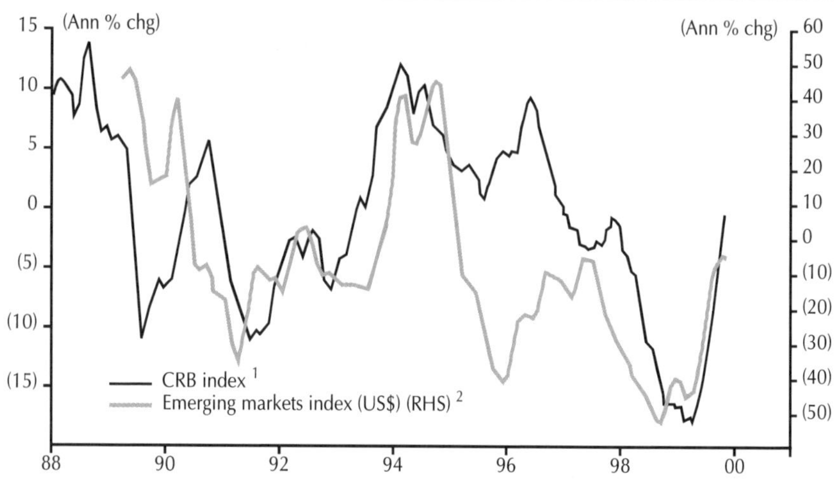

Note: [1] Commodity Research Bureau, [2] Morgan Stanley Capital International. Relative performance with the Nasdaq.
Source: BCA Publications Ltd.

I recently received an excellent report by my friend Robert Prechter, asking "Can the Fed Stop Deflation?". Prechter (author of the best-selling *Conquer the Crash*) makes the very valid case that the Fed or any other central bank *cannot* stop deflation. However, he adds a caveat at the end of his report by stating:

> While I discern no obvious forces that would counteract deflation, *after* deflation is another matter. At the bottom, when there is little credit left to destroy, currency inflation, perhaps even hyperinflation, could well come into play. In fact, I think this outcome has a fairly high probability in the next Kondratieff cycle. When a government embarks on a policy of currency hyperinflation - such as the Confederate States did in the 1860s, Germany did in the early 1920s or France did after World War II - the monetary path is utterly different from that of deflation, but ironically, the end result is about the same as that of a deflationary crash. At the end of hyperinflation, total bank accounts denominated in the hyperinflated currency are worth far less than they were, sometimes nothing at all. Total debts have shrunk or disappeared because the notes were denominated in depreciated money .... In this sense, even with hyperinflation, the end result is the destruction of money and credit, which is deflation.
>
> Robert Prechter, *The Elliott Wave Theorist*, April 2002

We dealt with domestic hyperinflation in 1980s Mexico and Latin America and simultaneous deflation through the exchange rate mechanism earlier in Chapter 10. In Prechter's opinion, there is perhaps some way that inflation could accelerate in the immediate future. He writes:

> How can you tell if my conclusion about deflation is wrong and that inflation or hyperinflation is taking place *instead of* deflation? There are two sensitive barometers of major monetary trends. One is the currency market. If the price of the Dollar against other currencies begins to plummet, then the market either fears Dollar inflation or that the value of the Dollar will not hold up in a climate of waning confidence. The other, which is more important, is the gold market. I hope to recommend gold at lower prices near the bottom of the deflationary trend, but if gold were to move above US$400 per ounce, I would probably be convinced that a major low had passed.

Well, while I agree with Prechter that the Fed cannot stop deflation, I am afraid that, in the US, deflation will not occur the same way it happened in the 1930s, when prices fell by around 30%. Rather, I believe it will occur, as Prechter points out, through the currency market, as a result of the Dollar depreciating sharply against a basket of commodities - if not "in the immediate future", at least within the next two to three years. The reason for this pessimism is simply that the US, with its huge debt burden, cannot afford deflation, as it would bankrupt the system almost instantly. Don't forget that the debt burden is far higher than in 1929, because (as can be seen in Chapter 6, Figure 3) the debt to GDP ratio rose sharply after 1929. Debt remained at about the same level, whereas GDP contracted by around 30%, which increased the ratio significantly.

But as a holder of gold shares and physical gold and foreign currencies, I sincerely hope that Prechter is right and that there will be genuine deflation in the domestic price level in the US. In such case, the economic mess will be complete, as the default rate among corporate borrowers will soar even further than it has over the past twelve months. At the same time, the confidence and blind faith of investors in the omnipotence of Alan Greenspan will finally collapse and lead to a panic. That gold prices could go through the roof in such an environment isn't difficult to envision. So, with or without inflation, investors should own some physical gold and silver, gold and silver shares, a basket of commodity futures and companies in resource-rich emerging economies.

Investors should never forget Law's experiment with paper money. Initially it was a great success and boosted the French economy. At his peak in 1719, Law was one of the most admired personalities in Europe. But the Mississippi Scheme failed, and Law fell from grace because the Banque Royale held too firm to the belief that it could solve every problem by increasing the supply of paper money. When Law finally realised that the enemy was a loss of confidence in paper money and accelerating inflation, the damage had already been done. He then tried to fix the price of the Mississippi stock, in the same way that some governments, in recent years, have supported their stock markets, while others are thinking about it. We should not forget that, following a January 2002 meeting of the Federal Open Market Committee (FOMC), a Fed official mentioned as an "unconventional measure" in case monetary policy became ineffective the "buying of US equities" and later indicated that the Fed "could theoretically buy anything to pump money into the system", including "state and local debt, real estate and gold mines - any asset".

That these measures would be doomed to fail as badly as Law's attempt to fix the price of the Mississippi stock at 9,000 livres is obvious. If the Fed implements such measures (and I'm sure they will, having learnt nothing whatsoever from Law's time), then Prechter's hyperinflation and currency-collapse scenario will shape our future economic environment. The fact that these "unconventional measures" even came up for discussion at an FOMC meeting makes me shudder as a believer in free markets and the capitalistic system, but the message is loud and clear. In fact, one could argue that the Fed has already tried to support the market by pushing down interest rates at an unprecedented speed (see Table 1) and massively increasing the money supply. Needless to say, the Fed will continue to do whatever it takes to avoid deflation, and this is why investors must prepare themselves for the financially suicidal consequences of such policies.

Table 1

COALS ON THE FIRE

Discount rate cuts in the United States

New era	Sequel	
2000	11 cuts over 12 months	6% to 1-1/4% or 475 bp
1929	8 cuts over 18 months	6% to 1-1/2% or 450 bp
1873	9 cuts over 8 months	9% to 2-1/2% or 650 bp

Source: *Pivotal Events*, 9 August 2002.

As a result, I think that, in due course, commodities, and gold and silver in particular will rise very significantly. I also believe that the US Dollar will depreciate - particularly against a basket of commodities, such as coffee, sugar, cotton and the grains (see Figure 9, which seems to indicate that a major bull move has already started for the grains). And I repeat here once again that rising commodity prices would be very beneficial for resource-rich emerging economies such as Brazil, Argentina, Indonesia, Russia, Malaysia, Thailand and Vietnam.

Figure 9

GRAZING BULLS

CRB futures price index[1]

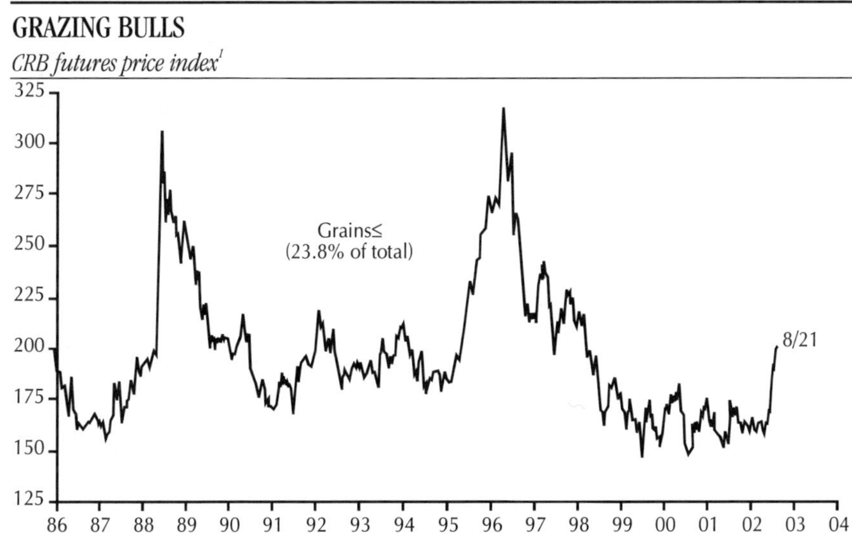

Note: [1] Nearby contract 5-day average of daily data. [2]Includes corn, soybeans and wheat. Source: Ed Yardeni / Prudential Securities (www.prudential.com).

The curse of empires

I have tried to make the point that if a bubble is created by excessive monetary and debt growth and it bursts, the danger is that - in order to support prices and avoid deflation - *too much* money is created, which leads to inflation and a depreciation of the currency. This is what happened in Weimar Germany in 1919-23, Latin America in the 1980s and at the time of the Mississippi Scheme. In weak economies, governments try to stimulate economic activity through budget deficits and with excessive monetary growth, which then leads to rising inflation rates and currency depreciation. In the case of the US, strong monetary and debt growth aside, I am concerned about another development, which could lead to a sharply lower Dollar.

Recently a number of articles in the American press have appeared to suggest that the US is not a mere superpower or hegemon, but a full-blown *empire* in the Roman and British sense (e.g., *International Herald Tribune* of 2 April 2002). And, according to columnist Charles Krauthammer, it is a fact "that no country has been as dominant culturally, economically, technologically and militarily in the history of the world since the Roman Empire". Even Paul Kennedy, who predicted not long ago America's ruin from overreach, now claims that, "nothing has ever existed like this disparity of power". According to Kennedy:

> ... the *Pax Britannica* was run on the cheap, Britain's army was much smaller than European armies and even the Royal Navy was equal only to the next two navies - right now all the other navies in the world combined could not dent American maritime supremacy. Napoleon's France and Philip II's Spain had powerful foes and were part of a multipolar system. Charlemagne's empire was merely Western European in its stretch. The Roman Empire stretched further afield, but there was another great empire in Persia and a larger one in China. There is no comparison.
>
> Kennedy, Paul, *The Rise and Fall of the Great Powers*, New York, 1987

The American journalist Robert Kaplan even suggests that America should embark on an imperialistic course.

> Our future leaders could do worse than be praised for their tenacity, their penetrating intellects and their ability to bring prosperity to distant parts of the

> world under America's soft imperial influence. The more successful our foreign policy, the more leverage America will have in the world. Thus, the more likely that future historians will look back on the 21st-Century United States as an empire as well as a republic, however different from that of Rome and every other empire throughout history.
>
> Robert Kaplan, *Warrior Politics: Why Leadership Demands a Pagan Ethos*, Random House, 2001

This is all great news because, as the *Wall Street Journal's* editorial features editor, Max Boot, wrote, the US is "an attractive empire, the one everyone wants to join". There is little doubt that, given the alternatives - such as a Chinese or Russian empire, which, while no longer communist, are still totalitarian in nature - a globally dominant US that can probably enforce some kind of a *Pax Americana*, may offer the best hope for economic and social development. European academics may not share this view, but I am certain that the average Tibetan, Saudi, Indonesian or Black African would be much better off if ruled by a US administration's "soft imperial influence" (though the Cambodians, whose country was carpet bombed by the US, may disagree with the word "soft") than by their own local governments and ruling classes, or by a foreign tyrant, as in the case of Tibet. The bad news, however, is an economic one. All the great empires experienced, over time, accelerating inflation, rising interest rates and a sharp depreciation of their currency.

In his introduction to *History of Interest Rates*, Sydney Homer quoted the Austrian economist Eugen Böhm von Bawerk (1851-1914), who declared that the cultural level of a nation is mirrored by its rate of interest. According to von Bawerk, the higher a people's intelligence and moral strength, the lower will be the rate of interest. Homer appropriately noted that von Bawerk was speaking of "free market rates" of interest, not of "controlled rates" of interest. (As an aside, if Bawerk were still alive today, he would also have made the distinction between "free market rates" and "manipulated rates", which occur when central banks intervene aggressively in the money market, and when the government issues quasi-guarantees for government-sponsored enterprises, which in the case of the US have kept mortgage rates artificially low.) Homer went on to explain that:

> If Böhm von Bawerk had said 'financial strength' instead of 'moral strength' and 'technological level' instead of 'cultural level', more people today would agree with him, but I think he meant exactly what he said. Indeed, if these substitutions had been suggested to him, he might well have responded that moral strength in a nation as a whole is a necessary precondition for financial strength and that a high cultural level is a necessary precondition for a high technological level.
>
> Sydney Homer, *A History of Interest Rates*, New Jersey, 1977

How true! Homer noted that the primary purpose of his history was:

> ... not to explore sociological or economic causes or effects of interest-rate fluctuations but rather simply to seek out, record, and analyse the prevailing rates of interest themselves over a long period of centuries in many countries. Nevertheless, the reader will not be able to avoid noticing sustained trends and repetitious patterns over the centuries. He may correlate them in his own mind with the rise and fall of nations and indeed of whole civilisations. The chapters on interest rates in ancient Babylonia, Greece, and Rome show, in each case, a progressive decline in interest rates as the nations or cultures developed and throve, and then a sharp rise in rates as each 'declined and fell' - a saucer formation. In our culture (Western Europe and North America), interest rates have declined most of the time since the Middle Ages. But now? Recent high rates have not lasted long enough to set a significant trend in the charts. But, will they?

If we look at Figure 4 in Chapter 7, the jury is still out on whether, based on long-term trends in interest rates, the American Empire has already passed its peak. But we note a very clear declining trend until the 1940s, then a steep rise until 1981, which decisively broke the downtrend, and a renewed decline in rates thereafter. But, where do we go from here - as Homer asked already in 1977? For sure, we shall not revisit the 2% yield level on US long-term government bonds we had in the 1940s, and, based on historical precedents and recently published inflation statistics, we need to be seriously concerned that the trend of rising inflation and interest rates will shortly reassert itself.

In this respect, a quick analysis of the monetary history of the Roman Empire might be helpful, in view of the fact that some pundits are now comparing the United States to Rome.

Until the rule of Augustus (who was installed as the first ruler of the

Roman Empire in 27 BC), the Romans only used pure gold and silver coins. In order to finance his vast infrastructure expenditures, Augustus ordered that government mines in Spain and France should be exploited 24 hours a day, a measure that increased the money supply significantly and it is estimated that between 27 BC and 6 BC, prices in Rome doubled. In the second part of his reign (6 BC to 14 AD), Augustus reduced coinage drastically, as he recognised what had led to the rise in prices. Upon his death in 14 AD, his stepson Tiberius, whom Augustus had married off to his colourful daughter Julia (who pursued a very successful career of nymphomania), was installed as emperor. Under Tiberius, the rate of new coinage was far inferior to that during Augustus's reign, which inevitably led to a real scarcity of money in the empire, but, at the same time, to a vast surplus in the coffers of the royal treasury (*fiscus*). Thus, when Tiberius was assassinated in 37 AD he left his insane successor Caligula with 700 million denarii - about 30 times the sum Augustus had left.

Caligula's lavish spending necessitated the expropriation of properties from a number of wealthy families he falsely accused of plotting against him. He was succeeded by the equally mad Claudius, then Nero. By then, the accumulated fiscal surpluses of Rome had been spent and the large trade deficits Rome maintained with its colonies led Nero to debase Rome's currency. In 64 AD, he made the *aureus* 10% lighter in weight. So, whereas in the past, 41 *aurei* had been minted from one pound of gold, the ratio now became 45. Nero also minted a new silver coin, which was not only lighter in weight but also contained about 10% of copper, which meant that the new *denarius* was worth about 25% less than the old one. Thus we can truly talk of Nero "fiddling" with the currency "while Rome burned".

From the start, the new coins traded at a discount to the old coins, as one can imagine, and led to inflation. Nero then tried to force a reminting of the old coinage - but this was only partially successful because the well to do either hid their wealth or emigrated to remote provinces and evaded the Roman tax collectors. However, Nero had set a precedent. Between his being deposed in 68 AD and the sacking of Rome in the second half of the 5th Century, a succession of emperors continued increasing the supply of money in the empire by debasing the *denarius*, which in the end only had a 0.02% silver content! A few years ago, Rolf Bertschi of Credit Suisse Private Banking, who writes an excellent daily technical comment (www.cspb.com/techresearch), produced a figure and table showing the gradual then total collapse of the Roman currency from the time of Augustus to 268 AD (see Table 2 and Figure 10).

Table 2

SHINING THE SILVER . . .

The debasement of the Roman denarius

Issuer	Year	% Silver
Nero	AD54	94
Vitellius	AD86	81
Domitian	AD81	92
Trajan	AD98	93
Hadrian	AD117	87
Antonius Pius	AD138	75
Marcus Aurelius	AD161	68
Septimus Severus	AD193	50
Elagenbalus	AD218	43
Alexander Severus	AD222	35
Gordian	AD244	28
Philip	AD244	0.5
Claudius Gothicus	AD268	0.02

Source: *Pivotal Events*, 9 August 2002.

Figure 10

. . . TIL THERE'S NOTHING LEFT

Roman Denarius, 54 to 268 AD

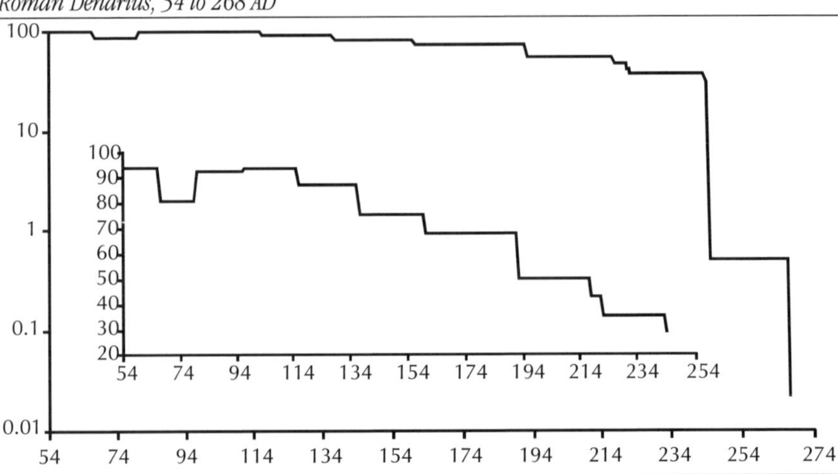

Source: Rolf Bertschi, Credit Suisse Private Banking.

A few more observations about the Roman Empire may be in order since the *Pax Americana* has been compared to the *Pax Romana*. At the zenith of the Roman Empire under Augustus, it is true that, for a short time at least, there was peace in most parts of the empire. But aside from this relatively short period, Rome was continuously engaged in wars along its borders or had to take care of uprisings in the provinces and even on the Italian peninsula. Moreover, for most of the duration of the empire, shipping was unsafe, since the Mediterranean Sea was infested with pirates. Thus, the *Pax Romana* was more of a myth than a reality. Also, it's no coincidence that Nero's currency devaluation occurred as the empire began to weaken. I suppose Nixon's closure of the gold window in August 1971 (after which US Dollars were no longer redeemable in gold for international settlements) also occurred after the US had reached its peak in terms of economic hegemony and led to a decade of accelerating inflation and a sharp depreciation of the Dollar. The view that the American Empire has already passed its peak would also be supported by Sydney Homer's remark that as empires decline, interest rates show a rising tendency. Based on this observation, the American peak would have to be placed in the 1940s or 1950s.

Also, while it is true that the US is at present militarily far superior to any other nation, as Paul Kennedy observed, and did win the Cold War, this is not necessarily a fact that should make us complacent. The Roman Empire also reached its largest extent under the emperor Trajan (98-116), but by then several wars to protect the empire had already been extremely costly in terms of human losses, and the economy on the Italian peninsula had already badly deteriorated. According to the historian William McNeill, under Domitian (81-96):

> ... a serious economic crisis manifested itself in Italy. The price of wine fell disastrously. The cause was probably the disappearance of an export market for Italian wine resulting from the spread of viticulture to the western provinces, and especially to Gaul. Thus while the prosperity of the western provinces - or at least of the landowning classes in those provinces - increased, economic decay manifested itself in Italy. ... [the] Italian population seemingly fell off, or at least ceased to grow. Italian recruits for the army could no longer be found in sufficient numbers; more and more soldiers and officials were recruited

> instead from the more Romanised of the western Provinces. As a result, Italy tended to lose the peculiar and privileged position it had enjoyed under Augustus and the early emperors
>
> William McNeill, *History of Western Civilisation*, Chicago, 1986, page 169.

So here we have another important parallel to the US. In the same way that Italian wines lost out to cultivators in other provinces of the Roman Empire, which brought about economic decay on the Italian peninsula, US manufacturing is gradually being undermined by new centres of production south of the border and in Asia, especially now in China. Finally, concerning Kaplan's observation that our leaders will be praised for their "tenacity, their penetrating intellects and their ability to bring prosperity to distant parts of the world", I can assure our readers that Roman emperors such as Trajan, Hadrian, Marcus Aurelius, Severus, Diocletian and Constantine were not only tenacious and of great intellect, but were also courageous and frequently stood at the helm of their armies in battle (Valerian died in the captivity of Persian King Shapur I and Crassus was killed in battle by Parthian King Mithradates III).

But what gradually broke the empire was a failure to adapt to a changing world. As Will Durant observed, "when the group or a civilisation declines, it is through no mystic limitation of a corporate life, but through the failure of its political or intellectual leaders to meet the challenges of change."

The next two "great" empires can be dealt with quickly. Under Carlos V and his successor, Philip II, 16th-Century Spain, especially after its unification with Portugal in 1580, had a huge empire spread through large parts of Western Europe, in the south to most of the African coast, in the east to the Philippines and parts of Indonesia, and in the Americas to Mexico and the entire Latin American continent. Philip II truly possessed an empire "upon which the sun never sets" - the largest territory a sovereign state has ever ruled. But prosperity was very short lived because all the gold and silver that flowed to Spain from its mines in Mexico and at Potosi was used for the defence of its empire and led to the decline of agriculture and manufacturing on the Iberian peninsula. The Spanish Crown had already defaulted on its loans in 1557, and further defaults occurred in 1575, 1596, 1607, 1627 and 1647.

Because of these defaults, major financial centres in Europe such as Antwerp, Genoa and Lyons, which had been the prime financiers of the Spanish loans, also experienced devastating financial crises. Moreover, the 16th Century was highly inflationary. Between 1500 and 1600, prices in Europe rose almost fivefold because of the huge increase in gold and silver in circulation (see Chapter 7, Figure 2). And when the shipments of precious metals began to diminish after 1580, the entire Spanish peninsula experienced a terrific depression, which lasted for a good part of the 17th Century. Other factors contributing to the decay of the Spanish Empire included Portugal's loss of its Eastern trading empire to the Dutch at the beginning of the 17th Century, the presence of pirates and privateers on the seas (the 16th Century equivalent of today's terrorists), uprisings in the low countries, and costly wars against just about every European nation and the Turks in the Mediterranean, which had totally drained Spain's human and natural resources.

The British Empire was in many ways probably the most successful in history, because, unlike Rome and Spain, it didn't *depend* on its colonies for its wealth. During the first half of the Industrial Revolution, its manufacturing sector was well ahead of other nations. As mentioned, Lancashire had more machines installed than the rest of the world combined in 1830. Moreover, Britain left a legacy of law and order in a large number of countries around the world. However, over time, the empire proved extremely costly and in the 20th Century it gradually had to give up its overseas possessions and lost out to other nations economically, a fact reflected in the pound's gradual depreciation against strong currencies (see Figure 11).

A further point that supports Sydney Homer's observation about declining empires and rising interest rates is the movement of British interest rates. From Figure 12, we can see that British rates bottomed out in 1896, when yields on consols fell to 2.21%. Consol yields never again reached these low levels, not even during the Depression and the Labour administration of the 1940s, which is quite different from the movement of US interest rates, which made new lows in the 1940s (see Chapter 7, Figure 4).

Figure 11

SUNSET OF EMPIRE 1

Pound Sterling versus Swiss Franc, 1915-1988

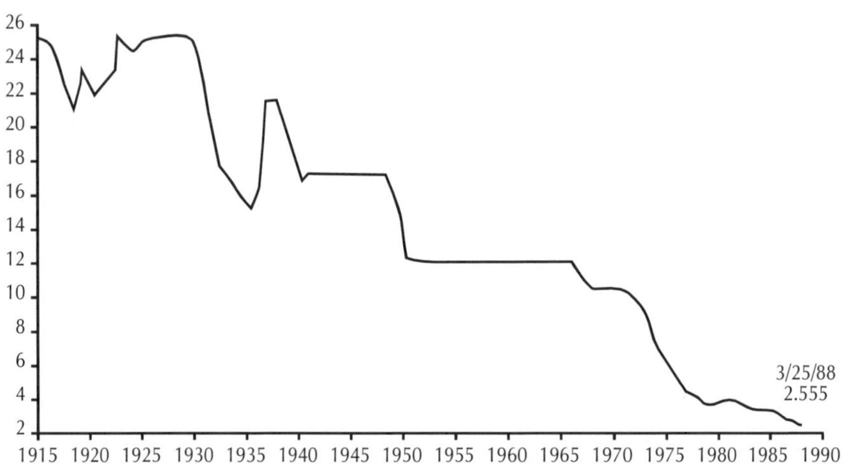

Source: Datastream.

Figure 12

SUNSET OF EMPIRE 2

Yields of long-term English government bonds, 1700-1975

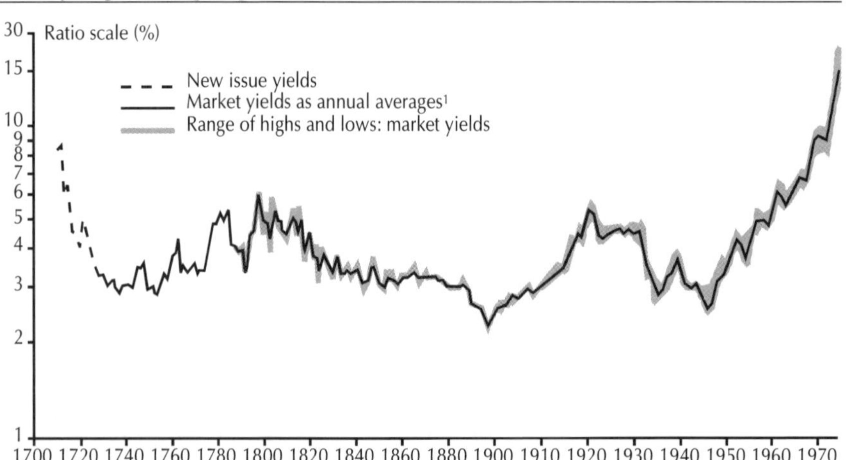

[1] 3% annuities and consols: 1725-1888; 2¾% consols: 1889-1902; 2½ consols: 1903-1975.
Source: Sydney Homer, *A History of Interest Rates.*

The impressive notion of "empire" is but an ill-fated ambition of large countries that sooner or later becomes a huge liability. Based on the historical evidence, I am surprised that anyone would wish to have an empire, because its maintenance proves in the long run to be ruinously costly. Inevitably, empires experience inflation, rising interest rates, a depreciating currency, default on their debts, or a combination thereof.

This is not to say that there are no good investment opportunities in empires. Even as empires disintegrated, there were always some cities or industrial sectors that thrived regardless. When the decline of the Roman Empire was well under way, Antioch became its most important and prosperous city in the Middle East, and when Constantine decided to take up residence in Constantinople in 330 AD, the city grew rapidly, its population soon exceeding that of Rome, which was by then already declining. The same was true of the Spanish/Portuguese Empire: several cities, such as Mexico, Bahia, Havana, Quito, Ouro Preto and Manaus, became economically important even as Spain and Portugal struggled. And despite the fading of the British Empire, no one can deny that there were some great investment opportunities in British companies and real estate over the last 100 years or so. But the fact remains that, over time, all empires experience rising inflation rates as well as, as Sydney Homer observed, rising interest rates, and that there are usually better long-term opportunities in places other than in empires that suffer from a weakening currency.

Pax Americana

Now, let us make the heretical assumption that the US Empire *is* already past its peak and that the analogous period to the golden era of the Roman Empire under Augustus was, in the US, the 1950s or early 1960s. This assumption does not in any way imply that the US is about to fall into an abyss, but it does imply rising inflation and interest rates and a weakening Dollar in the long term, and better investment opportunities in other parts of the world.

I have to admit inflation is an immensely complex issue, as some assets or prices can rise while simultaneously others decline. It is clear to me that the opening of China and of other low-cost producers of manufactured goods and services, such as India and now, increasingly, Vietnam, is bringing about a deflationary shock in many sectors of the economy. Conversely, I also see that huge pool of money pouring from the water bowl (Chapter 2), which is constantly growing as a result of an expanding money supply, and that this gigantic pool of liquidity or credit will produce inflation or bull markets in a variety of sectors of the economy. In fact, what I find disturbing is that when commodity prices and wages rise, people talk about inflation; but when stocks rise, the term "bull market" is used - when in reality both are simply price increases, the former for natural resources and the latter for financial assets. Thus, we need, once and for all, to clearly define what inflation is and what its symptoms might be.

According to the economist Ludwig von Mises, inflation, as this term was always used everywhere and especially in the US, means "increasing the quantity of money and bank notes in circulation and the quantity of bank deposits subject to check." But:

> ... people today use the term 'inflation' to refer to the phenomenon that is an inevitable consequence of inflation, that is the tendency of all prices and wage rates to rise. The result of this deplorable confusion is that there is no term left to signify the cause of this rise in prices and wages. There is no longer any word available to signify the phenomenon that has been, up to now, called inflation. ... As you cannot talk about something that has no name, you cannot fight it. Those who pretend to fight inflation are in fact only fighting what is the inevitable consequence of inflation, rising prices. Their ventures are doomed to failure because they do not attack the root of the evil. They try to keep prices low while firmly committed to a policy of increasing the quantity of money that must necessarily make them soar. As long as this terminological confusion is not entirely wiped out, there cannot be any question of stopping inflation.

Ludwig von Mises, "An Unworkable Fiscal Policy", in *Economic Freedom and Interventionism*, Foundation for Economic Freedom, 1990

If we accept von Mises' definition as a rise in money supply and not a general increase in the price of goods and services, then we can deduce that there has been considerable inflation in the US already, but that the increased supply of money has not yet found its way into goods prices. Import prices are still deflating because manufactured goods get cheaper and cheaper, largely due to Chinese products reaching global markets and to the strong Dollar. However, there have been plenty of price increases in other sectors of the US economy. Housing prices are up about 10% over the last 12 months and nationwide median home prices have risen by 40% since 1995. The price increases in some cities, such as Boston, San Francisco, San Diego and Denver are far higher and range between 70-96%. (In the United Kingdom, first-time buyers of homes are paying, on average, 14% more than a year ago and 18% more in London.)

Personally, I think there is a high probability that as we go into 2003, the rate of price increases in the US will accelerate significantly, whatever the economic scenario. If the global economy recovers, demand for commodities, which fell following the Asian Crisis, will revive and lead to far higher prices for non-ferrous metals, grains and soft commodities. Don't forget that, adjusted for inflation, commodities are near an all-time low (see Chapter 2, Figure 11) and many are selling for less than production cost. The US Department of Agriculture calculated that, in 1999, the average all-in cost of producing a pound of cotton in the US was 84 cents. Today, due to higher energy prices, this figure is likely to be closer to 90 cents. Thus, including a modest 3-5% profit margin, the equilibrium price of cotton would have to be around 95 cents. Yet cotton is trading at around 45 cents.

Moreover, it is entirely possible, as explained earlier, that commodity prices could rise even amidst a deflationary environment. From the low in 1932 to the 1934 high, commodity prices rose by 100% on average (see Chapter 2, Figure 11). And if the present recovery is aborted and the economy slips once again into a recession, or even just slows down, then higher inflation rates are even more likely down the road, because renewed economic weakness would lead (better, "mislead") the Fed into pursuing even more accommodative monetary policies. The argument would run that monetary policy was highly successful in keeping the housing industry and consumption up in 2001, but that they didn't remain loose long enough and that was the reason another dip occurred.

My view would be that, regardless of your outlook for the economy, rising inflation and interest rates will be the principal feature of the year 2003, if not sooner. This would be particularly true if, along with rising commodity prices, the US Dollar began to weaken - an event I regard as almost unavoidable within the next 12 to 18 months. This is so because a significant increase in commodity prices would certainly depress bonds. In turn, foreigners, who were major buyers of the American corporate bond market in the last two years, would suffer large losses and therefore almost certainly reduce their appetite for US denominated fixed interest securities, or exit the market altogether.

There is one more myth I should like to debunk. Based on the recent experience in Japan and memories of the Depression years in the 1930s, most people associate a weak economy with deflation and a strong economy with inflation. But the opposite is actually more the rule than the exception.

In weak economies, loose monetary policies usually accompany budget deficits. Combined with capital flight and the absence of foreign investors, this normally brings about a fall in the exchange rate, which in turn reinforces the domestic price increases. Thus, combating a weak economy with very easy money and fiscal deficits is frequently a recipe for disaster, as we experienced in Latin America and Mexico in the 1980s.

Table 3 shows the movement of Mexican shares in 1979-88, a period of severe recession, high inflation rates and a sharp depreciation of the currency. In local currency terms, the market moved sideward with a slight bias down from 1979-83. Thereafter, it took off (in local currency terms) because of very high inflation rates caused by excessively easy monetary policy. In local currency, the Mexican Stock Exchange Index shot up from a low of 1,066 in 1979 to a high of 343,545 in 1987! But in Dollar terms, the returns were quite different. From a high of 70 in 1979, the index collapsed to 5 in 1982-83 before rising to 234 in 1987 (see Table 3 and Figure 13). By 1988, however, the US Dollar index was at about the same level it had been in 1979, whereas the index in Peso terms was up by more than 100 times. Thus, it is obvious that in the 1980s, Mexico experienced very high inflation rates domestically. However, in Dollar terms, we had, until the mid-1980s, a period of severe deflation because of the continuous Peso depreciation that exceeded the rise in the domestic price level.

Table 3

PESO VOLATILTY

High/low of Mexican stock exchange index, 1979-1988

In Peso terms	1979	1980	1981	1982	1983	1984	1985	1986	1987	1988
High	1,651	1,432	1,479	786	2,452	4,366	11,197	47,101	343,545	214,154
Low	1,066	1,107	862	496	837	2,885	3,710	12,802	60,281	86,606
In US Dollar terms	**1979**	**1980**	**1981**	**1982**	**1983**	**1984**	**1985**	**1986**	**1987**	**1988**
High	70	62	63	29	15	24	25	51	234	93
Low	48	48	34	5	5	16	16	25	50	38

Source: Acciones y Valores.

Figure 13

STEADIER IN DOLLARS

Mexican stock exchange index (in US Dollar terms), 1982-1990

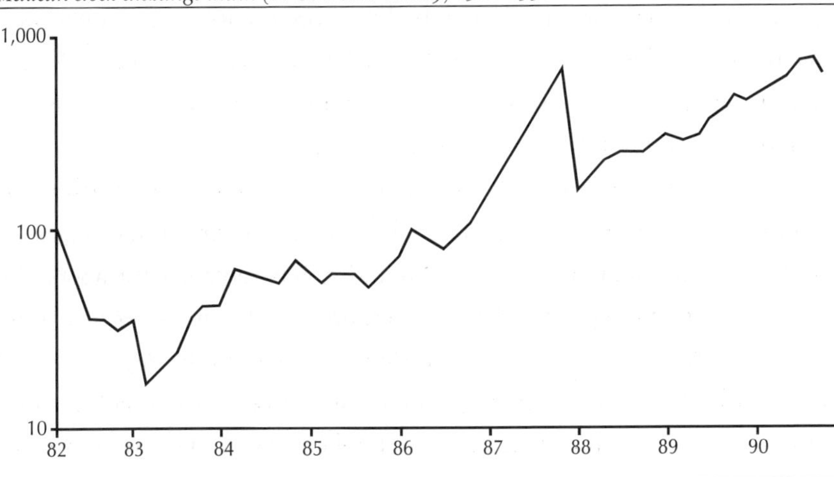

Source: Acciones y Valores.

Moreover, it isn't difficult to understand that, while from 1980 commodity prices fell in US Dollar terms (see Chapter 2, Figure 11), in Peso terms they increased several-fold. Therefore, I would like to reiterate my point that economic weakness can very well coexist with rapidly rising consumer prices and soaring commodity prices when rising prices are accompanied by a sharp currency depreciation, as was the case for Mexico and most of the Latin American countries in the 1980s - and more recently for Argentina where the gold price has shot up in Argentinean-currency terms (see Figure 1).

There is one last point I should like to make about Mexico and other Latin American countries in the 1980s. As they went into a highly inflationary recession at the beginning of the decade, it was best to stay out of their stock markets, because the currency depreciation more than offset the local-currency capital gains. However, the deadly combination of high inflation, recession and rapid currency depreciation also provided spectacular buying opportunities in mid-1980s Mexico and Chile and late-80s Argentina, Colombia, Peru and Brazil (as explained in detail in Chapter 10). As can be seen from Table 3 and Figure 13, within a couple of years after 1984, Mexican stocks soared by more than 50 times in Dollar terms! In sum, I would argue that it would be a grave mistake for today's investors to simply assume that if the US economy were to weaken once again, the CPI couldn't increase by much. The longer the economy fails to fully recuperate, the more prone to much higher monetary growth and inflation rates it will be, given the policies of the Fed.

Although the opening of China has brought a deflationary shock to the world, if we accept the Austrian school of measuring inflation as an increase in the money supply, we should not be complacent about the likelihood of renewed upward pressure on prices in future. In particular, we feel that commodity prices could rise significantly from the depressed level they reached in February. Bond prices are also close to a secular high after having been in a bull market since September 1981. Longer term, we can no longer be positive about US government bonds, as the Fed will take "extraordinary measures" to keep the economy up, which will spill over into price increases. Given America's serious imperial delusions, I also expect budget surpluses to be a thing of the past and the US Dollar soon to weaken considerably. But, as explained earlier, it is difficult to see the

US Dollar declining much against other currencies; so the most likely decline will be against a basket of commodities and especially gold, the latter being the only currency central bankers cannot tamper with. (they can sell the price down for a while, but obviously not forever).

In fact, I believe that "stagflation' is the most likely outcome of a relatively weak economy combined with excessive monetary, and now also fiscal, stimuli. The Fed cannot print its way out of any economic problem in the long term, but it can certainly print enough to generate the kind of Mexican domestic inflation discussed above, which resulted in hard-currency deflation because of the decline of the Mexican Peso. This is hardly a very appealing environment for US financial assets, given their still lofty valuations and the dimming prospects of a powerful earnings recovery.

In Chapter 13, I return to Asia, where I believe prospects for investors are best in a global context for the great variety of reasons outlined above. My focus is strongly on the consequences of China's coming global ascendancy. Finally, an Epilogue concludes this book with a discussion of the most serious economic challenge we shall have to deal with in the years to come, a challenge that tempers my optimism about the future - global wealth and income inequality.

CHAPTER THIRTEEN

Asia in transition

> Little else is requisite to carry a state to the highest degree of opulence from the lowest barbarism, but peace, easy taxes and a tolerable administration of justice.
>
> *ADAM SMITH (1723-1790)*

In the early 1990s, Asia entered a period of economic, social and political transition, which in my opinion will change its face in the years to come. Any visitor today, who had last visited Asia prior to the Second World War, would be stunned by the progress and change in the balance of power - but a visitor in the year 2020 will find a totally different landscape. By then, I suppose several countries who have hibernated economically under totalitarian rule (Myanmar, Vietnam, Laos, Cambodia, North Korea and China until quite recently) or xenophobia towards foreign investors (notably India) will have caught up with the rest of Asia or even overtaken some of today's centres of prosperity. Conversely, some of today's success stories, facing intense competition from the newcomers, could well succumb to absolute declines. This is what change is all about: It inevitably produces both winners and losers.

Following the Second World War several major trends became apparent in Asia: the end of colonial rule, the formation of sovereign nations and the rise of communism in countries like China, Vietnam and Burma. The end of colonial rule was initially accompanied by hostility towards the former colonial powers and a reluctance to let foreigners participate in the development of Asian economies. The priority was to build nations, not economic growth. Furthermore foreign investment was, for a long time, perceived as potentially destabilising.

The end of colonial rule also shaped the political systems of Asian countries. Since independence had frequently been gained through guerrilla warfare or after a period of civil strife, very close ties remained between political leaders and the army. In order to better understand this close relationship it is important to know that the opposition to colonial rule had only very limited resources (think of Mao's Red Army). Thus, the units of the revolutionary armies had to look after themselves for food and other supplies. There was no state with a military budget that could support the freedom fighters and, therefore, each army unit had to rely on one or several "supply officers" whose job it was to feed it. This was a delicate task: If too much was demanded of the local population, its support would have waned very quickly. Conversely enough had to be "collected" to keep the freedom fighters well equipped and content. Thus, we can say that the opposition armies were organised in a kind of a feudal system with each unit having the right to collect "taxes" from the region it operated in.

Not surprisingly, this system of privilege remained in place after independence, and we still find "feudal" political systems in some Asian countries. The leader of a country will assign privileges (monopolies, tax concessions, state loans, etc) to trusted followers (leading businessmen, influential local politicians and army generals) and they in turn give full support the ruling party. This system functioned quite well from 1950 to the mid 80s because it guaranteed peace and stability (albeit at the expense of individual freedom). Domestic stability in turn fostered economic growth. Until recently, this feudal system, incorporating political, economic and military power at the top, was accepted by the people because of the communist threat in the region and memories of "evil" colonial powers.

However, in the 1990s, cracks began to appear in Asia's feudal systems. More and more countries liberalised their economies and moved towards a capitalistic system with the participation of many foreign players via direct and portfolio investment. Free markets, capitalism and foreign investors, however, undermined the power of the feudal systems, as capitalism requires more structured political, legal and economic systems (see below). In addition, as political and social tensions eased in the Asian region (peace between Indonesia and Malaysia following President Sukarno's "crush Malaysia" policy in 1963, the end of the Vietnam war, the recent demise of communism, etc), governments could no longer justify tight control over the economy on grounds of domestic security. As a result Asia entered, in the 1990s, a transition phase characterised by significant change in the political sphere to more pluralistic societies where the rule of law increasingly challenged absolute state or military power.

I may add that Western countries, especially the US, supported totalitarian rule or military dictatorships in Asia (which ensured domestic stability) as long as the threat of communism existed. But when, in the 1980s, the threat receded and Western powers developed a strong interest in opening closed markets for exports, economic reform became a priority for Asia's industrialised countries because feudal systems based on monopolies and privileges were simply not conducive to free markets and free trade. Therefore, by pushing Asian countries to carry out economic reforms, Western countries encouraged the still-ongoing transition away from *ad hoc* feudal hierarchies towards more liberal, more structured, constitutional systems.

China's role

So far we have seen that the demise of communism in Asia had a favourable impact on the region as it diffused tension. However, the situation is not quite as simple as this. With the collapse of the Soviet Union, China had no pressure on its northern borders for the first time in modern history. Thus its military leadership began increasingly to focus on Southeast Asia and achieve some of its strategic objectives there. But what are China's strategic objectives exactly? In order to understand the issues involved we cannot look at Asia from a Western perspective alone but have to put ourselves in the position of the leadership in Beijing. From this vantage point we would likely look at Asia as follows:

We Chinese no longer feel pressure from the Soviet Union in the north. In fact our border trade with Russia is growing very rapidly and renewed friendship is a natural consequence of both our nations' envy and distrust of Western powers, especially the United States. (Although both our Russian friends and we have to recognise the superiority of a market-based economy over strict state economic planning, we still resent the West having emerged victoriously from the cold war.) Our economy is growing very rapidly and we repeatedly read in the Western press that in twenty years China will have the world's largest economy. However, our strong economic performance in recent years has also created some potentially destabilising problems. Domestic economic growth has eroded the power of our central government and led to rising autonomy in the provinces and among the entrepreneurial class; and we have become increasingly dependent on imports of natural resources, especially oil from the Middle East. This when the US seems increasingly concerned about our economic success and our growing military influence in the Pacific region. The Americans' response to our ascendancy has been a policy of containment for fear that one day we *may contain Asia (which explains America's support for Taiwan's independent stance and its strategic alliance with Japan).*

Our response to these potential problems is obvious. We must maintain our central government's power even if it means opening the party to some successful entrepreneurs; subdue democratic political trends; continue to modernise our army and bring Taiwan and Hong Kong back into our political fold. Furthermore, we cannot afford to have a hostile power strangle us economically by interrupting the flow of oil to China. To secure our shipping routes to the Middle East, we must establish strong military bases from the Persian Gulf to China's northern ports. In case of war, we must have direct access to the Andaman Sea through Myanmar and the Arabian Sea through Pakistan - both countries with whom we share common borders following our liberation of Tibet.

Finally we must get the American troublemakers out of our Southeast Asian backyard by becoming the Asian economies' most important customer and foreign investor. This won't be difficult, since we are resource-poor and can purchase our natural resource requirements from our Asian neighbours - oil and timber from Indonesia and Far East Russia, coffee from Vietnam, palm oil from Malaysia, rice from Thailand, copper from the Philippines and Mongolia, and all agricultural products from Australia and New Zealand. If our economy continues to grow at the present rate we shall become the world's largest buyers of most commodities - and by being Asia's best customer we shall also ensure open markets for our manufactured goods. Contrary to Western thinking, we are far less dependent on exports to the US for economic growth than the US depends on us for low-priced, high-quality products to keep its rate of inflation and interest rates low through deflating import prices. Total exports account for only 10% of our GDP and our domestic economy has huge potential for growth since housing and consumer markets are still largely undersupplied.

We therefore see that Asia is currently confronted with tremendous economic political crosscurrents. While intraregional tensions have abated, Chinese economic and military influence is increasingly becoming a threat - and at the same time, an opportunity. In Chapter 9, I discussed how China had squeezed other Asian countries from export markets in the 1990s (and was, therefore, one of the causes of the Asian Crisis) and how growing Chinese competitiveness in the manufacturing sector had diverted the flow of foreign investment away from other Asian countries. But at the same time, China is now also becoming Asia largest customer for its natural resource requirements, while its outbound holidaymakers are already in many countries the largest group of tourists. Figure 1 shows the growth in China's outbound traffic, which has trebled over the last six years, yet still represents less than 1% of its population. Since Asian countries such as Japan, South Korea and Taiwan have departure rates exceeding 10%, and the United Kingdom's rate is *above* 100% - it is not unrealistic to expect the Chinese rate to increase in the next 10-20 years to 5-10%, which would annually mean 60-100 million Chinese travellers abroad! In addition, Chinese companies are increasingly acquiring companies around Asia in order to spread their economic and political muscle. This also encourages Chinese nationals in countries such as Far East Russia and Myanmar, which they deem to be of strategic importance. The rise of China as Asia's dominant economic and political power raises a host of issues.

Figure 1

ON THE ROAD

China's foreign travellers

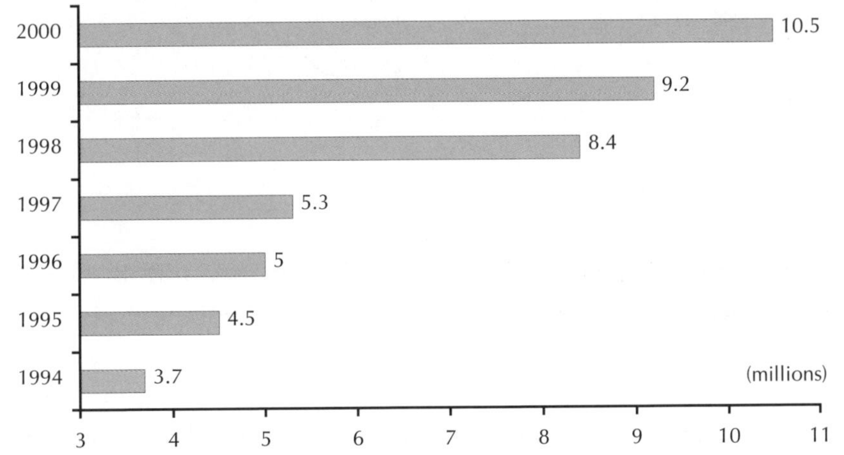

Year	(millions)
2000	10.5
1999	9.2
1998	8.4
1997	5.3
1996	5
1995	4.5
1994	3.7

3 4 5 6 7 8 9 10 11

Source: China National Tourism Administration.

It is obvious that with an increasingly affluent population of 1.2 billion, China will be the largest consumer in the world for most goods and services. It already has more refrigerators, mobile phones, TVs and motorcycles than the US and it is only a matter of time before it will have huge markets for just about any product. Its resource requirements will therefore rise very substantially and Chinese purchases of oil, coffee, copper and grains will move commodity prices dramatically. Just consider the following. Asia consumes 19 million barrels of oil daily with a population of about three billion. By contrast, 285 million Americans consume about 22 million barrels a day - a per-capita consumption more than ten times higher. But Asian consumption is now rising rapidly. For instance, Figure 2 shows that oil demand in China has doubled since 1992 to around 4.5 million barrels a day.

Figure 2

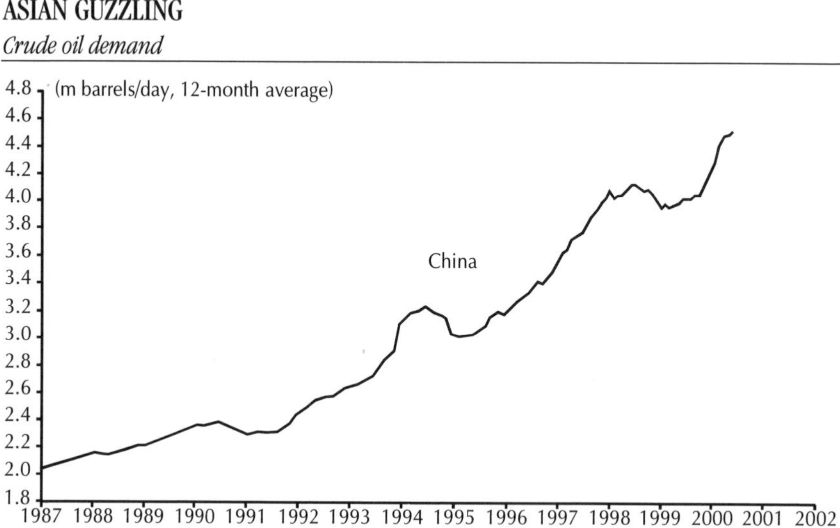

Source: Oil Market Intelligence, Ed Yardeni / Prudential Securities (www.prudential.com).

My guess is that oil consumption in Asia will double again over the next ten years or so to anywhere between 35 and 45 million barrels a day. At that level, per-capita consumption would still be inferior to the figure for Latin America. Therefore, I regard this estimate as fairly realistic given Asia's superior growth prospects, rapid industrialisation and steady increase in living standards in recently opened countries such as China and Vietnam. With such huge demand, by then largest of any economic bloc, Asia will revolutionise the geopolitics surrounding the oil producing regions of the world. Therefore, I expect China to become far more involved in the Middle East and Central Asia in the years to come, which could lead to some additional tensions in this volatile part of the world. In particular I regard as almost inevitable a clash of Chinese interests in the

Middle East and in Central Asia with American and possibly Russian interests. *Moreover a doubling of demand in Asia will inevitably lead to significantly higher oil prices in the second half of this decade when total global production is expected to peak.*

But Chinese economic growth will not only be felt in the oil market. Take for instance the per-capita consumption of food in China. I shall not compare it to food consumption in some Western countries, where obesity is endemic. But if we look at comparative meat, milk, fish, fruit and poultry consumption in China, Taiwan and Hong Kong it becomes obvious that rising standards of living in China will see it moving up to the pattern set by its wealthy compatriots in Hong Kong and Taiwan (see Table 1). Or compare coffee in China and Western countries. Annual per-capita consumption in Germany amounts to 8.6kg, in Switzerland it is 10.1kg and in Japan, where coffee consumption increased rapidly in the last 30 years, it is 2.3kg. But in China it is just 0.20kg. If it just rose to 1kg (a little less than in South Korea) then China would have a total consumption of 1.2 billion kg compared to around 70 million kg in Switzerland! What I really want to emphasise here is that if standards of living continue to rise in China, this country will have a huge impact on the world's commodity markets and is likely to push up commodity prices very considerably. In fact, I regard the purchase of a basket of commodities as the safest way to play the emergence of China as the world's dominant economic power.

Table 1

LOOKING FOR ITS SEAT AT THE TABLE

Food consumption in Asia - China vs Taiwan and Hong Kong

	China	Taiwan	Hong Kong
Meat	15	81	91
Poultry	2	*	29
Fish	4	59	57
Rice	154	85	60
Fruit	12	92	92
Liquid milk	6	39	52
Vegetables	19	70	78
Fruit juices	0	19	3

Per capita consumption of major food items kilograms per person except fruit juices in litres per person. *Included in meat. Source: *Consumer Asia* 1995.

Some readers will, of course, question my optimism about China's growth prospects and point out the problems the country faces. These relate largely to its financial system, large bad loans at state-owned banks, unfunded pension-fund liabilities, corruption and growing wealth inequality between its rural and urban populations. I am very familiar with all these problems, since I am usually invited at conferences around Asia to present the *bearish* case on China. My bearishness however usually rests more with the fact that it is extremely difficult for foreigners to make much money in China because of its deflationary and highly competitive environment in which foreigners - as was the case in the 19th Century American economy - are regularly taken to the cleaners. But in terms of China's own problems, which are incidentally endemic to almost all emerging economies, I believe that, while substantial in scope, they *can* be dealt with.

I emphasise "can" here because China has so far failed to deal effectively with most of the causes of its problems and has always postponed radical financial reform. However, I am convinced that sometime in the future it will experience a serious financial crisis, which will finally force its policymakers to deal with the bad-loan and pension-fund issues.

The reader should, however, not read too much into the financial crisis I am expecting. As we have seen in Chapters 4, 6 and 7, the American economy of the 19th Century also experienced a series of crises and even a civil war, yet its economy performed admirably well between 1800 and 1900 - and this in a deflationary environment. Moreover, I have found that all rapidly growing economies occasionally experience terrific temporary setbacks - a phenomenon that was already familiar to the father of the business-cycle theory, Clement Juglar, when he pointed out the riches of nations can be measured by the violence of the crises they experience.

As mentioned, the US economy's rapid expansion in the second half of the 19th Century was due to several factors, including a rapid increase in its population, the opening of new territories facilitated by the railroadisation of the country, and the application of new inventions to manufacturing, which boosted productivity dramatically. Thus, when we compare the US economy in the second half of the 19th Century to China at present, we should not overlook the fact that, in 1850, the US was well behind Europe in terms of industrialisation. A catch-up effect came into play. This is evident when we note that, from 1875 to 1890, US industrial production grew on average by 4.9% per annum, compared to just 1.2% for the UK and 2.5% for Germany. America's strong growth was typical of an emerging economy and is comparable to strong per-capita GDP growth in China between 1978 and 1995, averaging more than 5% while the world only averaged 1.11%. Moreover, by 1885, the US, which had hardly any industry at the beginning of the century, led the world in manufacturing, producing 28.9% of global output. Also, while the US hardly produced any cotton around 1800, its plantations supplied five-sixths of world supply by 1860! The point is simply this: If, from extremely humble beginnings, the US could become the world's dominant economic power in a century, I think, with the acceleration of the pace of change I have mentioned, it is quite probable that in 10-20 more years of modern development China will be by far the world's most important economy - no matter how many crises it has to deal with in the interim.

One problem I foresee, however, is that, because of its size and increasing economic and military importance, China will grow out of proportion for harmonious balance of power in Asia. When China becomes Asia's largest trading partner in both exports and imports, it will not only be an economic hegemon but also replace the US as Asia's most influential political power. That such a transition will lead at some point to serious tension between the US and Japan on one side and China on the other is obvious - the trend is there and in my opinion unstoppable.

Tension between Japan and China could also arise from nothing else than economic issues. In all markets the share of imports from Japan is shrinking whereas China's share is expanding rapidly (see Figure 3). Increasingly, Japan will be forced to shift its production of manufactured goods to China and other low-cost countries - which will continue to depress economic activity in Japan, but which could also increase the profitability of Japan's corporate sector. So, I should like to warn investors not to be overly negative about Japanese stocks at present. Ownership by individuals of equities as a percentage of financial assets is at a record low in Japan and, therefore, a reversal could lead to a surprisingly strong stock-market performance. This particularly in the case of an inflationary environment, which would lead to a collapse of Japanese bond prices, whose yield in 2002 is close to a record low, and bring about a shift of money flows from bonds to equities.

Figure 3

THE COMPETITIVE THREAT OF CHINA

Market share of US imports - Japan vs China

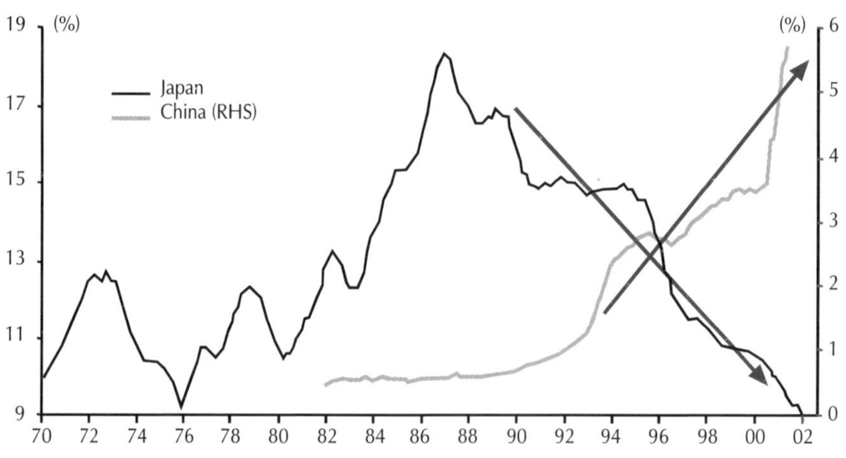

Source: Bridgewater Associates.

Although one must be highly sceptical of futurology, I think it is highly probable that, in ten to twenty years, Asia will depend far less on exports to the West than it does today. Trade within Asia will dominate, as the region hardly *requires* any Western products. Exports *to* the Western industrialised nations, however, are here to stay because Asian manufacturing and IT services are so competitive.

In addition, I should like to debunk another widespread myth among Westerners. I am frequently told that China and the rest of Asia still rely on Western knowledge and technology and that Asians are incapable of innovation and invention. When I hear such arguments I always have to smile. In India was invented the number zero, without which science in the

West could never have progressed at the pace it did. Francis Bacon thought that three inventions - paper and printing, gunpowder and the magnetic compass - had done more than any religious conviction, astrological influence or conqueror's achievement, to bring about the modern world and mark it off from the Middle Ages and antiquity. All three inventions came from China! Moreover, if I look at the achievements of Japan in the manufacturing sector over the last 30 years or so, there is simply no doubt that Asians can be great innovators as well. Not to mention that in just about every Western hi-tech company and leading research laboratory we find either Indian or Chinese scientists.

All Asia really needs to take off in terms of its own innovations is to create a more favourable social and political environment - such as catapulted Western Europe from the Dark Ages to the Industrial Revolution and the US from early-19th-Century agrarianism to 20th-Century world hegemony. The origin of progress and economic development in WesternEurope is extremely complex, but in essence it shows right away what Asia, to a large extent, still lacks. Still, I am hopeful that gradually the transition from the "Asian feudalistic capitalistic society" to a well-structured market economy and institutional capitalistic system will come to maturity. The reason I am reasonably optimistic is that a feudal system is based on a complete system in which political, economic and military power are one and the same and its objectives are security and stability rather than growth. The market economy and the capitalistic system, however, rest on equality and individual freedom and on institutions with dependable rules and laws (as opposed to the discretionary justice of manorial or royal courts) and its objective are not exploitation but growth and progress through innovations and creativity, and the "pursuit of profit, and forever renewed profit, by means of continuous, rational, capitalistic enterprise" (Weber, op. cit., 1930).

Now, I think that in Asia a new entrepreneurial class is emerging similar to the merchant class in the city-states of the Middle Ages, which brought about economic reforms that in turn led to wide-ranging political reform and replaced sovereign power with liberal representative governments. Many of the new Asian entrepreneurs have come from outside the established feudalistic capitalistic system, were not born to rich families and had no connections or access to capital from relatives, government or state banks. A good example of a sector that has thrived despite a horribly bureaucratic, corrupt and class-conscious government is the software and generic drug industry in India, which has proven that, no matter how bad a government is, market forces eventually can overcome just about any obstacle. Similarly, an entirely new entrepreneurial class has emerged in China outside the communist party or the state sector. Initially, these young entrepreneurs - many of who were educated in the West - only aspired to make money, to become rich and to gain social recognition. But especially as they come to pay taxes - it is only a matter of time before they also wish to have some governmental representation - and at that point we can expect a more structured capitalistic system in the spirit of Max Weber, which will also improve the transparency of Asian companies (not that transparency is any worse in Asia than in the US).

In this respect I am in particularly impressed by political developments in Taiwan. In 1996, Lee Teng-hui proved that Chinese people are *not* unsuited for democracy (as is still claimed today by most of Hong Kong's leading businessmen, including some Westerners, notably those with close business ties to China). The elections in Taiwan were a milestone in Asia's political history because they were truly free. President Lee demonstrated that the 21 million Chinese living in Taiwan had a strong determination to pursue freedom and democracy. He also recognised, as he put it, that vigorous economic development leads to independent thinking. According to Lee, "people hope to be able to fully satisfy their free will and see their rights fully protected. And then demand ensues for political reform. The vitality and energy such reform releases is the same force that drives economic growth. Thus economic reform and political reform must progress together." Lee also thought he had reason to believe that the mainland's policy of economic liberalisation would bring its own internal demands and pressure for political reform.

Clearly, Taiwan's political system of democracy, emphasising independent thinking and the will of the people, was at the time totally irreconcilable with China's authoritarian system of controlling the people and of imprisoning dissidents. And while President Zhang Zemin had offered reunification with Taiwan under the same "one country two systems" principle as Hong Kong (allowing Taiwan to keep its independent judiciary, government and army) Lee's view was that "China should be unified under freedom and democracy".

The tension between Taiwan and China arose because Beijing considers Taiwan to be a province of China (historically a claim with little basis), while Taiwan has given numerous indications that it aims for independence. For China, an independent Taiwan is not acceptable for strategic reasons (a hostile power could use it as a base to control shipping in the Taiwan Strait). Also, an independent Taiwan would set a precedent for other "provinces" (especially Tibet and Muslim Xinjiang) to seek independence as well. Moreover, China still strongly opposes democracy (as we know it) as a political system. Former Prime Minister Li Peng called it "the evil seed" he would not permit to be sown in Chinese soil. The "bourgeois democracy" of Hong Kong and Taiwan has also been repeatedly attacked in the *People's Liberation Army Daily*. Western parliamentary democracy has been denounced as fake, an instrument of capitalistic exploitation, while the readers of the *PLA Daily* were urged to "stick to the leadership of the Communist Party" to obviate "social turmoil".

Personally, however, I do not think there is any present risk of military action between China and Taiwan - largely because China lacks the military capability to launch an offensive. Business ties across the Strait have become extremely close, with most Taiwanese businesses establishing assembly plants and joint ventures with powerful mainlanders in China. So while the politicians will continue to argue about the fate of Taiwan, the businessmen will take a more pragmatic approach, which will lead to closer relations between the two peoples. In this respect the recent moves towards direct air-links are encouraging and show that, based on economic considerations, a relatively independent Taiwan and China's totalitarian leadership are compatible. It would seem that in the case of the Taiwan sovereignty issue, the words of Voltaire are applicable - when it comes to money, all people are of the same religion!

In sum I believe that the trend in Asia towards democracy and a true market economy and capitalistic system seems to be, from a historical perspective, irreversible. That the transition creates tensions should not be surprising. Countries with strong and forward-looking leaderships, such as Taiwan, South Korea and Singapore, may be able to sail through this difficult phase smoothly. Countries whose governments resist change may face a more uncertain future. Still, even Indonesia, which under Sukarno and Suharto was organised in a very feudalistic fashion, held fair elections in 2001, in which Megawati Sukarnoputri was elected by popular vote.

Moreover it is likely that we will also see big changes in China's political system sometime in the years to come. I would expect these changes to occur at the same time as the financial crisis I foreshadowed above, which will simultaneously bring about the necessary financial and economic reforms.

Another point gives me more reason for optimism. When former communist and socialist countries opened up in the 1980s and early 90s, they were ill prepared for the market economy and a competitive environment in the corporate sector. These transitional economies had not only a poor physical infrastructure, but lacked all the institutions necessary for capitalism to succeed. Just consider as an example that under the planned economy of communist regimes there was no system of taxation, as workers received a net salary and all corporations were owned by the state. Now, suddenly, these economies find themselves confronted with the market economy, where taxes need to be collected. One can, therefore, only imagine the complexity involved in the transition from communism to the market-based economy. Moreover, when these former communist countries opened up, their corporate sector was totally unprepared for international competition. Local companies lacked capital, management know-how, marketing skills, modern techniques of production and distribution channels. They also had practically no access to finance, as banks either extended no credit at all or only to state-owned enterprises.

No wonder Western multinationals that ventured into these transitional economies had such a huge competitive advantage. With the superior quality of their products, marketing skills and almost unlimited access to finance from the international capital markets, it was easy to quickly grab 50-70% of the market for their products. Indeed, the 1990s were highly favourable for companies such as Coca-Cola, Gillette, Procter & Gamble, Unilever, Nestlé, Nike, McDonald's, Kellogg's, Starbucks and so on. In addition, the profitability of many multinationals increased, as "outsourcing" became the order of the day. By closing down manufacturing facilities in high-cost Western countries and outsourcing their production to Asia, profit margins could be boosted.

But in the years to come I see vengeance coming from companies based in emerging economies. In the 1990s they learned their foreign competitors' methods for successfully running businesses, since many foreigners formed joint ventures that transferred knowledge, skills and manufacturing technology to the local partners. Through the process of outsourcing, local companies also acquired all the necessary technology to produce goods under their own brands. Therefore, I have no doubt that in time we shall see more and more Chinese and other brands gaining market share in their local markets and coming onto the world's markets to compete with established brands. Who, 30 years ago, had heard of *Samsung, Kia Motors, Hyundai, Daewoo, Acer, Shu Uemura, Issei Miyaki, Yamamoto, Shiseido and Red Bull* - and of companies such as Dr Reddy's, Wipro, Infosys, Reliance Industries, TSMC, UMC, Sampoerna, Posco, Legend, Konka, Haier and Singapore Airlines, just to name a few. From now on, life for the multinationals will be far more difficult, a fact already reflected in their recent poor stock-market performance.

There is one more point to consider with respect to the multinationals. Until recently, patents and licence fees were hardly discussed. But, with the rise of the anti-globalisation movement, patents have come under increasing pressure - particularly in the case of pharmaceutical companies whose drugs were in many cases not affordable in impoverished countries. In my opinion, Pandora's box has now been opened and more and more we shall see that emerging economies will either renegotiate patents and licence fees or simply disregard them. I simply cannot see under what scenario the billion or so Chinese and Indians would pay a few hundred dollars for Microsoft programs and around US$50 for Hewlett Packard printer ink cartridges when the latter can be produced for about one dollar apiece.

Another factor fosters my optimism about the Asian region and emerging markets in general. Because of the feudalistic capitalism I described above, and because of the perceived strength of the American economy in the 1990s, emerging economies suffered from significant capital flight. As a result, some private individuals and central banks have a vast pool of funds parked principally in the US capital market. If, however, the political, social and economic transition outlined above does indeed take place, conditions for a massive repatriation of funds held overseas will be created, which would lead to higher investment activity and boost local asset values. I would conservatively estimate that Indonesians hold assets of around US$100 billion outside the country. Argentineans hold at least US$50 billion in foreign bank accounts and Russian overseas assets must be very considerable as well.

Once again, I should like to remind readers that, following the Asian Crisis, price levels in Asia became extremely low compared to the industrialised economies and, therefore, repatriation of foreign holdings will make economic sense as soon as the market economy and the system of capitalism becomes more institutionalised. In addition, as can be seen from Figure 4, international banks, which all enthusiastically lent to Asian countries right up to the Crisis, cut their lending by around 50% soon after. I have no doubt that international bank lending will pick up again once perceptions about "Asian risk" as compared to the "safe haven" status of American financial assets changes.

Therefore, the combination of the repatriation of foreign assets by locals, the resumption of international bank lending and an improved climate in the international capital market for Asian borrowers is likely to create liquidity conditions in Asia sufficient to fuel a great new age of discovery in the region.

Figure 4

CUTTING OFF THE CREDIT

International bank lending (amounts outstanding)

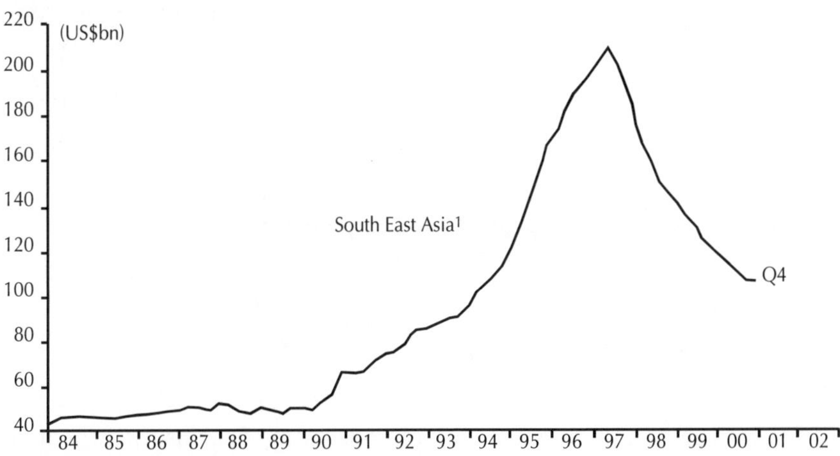

Note: [1] Includes Indonesia, Malaysia, Philippines and Thailand. Source: Bank for International Settlements, Ed Yardeni / Prudential Securities (www.prudential.com).

EPILOGUE

Wealth inequality - The great shadow

I could go on much longer with reasons for my optimism on the long-term prospects of the Asian region. But no matter how thorough such an analysis might be, it would remain superficial because of the extreme complexity of the issues under consideration and the vast social and economic differences we find in Asia. How can we generalise about Asia when we are dealing with well-developed countries such as Japan, South Korea, Taiwan and Singapore and at the same time grossly underdeveloped regions such as the rural sectors in India, China and all the other countries - as well as a country such as Bangladesh whose GDP with a population of more than 110 million is inferior to Singapore's with three million?

If we compare present-day Asia to Western Europe in the past and the present, what is striking is that Western Europe never had the kind of vast difference in the level of social and economic development we find now in Asia. Admittedly, there has long been a large difference between economic development in the United Kingdom and Germany on one side and Southern Italy, Greece and Portugal on the other. But, the gap in terms of income, wealth and level of industrialisation has always been far narrower than in Asia.

This disparity in the level of development both offers a tremendous opportunity on the one hand and creates problems on the other, which will have to be addressed. The opportunity lies of course in the exchange of goods and services as foreign trade is particularly beneficial between countries that have totally different comparative advantages - an insight already discovered by David Ricardo almost 200 years ago when making his case for free trade. It is obvious that trade between two equal countries such as Germany and France have a limited macroeconomic impact. If Germany imports an additional 100,000 French cars and France imports an additional 100,000 German cars, growth rates are not lifted. Admittedly some increased consumer satisfaction may occur as some Germans may desperately wish to drive French cars and vice versa. But compare this to trade in Asia between Japan and Bangladesh. Japan produces goods that are not manufactured in Bangladesh, while Bangladesh can, with its extremely low labour costs, produce labour-intensive goods whose production would be totally cost-inefficient in Japan. Therefore, foreign trade in this instance can boost both countries' growth rates and standards of living significantly.

Now, take the entire Asian economy and consider what an entirely free market would do for the whole region. Over time, trade and investment flows would be directed toward the sectors and regions around Asia that enjoy a comparative advantage and lift growth rates for the region as a whole. For this reason, I am quite confident that Asia will become, in future, far less dependent on exports to Western countries for its economic development. But the huge income and wealth inequality problem - not only in Asia but the entire world - will naturally also bring along a number of political and economic problems. In fact, I consider wealth and income inequality between the world's few rich and many poor countries to be the most serious economic challenge we must deal with in the years to come - and it is the one challenge that tempers my optimism about the future. Let me explain.

In 1998, Indonesia, a country with a population of around 200 million, had a GDP per capita of approximately US$300 (post-devaluation). Switzerland, with a population of around seven million, had a GDP per capita of almost US$40,000. Hence, Switzerland's GDP per capita was 133 times Indonesia's and its total GDP was more than four times. India has a population of around one billion and a GDP per capita of about US$400. At US$400 billion, its GDP is therefore just a tad above Switzerland's!

The US stock market capitalisation now exceeds US$11 trillion and accounts for 53% of the world's total. However, the US population, at 285 million, accounts for less than 5% of the world's population. Life expectancy in the most developed countries is close to 80 years, while in the poor countries of Asia and Africa it frequently does not exceed 50 years. Similarly, infant mortality is less than ten out of 1,000 live births in most developed countries, but above 100 in the world's poorest countries. In the United States, there are more than 2,000 doctors per million people; in countries like Indonesia, there are less than 100. Whereas 98% of children attend secondary school in the US, less than 10% do so in the poorest countries. Also, while multimillion-dollar pay packages for executives are common in industrialised countries, close to 1.5 billion people (25% of the world's population) earn less than US$1.60 per day.

Wealth and income inequality is nothing new; it has existed throughout history. But never before have there been such huge differences in living standards for such a large number of people across the globe. According to Richard Steckel, an Ohio State University Professor specialising in comparative economics, "Only in the 20th Century have we seen this amazing change - where populations in the developed countries with huge, efficient markets, like Europe and America and parts of Asia, have raced ahead of everyone else."

How have these unprecedented imbalances (albeit disputed by some academics) come about, and what might their impact be on the global economy in future? And, if the laws of *reversion to the mean* still hold, how will these imbalances eventually be redressed?

If we look at longer-term trends in global population and GDP, we see that there was practically no economic growth until the year 1000, then very slow growth until about 1750, and subsequently very strong growth up to this day (see Table 1). So, whereas world GDP increased by less than seven times between year 1 and about 1800, it subsequently rose by over 40 times in just 200 years. Equally, world population remained stagnant between year 1 and the year 1000, then grew slowly until 1800, but multiplied by close to six times between 1800 and today. These statistics are also supported by production and trade figures, which show little growth between the year 1000 and 1700, but strong growth thereafter - also on a per-capita basis (see Table 2).

Table 1

ERA OF EXPANSION 1

World economic growth to 1995

Year	1	1000	1500	1820	1995
The World - Population (m)	250	273	431	1,067	5,671
GDP (US$bn)[1]	106	115	235	720	29,423
The West - Population (m)	25	33	65	156	739
GDP (US$bn)[1]	11	13	40	179	14,773
The Rest - Population (m)	226	241	367	911	4,932
GDP (US$bn)[1]	95	102	195	541	14,651

[1] Total GDP in billions of 1990 international dollars. Note: These estimated draw on material for 1500-1995 in A. Maddison, 1995 and *Chinese Economic Performance in the Long Run*, 1998, published by the OECD Development Center, Paris. The time series for GDP were merged with estimated of 1990 GDP derived by use of purchasing power conversions rather than exchange rates and called here "international dollars". The tentative estimates for years before 1500 were specially prepared for this article. Source: Angus Maddison, *Monitoring the World Economy*, 1995.

Table 2

ERA OF EXPANSION 2

Global production and trade growth, 1000-1990

	Overall total		Per capita	
	1000-1700	1700-1990	1000-1700	1700-1990
Grain production	2-4x	14x	1-2x	2x
Iron & steel production	4-9x	2,000x	2-3x	260x
Textile production	2-4x	29x	1-2x	4x
Energy production	2-6x	280x	1-2x	36x
International trade	6-12x	920x	3-4x	120x
Total production	2-4x	44x	1-2x	6x
Population	2-3x	8x	-	-

Source: Paul Bairoch, *Victoires et déboires*, 1997.

Thus, as if a magic wand had touched the world's economy at the beginning of the 19th Century (the wand of capitalism and the Industrial Revolution), it began to grow at much higher rates than ever before and punctuated the economic equilibrium that had been in existence for several thousand years. Until the early 19th Century, all economies had been largely agricultural, with the level of urbanisation in 1750 not much different from what it had been 2000 years earlier. So, while it is estimated that the urbanisation rate averaged about 9-12% between 300 BC and 100 BC, by 1750 it was still only about 15%, even in Western Europe. But with the process of industrialisation, the urban population as a percentage of total population rose rapidly, reaching about 80% for OECD countries at present.

In fact, we may argue that the pre-Industrial Revolution age was characterised by the absence of many "very large" cities. By 1800, there were just six cities with more than 500,000 inhabitants (Beijing, London, Canton, Yedo (Tokyo), Constantinople and Paris) and only one (Beijing) with more than one million. This was so because poor usage of agricultural land, and inefficient as well as expensive transportation were constraining the expansion of cities. But with industrialisation and significantly improved transport (railroads lowered the cost of shipping food to the cities), large cities began to proliferate, resulting in close to 350 cities with more than one million inhabitants today. Astoundingly, the combined population of the five largest urban agglomerations today (Tokyo, New York, London, Chongqing and Shanghai) is equal to the combined population of the world's 2,000 or so cities with a population of more than 2,000 people in the year 1700!

The rate of progress has, however, been very uneven in different regions. If we look at GDP growth in the West (see Table 1) and compare it to the rest of the world, we find that while the former increased by over 80 times between 1820 and 1995 (from US$179 billion to US$14,773 billion), GDP in the rest of the world increased by just 27 times (from US$541 billion to US$14,651 billion). Now, the fact that Western countries grew about three times more rapidly than the rest of the world over the last 180 years or so is not particularly odd - after all, the process of industrialisation had its cradle in Western Europe and the United States - but more disconcerting is the way GDP per capita in the rich and poor countries has diverged since then. From Table 3, we note that, whereas in 1800, incomes in the most-developed countries (MDCs) and the least-developed countries (LDCs) were not markedly different, after which time income inequality widened significantly. Between 1800 and 1995, GDP per capita in the MDCs rose over 21 times, but in the LDCs it only increased by 2.5 times. So, whereas in the MDCs it was 1.2 times higher than in the LDCs in 1800, today the ratio is more than ten times.

Table 3

THE RICH GET RICHER

Per capita GDP, 1750-1995 (in 1960 US Dollars)

	Most developed countries	Developed countries	Less developed countries	World
1750	230	182	188	188
1800	242	198	188	190
1860	575	324	174	218
1913	1,350	662	192	560
1950	2,420	1,050	200	590
1995	5,230	3,320[1]	480[2]	1,100

[1] Up 21 times. [2] Up 2.5 times. Source: Paul Bairoch, *Victoires et déboires*, 1997.

An even wider divergence is apparent in the economic performance of the richest versus the poorest nations. In 1800, the United Kingdom, then the world's richest country, had a GDP per capita slightly less than twice as large as that of the world's poorest nations. But now, the richest countries have a per-capita GDP 50 times larger than that of the world's five poorest countries (purchasing power parity (PPP) adjusted).

Someone could rightly question these statistics. However, if we look at infant mortality rates, life expectancy, calorie consumption, crop yields, urbanisation rates, energy consumption and steel production (all indicators of economic development) in Europe and the rest of the world in 1800, it is evident that Europe was better off than the world's poorest nations - but not by all that much. In 1800, life expectancy at birth was about 40 years in Europe and only 35 years in the rest of the world. Infant mortality was about the same, as was the level of urbanisation and crop yields. Therefore, while there could be some dispute about whether 1800 GDP per capita was 1.5 or 3 times higher in the UK than in the world's then poorest countries, there is no disputing the fact that, *until about 1800, everyone in the world was basically poor with the exception of a few rich aristocrats, landowners, artisans and merchants.*

In fact, in *A History of Technology*, Charles Singer (Oxford, 1954) points out that up to the 16th Century the Near East was superior to the

West in skill and inventiveness, and the Far East was superior to both; technologically, the West had little to offer the East. Yield rates per man and per unit of land were higher in India than in the more progressive Western European countries in the 17th Century. Furthermore, seed-yield ratios for individual crops were superior in India, which had larger and richer urban areas than Europe before the Industrial Revolution. However, because of the congenial weather and abundant natural resources in India, there was no pressure to improve agricultural productivity. In northern European countries, conversely, very harsh and unfavourable climatic conditions and the growing population demanded improvements in productive techniques, which in turn fostered the development of modern technology. In fact, as Karl Marx explained in *Das Kapital* (Hamburg, 1867), the development of industry in the West was a consequence of society's need to bring nature under control.

Thus, the Industrial Revolution and rise of the West can be partly explained as a consequence of huge improvements in agricultural productivity that took place in Western Europe, which actually forced workers off their farms to look for employment in the manufacturing sector. So while until 1750 it had taken about 3,500 hours of work to produce 100 bushels of wheat, by 1840 it took only 250 man-hours to do the same job; by 1925, the figure was 74, and by 1990, just seven. As a side-note I may add that, over the last 200 years, hardly any sector has seen productivity improvements as dramatic as agriculture, yet nobody could claim that agriculture was a particularly profitable sector in the economy - certainly not in Europe following the opening of the American western territories. From Figure 1, we can see that farm productivity has far outstripped non-farm productivity since 1950. I am mentioning this because some pundits have argued that because of large productivity improvements, US equities deserve a higher valuation than in the past.

Figure 1

WORKING HARDER ON THE FARM

Farm and nonfarm productivity real output per hour

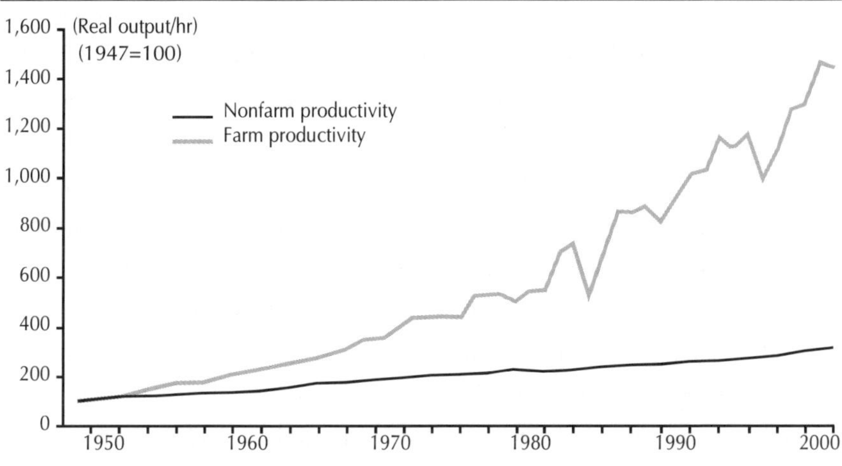

Source: Bureau of Labor Statistics, Bureau of Economic Analysis and Gary Shilling.

Of particular importance for the rise of Western Europe may have also been the acceptance of the idea of "equality of opportunity", which enables individuals to achieve their highest potential and led, in several European countries, to the introduction of compulsory primary schooling by the beginning of the 19th Century. In this respect, it must be pointed out that, *while at the dawn of the Industrial Revolution, Europe was not much richer than other regions of the world, and the diffusion of knowledge there was far superior.* So, whereas in 1800, in some advanced European countries like England, close to 90% of people could read and write - in other less-developed countries, 90% were illiterate. Indeed, it would appear that, thanks to superior knowledge, several European countries and America had a tremendous head start. Relatively high standards of education allowed rural workers to migrate to the cities and be integrated into the industrial process. Simply put, at the beginning of the 19th Century, advanced European countries had a far superior "capacity for change" than did poor countries. (We use the term "advanced European countries" because a number of European countries, such as Serbia, Greece and Portugal, were as underdeveloped and poor as Third World countries.)

I may add that the lack of education in rural areas of emerging economies remains a huge problem as it hampers or makes altogether impossible their integration into the modern economy.

The Industrial Revolution in Europe and America in the 19th Century had some undesirable consequences for the then less-developed countries. Because of the West's enormous productivity gains in agriculture and industry, products from LDCs became far less competitive. For example, by 1830 in England, labour productivity in cotton spinning was already about 14 times higher than in India. As a result of these productivity gains - and, possibly, the colonial system - the LDCs experienced *deindustrialisation* in the 19th Century. According to a recent study of the deindustrialisation of India, the proportion of industrial to total population in Bihar fell from 18.6% around 1809-13 to 8.5% in 1901. Similarly in India, the proportion of the workforce engaged in manufacturing and construction fell by half between 1881 and 1911, from 35% to 17%.

Another contributing factor in the relative decline of the LDCs in the last 100 years had to do with inventions, which lessened the need for raw materials on which the LDCs had depended. Thus, in the 20th Century, synthetic plastics and fibres gradually displaced rubber and natural fibres in the production of tyres and textiles (see Table 4). The rapid productivity gains in the MDCs and deindustrialisation in the LDCs, therefore, led to a rise in wealth inequality. According to the economic historian, Paul Bairoch, (*Disparities in Economic Development since the Industrial Revolution*, New York, 1981), the daily wage of an English urban worker in 1780 bought about 6-7 kilograms of wheat. At the same time, he estimates that Indian workers, as well as workers in other Third World countries, had daily wages which bought them about 5-6 kilograms of wheat. However, by 1910, the English worker's wage had risen substantially and enabled him to buy 33kg; whereas in India, it had hardly moved and still only enabled them to buy 5-6kg. (According to some estimates, Indian salaries had actually declined in terms of their purchasing power.) Today, in industrialised countries, a worker earning US$100 per day could buy with his daily wage 1,250kg of wheat, while an Indian worker earning, say,

US$3 per day could buy 37kg. This illustrates that income inequalities have further increased in the course of the 20th Century.

Table 4

AU NATUREL NO MORE

Global production of rubber and textiles, 1913-1990

Ratio of synthetic fibres in . . .	Rubber (%)	Textile fibres (%)
1913	0.0	0.2
1928	0.0	1.4
1936	0.5	5.0
1950	29.0	12.0
1960	48.0	16.0
1970	63.0	24.0
1980	65.0	40.0
1990	65.2	39.0

Source: Paul Bairoch, *Victoires et déboires*, 1997.

To explain the causes of this growing wealth and income inequality between rich and poor countries is extremely complex and has been attempted with mixed results by numerous sociologists and economists. It is easy to see that Europe and the United States raced ahead because of their enormous progress in agricultural productivity and early industrialisation. But why did industrialisation occur there in the 19th Century and not in other regions of the world at a much earlier time? Some economists explain the 19th Century Industrial Revolution in the West as an historical accident. After all, societies like the Romans and, later, the Chinese had developed "modern technologies" and with their skills could have industrialised. Why did they fail to do so? Furthermore, why did the rest of the world not just copy the production techniques developed in Western Europe and the United States in the 19th Century and industrialise the way Japan did at the end of the 19th Century?

We have seen above that, thanks to superior "knowledge" and a favourable moral background, Western Europe already had a head start at the onset of the 19th Century. Knowledge and special skills were certainly also a factor in the industrialisation of Japan. But another factor was the "capacity for change", which seems to have been inferior in poor nations than in affluent societies. In addition, there seems to exist a first-mover advantage, as countries that *initially* acquire wealth have an advantage in generating additional prosperity over countries that lag behind. The rich countries have in all instances stronger bargaining power and can get favourable terms for every kind of contract by bribing just one individual in a powerful position - which may be unfavourable for the emerging economy involved, but of great advantage to the individual facilitating the transaction. (Large inequality of wealth fosters corruption as companies based in rich countries can easily buy favours from poor local government officials and corporate officers - a practice common in the physical commodities markets and large-scale infrastructure and resource projects!) In addition, the rich countries have greater ability than the poor to finance high standards of education and health care and to implement new technologies

Now we ought to consider the following. We have seen that, since the beginning of the 19th Century, the most-developed countries have grown at a far superior rate than the less-developed countries. In fact, according to some studies, the US economy outperformed the global economy in the late 1990s by the largest margin ever. Furthermore, per-capita incomes in the MDCs have increased at a rate about ten times higher than in the LDCs. But while the abyss between rich and poor countries may continue to widen, it is clear that in the very, very long run, no region, country or company can grow faster than the rate of growth for the world as a whole. I therefore, believe that there will eventually be either an acceleration of global growth and significant improvement of economic conditions among the developing countries, or a slowdown in economic growth in the most developed countries - specifically the United States. A combination thereof is another possibility.

Finding a balance

So, what are the prospects for faster economic growth in the LDCs? As indicated in Chapter 9, economic growth in emerging economies depends on exports, foreign direct investment and domestic spending and investment. Export growth should accelerate somewhat for resource-based emerging economies, if I am right about rising commodity prices in the years to come. Conversely, we cannot expect much improvement for exports of manufactured products since their prices are deflating and demand in the Western industrialised countries is likely to remain anaemic for the foreseeable future. Foreign direct investment, which fell after 1997 (except in the case of China, the former Soviet Union and Vietnam), may stabilise, but is unlikely to pick up dramatically because of existing overcapacity. However, domestic spending and investment could well improve - particularly in Asia as the debt level has been reduced over the last five years and the need for housing remains high. In particular, the urbanisation of Asia, which will lead to a rapid expansion of very large cities, should be extremely beneficial for the housing industry (see Figure 2). So, while the emerging economies may have reached the bottom of the valley (this may not yet be the case in Latin America) after falling off a cliff since 1997, very significant improvement in their growth rates is unlikely in the near term.

Figure 2

GOING TO TOWN

Number of cities with an urban population above 10 million

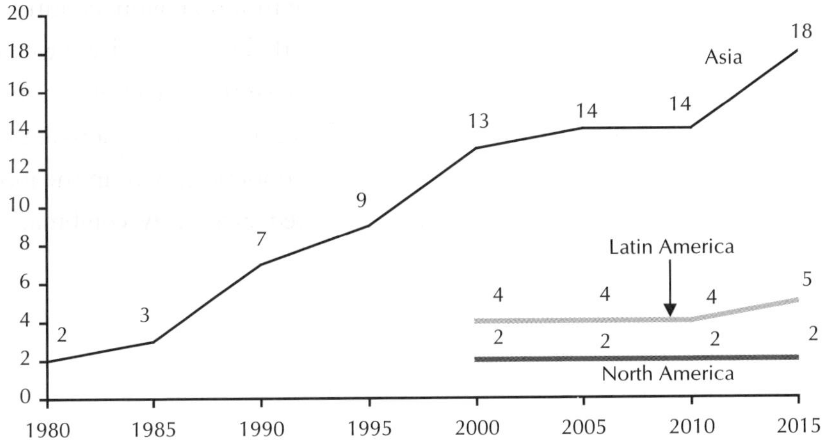

Source: United Nations.

In my opinion, the crux of the problem, not only for the LDCs but also for the global economy, is the depressed level of unskilled workers' incomes (even more so after the recent devaluations); which makes for insufficient purchasing power, which leads to underconsumption (see Hobson's theory in Chapter 6). For a while in the 1990s, when the industrialised countries were willing to lend the LDCs money and domestic credit expanded at phenomenal rates, consumption increased rapidly. But once the credit cycle turned down, consumption collapsed and has since then improved only moderately. Now, assuming that the depressed state of wages for unskilled workers in the LDCs is the main problem (among many others), where does that leave us? It could be argued that with globalisation, wages in LDCs will show a rising tendency. Unfortunately, that may not be the case.

Take, for instance, highly productive modern production methods that require a very limited workforce. The size and scope of such processes enable the modern and efficient corporation to produce and market goods at a lower unit price than smaller companies in the host countries. Furthermore, these powerful and financially strong companies can engage in dumping in order to gain market share, or even eliminate local competitors. This can be achieved easily for an international company as long as its profits in other countries are large enough to cover a loss in the host country. Later, once the local competitor is eliminated, prices can be increased substantially to turn a profit. Hence, foreign direct investment by efficient and large corporations in emerging economies may actually lead to a *decline in employment*! The optimists might think, "great!" and argue that as productivity improvements in agriculture at the beginning of the 19th Century in Europe freed labour to work in factories (see above), then productivity improvements in LDCs will free their workers to find employment as software engineers, Disney Park attendants, or in research labs. "A catastrophe", will be the opinion of the pessimists, who will point to the deindustrialisation of India in the 19th Century, which resulted from enormous productivity gains in Britain.

Clearly, there is a problem with modern, labour-saving production methods. Take, for instance, China. Its state-owned enterprises are highly inefficient but they employ about 110 million people. If China had a totally free market without state subsidies (in the form of bank loans, which are not repaid), 80% of these workers would have to be laid off. But, since urban unemployment rates are already at around 15% or higher, a major social problem would arise. The truth probably lies somewhere in between these extreme views, but there is little doubt that, in the case of China, the sudden dismantling of the state-owned enterprise system would lead to massive temporary dislocations (which accounts for the continuous postponement of reform).

Another way to redress the low-wage problem in LDCs would be to reduce the prices of goods and services dramatically, and make them affordable by the world's poor countries. Thus, if the prices of personal computers, cellular phones, pharmaceuticals, cars, Boeing 747s and other manufactured goods totally collapsed, demand would increase rapidly and create a "deflationary boom". Hopefully this process - which to some extent has begun - will become a long-term trend. It is probably the only way out of the wealth inequity dilemma. But I doubt that Western governments and multinationals will regard such a development favourably as their product prices would decline and profitability would suffer!

What can we expect if the wealth and income inequities between MDCs and LDCs increase even further? I suppose that in such a case, something will eventually give. Either global economic growth will subside, as it has recently, or social and political tension will increase even further. In the past, societies whose wealth inequality grew to an extreme level eventually experienced revolution - or at the very least, social upheaval (inequality was certainly a factor in Rome's decay). As Will Durant pointed out, "the concentration (of wealth) may reach a point where the strength of number in the many poor rivals the strength of ability in the few rich; then the unstable equilibrium generates a critical situation, which history has diversely met by legislation redistributing wealth or by revolution distributing poverty."

Thus, the problem of the current, unprecedented wealth and income inequality remains, in my opinion, the most pressing issue facing economic policymakers. Yet, many appear to be either unaware of the problem or unqualified to find a solution that will redress the existing imbalances. In fact, there are even some academics who claim that, in recent years, wealth inequality in the world has diminished. But this is certainly not my view given the severe currency depreciations emerging economies experienced in the last few years, which reduced peoples' Dollar incomes. Moreover, just remember that in 1914, Henry Ford increased the daily wage of autoworkers from US$2.34 for a nine-hour shift to US$5 for an eight-hour shift (approximately US$1,250 per annum). With such a high wage (*The Wall Street Journal* referred to it as an economic crime), a Ford worker was in a position to buy more than two Model-T automobiles (which sold for around US$360) every year. By contrast, most workers engaged today in manufacturing in emerging countries earn less than US$600 per annum - a little more than half the monthly cost of parking my motorcycle in the late 1990s in Hong Kong's New World Tower! Hence, most workers in developing countries can only dream of purchasing a car at a cost of around US$15,000.

In my opinion, the deep ravine separating the poor of this world from the rich will require us to think more carefully on how we can strike a balance between progress and wealth in our highly developed Western civilisation and the large number of destitute people in the world who have very little means of subsistence and no other means to fight and express their grievances than through acts of atrocity.

* * *

Despite these concerns and despite my pessimism on the US economy, I do remain optimistic about the future. This may come as a surprise to readers who associate my name with doom and gloom. But as I wrote in my introduction, this book is not about predicting economic disasters or colossal booms, it is about highlighting opportunities in a world where economic, political and social conditions are continuously changing, ever-faster, thanks to improvements in transport, communication and the global transfer of information.

I have tried to show that the global economic equilibrium that existed before communism's demise and the rise of globalisation has been disturbed - and that we are experiencing changes as dramatic as the ones that followed the Discovery Voyages and the Industrial Revolution. The acceleration of change itself - nowhere more evident than when regions open up, enter the market economy and industrialise - combined with the fact that so many population-rich countries (the former Soviet Union, China and India) are joining the free global, capitalistic system, will truly create a "new world order".

In Asia's new age of self-discovery, it is not difficult to expect such colossal transformation to create a "win-win" situations everywhere. Some sectors and regions must lose out, while others stand greatly to gain. New cities, low-cost industrial regions and dynamic companies will emerge to displace established centres of prosperity and successful businesses. Similarly, some financial markets will expand and thrive while others trade sidewards - or even decline like Japan's since 1990.

It is still unclear whether this new world order will bring about widespread deflation, as feared by some pundits, or a new wave of inflation. I am leaning toward the view that some sectors and regions will deflate - either through absolute price falls or currency depreciation - while those already extremely deflated will rise in price. So inflation and deflation could coexist for quite some time. Moreover, it should not be forgotten that, even in a strongly deflationary environment, some commodities and assets can appreciate rapidly as their respective prices are determined not by the overall macroeconomic price trend, but rather by demand and supply forces specific to their particular markets. As an example, the southern Californian real estate boom of 1882-86 took place in the midst of the longest and most pronounced deflationary periods the US ever experienced - a deflationary boom from 1864 to the end of the 19th century. Therefore, while the overall future price trend will have significant implications for holders of fixed-interest securities and on the valuation of equities, I find it more important for the investor to consider carefully what markets could appreciate under almost any kind of macroeconomic scenario. I dealt with this subject when discussing the outlook for commodities and emerging economies. Under the worst imaginable economic scenario, the emphasis on picking lowest-cost producers would be of crucial importance, as in today's highly competitive environment, only the very fittest can survive.

There is a final point I wish to make. In Chapter Two, I tried to show that while central bankers control the volume of liquidity flowing into the global economy, they can not control where the money flows once it comes to earth. This is important in the context of the US Fed and other central banks' present extreme expansionary monetary policies, which are designed to avoid recession and deflation *à tout prix* . In an almost borderless global economic system, it is conceivable that such monetary policies could reinforce the deflationary pressures because artificially low interest rates could lead to even greater capacity expansion in countries with very low price levels, such as China, Vietnam and India.

Therefore, low interest rates that lead to additional capacity, which produce additional supplies of manufactured products and services in already glutted markets, could be totally counterproductive. In a deflationary environment, the medicine ought to aim at reducing producion capacity as quickly as possible – requiring willpower whose absence in Japan in the past ten years is largely responsible for the present economic mess in that country.

What I am driving at is that, if monetary policies and central-bank interventions in the market economy should now fail - as I believe they will - the economic textbooks of the post Second World War period, which emphasised monetary and fiscal policies as the core of economics, will have to be rewritten. I would also expect the power of central banks to be significantly curtailed. It will finally dawn on even the starchiest supporters of central banking, who believe that "monetary policies always work", that as former Fed governor Wayne Angell recently uttered on CNBC, in economics only market forces "always" work. Interventions in the market always bring about additional maladjustments and unintended consequences. The public is brainwashed by fast-talking commentators and pseudo-economists who spread economic sophism spouting the omnipotence of central bankers and especially of Alan Greenspan. But when it finally realises that central bankers are no wiser than the central planners of former communist regimes, the tide will turn and monetary reform will come to the fore. At that time, the present loose monetary "arrangements" will be replaced by a disciplined monetary system with automatic stabilisers, checks and balances. Central bankers will no longer be able to tamper at the whim of questionable, government-doctored economic statistics. I suppose that in such a future monetary system, gold - the only currency whose supply cannot be increased ad infinitum - will have an important role to play.

So, I would expect that the new world order will not only come as a result of the enormous changes I envision for the global economic landscape, but also as a result of new economic theories far more aligned to the Austrian School of Economics. This should also explain my long-term optimism about the future, since I regard it as crucial that market forces drive economic activity, and not some kind of central planner: regardless whether they stand forth as senior officials of totalitarian regimes - or come cleverly disguised as central bankers.

Bibliography

Aftalion, Albert, *Les crises périodiques de surproduction*, Paris, 1913

Anderson, *History of Commerce*, London, 1788

Ashton, T. S., *Iron And Steel In The Industrial Revolution*, Manchester, 1924

Ashton, T. S., *Economic Fluctuations In England 1700-1800*, Oxford, 1959

Bairoch, Paul and Levy-Leboyer, Maurice, *Disparities in Economic Development since the Industrial Revolution*, New York, 1981

Bairoch, Paul, *Victoires et déboires*, Éditions Gallimard, 1997

Badger, Ralph, E., *Investment Principles and Practices*, New York, 1935

Beer, A., *Geschichte des Welthandels*, Wien, 1864

Benner, Samuel, *Benner's Prophecies of Future Ups and Downs in Prices*, Cincinnati, 1884

Bernstein, Peter, *Against The Gods*, New York, 1996

Bernstein, Peter, *The Power Of Gold*, New York, 2000

Blanqui, A., *Résume de L'histoire du Commerce et de L'industrie*, Paris, 1826

Board of Governors of the Federal Reserve System, International Discussion Paper, *Preventing Deflation; Lessons from Japan's Experience in the 1990s*, No. 729, June 2002

Böhm Bawerk, Eugen (von), *Kapital und Kapitalzins*, Jena, 1921

Braudel, Fernand, *The Mediterranean*, New York, 1972

Braudel, Fernand, *Civilisation and Capitalism 15th-18th Century*, New York, 1979

Bresciani-Turroni, Constantino, *The Economics of Inflation*, August M. Kelley, 1968 (first published by Universita Bocconi in 1931)

Brooks, John, *Once in Golconda*, New York, 1969

Bullock, Hugh, *The Story of Investment Companies*, New York, 1959

Burton, Theodore, *Financial Crises*, New York, 1910

The Cambridge Economic History of Europe, Cambridge, 1965

The Cambridge Economic History of India, Cambridge, 1982

The Cambridge History of China, Cambridge, 1980

The Cambridge History of Southeast Asia, Cambridge, 1992

Cannan, Edwin, *A History of the Theories of Production and Distribution*, London 1893

Chancellor, Edward, *Devil Take The Hindmost*, New York, 1999

Chandler, Tertius, *Four Thousand Years of Urban Growth*, New York, 1987

Chi, C., *Key Economic Areas in Chinese History*, New York, 1970

Cipolla, Carlo, *The Economic History of World Population*, Baltimore, 1962

Cipolla, Carlo, *Guns, Sails and Empires*, Minerva Press, 1965

Cipolla, Carlo, *The Fontana Economic History of Europe*, Collins/Fontana Books, 1976

Cipolla, Carlo, *Before The Industrial Revolution*, New York, 1993

Clough, Shephard, and Cole, Charles, *Economic History of Europe*, Boston, 1952

Clark, John, J., and Cohen, Morris, *Business Fluctuations, Growth, and Economic Stabilisation*, New York, 1963

Cootner, Paul, H., *The Random Character Of Stock Market Prices*, Cambridge, MA, 1964

Cowles, Virginia, *The Great Swindle*, London 1960

Derry, T. K. and Williams, Trevor, *A Short History of Technology*, Oxford, 1960

Dewey, Edward, *Cycles - The Science of Predictions*, New York, 1947

Diamond, Jared, *Guns, Germs, And Steel,* New York, 1997

Doolittle, Justus, *Social Life of the Chinese*, London, 1868

Douglas, P. H., *Controlling Depressions*, New York, 1935

Dreman, David, *Psychology and the Stock Market*, New York, 1977

Durant, Will, *The Story of Civilisation*, New York, 1954

Encyclopaedia Britannica

Engels, Frederik, *Socialism: Utopian and Scientific* (translated by E Aveling) London, 1892

Estey, James, A., *Business Cycles*, New York, 1941

Etherton, P. T., and Tiltman Hessell, *Manchuria, The Cockpit of Asia*, London, 1933

Evans, Morier, D., *The History of the Commercial Crisis, 1857-58 and the Stock Exchange Panic of 1859*, New York, London 1859 (reprinted New York, 1969)

Fisher, Irving, *The Stock Market Crash - And After*, New York, 1930

Fisher, Irving, *Booms and Depressions*, New York, 1932

Fisher, Irving, *The Debt-Deflation Theory of the Great Depression*, London, 1933

Fisher, Irving, *Inflation?*, London, 1933

Foxwell, (ed), Jevons, W. Stanley, *Investigations in Currency and Finance*, London, 1884

Frasca, Charles, *Stock Swindlers And Their Methods*, New York, 1931

Fridson, Martin, S., *It Was a Very Good Year*, New York, 1998

Friedman, Milton, and Schwartz, Anna, *A Monetary History of the United States, 1867-1960*, Princeton, 1963

Gaettens, Richard, *Inflationen*, München, 1955

Galbraith, John Kenneth, *The Great Crash 1929*, Boston, 1988

Garnier, J., *Du Principe de Population*, Paris, 1857

Gayer, A. D., *Monetary Policy and Economic Stabilisation*, New York, 1935

Gernet, J., *A History of Chinese Civilisation*, Cambridge, 1982

Gibbon, E., *The History of the Decline and Fall of the Roman Empire*, London, 1780

Gibson, Alexander, *Economic Geography*, New Jersey, 1979

Graham, Frank, D., *Exchange, Prices, And Production in Hyper-Inflation: Germany, 1920-1923*, New York, 1930

Guyot, Yves, *La Science Économique*, Paris, 1881

Haberler, Gottfried, *Prosperity And Depression*, New York, 1946

Haberler, Gottfried, *Readings in Business Cycle Theory*, London, 1950

Hall, Peter, *Cities In Civilisation*, New York, 1998

Halley Stewart Lecture, *The World's Economic Crisis*, London, 1931

Harrod, R.F., *The Trade Cycle*, Oxford, 1936

Hayek, Friedrich, A., *Monetary Theory and the Trade Cycle*, London, 1933

Hayek, Friedrich, A., *Prices and Production*, London, 1931

Hicks, J. R., *A Contribution to the Theory of the Trade Cycle*, Oxford, 1950

Hicks, J. R., *Essays in World Economics*, Oxford, 1959

Hippocrates, "Influence of Atmosphere, Water, and Situation" in *Greek Historical Thought from Homer to the Age of Heraclius*, translated by AJ Toynbee, 1924

Hobson, John A., *The Evolution of Modern Capitalism*, London, 1894

Hobson, John A., *Free-Thought In The Social Sciences*, New York, 1926

Hobson, John A., *The Economics of Unemployment*, London, 1931

Hobson, John A., *Confessions of an Economic Heretic*, London 1938

Homer, Sydney, *A History of Interest Rates*, New Jersey, 1977

Homer, Sydney, *The Great American Bond Market, Selected Speeches*, Dow Jones-Irwin, 1978

Huntington, Ellsworth, *World Power and Evolution*, New Haven, 1919

Hunold, Albert, *Vollbeschäftigung, Inflation und Planwirtschaft*, Aufsätze von verschiedenen Oekonomen, Zürich, 1951

Hyndman, H. M., *Commercial Crises of the Nineteenth Century*, London, 1892 (reprinted New York, 1967)

Issawi, C., *The Economic History of the Middle East*, Chicago, 1966

Jacobs, Jane, *The Economy of Cities*, New York, 1969

Jerome, Harry, *Migration And Business Cycles*, New York, 1926

Jevons, Stanley, William., *The Theory of Political Economy*, London 1888

Jones, Edward, *Economic Crises*, New York, 1900

Juglar, Clément, *Des crises commerciales et de leur retour périodique en France, en Angleterre et aux États-Unis*, 2nd ed., Paris, 1889

Kaufman, Henry, *Interest Rates, the Markets, and the New Financial World*, New York, 1986

Kaufman, Henry, *On Money And Markets*, New York, 2000

Keynes, John Maynard, *The Economic Consequences Of The Peace*, London, 1919

Keynes, John Maynard, *A Tract On Monetary Reform*, London, 1923

Keynes, John, Maynard, *A Treatise On Money*, London, 1930

Keynes, John, Maynard, *The General Theory of Employment Interest And Money*, London, 1936

Kindleberger, Charles, *Manias, Panics, And Crashes*, New York, 1978

Kindleberger, Charles, *A Financial History of Western Europe*, New York, 1993

Kennedy, Paul, *The Rise and Fall of the Great Powers*, New York, 1987

Kondratieff, Nikolai, *The Long Wave Cycle*, (translated by Guy Daniels), New York, 1984

Landes, David, S., *The Wealth and the Poverty of Nations*, New York, 1998

Lavington, F., *The Trade Cycle*, London, 1925

Le Bon, Gustave, *The Crowd*, Norman S Berg, Publisher, Sellanraa, Dunwoody, Georgia

Levy, Jerome, *Economics Is An Exact Science*, New York, 1943

Mackay, Charles, *Extraordinary Popular Delusions and the Madness of Crowds*, New York, 1993

McCulloch, J. R., *The Principles of Political Economy*, 2nd ed. London 1830

McCulloch, J. R., Treatises And Essays on Subjects Connected With Economical Policy, Edinburgh, 1833

McNeill, William, *The Rise of the West*, Chicago, 1963

McNeill, William, *Plagues and Peoples*, New York, 1976

McNeill, William, *The Pursuit of Power*, Chicago, 1982

McNeill, William, *History of Western Civilisation*, Chicago, 1986

Maddison, A, *Monitoring the World Economy*, 1995

Marx, Karl, *Capital*, first published posthumously in German in 1885

Meason, Malcolm, R.L., *The Profits Of Panics*, London, 1866

Mill, James, *The History of British India*, London, 1826

Mill, John Stuart, *Principles of Political Economy*, 7th ed., London, 1871

Mises, Ludwig (von), *The Theory of Money and Credit*, New York, 1935

Mitchell, Wesley Clair, *Business Cycles*, Berkley, 1913

Mitchell Wesley, Clair, *What Happens During Business Cycles*, National Bureau of Economic Research, New York, 1951

Morgenstern, Oskar, *The Limits Of Economics*, London, 1937

Mulhall, Michael, *History of Prices Since The Year 1850*, London, 1885

Nairn, Alasdair, *Engines That Move Markets*, John Wiley & Sons, 2002

Naisbitt, John, *Global Paradox*, London 1994

National Bureau of Economic Research, *Conference on Business Cycles*, New York, 1951

Necker, M., *De L'Administration des Finances de France*, 1789

Neill, Humphrey, *The Art Of Contrary Thinking*, Caldwell, 1954

Nisbet, Robert, *History Of The Idea Of Progress*, New York, 1980

Noel, O., *Histoire du Commerce du Monde*, Paris, 1894

North, S.N.D., *A Century of Population Growth*, Washington, 1909

Norwich, John, J. *A History of Venice*, New York, 1982

Olson, M., *The Rise and Decline of Nations*, New Haven, 1982

Pacey, Arnold, *Technology in World Civilisation*, Oxford, 1990

Paepke, Owens, C., *The Evolution of Progress*, New York, 1993

Pares, B., *A History of Russia*, London, 1949

Parnell, Henry, *On Financial Reform*, London, 1830

Pigou, A. C., *The Economics of Welfare*, London, 1920

Pigou, A. C., *Industrial Fluctuations*, London, 1927

Pigou, A. C., *The Economics of Stationary States*, London, 1935

Pigou, A. C., *Employment and Equilibrium*, London, 1949

Pigou, A. C., *Income*, London, 1955

Pokrovsky, M. N., *Brief History of Russia*, London, 1933

Pratt, Sereno, *The Work of Wall Street*, New York, 1921

Prechter, Robert, and Frost, Alfred, *Elliott Wave Principle*, Georgia, 1978

Prechter, Robert, *At the Crest of the Tidal Wave*, Georgia, 1995

Remer, C. F., *Foreign Investments in China*, New York, 1933

Riesman, David, *The Lonely Crowd*, New Haven, 1950

Roll, Erich, *A History Of Economic Thought*, London, 1938

Rogers, James, E., *The Economic Interpretation of History*, London, 1895

Röpke, Wilhelm, *Crises and Cycles*, London, 1936

Röpke, Wilhelm, *Jenseits von Angebot und Nachfrage*, Zürich, 1966

Rosenberg, Nathan and Birdzell, L. E. Jr., *How the West Grew Rich*, New York, 1986

Rothbard, Murray, *The Panic of 1819*, New York, 1962

Salvatore, Dominick, *World Population Trends And Their Impact On Economic Development*, New York, 1988

Say, Jean-Baptiste, *Cours Complet D'Economie Politique*, Bruxelles, 1844

Schumpeter, Joseph, "The Analysis of Economic Change", *The Review of Economic Statistics*, Vol. 17, No. 4, May 1935

Schumpeter, Joseph, *Business Cycles*, Philadelphia, 1939

Schumpeter, Joseph, *Capitalism, Socialism, and Democracy*, New York, 1942

Schumpeter, Joseph, *History of Economic Analysis*, London, 1954

Seligman, Edwin, *The Economic Interpretation of History*, New York, 1924

Shilling, Gary, A., *Deflation*, New Jersey, 1998

Singer, Charles, Hall, A. R., Williams, Trevor, *A History of Technology* (5 volumes), Oxford, 1954-8

Slater, F. R., *Sir Thomas Gresham*, London, 1925

Smith, Walter, & Cole, Arthur, *Fluctuations in American Business, 1790-1860*, Cambridge, 1935

Sobel, Robert, *The Big Board*, New York, 1965

Sobel, Robert, *Panic On Wall Street*, New York 1968

Sombart, W., Der Moderne Kapitalismus, Leipzig, 1928

Speck, E., *Handelsgeschichte des Altrertums*, Leipzig, 1906

Temple, Robert, *The Genius of China*, New York, 1986

Temple, William *Observations upon the Provinces of the United Netherlands*, 1720 (reprinted Cambridge, 1932)

Thompson, Robert, L., *Wiring A Continent*, Princeton, 1947

Thornton, Henry, *An Inquiry into The Nature and Effects of The Paper Credit of Great Britain*, London,1802

Timoshenko, V.P., *World Agriculture and the Depression*, Michigan Business Studies, Vol.V, No. 5, 1953

Tinbergen, Jan, *The Dynamics of Business Cycles*, London, 1950

Tooke, Thomas, *Thoughts and Details on the High And Low Prices of The Last Thirty Years*, London, 1823

Tooke, Thomas, *A History of Prices*, London, 1838

Toynbee, Arnold, J., *A Study of History, London 1947*, Toynbee (see especially his chapter entitled "The Comparability of Societies")

Tracy, (Comte) Destutt, *Traite D'Economie Politique*, Paris, 1825

Trollope, Anthony, *The Way We Live Now*, New York, 1996

Tugan-Baranowsky, Michael, *Studian zur Theorie und Geschichte der Handelskrisen in England*, Jena, 1901

Underwood Faulkner, Harold, *American Economic History*, New York, 1935

US Department of Commerce and Labour, *A Century of Population Growth*, Washington, 1909

Veblen, Thorstein, *The Theory of the Leisure Class*, New York, 1899

Veblen, Thorstein, *The Theory of Business Enterprises*, New York, 1904

Veblen, Thorstein, *The Higher Learning In America*, New York, 1918

Von Wieser, Friedrich, *Das Gesetz der Macht*, Wien, 1926

Weber, Max, *Wirtschaftsgeschichte*, Leipzig, 1923

Weber, Max, *Protestant Ethic and the Spirit of Capitalism*, New York, 1930

Wicksell, Knut, *Interest and Prices*, London, 1936

Wigmore, Barrie, A., *The Crash and Its Aftermath*, Westport, 1985

Wise, Murray, *Investing in Farmland*, Chicago, 1989

Wirth, Max, *Geschichte der Handelskrisen*, Frankfurt, 1874

Zahorchack, Michael, (ed), *Climate, The Key to Understanding Business Cycles*, New Jersey, Tide Press, 1980

Index

A

C

I

N

O

P

Q

R

S

T

U

- first gains are the most spectacular
- be cautious investing in widely accepted, highly popular theme
- outstanding opportunities arise elsewhere — when noone is looking
- watch what makes up the smallest % of the S&P
  how has this % Δed?
- is monetary policy accomodative or not
- Knowing what to avoid is also important
- dont just look within the US - look at different asset classes p18
- where is the negative sentiment?
- In an environment when the Fed is trying to prevent deflation (ie pumping liquidity into the markets), it is unlikeley bonds will do well (especially if rates are already low (p23)
- mkts bottom w/ low turnover & low volume
- over ~~capacity~~ investment leads to overcapacity
- purchase basket of commodity futures